# Commodity Advertising and Promotion

# Commodity Advertising and Promotion

EDITED BY

**Henry W. Kinnucan**
**Stanley R. Thompson**
**Hui-Shung Chang**

WITHDRAWN

IOWA STATE UNIVERSITY PRESS / AMES

**HENRY W. KINNUCAN** is Associate Professor of Agricultural Economics, Auburn University.
**STANLEY R. THOMPSON** is Professor and Chairman, Department of Agricultural Economics and Rural Sociology, The Ohio State University.
**HUI-SHUNG CHANG** is Visiting Assistant Professor, Department of Agricultural Economics and Rural Sociology, Auburn University.

© 1992 Iowa State University Press, Ames, Iowa 50010

First edition, 1992

Library of Congress Cataloging-in-Publication Data

Commodity advertising and promotion / edited by Henry W. Kinnucan, Stanley R. Thompson, Hui-Shung Chang—1st ed.
    p.   cm.
  Includes bibliographical references and index.
  ISBN 0-8138-1297-6 (alk. paper)
  1. Advertising—Food. I. Kinnucan, Henry W. II. Thompson, Stanley R. III. Chang, Hui-Shung.
HF6161.F616.C65 1992
659.1′96413—dc20                                         90-29254

# CONTENTS

## 6. Future Directions for Advertising Research

# CONTRIBUTORS

**STEVEN BEARE** is a senior economist, Australian Bureau of Agricultural and Resource Economics, Canberra, Australia.

**JAMES R. BLAYLOCK** is an economist, Economic Research Service, U.S. Department of Agriculture.

**CHARLES R. BRADER** is Director, Fruit and Vegetable Division, Agricultural Marketing Service, U.S. Department of Agriculture.

**MARK G. BROWN** is a research economist, Florida Department of Citrus, and adjunct assistant professor, Food and Resource Economics Department, University of Florida.

**ORAL CAPPS, JR.,** is Professor, Department of Agricultural Economics, Texas A&M University.

**HUI-SHUNG CHANG** is Visiting Assistant Professor, Department of Agricultural Economics and Rural Sociology, Auburn University.

**YANG CHOI** is a graduate research assistant, Department of Agricultural Economics and Rural Sociology, The Ohio State University.

**JON M. CONRAD** is Professor, Department of Agricultural Economics, Cornell University.

**THOMAS L. COX** is Associate Professor, Department of Agricultural Economics, University of Wisconsin-Madison.

**BRIAN COZZARIN** is a graduate research assistant, Department of Agricultural Economics and Business, University of Guelph.

**JOE DEWBRE** is a senior economist, Australian Bureau of Agricultural and Resource Economics, Canberra, Australia.

**BRUCE DIXON** is Professor, Department of Agricultural Economics, University of Arkansas.

**OLAN D. FORKER** is Professor, Department of Agricultural Economics, Cornell University.

**DHANESHWAR GHURA** is a graduate research assistant, Department of Economics, North Carolina State University, Raleigh.

**ELLEN GODDARD** is Associate Professor, Department of Agricultural Economics and Business, University of Guelph.

**PETER GOULD** is an economist, Ontario Milk Marketing Board, Canada.

**RICHARD GREEN** is Professor, Department of Agricultural Economics, University of California-Davis.

**ERIC GRUNDMEIER** is a research associate, Center for Agricultural and Rural Development, Iowa State University.

**DAVID E. HAHN** is Professor, Department of Agricultural Economics and Rural Sociology, The Ohio State University.

**MARVIN HAYENGA** is Professor, Department of Economics, Iowa State University.

**DERMOT HAYES** is Assistant Professor, Department of Economics, Iowa State University.

**SUE HOOVER** is a graduate research assistant, Department of Economics, Iowa State University.

**HELEN H. JENSEN** is Associate Professor, Center of Agricultural and Rural Development, Iowa State University.

**STANLEY R. JOHNSON** is Director, Center of Agricultural and Rural Development, Iowa State University.

**EUGENE JONES** is Assistant Professor, Department of Agricultural Economics and Rural Sociology, The Ohio State University.

**HARRY M. KAISER** is Associate Professor, Department of Agricultural Economics, Cornell University.

**KEVIN KESECKER** is an economist, Economic Research Service, U.S. Department of Agriculture.

**HENRY W. KINNUCAN** is Associate Professor, Department of Agricultural Economics and Rural Sociology, Auburn University.

**JONQ-YING LEE** is a research economist, Florida Department of Citrus, and Adjunct Assistant Professor, Food and Resource Economics Department, University of Florida.

**DONALD J. LIU** is Assistant Professor, Department of Economics, Iowa State University.

**ARCHIE MACDONALD** is Vice President, Economic and Market Research, Dairy Bureau of Canada.

**DANIEL S. MOEN** is a business analyst, Tri-Valley Growers, San Francisco, California.

**TIMOTHY D. MOUNT** is Professor, Department of Agricultural Economics, Cornell University.

**BARRY D. PFOUTS** is Director, Consumer Marketing, National Pork Producers Council.

**HAROLD S. RICKER** is Deputy Director, Agricultural Marketing Service, U.S. Department of Agriculture.

**RONALD A. SCHRIMPER** is Professor, Department of Economics, North Carolina State University, Raleigh.

**JOHN R. SCHROETER** is Associate Professor, Department of Economics, Iowa State University.

**K. SKOLD** is a graduate research assistant, Department of Economics, Iowa State University.

**CAMERON S. THRAEN** is Associate Professor, Department of Agricultural Economics and Rural Sociology, The Ohio State University.

**RONALD W. WARD** is Professor, Department of Food and Resource Economics, University of Florida.

# FOREWORD

This volume is a landmark in the evolution and advancement of research on commodity advertising and promotion. In the early 1980s a small group of agricultural economists from universities, the government, and industries organized an ad hoc committee that came to be known as NEC-63, to plan a conference on commodity promotion programs and research. That conference was held in the spring of 1985. The papers were published by the Farm Foundation in a proceeding titled "Research on Effectiveness of Agricultural Commodity Promotion," edited by Walter J. Armbruster and Lester H. Myers.

The committee that arranged the 1985 conference evolved officially into NEC-63, formally established that year by the directors of the Northeast Experiment Stations. Academicians and interested persons in the United States and other countries are welcome to participate in this national committee. The committee meets two times each year. Presentations or discussions are arranged so that each meeting focuses on some important aspect of commodity promotion research. The committee's purpose, simply stated, is to provide an opportunity for anyone and everyone interested in the economics of generic advertising and promotion to meet and discuss issues of common interest.

Only two commodities were discussed at the 1985 conference. All of the references to empirical work were from the citrus and dairy promotion programs. In the proceedings are papers about the economics of advertising apples, beef, eggs, fats and oils, potatoes, pork, and wool. All of the research involved single-equation, single-commodity models.

The papers in this book were first presented at a Commodity Advertising and Promotion conference in 1989 sponsored by NEC-63. They represent substantial progress in research methods. Several papers are based on multiple-equation and multiple-commodity models, and the papers cover more commodities than previously considered. The progress and evolution represented by the research in the present volume are important to farmers, the agricultural industry, politicians, and society because it is fostering a better understanding of the economics of commodity and generic advertising and promotion.

Farmers want to know whether their investment is having a positive impact on the marketing of the commodity they produce. Farmers also want to make sure that the managers of their promotion organizations have the needed information to run the best program possible.

Businesses that process food, especially those with strong brand franchises, generally hold unfavorable views of generic advertising. The true relationship between brand and generic advertising needs to be clarified for their benefit.

Politicians and society have supported commodity promotion programs by granting authority for mandatory assessments. They need to be provided with information and analyses indicating the appropriateness or inappropriateness of this policy.

During the past ten years the investment in commodity promotion efforts has increased dramatically, and the number of commodities covered by some form of mandatory assessment has increased substantially.

The commodity check-off concept dates as far back as 1880, when several state legislatures passed laws enabling commodity groups to receive state funds for promotion purposes. These state programs were justified in the name of economic development and were held to be constitutional by state courts (Armbruster and Myers 1985).

Since the amount of money available from state governments was modest, several commodity groups organized voluntary programs. But, inherent in the voluntary arrangement is the "free rider" problem. In addition to the inequity involved, the "free rider" issue made it difficult to collect enough money to develop effective programs. This "free rider" problem caused those in favor of promotion to push for legislation to require all farmers marketing a commodity to contribute in proportion to their sales volume, the argument being that all producers of a commodity benefit from effective promotion so everyone should pay.

State governments were the first to introduce legislation for mandatory nonrefundable assessments. In some cases this authority dates back to the 1930s. The Florida Citrus Commission was established in 1935 with the authority to establish mandatory nonrefundable assessments on all citrus marketed.

The amount of money earmarked for generic promotion increased dramatically when Congress passed the 1983 Dairy and Tobacco Adjustment Act, which authorized mandatory assessments on milk. This nonrefundable assessment on the dairy industry raises about $200 million annually for promotion. About $145 million is invested in media advertising; the balance is invested in research, new product development, nutrition research, and administration. In 1985 Congress authorized mandatory check-off programs for beef, pork, and honey. Since 1985, Congress has granted assessment authority to additional commodity groups.

In 1988 the funds contributed toward generic commodity advertising and promotion activities by commodity promotion organizations under various authorities, by voluntary arrangements, and by federal and state governments (for export promotion) easily exceeded $750 million. This probably is a sevenfold or eightfold increase over the amount available seven years earlier. This number, although large in absolute terms, is small when compared to the over $9 billion invested in brand advertising by the food industry. But it is a large and important number relative to net farm income and to the income of individual farmers. The assessment is subtracted from the price farmers receive when they sell; although some farmers view this as an expense and just write it off, others view it as an investment. They would like to be assured of a good return. In the view of many farm producers, commodity promotion is an important marketing tool that they wish to fully understand and effectively use. More leaders throughout the agricultural community are beginning to view generic promotion as an investment and as one of several important tools for market development.

The Commodity Advertising and Promotion conference was designed to address several important questions. The papers in this book address methodological issues as well as provide empirical evidence of the economic implications of commodity promotion activities. Some of the specific questions addressed include, but are not limited to, the following: What research methods work best in our attempt to provide empirical estimates of the theoretical relationship between promotion and consumer behavior? What is the empirical evidence concerning the many hypotheses or questions about the impact of generic advertising and promotion? Does generic advertising have a positive impact on consumption or sales? What is the effect of advertising on the structure of the demand system? What does advertising do to consumer attitudes and how do attitude changes relate to sales? Do producers increase supplies in response to the increased returns from advertising and does this supply response offset any of the benefits? Is it possible to manage available funds in some optimal way?

All of these are very important questions. Answers are essential in order that farmers who provide the funds and the managers who manage the funds might have the best information available in making policy, allocation, and program implementation decisions. Answers are essential to food industry processors and distributors so that they might have the information that will enable them to design the best possible brand advertising campaigns and in a way that will obtain the greatest possible synergism from the combined brand and generic promotion programs. Answers are essential to the public and politicians so that policy can be modified if necessary to enable the promotion programs to be most effective in achieving goals of economic health and development for the agricultural sector of the economy.

The papers in this book will provide answers at least in part to the questions posed above. They provide useful information for farmers, food industry leaders, food processors and distributors, and policymakers in industry and government.

OLAN D. FORKER
Chairman, Research
Committee on Commodity
Promotion Programs (NEC-63)

# 1 Ongoing Empirical Research on Generic Advertising

# 1     Newspaper Advertising of Apples in North Carolina: Characteristics and Comparisons across Cities and Time

DHANESHWAR GHURA and RONALD A. SCHRIMPER

Advertising is widely used to promote sales of agricultural products. Specific agricultural products are advertised by local, regional, and national associations, by processors and manufacturers as well as by retailers via local newspapers, radio, television, and magazines (Morrison 1984).

In recent years there has been considerable interest in evaluating the various techniques and vehicles of commodity promotion. Useful theoretical considerations about the impact of advertising on product prices, demand, and consumer behavior include the work of Stigler and Becker (1977), and Green (1985). Most of the empirical research evaluating advertising of agricultural commodities consists of examining how the value, quantity, sales, or consumption of particular products has responded to some measure of advertising (Nerlove and Waugh 1961; Kinnucan and Forker 1986; Blaylock and Blisard 1988; Liu and Forker 1988; Ward and Dixon 1988). Invariably in such efforts researchers face the task of quantifying advertising in order to estimate responses.

Promotion expenditures are a frequent measure of advertising activities. This measure implicitly assumes every nominal, deflated, or adjusted dollar spent on advertising is an identical treatment regardless of the message being conveyed or media selected. If advertising messages conveyed for the same product are not identical even for the same level of expenditure, different effects on consumer behavior might be expected.

Changes in the intensity and type of advertising messages reflect the outcome of business decisions about how to stimulate favorable consumer responses. Different advertising messages may reflect how particular product characteristics are presented to the public as well as how specific media are utilized. The present study examines changes in the type of advertising of apples through newspaper food ads in two cities in North Carolina for two seasons.

Local newspapers are an important vehicle for all types of advertising. In the ten years from the mid-1970s to the mid-1980s, newspapers accounted for approximately one fourth of all advertising expenditures (U.S. Department of Commerce 1987). Local newspapers account for a significant amount of food advertisements. In 1985, local newspapers accounted for 17 percent of all food marketing advertising expenditures (U.S. Department of Agriculture 1987).

## Nature of Data Set

This study is based on a data set that indicates the characteristics of newspaper advertisements featuring fresh apples during parts of two years in Charlotte and Raleigh, North Carolina, newspapers. These cities were chosen because they are the two largest metropolitan areas in the state. Of particular interest was the frequency with which North Carolina apples were promoted relative to those produced in the other areas of the country.

The basic data were complied by examining daily copies of the *Charlotte Observer* and the *Raleigh News and Observer* for August through January of 1976–77 and 1986–87 to determine how frequently fresh apples were included in retail food store advertisements. When information about fresh apples was observed in a food ad, various details about the advertisement were recorded. The observed characteristics were classified into two general categories: characteristics pertaining to the apples being advertised and characteristics about the ads themselves.

The characteristics of the apples being advertised included location of production of apples (North Carolina); variety (Red Delicious); grade and/or size (Fancy); retail price (48 cents per lb); and packaging type (3-lb bags).

The characteristics of the ads included the timing of the ad (day of the week and month), the space (in square inches) allocated to apple ads, the size (in square inches) of the total food ad, location of the apple information in the overall food ad, whether a pictorial representation was used to draw readers' attention to apples, and whether the overall food ad was part of the regular newspaper or a special insert within the newspaper. The period August through January was selected for each season of interest because it is the time of the year when North Carolina fresh apples are in most abundant supply. This is also the time of the year when consumers spend the highest proportion of their weekly grocery budget on apples (U.S. Department of Agricultural 1983).

The two periods of time selected for study included the most recent season (1986–87) when data collection was initiated as well as the same period of time a decade earlier. This made it possible to compare apple advertisements in the selected cities to identify possible changes in advertising messages over the decade.

An obvious question with respect to the two years selected for analysis is whether there was anything unusual about total apple production and prices in these two periods that might account for unusual advertising behavior relative to other years. Annual apple production and prices in real and nominal terms for the United States and North Carolina for 1970–87 are presented in Table 1.1. A common characteristic noted about the two periods selected is that production in both the United States and North

Table 1.1.  U.S. and North Carolina apple production and prices, 1970–87

| Year | Total production commercial crop | | Average prices | | | |
|------|------|------|------|------|------|------|
| | U.S. | N.C. | U.S. | | N.C. | |
| | | | Nominal | Real[a] | Nominal | Real[a] |
| | (million lb) | | (cents per lb) | | | |
| 1970 | 6257 | 223 | 4.5 | 4.5 | 4.1 | 4.1 |
| 1970 | 6081 | 185 | 4.9 | 4.7 | 4.2 | 4.0 |
| 1972 | 5870 | 245 | 6.4 | 5.9 | 4.6 | 4.3 |
| 1973 | 6225 | 210 | 8.8 | 7.7 | 6.4 | 5.6 |
| 1974 | 6484 | 295 | 8.4 | 6.6 | 6.2 | 4.9 |
| 1975 | 7530 | 280 | 6.5 | 4.7 | 5.9 | 4.3 |
| 1976 | 6479 | 265 | 9.1 | 6.2 | 9.1 | 6.2 |
| 1977 | 6656 | 270 | 10.5 | 6.7 | 8.7 | 5.6 |
| 1978 | 7597 | 324 | 10.4 | 6.2 | 7.9 | 4.7 |
| 1979 | 8143 | 362 | 10.9 | 5.8 | 7.2 | 3.9 |
| 1980 | 8824 | 410 | 8.7 | 4.1 | 6.7 | 3.2 |
| 1981 | 7754 | 375 | 11.1 | 4.7 | 7.5 | 3.2 |
| 1982 | 8110 | 170 | 9.9 | 4.0 | 8.1 | 3.3 |
| 1983 | 8379 | 415 | 10.5 | 4.1 | 6.3 | 2.5 |
| 1984 | 8331 | 360 | 11.2 | 4.2 | 6.6 | 2.5 |
| 1985 | 7921 | 275 | 11.6 | 4.2 | 7.4 | 2.7 |
| 1986 | 7891 | 120 | 13.6 | 4.8 | 8.5 | 3.0 |
| 1987 | 10534 | 390 | 13.0 | 4.4 | 6.4 | 2.2 |

SOURCES:  1970–86 total production and prices obtained from selected issues, *Agricultural Statistics,* Washington, D.C.: U.S. Department of Agriculture. 1987 production data obtained from *Crop Production,* October 12, 1988. Washington, D.C.: U.S. Department of Agriculture. 1987 prices obtained from North Carolina Department of Agricultural Statistics Division. U.S. CPI data obtained from selected issues, *International Financial Statistics.* Washington, D.C.: International Monetary Fund.

[a]Nominal price deflated by U.S. CPI (1970 = base).

Carolina was lower than average while prices were higher than average. In 1976 total U.S. apple production was below the large crop of 1975 but fairly similar to the 1974, 1977, and 1978 crops. The U.S. average real price of apples in 1976 was higher than that of 1975 but about the same as 1974, 1977, and 1978. On the other hand, in 1986 total U.S. production was smaller than any of the previous four years. Consequently, the 1986 real price of apples was higher than any year since the 1970s.

In 1976 North Carolina apple production was smaller than in any year between 1974 and 1981. It is therefore not surprising the 1976 North Carolina prices (real and nominal) were the highest observed between 1970 and 1987. North Carolina apple production in 1986 was under half the average production for the 1981–86 period. The 1986 North Carolina real and nominal apple prices were higher than those of the previous three years.

It is important in the context of this study to clearly define the meaning of a newspaper apple ad. In most cases, specific space in the food ad was allocated to indicate a single price, variety, and/or production location of apples, and this information could be considered as a single observation. Sometime, however, the same food ad contained information about multiple types of apples. If apples from more than one geographic area of production with different prices were featured in the same ad, each production area and price combination was considered as a separate apple ad. If production location information was not present in the ad but multiple apple prices were indicated to distinguish different varieties of apples or type of package, each price-variety or price-package combination was considered to be a separate apple ad. In most cases when multiple types of apple ads were present, the space for each ad was clearly delineated. In a few instances where multiple ad information was presented closely together in the food ad and the space for each ad could not be easily identified, the total advertising space for apples was divided evenly among the different combinations.

## Frequency and Retail Source of Ads

Tabulations from the data set indicate that the number of newspaper apple ads decreased from the mid-1970s to the mid-1980s in Charlotte but increased in Raleigh. The number of such ads decreased in Charlotte by 25 percent (from 263 to 197) but increased in Raleigh by 27 percent (from 150 to 190). The fact that a different directional change in the number of apple ads was observed in each city indicates that factors other than the changes in total production and average price of apples influenced the frequency of advertising.

The frequency of multiple apple advertisements within the same food ad was fairly similar in both cities and relatively constant over time. In the earlier period multiple apple ads accounted for 16 and 17 percent of total apple ads in Raleigh and Charlotte. For the latter period the proportion of multiple ads stayed the same for Raleigh and increased slightly in Charlotte to 25 percent. These proportions indicate that approximately one of every four to six times, retailers elected to include multiple types of apples with different prices in the same ad.

Fifteen different retailers accounted for the newspaper ads in Charlotte in 1976–77 (Table 1.2). The number of retailers advertising apples in Charlotte decreased by two by 1986–87. In Raleigh, nine retailers advertised apples in 1976–77 with the number increasing to eleven by 1986–87.

Winn Dixie and A&P were the most frequent advertisers in both cities in 1976–77. These two chains accounted for 33 percent of the total apple in Charlotte ads and 51 percent in Raleigh. In 1986–87 the Park-n-Shop chain had the most newspaper apple ads in Charlotte accounting for 29

**Table 1.2. Number of fresh apple ads by retail store in *Charlotte Observer* and *Raleigh News and Observer* for 1976–77 and 1986–87**

| Store | 1976–77 | | 1986–87 | |
|---|---|---|---|---|
| | Charlotte | Raleigh | Charlotte | Raleigh |
| A&P | 39 | 40 | 16 | 17 |
| Big M | 4 | 0 | 0 | 0 |
| Big Star | 18 | 8 | 0 | 30 |
| Bi-Lo | 19 | 0 | 9 | 0 |
| Cashions FM | 1 | 0 | 0 | 0 |
| Colonial | 0 | 15 | 0 | 0 |
| Farm Fresh | 0 | 0 | 0 | 27 |
| Food Lion | 29 | 12 | 15 | 10 |
| Food Mark | 4 | 0 | 0 | 0 |
| Food-A-Rama | 0 | 0 | 11 | 0 |
| Food World | 0 | 12 | 0 | 0 |
| Fresh Market | 0 | 0 | 5 | 0 |
| Giant Genie | 7 | 0 | 11 | 0 |
| Harris Teeter | 30 | 0 | 14 | 14 |
| Hillbilly | 0 | 0 | 5 | 0 |
| IGA | 0 | 5 | 0 | 15 |
| Kroger | 0 | 0 | 17 | 15 |
| Loves | 0 | 0 | 2 | 0 |
| Lyons | 0 | 0 | 0 | 1 |
| New Gambles | 17 | 0 | 0 | 0 |
| Park-N-Shop | 28 | 0 | 58 | 0 |
| Piggly Wiggly | 0 | 13 | 0 | 4 |
| Red & White | 6 | 8 | 0 | 17 |
| Trade Winds | 10 | 0 | 0 | 0 |
| Village Market | 0 | 0 | 7 | 0 |
| Winn Dixie | 49 | 37 | 27 | 40 |
| Wrigley | 2 | 0 | 0 | 0 |
| Total | 263 | 150 | 197 | 190 |

percent of the total. Winn Dixie was the second largest advertiser of apples in Charlotte in 1986–87. Some of the decrease in the total number of ads in Charlotte from the mid-1970s to the mid-1980s was due to Winn Dixie, A&P, Food Lion, and Harris Teeter reducing their number of apple ads. Also, Big Star and New Gambles did not have any apple advertisements in the latter period in Charlotte. In Raleigh in 1986–87, Winn Dixie had the largest number of apple ads with 21 percent followed by Big Star (16 percent) and Farm Fresh (14 percent). The increase in total number of ads in Raleigh from 1976–77 to 1986–87 was due in large part to four retailers — Farm Fresh, Harris Teeter, Kroger, and Red and White. These four stores did not account for any newspaper apple ads in 1976–77 but accounted for 38 percent of the Raleigh total in 1986–87.

## Characteristics of Apples Being Advertised

### GEOGRAPHIC ORIGIN OF APPLES

Over the ten-year period there was a significant increase in the frequency with which geographic location of apple production information appeared in ads (Table 1.3). In Charlotte, the proportion of apple ads including geographic information increased from 67 percent (177 of 263) in 1976–77 to 73 percent (144 of 197) in 1986–87. In Raleigh, the share of apple ads that included information about geographic origin increased from 45 percent (78 of 150) to 71 percent (135 of 190) from 1976 to 1986. It is not clear whether these changes reflect the perceived importance of particular types of apples to consumers or more aggressive participation of some producer organizations in helping finance promotional efforts.

The increase in the proportion of ads featuring Washington State apples accounted for most of the increases in both cities during the decade. The share of ads featuring Washington State apples increased from 26 percent (68 of 263) to 46 percent (96 of 197) in Charlotte and from 37 percent (55 of 150) to 41 percent (78 of 190) in Raleigh. The proportion of ads featuring North Carolina apples declined between 1976–77 and 1986–87 in both cities. In Raleigh, such ads declined from 11 percent (17 of 150) to 4 percent (7 of 190); in Charlotte, from 13 percent (34 of 263) to 3 percent (5 of 197).

The proportion of food ads featuring Western apples also increased in both Raleigh and Charlotte between 1976–77 and 1986–87. For Raleigh the increase was from nil to 6 percent (12 of 190) and in Charlotte that increase was from 8 percent (22 of 263) to 12 percent (23 of 197).

In Raleigh, there was a large increase in the number of ads featuring Eastern apples from 1976–77 to 1986–87. In the earlier period only 2

Table 1.3. Number of fresh apple ads by location of production in *Charlotte Observer* and *Raleigh News and Observer* for 1976–77 and 1986–87

| Location | 1976–77 | | 1986–87 | |
|---|---|---|---|---|
| | Charlotte | Raleigh | Charlotte | Raleigh |
| North Carolina | 34 | 17 | 5 | 7 |
| Eastern | 40 | 3 | 17 | 30 |
| Washington | 68 | 55 | 96 | 78 |
| Western | 22 | 0 | 23 | 12 |
| Virginia | 10 | 2 | 2 | 7 |
| Others | 3[a] | 1[b] | 1[a] | 1[c] |
| Subtotal of locations | 177 | 78 | 144 | 135 |
| No locations given | 86 | 72 | 53 | 55 |
| Total | 263 | 150 | 197 | 190 |

[a]Montana.
[b]Michigan.
[c]New Zealand.

percent of the ads featured Eastern apples. In the latter period, this share increased to 16 percent. In Charlotte, the pattern was quite different. For that city the share of Eastern apples remained virtually insignificant.

The share of ads featuring Virginia apples was fairly small in both cities and time periods. In Charlotte, the share of ads featuring Virginia apples dropped from 4 percent (10 of 263) in 1976–77 to nil in 1986–87. In Raleigh, there was a slight increase in the number of ads featuring Virginia apples.

## APPLE VARIETY

In both cities for both time periods, a much larger fraction of the fresh apple ads included information about varieties than about a specific location of production (Table 1.4). The varieties which dominated the ads were Red Delicious or a combination of Red and Golden Delicious. These variety combinations accounted for well over two-thirds of the total ads in each city in both periods. The proportion of ads featuring these two varieties rose in both cities between the two periods. Red Delicious apples had a leading role in both cities in 1986–87 with 49 percent (92 of 187) of the apple ads in Charlotte and 46 percent (82 of 179) in Raleigh including this variety. This was also true for Charlotte in 1976–77. In Raleigh, however, ads with the combined variety of Red and Golden Delicious apples were the most frequent in the earlier period.

**Table 1.4. Number of fresh apple ads by variety in *Charlotte Observer* and *Raleigh News and Observer* for 1976–77 and 1986–87**

| Variety | 1976–77 | | 1986–87 | |
|---|---|---|---|---|
| | Charlotte | Raleigh | Charlotte | Raleigh |
| Red Delicious | 100 | 46 | 92 | 82 |
| Red or Golden Delicious | 89 | 56 | 59 | 69 |
| Golden Delicious | 37 | 11 | 16 | 5 |
| Others | 26 | 29 | 20 | 23 |
| No variety information specified | 11 | 8 | 10 | 11 |
| Total | 263 | 150 | 197 | 190 |

Golden Delicious was advertised relatively infrequently by itself and its share went down in both cities. Ten to 20 percent of the ads featured several other varieties. Two varieties — Granny Smith and Jonathan — which were not advertised at all in 1976–77 appeared in some food ads in 1986–87 although the frequency of such ads was very low.

## TYPES OF PACKAGING

A major change in apple promotion observed between 1976–77 and 1986–87 in Raleigh and Charlotte newspapers was in the type of package unit emphasized in the advertisements (Table 1.5). For purposes of comparing the ads, two categories of packaging were considered. The first category (NOCHOICE) includes apples sold by the bag, bushel, case, or essentially in units where consumers had no choice about particular apples in the package. The second category (CHOICE) includes apples sold by the pound or per apple or at a fixed price for a specified number of apples. In both cities, the share of ads featuring the CHOICE category increased. In Charlotte, the share of the ads in the CHOICE category increased from 32 percent (84 of 263) to 72 percent (142 of 197) and in Raleigh from 23 percent (34 of 150) to 58 percent (111 of 190).

A high proportion of the increase in the number of apple ads in the CHOICE category in both cities between 1976–77 and 1986–87 consisted of Red Delicious apples from Washington sold by the pound. In Charlotte, there was also an increase in the frequency of ads containing Western apples sold on a per pound basis.

Advertisements of eastern apples continued to be the primary bagged apples in 1986–87 in both cities. Three out of the five North Carolina apple

**Table 1.5. Number of fresh apple ads by packaging type in *Charlotte Observer* and *Raleigh News and Observer* for 1976–77 and 1986–87**

| | 1976–77 | | 1986–87 | |
|---|---|---|---|---|
| Category | Charlotte | Raleigh | Charlotte | Raleigh |
| Choice[a] | 84 | 34 | 142 | 111 |
| No choice[b] | 179 | 116 | 55 | 79 |
| Total | 263 | 150 | 197 | 190 |

[a] Includes apples sold per pound, per apple, or specific number of apples.
[b] Includes prepackaged apples sold in plastic bags, wrapped trays, bushels, and cases.

ads in Charlotte in 1986–87 featured apples in 3-lb bags. In Raleigh, all seven apple ads for North Carolina apples in 1986–87 were on a per pound basis. This is in contrast to 1976–77 when most of the North Carolina apple ads featured bags.

## GRADE AND/OR SIZE

Information about apple grade and/or size was included relatively infrequently in the newspaper ads of Raleigh and Charlotte in both periods (Table 1.6). There was a moderate increase in the frequency of apple ads containing information about grade and/or size in Charlotte between 1976–77 and 1986–87. A slight increase in such types of ads occurred in Raleigh. Nevertheless, more than 60 to 70 percent of the apple ads in 1986–87 did not specify grade or size information. This kind of information was included relatively more frequently in Charlotte than Raleigh in both periods. Grade information was included more frequently than size in the ads.

**Table 1.6. Number of fresh apple ads by grade/size in *Charlotte Observer* and *Raleigh News and Observer* for 1976–77 and 1986–87**

| | 1976–77 | | 1986–87 | |
|---|---|---|---|---|
| Grade/size | Charlotte | Raleigh | Charlotte | Raleigh |
| Extra fancy | 28 | 9 | 15 | 18 |
| Fancy | 17 | 3 | 36 | 5 |
| Other grade and/or size | 8 | 4 | 19 | 13 |
| No grade or size information specified | 210 | 134 | 127 | 154 |
| Total | 263 | 150 | 197 | 190 |

## PRICE OF APPLES ADVERTISED

The real price of advertised apples is summarized in Table 1.7 for those observations for which prices could be expressed on a per pound basis. Retail apple prices were consistently a few pennies less per pound in Charlotte than Raleigh in November, December, and January in both periods. For some of the other months, prices were higher in Charlotte than in Raleigh.

Table 1.7. Average real retail prices of fresh apple by month in *Charlotte Observer* and *Raleigh News and Observer* for 1976–77 and 1986–87[a]

| Month | 1976–77 | | 1986–87 | |
|---|---|---|---|---|
| | Charlotte | Raleigh | Charlotte | Raleigh |
| August | 20 | 18 | 19 | 19 |
| September | 15 | 18 | 16 | 15 |
| October | 21 | 18 | 16 | 18 |
| November | 16 | 20 | 15 | 17 |
| December | 17 | 19 | 16 | 18 |
| January | 19 | 20 | 16 | 19 |

[a] Expressed in 1970 values using CPI as the deflator. The monthly figures for CPI were obtained from Board of Governors of the Federal Reserve System, *Federal Reserve Bulletin*, Washington, D.C.

## CHARACTERISTICS OF APPLE ADVERTISEMENTS

### Timing of Ads

In 1976–77 the number of apple ads was fairly evenly distributed among September through January in Charlotte and Raleigh (Table 1.8). In 1986–87, however, October accounted for nearly twice as many apple ads as the other months in each city. For the other months in the latter period, the number of ads was fairly evenly distributed in both cities. Relatively few apple ads appeared in August in either time period. There is no readily available explanation for the sharp change in seasonality of apple ads in the 1986–87 season.

Thursday was the most popular day for apple advertisements in both cities during the 1976–77 season. Over 60 percent of the ads in Charlotte and Raleigh in the mid-1970s appeared in Thursday newspapers. By the mid-1980s, Wednesday had supplanted Thursday as the most popular day for apple ads in Charlotte. Wednesdays accounted for 65 percent of the apple ads in 1986–87 in Charlotte. In Raleigh, Thursday remained the most

**Table 1.8. Monthly distribution of fresh apple by month in *Charlotte Observer* and *Raleigh News and Observer* for 1976–77 and 1986–87**

| Month | 1976–77 | | 1986–87 | |
|---|---|---|---|---|
| | Charlotte | Raleigh | Charlotte | Raleigh |
| August | 12 | 6 | 2 | 5 |
| September | 50 | 25 | 30 | 27 |
| October | 46 | 28 | 69 | 65 |
| November | 48 | 32 | 39 | 32 |
| December | 55 | 27 | 28 | 28 |
| January | 52 | 32 | 29 | 33 |
| Total | 263 | 150 | 197 | 190 |

popular day for apple ads in the mid-1980s. There was also an increase in the number of apple ads in Sunday newspapers and a decrease in Mondays for both cities in the latter period relative to the mid-1970s.

## Space Allocated to Apples

The average size of apple ads increased in both cities over time (Table 1.9). In 1986–87 the average apple ad was 6.2 and 8.4 square inches in Charlotte and Raleigh respectively. These values were substantially larger than the 4.7 and 4.5 square inches observed for ads ten years earlier. The increase in the size of the apple ads over time occurred nearly for all months. The only exception was for the month of August in Charlotte. While the average size of newspaper ad space for apples in both cities increased, the share of total newspaper food advertising space allocated to apples decreased a little in Charlotte and increased slightly in Raleigh. In Charlotte the percentage of the total food ad space allocated to apples fell from 1.3 percent to 1.1 percent. In Raleigh the corresponding percentage increased from 1.2 percent to 1.3 percent between 1976–77 and 1986–87.

**Table 1.9. Average space allocated to fresh apple ads in *Charlotte Observer* and *Raleigh News and Observer* for 1976–77 and 1986–87**

| Category | 1976–77 | | 1986–87 | |
|---|---|---|---|---|
| | Charlotte | Raleigh | Charlotte | Raleigh |
| Apple ad | 4.7 | 4.5 | 6.2 | 8.4 |
| Proportion of total food ad | 1.3 | 1.2 | 1.1 | 1.3 |

Most of the percentages mentioned above tended to be slightly higher than the proportion of average weekly household food expenditures spent on apples. Information from the 1977–78 Household Food Consumption Survey indicated the U.S. households allocated about 1.2 percent of their total food expenditures to apples in the fall season (U.S. Department of Agriculture 1983). The corresponding proportion for U.S. urban households in 1981 based on the Continuing Consumer Expenditure Survey was 1.1 percent (Smallwood and Blaylock 1983).

The comparison between expenditure proportions and allocation of ad space is a little misleading because food ads that did not contain any information about apples were excluded in this study. Consequently if all food ads had been taken into account, the proportion of total newspaper food ad space allocated to apples would be lower than the proportions indicated above. Thus it appears that newspaper ad space allocated to apples is not necessarily the same as the way households allocate their food expenditures even for that part of the year when fresh apples are in most abundant supply.

## SPECIAL INSERTS AND PICTURES

Two major changes in the kind of apple advertisements were noted between 1976–77 and 1986–87. One was a substantial increase in the use of pictorial information about apples in the ads to catch readers' attention (Table 1.10). In 1976–77, less than 37 percent of apple ads in both Charlotte and Raleigh contained pictures. By 1986–87 the proportion of apple ads including pictures was 57 percent in Charlotte and 64 percent in Raleigh.

Table 1.10. Number of fresh apple ads with pictures in *Charlotte Observer* and *Raleigh News and Observer* for 1976–77 and 1986–87

| Category | 1976–77 | | 1986–87 | |
|---|---|---|---|---|
| | Charlotte | Raleigh | Charlotte | Raleigh |
| Picture | 70 | 56 | 112 | 121 |
| No picture | 193 | 94 | 85 | 69 |
| Total | 263 | 150 | 197 | 190 |

The other change was a major shift in the use of special inserts for food ads rather than using regular parts or food sections of newspapers (Table 1.11). In the early period only one or two percent of the apple ads appeared in special inserts. That percentage increased fairly substantially by 1986–87. In the latter period, more than 30 percent of the apple ads in Raleigh were in food ads appearing in irregular sized special inserts. The proportion of ads in special inserts increased to 9 percent in Charlotte by 1986–87.

**Table 1.11.  Number of fresh apple ads with inserts in *Charlotte Observer* and *Raleigh News and Observer* for 1976–77 and 1986–87**

| Category | 1976–77 | | 1986–87 | |
|---|---|---|---|---|
|  | Charlotte | Raleigh | Charlotte | Raleigh |
| Insert | 4 | 2 | 18 | 58 |
| No insert | 259 | 148 | 179 | 132 |
| Total | 263 | 150 | 197 | 190 |

## LOCATION OF APPLE INFORMATION IN OVERALL FOOD AD

Three location categories were used to classify where the information about apples appeared within each food ad: top, middle, or bottom. Use of this classification scheme indicated that apple information tended to be located higher in the food ads in the mid-1980s relative to a decade earlier (Table 1.12). In 1976–77, the most favorite location for apple advertising was the bottom one-third of food ads. The second most favorite location for the 1976–77 season was the middle one-third of the ads. The least favorite apple ad location was the top third of the food ad section in 1976–77 in both cities.

**Table 1.12.  Number of fresh apple ads by location in food ads in *Charlotte Observer* and *Raleigh News and Observer* for 1976–77 and 1986–87**

| Location in food ad | 1976–77 | | 1986–87 | |
|---|---|---|---|---|
|  | Charlotte | Raleigh | Charlotte | Raleigh |
| Top | 43 | 12 | 48 | 44 |
| Middle | 103 | 54 | 101 | 88 |
| Bottom | 117 | 84 | 48 | 58 |
| Total | 263 | 150 | 197 | 190 |

By 1986–87, the middle third of the food ads became the most common location for apple advertising. The respective shares for the middle one-third of the food ads in Charlotte and Raleigh were 51 percent and 46 percent. In Charlotte, the top and bottom thirds of the food ad tied for the second most favorite apple ad locations in 1986–87. In Raleigh, the second most favorite location for apple ads was the bottom third in 1986–87.

## Factors Related to Size of Ads for Apples

This section of the paper is based on a behavioral equation postulated to explore the importance of factors related to the square inches of space allocated to fresh apple advertisements in local newspapers. It is hypothesized that space allocation depends on the characteristics of the apples being advertised and the characteristics of the ads themselves as well as special store effects.

The following functional form was assumed for the relationship between apple advertising space and apple and ad characteristics.

$$\log_e(s_i) = a + b\,\log_e(p_i) + \Sigma_{j=1}^{J}\pi_j D_{ji} + \Sigma_{k=1}^{K}\theta_k\,\text{STORE}_{ki} + u_i \qquad (1.1)$$

where $s_i$ is the space (in square inches) allocated to an apple ad in the $i$th overall food ad, $p_i$ is the price per pound of apples in the $i$th apple ad; $D_{ji}$ is the $j$th dummy to account for the presence of the $j$th product or ad characteristic associated with the $i$th observation; $\text{STORE}_{ki}$ is a dummy variable for store $k$ indicating which retail outlet was responsible for the $i$th observation: $u_i$ is a random disturbance assumed to have a mean of zero and constant variance. The parameters to be estimated include $a$, $b$, and the $\pi_j$'s and $\theta_k$'s. A list of the characteristics used for specifying the dummy variables ($D$'s) is given in Table 1.13.

In addition to the variables identified in Table 1.13, other variables representing total ad size, use of inserts, and particular day of the week were included in preliminary analyses. The lack of statistical significance for any of the latter variables resulted in their deletion from the results reported in this paper. Also, the results of a simple linear specification of the above variables were examined. The signs of the estimated coefficients were very similar for both specifications, but the statistical level of significance of the individual effects were better with equation (1.1).

To investigate how ad space for apples might be related to price it was necessary to restrict the sample to a smaller set of observations than used for most of the tabulations presented earlier. The smaller set of observations were restricted to those for which a standardized price measure could be computed. This meant that apple ads which featured apples for sale in units other than on a per-pound, per-bag, or per-tray basis were not used in the empirical analysis because prices could not be converted to a per-pound price. For 1976–77, twenty-one such ads in Raleigh and forty ads in Charlotte were dropped from the analysis. Only three such ads in Raleigh and seven ads in Charlotte had to be deleted for 1986–87.

Table 1.13. Definition of variables in equation (1.1)

| Effect/variable | Definition |
| --- | --- |
| Location | |
| LOCAWASH | 1 if apples were from Washington |
| LOCAWEST | 1 if apples were from the West |
| LOCANC | 1 if apples were from North Carolina |
| LOCAEAST | 1 if apples were from the East |
| LOCAVIRG | 1 if apples were from Virginia |
| LOCAMICH | 1 if apples were from Michigan |
| LOCANEWZ | 1 if apples were from New Zealand |
| LOANOINF | 1 if no information about location was given (BASE = LOCANOINF) |
| Variety | |
| VARRD | 1 if variety was Red Delicious |
| VARRGD | 1 if variety was combination Red or Golden Delicious |
| VARGD | 1 if variety was Golden Delicious |
| VARINF | 1 if information about variety other than above was given |
| VARNOINF | 1 if no information about variety was given (BASE = VAROINF) |
| Grade/size | |
| GRADEXF | 1 if grade was extra fancy |
| GRADEFCY | 1 if grade was fancy |
| GRADESIZ | 1 if some combined grade and size information or if only size information was given |
| GRANOINF | 1 if no information about grade and/or size was given (BASE = GRANOINF) |
| Packaging | |
| CHOICE | 1 if apples were sold by the pound |
| NOCHOICE | 1 if apples were sold in bags or prepackaged trays (BASE = NOCHOICE) |
| Pictures | |
| PICTURE | 1 if a picture was included in the apple ad |
| NOPICTU | 1 if no picture was included in the apple ad (BASE = NOPICTU) |
| Ad location | |
| TOP | 1 if ad was at the top one-third of food ad |
| MIDDLE | 1 if ad was in the middle one-third of food ad |
| BOTTOM | 1 if ad was at the bottom one-third of food ad (BASE = BOTTOM) |

**Table 1.13.  (cont.)**

| Effect/variable | Definition |
| --- | --- |
| Multiple ad | |
| SAMEAD | 1 if multiple apple ads were included in the same food ad |
| SINGLEAD | 1 if only one apple ad was included in the food ad |
| | (BASE = SINGLEAD) |
| Seasonality | |
| AUG | 1 if ad appeared in August |
| SEP | 1 if ad appeared in September |
| OCT | 1 if ad appeared in October |
| NOV | 1 if ad appeared in November |
| DEC | 1 if ad appeared in December |
| JAN | 1 if ad appeared in January |
| | (BASE = SEP) |
| Store | The individual retail store names are listed in Table 1.14. |

## EMPIRICAL RESULTS

The parameter estimates for the above model based on data from Charlotte and Raleigh are reported in Table 1.14. The explanatory power of the models was fairly high for cross-sectional data sets ranging from 59 to 73 percent. The explanatory power was slightly higher for the Charlotte data than for the Raleigh observations. Additional analyses support the hypothesis that the inclusion of product attributes over and above the characteristics of the ads and the store variables contribute a significant amount of explanatory power in both Raleigh and Charlotte. The set of variables excluding product characteristics accounted for 67 percent and 60 percent of the variation in the dependent variable in Raleigh and in Charlotte in 1976–77 respectively. For the 1986–87 period the proportions were 58 percent in Raleigh and 68 percent in Charlotte. Adding the characteristics of the apples to the models added 7 percent to the explanation power for apple ad space in Raleigh and 13 percent in Charlotte in 1976–77. The addition to explanatory power from apple characteristics in 1986–87 were 9 percent in Raleigh and 10 percent in Charlotte in 1976–77.

The apple characteristic most consistently associated with ad size was the price variable. Estimated coefficients for this variable were highly significant and negative in all four cases. The negative coefficients suggest an inverse relationship between the price of apples and the amount of space allocated to apples in food ads of local newspapers. This result seems very plausible since products that appear to be especially good bargains are likely to be given more exposure by retailers in order to increase store traffic. Variation in the coefficients of the price variable, ranging from −.37 to

Table 1.14. Estimated coefficients and *t*-ratios (in parentheses) for the apple advertising space model based on Charlotte and Raleigh data for 1976–77 and 1986–87

| Effect/ variable | 1976–77 | | | | 1986–87 | | | |
|---|---|---|---|---|---|---|---|---|
| | Charlotte | | Raleigh | | Charlotte | | Raleigh | |
| Price | -.37* | (2.09) | -1.12* | (2.57) | -1.41* | (5.32) | -1.03* | (2.63) |
| **Location** (BASE = LOCANOINF) | | | | | | | | |
| LOCAWASH | .73* | (4.44) | .15 | (.93) | .51* | (3.39) | .60* | (2.26) |
| LOCAWEST | .19 | (.63) | a | | .35 | (1.96) | .61* | (2.15) |
| LOCANC | .10 | (.69) | -.02 | (.12) | .12 | (.46) | -.03 | (.10) |
| LOCAEAST | -.28 | (1.38) | .11 | (.28) | .31 | (1.75) | -.09 | (.45) |
| LOCAVIRG | -.20 | (.65) | .72 | (.33) | -.20 | (.50) | -.06 | (.19) |
| LOCAMICH | a | | .98 | (1.40) | a | | a | |
| LOCANEWZ | a | | a | | a | | -1.27 | (1.56) |
| **Variety** (BASE = VARNOINF) | | | | | | | | |
| VARRD | 1.35* | (4.82) | .28 | (1.21) | .14 | (.66) | .81* | (3.30) |
| VARRGD | 1.38* | (4.74) | .45 | (1.65) | .23 | (1.12) | .54* | (2.02) |
| VARGD | 1.29* | (4.35) | .08 | (.25) | .35* | (2.03) | 1.07* | (2.71) |
| VARINF | .97* | (3.38) | -.02 | (.07) | .30 | (1.43) | .57* | (2.07) |
| **Grade** (BASE = GRANOINF) | | | | | | | | |
| GRADEXF | -.03 | (.15) | .64* | (2.84) | -.10 | (.45) | -.14 | (.63) |
| GRADEFCY | .11 | (.18) | -.64 | (1.57) | .42* | (3.23) | .15 | (.46) |
| GRADESIZ | -.02 | (.06) | .76 | (1.06) | .01 | (.04) | .18 | (.51) |
| **Packaging** (BASE = NOCHOICE) | | | | | | | | |
| CHOICE | .20 | (1.45) | .34 | (1.37) | .58* | (3.26) | .15 | (.51) |
| **Pictures** (BASE = NOPICTU) | | | | | | | | |
| PICTURE | .73* | (6.10) | 1.02* | (8.16) | .57* | (5.26) | .83* | (5.59) |
| **Adlocation** (BASE = BOTTOM) | | | | | | | | |
| TOP | .33* | (2.13) | .04 | (.21) | .19 | (1.43) | .42* | (2.50) |
| MIDDLE | .03 | (.21) | -.06 | (.46) | .09 | (.85) | .06 | (.44) |
| **Miltiplead** (BASE = SINGLEAD) | | | | | | | | |
| SAMEAD | .02 | (.12) | .04 | (.19) | .10 | (.89) | -.39* | (2.46) |

Table 1.14. (cont.)

| Effect/ variable | 1976–77 | | | | 1986–87 | | | |
|---|---|---|---|---|---|---|---|---|
| | Charlotte | | Raleigh | | Charlotte | | Raleigh | |
| **Seasonality** | | | | | | | | |
| **(BASE = SEP)** | | | | | | | | |
| AUG | .08 | (.33) | .01 | (.04) | -.44 | (1.22) | .08 | (.20) |
| OCT | .11 | (.78) | .26 | (1.53) | -.46* | (3.24) | -.17 | (.89) |
| NOV | -.29 | (1.83) | .03 | (.14) | -.84* | (4.99) | -.05 | (.24) |
| DEC | -.39 | (2.40) | -.04 | (.18) | -.69* | (3.92) | -.28 | (1.09) |
| JAN | -.19 | (1.10) | .82* | (3.86) | -.53* | (3.15) | -.20 | (.86) |
| **Store** | | | | | | | | |
| **(BASE = WINN DIXIE)** | | | | | | | | |
| A&P | .93* | (4.20) | .66* | (3.33) | .42* | (2.22) | .53 | (1.91) |
| BIG M | 1.08* | (2.74) | a | | a | | a | |
| BIG STAR | .66* | (2.47) | .66* | (.238) | a | | .46 | (1.70) |
| BI-LO | .40 | (1.39) | a | | .10 | (.32) | a | |
| CASHIONS FM | 1.67* | (2.54) | a | | a | | a | |
| COLONIAL | a | | .17 | (.85) | a | | a | |
| FARM FRESH | a | | a | | a | | .63* | (2.19) |
| FOOD LION | -.32 | (1.02) | -1.25* | (2.07) | .35 | (1.75) | .60 | (1.86) |
| FOOD MART | .74 | (1.91) | a | | a | | a | |
| FOOD-A-RAMA | a | | a | | -1.60* | (6.23) | a | |
| FOOD WORLD | a | | .55* | (2.65) | a | | a | |
| FRESH MARKET | a | | a | | .05 | (.20) | a | |
| GIANT GENIE | -.48 | (1.37) | a | | -1.23* | (4.91) | a | |
| HARRIS TEETER | .61* | (2.47) | a | | -.16 | (.73) | -.10 | (.39) |
| HILLBILLY | a | | a | | -1.44* | (4.58) | a | |
| IGA | a | | -.20 | (.67) | a | | -.92* | (2.83) |
| KROGER | a | | a | | .45* | (2.13) | .81* | (2.63) |
| LYONS | a | | a | | a | | -.26 | (.35) |
| NEWGAMBLES | .91* | (3.39) | a | | a | | a | |
| PARK-N-SHOP | 1.24* | (4.48) | a | | -1.17* | (6.31) | a | |
| PIGGLY WIGGLY | a | | .14 | (.61) | a | | -.43 | (.98) |
| RED & WHITE | 1.08* | (2.80) | .07 | (.27) | a | | .25 | (.91) |
| TRADE WINDS | .55 | (1.52) | a | | a | | a | |
| VILLAGE MKT | a | | a | | -.92* | (3.40) | a | |
| WRIGLEY | .93 | (1.96) | a | | a | | a | |
| $\bar{R}^2$ | .67 | | .65 | | .73 | | .59 | |
| Degrees of Freedom | 185 | | 97 | | 154 | | 152 | |

a No observations present in given city in given year.
* Denotes that the coefficients are significant at the 5 percent level.

−1.4, indicates considerable uncertainty about the magnitude of an association between ad space and product price.

There was no single other apple characteristic consistently significant in all models. In three of the four cases, ads for Washington State apples appeared to be significantly larger than for several other kinds of apples. Western apples also received significantly more space in food ads in Raleigh in 1986−87 relative to ads that did not include a specific location.

For two of the models there was strong statistical evidence that more space was allocated to apple ads when a specific variety was mentioned relative to ads without a specific variety being included. Inclusion of grade and/or size information seemed to have little effect on size of apple ads. This is not too surprising given the relatively small proportion of observations that had this information included. Finally, there is limited support for ad size being positively associated with apples being sold in units where consumers choose their apples relative to prepackaged units. Only in Charlotte in 1986−87 was this effect statistically significant.

Pictures are the most prominent ad characteristics related to ad space. Signs of the picture variables are all positive indicating that when pictures were used more space was allocated to apple ads. This result is consistent with pictures being generally space intensive relative to words or numbers.

Only in isolated instances, did other variables representing characteristics of the ad appear to have any significant effects on ad space. For two of the models, the evidence suggested that when apples appeared in the top third of the food ads, more space was given to apples relative to such information being included in the bottom third of food ads.

There was not much difference in the amount of space allocated to apple ads in the middle third of the food ads compared to the bottom third of food ads.

In 1986−87 apple ad space was smaller for most months relative to September. Only in Charlotte, however, were the differences for October through January significantly different from September. The estimated seasonal effects for 1976−77 were not as consistent as for 1986−87. Similarly it is difficult to detect many systematic relationships between ad size and individual retail outlets. One tendency based on the results for both cities and both periods was that A&P tended to have larger ads relative to several other stores after adjusting for the effects of other variables. Several other coefficients for individual stores were significantly different from zero suggesting substantial individual management decisions about how much space to allocate to apple advertising over and above decisions about the kinds of particular information about apples to communicate to potential customers.

## Summary and Conclusions

Several important changes were noted in the newspaper advertisements of apples between 1876–77 and 1986–87. For example the number of newspaper apple ads in Charlotte declined whereas a substantial increase in the number of such ads was observed for Raleigh. Also there were some substantial changes in the type of information about apples communicated through newspaper ads in the eighties compared to a decade earlier in Raleigh and Charlotte. In the mid-1980s, more emphasis was placed on identifying the apples being advertised by specific geographic origin in both cities than in the earlier period. Also, in both cities, there was a moderate increase in the frequency of ads including information about apple grade and/or size although the proportion of such ads remained low even in the latter period. Furthermore, a rise in the share of ads promoting apples sold in non-bag units was noted between the mid-1970s and mid-1980s.

Some strategies used by retailers in advertising apples seemed to be maintained over time. For instance, the dominance of Washington State apples in both the 1976–77 and the 1986–87 seasons (especially in the latter period) was noted in Raleigh and Charlotte. Also, in both 1976–77 and 1986–87, Red Delicious apples was the most frequently advertised variety in Charlotte. The combination of Red and Golden Delicious apples had a higher frequency of advertisement in Raleigh in the same periods.

Other results of this study indicate changes in techniques used to draw consumers' attention to fresh apples. Not only was there a tendency for retailers to move the apple ads to the middle of the food ad, also more space was given to apple ads even though the proportion of apple ad space to total food ad space does not vary that much. More apple ads were also included in special newspaper inserts. There was also an increase in the use of pictorial representations to emphasize apples being advertised.

The exploratory econometric investigation of the relationship between apple ad space and characteristics of the apples and ads indicated an inverse relationship between ad size and price and a positive relationship between space and pictorial representation. These were the most consistent findings for the models estimated. The tendency for ads featuring Washington State apples to be a little bigger than other apple ads should be of interest to apple growers. The lack of consistent associations between apple ad space and other characteristics over time and between cities indicates there is considerable opportunity for more study of factors affecting advertising decisions.

It would be of interest to know whether the results of this study hold for other major cities and other products. Also it would be of interest to expand the data set for other years to permit a better analysis of trends in apple advertising strategies by North Carolina retailers instead of relying on just two particular years.

# 2 Assessing the Impact of Generic Advertising of Fluid Milk Products in Texas

ORAL CAPPS, JR., and DANIEL S. MOEN

U.S. dairy farmers invest about $200 million annually to advertise and promote the sales of their products on a nonbrand basis.

Milk advertising programs occur through a number of federal milk marketing orders and state and regional agencies. (Marketing orders are government sanctioned monopolies designed to give producers greater control over prices, incomes, and product distribution.) Advertising and promotion expenditures are financed through a 15-cent per hundredweight assessment authorized under the 1983 Dairy and Tobacco Adjustment Act. Up to 10 cents can be applied to regional programs, while at least 5 cents must remain with the National Dairy Promotion and Research Board to underwrite national efforts (Ward 1988).

In agreement with Liu and Forker (1988), and in light of the large investment on the part of dairy farmers, the impact of generic milk advertising and promotion on demand is a key issue for the dairy industry. Evidence exists to indicate that generic advertising, with appropriate lags, affects consumption of fluid milk (Thompson and Eiler 1977; Kinnucan 1986; Kinnucan and Forker 1988; Ward and McDonald 1986; Kinnucan, 1987; Liu and Forker 1988). Except for the Ward and McDonald study, the markets typically studied have been either Buffalo or New York City. Ward and McDonald, however, consider ten milk market order regions (eastern Colorado; southeastern Florida; Georgia; the Great Basin; Greater Kansas City; southern Michigan; New England; Middle Atlantic; the Upper Midwest; and Virginia). In the various studies, the impacts of generic advertising specifically on whole milk and lowfat milk were not analyzed. Moreover, in the respective studies, advertising expenditures were not disaggregated by medium (that is, television and radio).

In this light, the focus of this paper is on assessing the impacts of generic advertising by medium on the sales of whole milk and lowfat milk, separately, for the Texas milk market order. The time period in question is

1980 to 1985. The chief concern is to determine whether television and radio advertising expenditures result in increases in the sales of whole milk and lowfat milk within the Texas order. This paper differs from the aforementioned research in three ways: (1) the disaggregation of advertising expenditures by medium; (2) the disaggregation of fluid milk into whole milk and lowfat milk; and (3) the attention on the Texas order.

Per capita fluid milk consumption in the United States declined roughly 2 percent over the 1980–85 period. However, diverse consumption trends were evident for whole milk and other milk products. The consumption of whole milk decreased approximately 15 percent over the period, while the consumption of other milk beverages increased roughly 16 percent (Agricultural Marketing Service). Corresponding patterns exist in Texas. Between 1980 and 1985, total per capita consumption of fluid milk dropped slightly more than 1 percent. The consumption of whole milk declined by nearly 6 percent, but the consumption of lowfat milk increased by almost 21 percent. Relative to the United States as a whole, the decline in the consumption of whole milk in Texas has been less dramatic during the 1980s (Texas Milk Market Report). Previous research suggests that consumption patterns for dairy products may differ substantially among regions in the United States (Boehm 1975; Boehm and Babb 1975; Huang and Raunikar 1983). Huang and Raunikar note that regional differences in consumption patterns may arise from variations in demographic composition and characteristics, income levels, relative price levels, and tastes and preferences.

Four federal marketing orders currently operate in Texas (Texas, Texas Panhandle, Lubbock-Plainview, and Rio Grande Valley). Formerly there were five orders, but the Red River Valley order became part of the Texas order as of the last quarter of 1982 (Schwart 1988). The Texas order, however, encompasses more producers, handlers, and consumers than the other three Texas orders combined (Knutson, Hunter and Schwart 1981). The Texas order incorporates six of the largest standard metropolitan statistical areas (SMSAs) in the state (Figure 2.1). Between 80 and 85 percent of Texas's population lives the boundaries of the Texas order (Seton 1985; Knutson, Schwart, and Smith 1988).

## Model Development

According to Kinnucan (1985), four modeling issues associated with advertising and promotion of farm products warrant attention: (1) choosing appropriate functional forms; (2) incorporating carryover effects; (3)

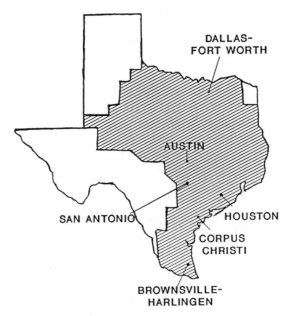

DALLAS-
FORT WORTH

AUSTIN

SAN ANTONIO   HOUSTON

CORPUS
CHRISTI

BROWNSVILLE-
HARLINGEN

The geographical area of the Texas milk marketing order is the shaded portion of the map.

**Figure 2.1. The Texas milk marketing order and major metropolitan markets served.**

controlling for confounding influences; and (4) identifying seasonality effects. Much of the literature on commodity promotion suggests the existence of diminishing marginal returns to advertising (Simon and Arndt 1980). Commonly used functions that permit marginal returns to advertising to diminish with increases in expenditure are the double-logarithmic, semilogarithmic, and logarithmic-inverse forms. The functional form chosen for this analysis is the double-logarithmic form. With this functional form, the structural parameter estimates are elasticities.

In addition, the total impact of advertising expenditures may not be realized immediately, but instead may be distributed over time. Analyses of various dairy-product promotional programs based on monthly data support the notion of a hump-shaped lag pattern (Kinnucan 1986, 1987; Thompson and Eiler 1977; Ward and McDonald 1986). The estimated lag structures from these studies yield small initial period responses in relation to the total response. The peak effect usually occurs two to four months beyond the initial expenditure. The availability of time-series data permits the application of distributed lag models to obtain estimates of both short-run and long-run effects of advertising on sales. In fact, most econometric studies of advertising use a distributed lag specification with variables expressed in logarithms (for example, Thompson and Eiler 1977, third degree polynomial with lag length of five months; Ward and McDonald 1986, second degree polynomial with lag length of twelve months; Thompson and Eiler 1975, second degree polynomial with lag length of six months; and Kinnucan 1986, 1987, second degree polynomial with lag length of six months).

An alternative approach, suggested by the Nerlove and Arrow (1962) treatment of advertising expenditures, is to specify in the demand equation a single variable, "goodwill." In this approach, the goodwill variable is a weighted average of current and past advertising expenditures. Typically, the weights follow a Pascal distribution and sum to unity (Kinnucan and Forker 1986).

The length of the lag structure for advertising expenditures is an empirical question (Myers 1987). For dairy products, according to Liu and Forker (1988), the full effect of fluid milk advertising is not apparent until two months after the initial exposure. The carryover effect for fluid milk products, where advertising continues to affect consumption beyond the initial impact, lasts roughly six months. Studies of generic advertising of fluid milk conducted by Kinnucan (1986, 1987) in two different cities — Buffalo and New York City — indicate lag lengths of six months. Moreover, Clarke (1976) concluded that 90 percent of the cumulative effects of advertising for frequently purchased products, such as fluid milk, are captured within three to nine months.

It is not uncommon for zero levels of advertising expenditures to exist for some observation periods. With the use of logarithmic transformations, however, problems arise when zero levels of advertising occur. To circumvent this problem, arbitrarily "low" values are usually employed. For example, Thompson and Eiler (1977) use a "very small" monthly per capita advertising level of $.0001. However, according to Wu, Kesecker, and Meinhold (1985), the empirical results can be sensitive to the arbitrary values selected.

Over the period 1980 to 1985, the level of generic advertising in the Texas order ranged from $0 to over $254,000 per month for television and $0 to over $198,000 per month for radio. Strikingly, as exhibited in Table 2.1, the number of zero observations for television advertising was 53 (72 percent), and the number of zero observations for radio advertising was 33 (45 percent). No information exists on brand advertising in the Texas order.

**Table 2.1. Nominal monthly generic advertising expenditures in the Texas order for fluid milk by medium, January 1980 to January 1986**

| Time period | Television | Radio | Total |
|---|---|---|---|
| 1980 | | (dollars) | |
| January | 0 | 0 | 0 |
| February | 0 | 0 | 0 |
| March | 0 | 0 | 0 |
| April | 0 | 0 | 0 |
| May | 0 | 0 | 0 |
| June | 0 | 0 | 0 |
| July | 0 | 0 | 0 |
| August | 0 | 0 | 0 |
| September | 0 | 0 | 0 |
| October | 0 | 0 | 0 |
| November | 0 | 0 | 0 |
| December | 0 | 0 | 0 |
| | | | |
| 1981 | | | |
| January | 0 | 0 | 0 |
| February | 0 | 0 | 0 |
| March | 0 | 0 | 0 |
| April | 0 | 0 | 0 |
| May | 0 | 0 | 0 |
| June | 105,723 | 38,094 | 143,817 |
| July | 109,146 | 30,360 | 139,506 |
| August | 0 | 48,697 | 48,697 |
| September | 0 | 0 | 0 |
| October | 0 | 83,754 | 83,754 |
| November | 0 | 139,563 | 139,563 |
| December | 52,594 | 0 | 52,594 |
| | | | |
| 1982 | | | |
| January | 39,380 | 0 | 39,380 |
| February | 49,319 | 0 | 49,319 |
| March | 187,227 | 0 | 187,227 |
| April | 153,826 | 0 | 153,826 |
| May | 153,956 | 57,679 | 211,635 |
| June | 0 | 18,987 | 18,987 |
| July | 0 | 0 | 0 |
| August | 0 | 84,233 | 84,233 |
| September | 0 | 70,549 | 70,549 |
| October | 0 | 149,362 | 149,362 |
| November | 0 | 131,338 | 131,338 |
| December | 0 | 59,938 | 59,938 |
| | | | |
| 1983 | | | |
| January | 0 | 43,032 | 43,032 |
| February | 0 | 185,211 | 185,211 |
| March | 0 | 91,694 | 91,694 |

**Table 2.1.  (cont.)**

| Time period | Television | Radio | Total |
|-------------|-----------|-------|-------|
|             |           | (dollars) |     |
| April       | 0         | 59,130  | 59,130 |
| May         | 0         | 82,131  | 82,131 |
| June        | 0         | 69,323  | 69,323 |
| July        | 0         | 106,979 | 106,979 |
| August      | 0         | 32,102  | 32,102 |
| September   | 0         | 74,225  | 74,225 |
| October     | 0         | 112,782 | 112,782 |
| November    | 0         | 128,300 | 128,300 |
| December    | 0         | 83,371  | 83,371 |
|             |           |         |        |
| 1984        |           |         |        |
| January     | 253,797   | 36,914  | 290,711 |
| February    | 0         | 51,287  | 51,287 |
| March       | 0         | 81,765  | 81,765 |
| April       | 203,277   | 0       | 203,277 |
| May         | 78,981    | 0       | 78,981 |
| June        | 203,598   | 0       | 203,598 |
| July        | 0         | 0       | 0 |
| August      | 0         | 0       | 0 |
| September   | 115,965   | 109,726 | 225,691 |
| October     | 90,875    | 198,302 | 289,177 |
| November    | 59,925    | 102,224 | 162,149 |
| December    | 130,531   | 133,806 | 264,337 |
|             |           |         |        |
| 1985        |           |         |        |
| January     | 0         | 0       | 0 |
| February    | 0         | 66,911  | 66,911 |
| March       | 0         | 89,361  | 89,361 |
| April       | 0         | 72,234  | 72,234 |
| May         | 0         | 50,600  | 50,600 |
| June        | 0         | 95,415  | 95,415 |
| July        | 0         | 0       | 0 |
| August      | 104,191   | 0       | 104,191 |
| September   | 203,668   | 14,224  | 217,892 |
| October     | 4,250     | 5,525   | 9,775 |
| November    | 37,033    | 81,803  | 118,836 |
| December    | 0         | 0       | 0 |

SOURCE: Ward, Ronald W., and Bruce Dixon 1988.

Advertising of fluid milk by the National Dairy Board commenced September 1984. However, this analysis excludes the national advertising that appears in various Texas television markets. The markets make up about 5.5

percent of the television households in the United States (personal correspondence with Judy Hage, Associated Milk Producers, Inc.). While this omission technically results in specification bias, the magnitude of this bias is assumed to be negligible.

In this study, to allow the use of the double-logarithmic model when zero levels of advertising occur, the respective zero levels are set to one. The rationale for this representation lies in the fact that the natural logarithm of one is zero. This representation works well as long as advertising expenditures are not placed on a per capita basis.

In agreement with Ward (1988), deflating advertising expenditures is a data issue that should not be treated lightly. Because of the relatively large number of zero observations, and in light of the preceding discussion, deflated advertising expenditures were *not* placed on a per capita basis. Additionally, because appropriate media cost indices in which to deflate advertising expenditures were difficult to construct due to lack of pertinent information, the Consumer Price Index for all items (1967 = 100) was used.

Based on previous research, the impacts of both television and radio advertising on the consumption of whole milk and lowfat milk in this study are hypothesized to be positive. The length of the lag structure, although an empirical question, is hypothesized to range from two to nine months. Alternative polynomial lag specifications for both radio and television advertising expenditures were estimated. However, perhaps due to collinearity among the regressors (see subsequent parts of this section) or to the relatively large percentage of zero observations for advertising expenditures, the coefficients associated with current and lagged effects of advertising were predominantly negative and statistically insignificant. Similarly, attempts to use the goodwill variable specification (Kinnucan and Forker 1986), where the weights $w_i$ follow a Pascal distribution ($w_i = (i + 1)(1 - \lambda)^2\lambda^i$; $0 < \lambda < 1$; $i = 0, 1, 2, \ldots, n$; and $n$ represents the length of the lag structure), were not successful. Although the use of the goodwill specification reduces the magnitude of the collinearity problem, the coefficients associated with the measure of goodwill for various values of $\lambda$ and $n$ (parameters to be estimated) were nonetheless mostly negative and statistically insignificant.

Due to the shortcomings of traditional ways to capture the effect of generic advertising in demand relationships, no assumption is made regarding the form of the distribution of the weights. This assumption is equivalent to the work of Alt (1942) in the use of distributed lag models in that the weights do not follow a priori structure. The lag lengths may still be different for the respective media and for the respective commodities.

We are in agreement with Kinnucan (1985), "An important measurement problem associated with time-series analysis of commodity promotion programs is that of controlling for confounding influences such as income, population, price, and demographic changes." Because this study relies on monthly time-series observations, demographic factors such as household size and ethnicity are not considered.

Haidacher, Blaylock, and Myers (1988) conclude that although the demand for dairy products was sensitive to a number of factors, sensitivity to changes in relative prices and income was most pronounced. Own-price effects are expected to be negative. In an investigation of fluid milk demand in Pennsylvania, Kirkland and Sipple (1987) found own-price effects to be negative for whole milk and 2 percent milk but positive for 1 percent milk and skim milk. As well, Kirkland and Sipple found whole milk, 2 percent milk, 1 percent milk, and skim milk to be complements in lieu of substitutes. On this basis, whole milk and lowfat milk are hypothesized to be complements.

Prior milk demand studies have utilized an index of coffee, tea, and cola prices as well as an index of beverage prices to determine cross-price effects of competing products (Wilson and Thompson 1967; Prato 1973). A major problem in demand analyses is in defining plausible substitutes for milk. Milk is unique in that it is not only a beverage but also a highly nutritional commodity essential to healthy body development. In this study, cola is hypothesized to be a substitute for both whole milk and lowfat milk. Yogurt is also hypothesized to be a substitute for lowfat milk because of the association with health and nutrition. Other nonmilk dairy products (cheese, margarine) and products outside the dairy group (coffee) may be substitutes or complements to fluid milk products (Huang 1985; Heien and Wessells 1988). However, due to data limitations, these products are omitted from the analysis.

Following Boehm (1975), Salathe (1979), Blaylock and Smallwood (1983), and Huang and Raunikar (1983), income effects are hypothesized to be negative for whole milk and positive for lowfat milk. Although there has been considerable discussion of how concerns over nutrition and health affect the demand for dairy products, few empirical studies quantitatively link these concerns with demand. The dairy industry has spent millions of dollars on nutrition related research and on promoting the health related aspects of dairy products. Concern for reducing fat intake has been cited as a major factor influencing the trend away from whole milk toward lowfat and skim milk (Jones and Weimer 1980). Following Liu and Forker (1988), a trend variable is used to capture structural changes in consumer perceptions toward dairy products. The coefficient associated with the trend variable is hypothesized to be negative for whole milk consumption and positive for lowfat milk consumption.

Seasonal patterns are evident for fluid milk consumption. A viable approach to capture seasonal effects is to include dummy variables (either monthly or quarterly) in the model. Monthly dummy variables are commonly used to represent seasonality. However, a relatively large number of degrees of freedom are consumed with the use of monthly dummy variables. Consequently, quarterly dummy variables are used in this study. Doran and Quilkey (1972) suggest using the harmonic variable format as an alternative to the use of dummy variables when the seasonal demand for the good in question follows a regular pattern from year to year. Harmonic variables, constructed as sine and cosine functions of trend, have been found to be especially useful in cases where interaction effects between advertising and seasons are thought to be present. The use of slope dummies to investigate seasonal variations in the coefficients of advertising for television and radio may be worthwhile (Kinnucan and Forker 1986). Slope dummy variables are not used in this study.

In light of the preceding discussion, the specification of the respective demand relationships for whole milk and lowfat milk in this study is as follows:

$$\log SW_t = f(\log PWD_t, \log PLF_t, \log PC_t, \log INC_t, \qquad (2.1)$$
$$\log LTV_t, \log LRAD_t, APRJUN, JULSEP, OCTDEC,$$
$$TREND) \quad \text{and}$$

$$\log SLF_t = g(\log PLF_t, \log PWD_t, \log PC_t, \log PY_t, \qquad (2.2)$$
$$\log INC_t, \log LTV_t, \log LRAD_t, APRJUN,$$
$$JULSEP, OCTDEC, TREND)$$

where

log SW = natural logarithm per capita real sales of whole milk in the Texas order ($);

log SLF = natural logarithm per capita real sales of lowfat milk in the Texas order ($);

log PWD = natural logarithm of real price in Dallas of whole milk ($/half gallon);

log PLF = natural logarithm of real price in Dallas of lowfat milk ($/half gallon);

log PC = natural logarithm of real price in Dallas of cola ($/12 oz can);

log PY = natural logarithm of real price in Dallas of yogurt ($/half pint);

log INC = natural logarithm of real per capita income in Texas ($);

log LTV = natural logarithm of appropriate lag(s) of television advertising in real terms ($) (i.e., $\log TV_t, \log TV_{t-1}, \ldots, \log TV_{t-p}$);

log LRAD = natural logarithm of appropriate lag(s) of radio advertising in real terms ($) (i.e., $\log RAD_t, \log RAD_{t-1} \ldots, \log RAD_{t-m}$);

APRJUN = 1 if month either April, May, or June, 0 otherwise;
JULSEP = 1 if month either July, August, or September, 0 otherwise;
OCTDEC = 1 if month either October, November, or December, 0
    otherwise; and
TREND = chronological number of each month.

## Descriptive Statistics and Statistical Procedures

Monthly time-series observations from January 1980 to January 1986 are used in this study. The data are available from the authors upon request. To avoid "data interval bias" in the estimation of advertising effects, Clarke (1976) recommends the use of monthly data in most situations. Descriptive statistics of the continuous variables in the model are exhibited in Table 2.2. On average over this sample period, consumers in the Texas order spent roughly three and a half times more on whole milk than on lowfat milk on a monthly basis. The plot of per capita fluid milk sales in the Texas order over the sample period in question is exhibited in Figure 2.2. Seasonal and trend patterns are evident from this diagram.

Table 2.2. Descriptive statistics of the continuous variables in the model[a]

| Variable | Mean | Standard deviation | Minimum | Maximum |
| --- | --- | --- | --- | --- |
| Endogenous variables | | | | |
| SW | 1.4135 | 0.0954 | 1.1369 | 1.6815 |
| SLF | 0.3847 | 0.0427 | 0.3034 | 0.4850 |
| Exogenous variables | | | | |
| PWD | 0.4395 | 0.0156 | 0.3770 | 0.4720 |
| PLF | 0.4208 | 0.0121 | 0.3990 | 0.4500 |
| PC | 0.1636 | 0.0048 | 0.1530 | 0.1750 |
| PY | 0.1800 | 0.0054 | 0.1670 | 0.1910 |
| TV | 10853 | 21308 | 0 | 84769 |
| RAD | 14844 | 17537 | 0 | 65145 |
| INC | 4075.8 | 166.48 | 3784 | 4355 |

[a]All variables are in real terms, 1967 dollars.

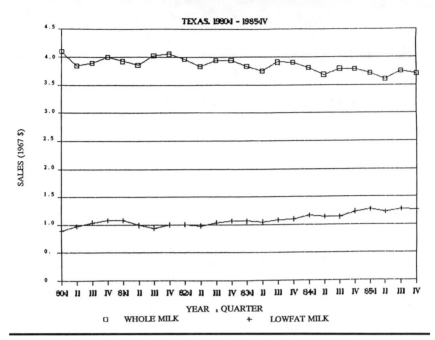

**Figure 2.2. Per capita fluid milk sales in the Texas order, 1980–1985.**

Included as independent variables are retail fluid milk prices (dollars per ½ gallon); the price of cola (dollars per 12 oz can); the price of yogurt (dollars per ½ pint); per capita income of Texas residents (dollars); advertising expenditure, both television and radio (dollars per month); quarterly dummy variables to capture seasonality effects; and a trend variable. Adjustments were made to convert nominal values to real values using the Consumer Price Index (1967 = 100).

In real terms, the average price of whole milk was nearly 44 cents, just 2 cents above the average price of lowfat milk. Over the period 1980 to 1985 in the Texas order, real prices for both whole milk and lowfat milk declined. The decline in the real price of whole milk was on the order of 10 percent, and the decline in the real price of lowfat milk was on the order of 7 percent. The average real price of cola was about 16 cents per 12 ounce can, and the average price of yogurt in real terms was almost 18 cents per half pint. Real expenditures on television advertising for fluid milk averaged $10,850 per month, while real expenditures on radio advertising averaged close to $14,850 per month. The share of expenditures on radio advertising is 58 percent, while the share on television advertising is 42 percent. Real per capita income, on average, was almost $4,100.

The problem of simultaneity may exist between advertising expenditures and sales, particularly with the use of time-series data (Schmalensee 1972). However, in the Texas order, because the level of sales for whole milk and for lowfat milk has no influence on direct consumer advertising expenditures, this issue is not relevant.

Assuming that supply is perfectly elastic, ordinary least squares (OLS) is used to obtain structural parameter estimates. It may be argued that a seemingly unrelated regression (SUR) procedure may be used in this situation. Indeed, exogenous factors such as the general level of economic activity, prices of other dairy products, demographic variables, or other omitted factors may affect the sales of the respective fluid milk products apart from the specified predetermined variables. Consequently, the disturbance terms of the respective equations may be contemporaneously correlated. In this analysis, however, the gains in estimation efficiency are minimal. Therefore, the OLS procedure, not the SUR procedure, is used.

Yet, attempts to estimate the respective demand relationships using OLS were plagued by deleterious collinearity problems. Collinearity adversely affects the reliability of the structural parameter estimates. The presence of collinearity was confirmed by examination of the singular value decomposition of the data matrix, the variance decompositon proportions, and the variance inflation factors. Strong variable intercorrelations exist in the case of condition indices in excess of 30, variance decomposition proportions in excess of 0.5, and variance inflation factors in excess of 10 (Belsley, Kuh, and Welsch 1980).

To overcome the effects of collinearity in the single-equation specifications, this study employs ridge regression (Fomby, Hill, and Johnson 1984). In brief, the procedure entails the addition of small positive increments, $k$-values (biasing parameters), to the diagonal elements of the correlation matrices of the set of exogenous variables. Stochastic and nonstochastic procedures are available for determining biasing parameters. In this analysis, the selection of the $k$-values for the respective equations rests on the basis of the ridge trace (Hoerl and Kennard 1970), which is a plot of the estimated structural coefficients versus various $k$-values. The choice of the $k$-values occurs where the estimates of the structural parameters begin to stabilize. The major drawback to this criterion is the subjectivity of the selection process.

## Empirical Results

The parameter estimates and associated pseudo $t$-statistics obtained from the ridge regression procedure are exhibited in Table 2.3. Because the ridge regression procedure gives rise to biased parameter estimates, strictly speaking, the $t$-statistics are not applicable. However, the $t$-statistics provide crude indicators of significance. The $\bar{R}^2$ measure for the whole milk relationship is .5777, and the $\bar{R}^2$ measure for the lowfat milk relationship is .6045. On the basis of the ridge trace, the $k$-value chosen for the whole milk relationship is 0.15, while the $k$-value chosen for the lowfat milk relationship is 0.75. The .10 level of significance is chosen for the statistical tests.

**Table 2.3. Parameter estimates and associated standard errors obtained from the ridge regression procedure**

| Variable | Whole milk | Lowfat milk |
|---|---|---|
| log PWD$_t$ | 0.5854[a,c] | -0.1290 |
|  | (3.26)[b] | (-1.06) |
| log PLF$_t$ | -0.2737[c] | 0.7654[c] |
|  | (-1.38) | (4.26) |
| log PC$_t$ | 0.0793 | -0.5438[c] |
|  | (0.42) | (-3.65) |
| log PY$_t$ | ------ | 0.5154[c] |
|  |  | (3.06) |
| log INC$_t$ | -0.1731[c] | 0.2922[c] |
|  | (-1.31) | (3.05) |
| log RAD$_{t-2}$ | 0.0013[c] | ------ |
|  | (1.29) |  |
| log RAD$_{t-3}$ | ------ | 0.0004 |
|  |  | (0.38) |
| log TV$_{t-4}$ | 0.0015[c] | 0.0019[c] |
|  | (1.45) | (1.62) |
| APRJUN | -0.0194[c] | -0.0238[c] |
|  | (-1.65) | (-1.96) |
| JULSEP | 0.0232[c] | -0.0257[c] |
|  | (1.99) | (-2.30) |
| OCTDEC | 0.0220[c] | 0.0007 |
|  | (1.89) | (0.06) |
| TREND | -0.0012[c] | 0.0013[c] |
|  | (-5.48) | (7.75) |
| INTERCEPT | 2.1969[c] | -2.9730[c] |
|  | (2.25) | (-3.45) |
| Regression diagnostics |  |  |
|   $k$-value | 0.15 | 0.75 |
|   $\bar{R}^2$ | 0.5777 | 0.6045 |

[a]Parameter estimate.
[b]Pseudo $t$-statistic.
[c]Significant at the .10 level.

Based on the explanatory power of the model and the significance of the estimated coefficients, a two-period lag for radio advertising and a four-period lag for television advertising best fit the data in regard to the model for whole milk; a three-period lag for radio advertising and a four-period lag for television advertising best fit the data in regard to the model for lowfat milk. For whole milk and lowfat milk, the effect of advertising on television occurs four months beyond the initial expenditure. The elasticity of television advertising for whole milk is .0015, for lowfat milk .0019. For whole milk, the effect of radio advertising occurs two months beyond the initial expenditure. The elasticity of radio advertising for whole milk is .0013. However, for lowfat milk, the effect of radio advertising is not statistically different from zero.

The respective lags associated with television and radio advertising are similar across commodities. The lag lengths are within the limits reported in the literature. Specific studies relating to milk demand typically indicate a sales-advertising lag ranging from two to six months. Importantly, however, the estimated advertising effects in this analysis are simply lags; consequently the lags reported refer to the number of months before a response occurs. The lags of two to six months mentioned in the literature refer to the number of months in which carryover is observed.

Markets unequivocally differ in their responsiveness to advertising efforts. Yet, the elasticities of advertising from this analysis are similar to those reported by Liu and Forker (1988) (short-run elasticity of .0017, long-run elasticity of .0028) and by Ward and McDonald (1986) (short-run elasticity of .0039, long-run elasticity of .0085). The Liu and Forker study deals with monthly time-series data for the New York City market over the period 1971 to 1984. The Ward and McDonald study deals with pooled time-series and cross-sectional data from 10 milk market order regions over the period 1976 to 1983.

The own-price elasticities for whole milk and lowfat milk in the Texas order are −.4146 and −.2346 respectively. By comparison, Boehm (1975) found the own-price elasticity of whole milk (lowfat milk) to be −.37 (−.55); Kirkland and Sipple (1977) found the own-price elasticity of whole milk (lowfat milk) to be −.97 (−.99). The cross-price elasticity of whole milk with respect to lowfat milk is −.2737, while the cross-price elasticity of lowfat milk with respect to whole milk, although negative, is not statistically different from zero. Because similar complementary relationships were found in the Kirkland and Sipple study for Pennsylvania, this particular finding is not unprecedented.

The cross-price elasticity of whole milk (lowfat milk) with respect to cola is .0793 (−.5438), and the cross-price elasticity of lowfat milk with respect to yogurt is .5154. Cola and whole milk in the Texas order are very weak substitutes. Yogurt and lowfat milk are indeed substitutes. However, contrary to prior beliefs, lowfat milk and cola are complements.

As expected, the income effect was negative for whole milk and positive for lowfat milk. For the Texas order, the income elasticity for whole milk is −.1731, while the income elasticity for lowfat milk is .2922. Boehm found the income elasticity for whole milk (lowfat milk) to be −.07 (.16). Salathe

(1979) found the income elasticity for whole milk (lowfat milk) to be −.09 (.36). Finally, Huang and Raunikar (1983) found the income elasticity for lowfat milk to be .29. The income elasticities for the Texas order compare favorably with those in the literature.

The seasonality patterns of sales of whole milk and lowfat milk are indeed different in the Texas order. Relative to the January–March period, sales of whole milk are significantly higher in the July–September and October–December periods. On the other hand, the sales of lowfat milk are significantly lower in the April–June and July–September periods relative to the January–March period. As expected, *ceteris paribus,* a significant negative (positive) trend exists in the sales of whole milk (lowfat milk) in the Texas order.

## Concluding Remarks

The purpose of this paper is to determine whether television and radio advertising expenditures result in increases in the sales of whole milk and lowfat milk within the Texas milk market order. Monthly time-series observations over the period January 1980 to January 1986 were used. *Ceteris paribus,* both radio and television advertising bolstered real sales of whole milk, while only television advertising bolstered real sales of lowfat milk. The lag structure associated with generic advertising expenditures differed across media types; a two-month lag for radio advertising and a four-month lag for television advertising were identified; however, the lag structure was similar for the respective fluid milk products.

Own-price elasticities for whole milk and lowfat milk were negative, statistically significant, and in the inelastic range. In the Texas order, cross-price effects of the fluid milk products were negative, indicative of complements. With regard to additional cross-price effects, cola was a substitute (complement) for whole milk (lowfat milk), and yogurt was a substitute for lowfat milk. Seasonal sales patterns were evident for whole milk and lowfat milk, but the patterns were dissimilar for the fluid milk products.

Certain areas of concern remain. Although the disaggregation of advertising expenditures by medium is certainly worthwhile, the numerous zero levels of expenditure are indeed a limitation in this analysis. As well, severe collinearity among the regressors is another key limitation. To circumvent these limitations and similar to the work by Ward and McDonald (1986), it is of interest to pool time-series and cross-sectional observations for various milk marketing orders. By pooling, greater variability in advertising and other demand variables can be observed. However, if data are pooled, it is no longer possible to consider the effectiveness of generic advertising in specific markets.

Additionally, although this effort establishes a link between advertising and fluid milk sales, this work fails: (1) to ascertain whether the benefits of advertising exceed the cost of the program, and (2) to determine whether the allocation of funds for advertising is economically efficient. Additional work to address these issues is certainly worthwhile.

The analysis in this paper constitutes a first step in assessing the effectiveness of generic advertising for fresh fluid milk products in the Texas order. Given that consumption (sales) patterns generally differ among regions in the United States, further studies should pay dividends to the dairy industry for this area of Texas.

# 3    Impacts of Dairy Promotion from Consumer Demand to Farm Supply

HARRY M. KAISER, DONALD J. LIU,
TIMOTHY D. MOUNT, and OLAN D. FORKER

The funds available to national and state organizations from the national dairy promotion program have averaged over $200 million annually since its inception in 1983. Given the magnitude of money involved, which comes from an assessment of 15 cents per cwt on all milk sold by dairy farmers, there is an obvious need for sound program evaluation.

This paper examines the effects of the generic dairy promotion program within a multiple dairy market context. The analysis is based on a quarterly simulation of the national dairy industry that uses the estimated equations of an econometric model developed in Liu et al. (1988). The econometric model divides the national dairy market into three sectors (a retail, wholesale, and farm sector) and is estimated by a switching simultaneous system (SSS) procedure. The SSS method corrects for potential selectivity bias caused by the existence of two possible market solutions at any point in time: a competitive equilibrium regime, which occurs if the market price determined through supply and demand conditions is above the government support price for dairy products, and a government support regime, which occurs if the market price is at or below the support price. In the latter case, the government purchases unlimited amounts of dairy products at the purchase price until the market price is bid up to the government price.

The determination of a competitive vs. a government support regime is based on the relationship between the market price and the government purchase price for manufactured products rather than on the basis of

The authors thank Mary Jo DuBrava for her assistance in preparing this paper. This research was funded by Hatch Projects 427, 433, and the New York Milk Promotion order.

Material from this chapter has been published in D. J. Liu, H. M. Kaiser, O. D. Forker, and T. D. Mount, "An Economic Analysis of the U.S. Generic Dairy Advertising Program Using an Industry Model," *Northeastern Journal of Agricultural and Resource Economics* 19(1990): 37–48.

whether or not the government is buying products through the dairy price support program. This is because the government may purchase dairy products from plants set up to sell only to the government even when the market is competitive (market price above government price). These specialty plants package their products according to Commodity Credit Corporation standards and are not equipped to sell in commercial markets. The existence of the specialty plants and the government's patronage throughout the 1980s may lead to the erroneous conclusion that the decade has been dominated by government support regimes.

The SSS model extends the Tobit two-stage least squares procedure (Maddala 1983) from a single market to a systems context of multiple sectors within the dairy market (Liu et al. 1988). The model is used to simulate price and quantity values for all sectors under various advertising expenditure level scenarios. The first set of scenarios simulate the effects of: (1) fluid-only advertising, (2) manufactured-only advertising, and (3) combined advertising on prices and quantities. The second set of scenarios simulate the marginal impacts of the promotion program for alternative funding amounts ranging from 10 percent to 200 percent of historical levels. The results of both sets of scenarios are used to derive the welfare impacts of the various promotion strategies.

## Background

Numerous studies have been carried out to investigate the impact of dairy promotion on the demand for dairy products. Much of this research has focused on the impact of fluid product advertising on regional consumption. For example, Liu and Forker (1988) studied the impact of the New York City fluid promotion program on demand and farm revenue. They estimated a fluid demand equation for New York City using a transfer function approach. Their results indicated that generic fluid advertising had a significant positive impact on demand. Liu and Forker also conducted a dynamic simulation of alternative promotion levels and concluded that current advertising levels for New York City should be reduced by 35 percent to be optimal in a marginal sense. In another study of fluid promotion, Ward and Dixon (1988) examined the advertising impacts on demand based on data drawn from twelve milk marketing regions. They also concluded that fluid advertising had a significant positive impact on demand. Based on simulations of the estimated fluid demand equation, Ward and Dixon concluded that there are gains in sales attributed to advertising, but the gains diminished as advertising levels increased.

With respect to manufactured product advertising, Blaylock and Blisard

(1988) studied the impact of brand and generic cheese promotion on demand for cheese. They estimated demand equations for natural and processed cheese based on at-home consumption panel data provided by Market Research Corporation of America. The estimated effect of generic natural cheese advertising on demand was positive and statistically different from zero. Blaylock and Blisard also found the combined effect of brand and generic processed cheese advertising on demand to be positive and statistically significant. Brand and generic advertising, in the case of processed cheese, were aggregated because one company dominated branded advertising of processed cheese. Kinnucan and Fearon (1986) examined the effect of brand and generic cheese advertising on sales in New York City. They concluded that both brand and generic cheese advertising increased cheese sales and that there was a significant interaction effect between both types of advertising. Kinnucan and Fearon's results suggest that when launched during periods of heavy brand advertising, the impact of generic advertising could be substantially enhanced.

The studies mentioned above, and others, contribute to our overall understanding of the impact of generic dairy promotion. Several important issues, however, remain to be addressed. First, previous research has focused on fluid advertising in isolation from manufactured dairy product advertising, or vice versa. Since both fluid and manufactured dairy products have to compete against each other for a limited farm milk supply, it is desirable to investigate program impacts on both sectors simultaneously.

Second, previous studies have estimated retail demand equations, but have ignored retail supply. Hence, retail prices for milk and dairy products are not affected by the increase in demand generated by advertising. Using single-equation models in analyzing the impacts of promotion may suffer from simultaneity bias in model estimation. Additionally, such models may also cause the simulated impact of advertising on demand to be biased upward.

Third, the link between the impact of advertising on the retail sector and the subsequent impact on the farm sector has not been explicitly modeled in past research. By not modeling the sectors of the dairy market together, the tracing back of the promotion effects at the retail level to the farm level cannot be appropriately analyzed.

Fourth, the role of the government dairy price support program has not been incorporated in any models. It will be shown that the promotion program has different effects depending on whether a competitive regime or a government support regime prevails. Finally, with few exceptions, previous studies have not considered the effect of advertising on farm supply response. If the promotion program indeed increases the demand for milk and, hence, farm revenue, farmers will be encouraged to increase supply and this might eventually wipe out any short-term gains. Our model addresses the above issues and methodological limitations.

## The Simulation Model

The conceptual model of the national dairy industry consists of three markets.

Retail Fluid Market:
$$RFD = RFD(RFP \mid GFA) \tag{3.1.1}$$
$$RFS = RFS(RFP, WFP) \tag{3.1.2}$$
$$RFD = RFS \equiv Q1 \tag{3.1.3}$$

Retail Manufactured Product Market:
$$RMD = RMD(RMP \mid GMA) \tag{3.2.1}$$
$$RMS = RMS(RMP, WMP) \tag{3.2.2}$$
$$RMD = RMS \equiv Q2 \tag{3.2.3}$$

Wholesale Fluid Market:
$$WFS = WFS(WFP, P2 + DIFF) \tag{3.3.1}$$
$$WFD = Q1 \tag{3.3.2}$$
$$WFS = WFD \tag{3.3.3}$$

Wholesale Manufactured Product Market:
$$WMS = WMS(WMP, P2) \tag{3.4.1}$$
$$WMD = Q2 \tag{3.4.2}$$
$$WMS = WMD + QG + \Delta INV + QSP \tag{3.4.3}$$

Competitive regime:
$$WMP > PG \tag{3.5.1}$$
$$QG = 0 \tag{3.5.2}$$

Government support regime:
$$WMP = PG \tag{3.5.1'}$$
$$QG > 0 \tag{3.5.2'}$$

Farm Raw Milk Market:

$$AMP = \frac{(P2 + DIFF) * WFS + P2 * (QMILK - FUSE - WFS)}{(QMILK - FUSE)} \tag{3.6.1}$$

$$QMILK = f(AMP\text{-}1) \tag{3.6.2}$$
$$QMILK = FUSE + WFS + WMS \tag{3.6.3}$$

where:

| | | |
|---|---|---|
| RFD | = | Retail demand for fluid products; |
| RFP | = | Retail price of fluid products; |
| GFA | = | Generic fluid advertising expenditures; |
| RFS | = | Retail supply of fluid products; |
| WFP | = | Wholesale price of fluid products; |
| Q1 | = | Equilibrium quantity of fluid products; |
| RMD | = | Retail demand for manufactured dairy products; |
| RMP | = | Retail price of manufactured dairy products; |
| GMA | = | Generic manufactured product advertising expenditures; |
| RMS | = | Retail supply of manufactured dairy products; |
| WMP | = | Wholesale price of manufactured dairy products; |
| Q2 | = | Equilibrium quantity of manufactured dairy products; |
| WFS | = | Wholesale supply of fluid products; |
| P2 | = | Class 2 price for raw milk; |
| DIFF | = | Class 1 fixed fluid differential (exogenous); |
| WFD | = | Wholesale demand for fluid products; |
| WMS | = | Wholesale supply of manufactured dairy products; |
| WMD | = | Wholesale demand for manufactured dairy products; |
| QG | = | Government purchases of surplus dairy products; |
| $\Delta$INV | = | Change in commercial inventories (exogenous); |
| QSP | = | Government purchases of dairy products from plants specializing in selling only to the government (exogenous); |
| PG | = | Minimum government purchase price (exogenous); |
| AMP | = | Average milk price received by farmers; |
| QMILK | = | Farm production of raw milk (predetermined); and |
| FUSE | = | On-farm use of raw milk (exogenous). |

In the retail market, fluid and manufactured product retailers buy their products from fluid and manufactured product wholesalers at wholesale prices and sell to consumers. The retail fluid and manufactured product markets are characterized by the supply, demand, and equilibrium conditions reflected in equations (3.1.1) through (3.2.3). For both products, retail demand is a function of the retail price and other demand shifters including generic advertising variables; retail supply is a function of the retail price, the wholesale price, and other supply shifters; and the equilibrium condition is that demand equals supply.

In the wholesale fluid market, processors buy raw milk from dairy farmers. They pay the Class 2 price plus an exogenous fluid differential, and sell to fluid retailers. The wholesale fluid supply, demand, and equilibrium conditions are quantified by equations (3.3.1) through (3.3.3). In the wholesale market all quantities are expressed on a milk equivalent basis and demand is derived from the retail market and is equal to the equilibrium quantity in the retail fluid market. Similarly, in the manufactured market wholesale processors convert the raw milk into nonfluid products and sell either to nonfluid retailers or the government, depending upon whether the market price is above or at the minimum government purchase price, as depicted in equations (3.4.1) through (3.5.2). The equilibrium condition in (3.4.3) is different from those in other markets in that wholesale supply is equal to commercial demand plus government purchases plus change in commercial inventories plus products sold by plants specializing in selling to the government. Since the magnitudes of the latter two variables are quite small, they are treated as being exogenous.

The supply of raw milk by farmers is a function of the expected average milk price and other supply shifters. Since milk used for fluid and manufactured product purposes commands different prices, the average milk price received by farmers is the weighted average price given by equation 3.6.1. It is assumed that farmers have naive price expectations in the sense that the expected next period's price is equal to the current price. As such, the farm milk supply is lagged one period and hence is "predetermined," as expressed in equation 3.6.2. The equilibrium condition is that farm supply equals on-farm usage of milk plus the wholesalers' farm demand, which is equal to the fluid and manufactured supply in the wholesale market (3.6.3). Since on-farm use of milk is very small, it is treated as being exogenous.

With the predetermined raw milk supply in (3.6.2), all equations must be solved simultaneously to obtain solutions for the endogenous variables in the retail and wholesale markets. Then, the average milk price received by farmers can be determined through (3.6.1) which, in turn, determines the next period's farm milk supply.

The estimated structural equations are presented below. The retail and wholesale market equations are estimated using the switching simultaneous systems procedure and the farm supply equation is estimated by ordinary least squares. The estimated coefficients of all the included variables have the expected signs, and most $t$-values are statistically significant at conventional levels. The model is dynamically simulated using historical advertising expenditures. When compared with the historical endogenous variables, the root-mean-square simulation errors are very small (about 3 percent for most variables). For more details on the simulation procedures, validation results, and the data, see Liu et al. (1989).

Retail Fluid Demand:

$$\ln \text{RFD} = \underset{(-2.03)}{-0.536} \ln (\text{RFP/PFOOD}) + \underset{(2.87)}{0.341} \ln \text{RFD}_{-1} + \underset{(5.37)}{0.409} \ln \text{DINC}$$
$$+ \underset{(3.03)}{0.019} \ln \text{DGFA} - \underset{(-4.52)}{0.007} \text{TREND} + \underset{(10.65)}{0.073} \text{COS1} - \underset{(-5.16)}{0.057} \text{SIN1} + U$$
$$\bar{R}^2 = 0.89; \text{D.W.} = 2.00$$

Retail Fluid Supply:

$$\ln \text{RFS} = \underset{(4.37)}{1.403} + \underset{(2.18)}{0.319} \ln (\text{RFP/WFP}) + \underset{(5.17)}{0.538} \ln \text{RFS}_{-1} - \underset{(-2.97)}{0.077} \ln \text{DPFE}$$
$$- \underset{(-2.53)}{0.074} \ln \text{UNEMP} + \underset{(12.17)}{0.071} \text{COS1} - \underset{(-6.34)}{0.068} \text{SIN1} + U$$
$$\bar{R}^2 = 0.90; \text{D.W.} = 1.92$$

Retail Manufactured Demand:

$$\ln \text{RMD} = \underset{(-1.92)}{-0.906} \ln (\text{RMP/PFOOD}) + \underset{(0.42)}{0.064} \ln \text{RMD}_{-1} + \underset{(6.10)}{0.579} \ln \text{DINC}$$
$$+ \underset{(3.93)}{0.009} \ln \text{DGMA} + \underset{(3.18)}{0.082} \text{DUM} - \underset{(-5.41)}{0.079} \text{COS1} - \underset{(-2.56)}{0.048} \text{SIN1} + U$$
$$\bar{R}^2 = 0.87; \text{D.W.} = 2.02$$

Retail Manufactured Supply:

$$\ln \text{RMS} = \underset{(5.30)}{0.553} \ln (\text{RMP/WMP}) + \underset{(2.31)}{0.309} \ln \text{RMS}_{-1} + \underset{(3.16)}{0.074} \ln \text{TREND}$$
$$- \underset{(-7.78)}{0.104} \text{COS1} - \underset{(-1.32)}{0.023} \text{SIN1} + \underset{(1.46)}{0.012} \text{COS2} + U$$
$$\bar{R}^2 = 0.86; \text{D.W.} = 1.93$$

Wholesale Fluid Supply:

$$\ln \text{WFS} = \underset{(2.54)}{0.139} \ln (\text{WFP/(P2+DIFF)}) + \underset{(17.56)}{0.875} \ln \text{WFS}_{-1} - \underset{(-1.41)}{0.004} \text{UNEMP}$$
$$+ \underset{(10.79)}{0.062} \text{COS1} - \underset{(-12.56)}{0.095} \text{SIN1} - \underset{(-1.67)}{0.246} U_{-1} + U$$
$$\bar{R}^2 = 0.89; \text{D.W.} = 1.93$$

Wholesale Manufactured Supply:

$$\ln WMS = -7.106 + 0.254 \ln (WMP/P2) + 0.500 \ln WMS_{-1}$$
$$\phantom{\ln WMS =} (-5.73) \quad (0.41) \phantom{\ln (WMP/P2) +} (6.64)$$
$$-2.379 \ln DMWAGE - 0.072 \text{ POLDUM} - 0.177 \text{ COS1}$$
$$(-6.18) \phantom{\ln DMWAGE} (-3.52) \phantom{POLDUM} (-17.00)$$
$$+0.110 \text{ SIN1} + U$$
$$(7.25)$$

$$\overline{R}^2 = 0.95; \text{ D.W.} = 1.72$$

Raw Milk Farm Supply:

$$\ln QMILK = 1.835 + 0.059 \ln (AMP/FC)_{-1} + 0.445 \ln QMILK_{-1}$$
$$\phantom{\ln QMILK =} (5.68) \quad (2.28) \phantom{\ln (AMP/FC)_{-1} +} (4.47)$$
$$-0.251 \ln DFWAGE + 0.002 \text{ TREND} - 0.028 \text{ POLDUM} - 0.070 \text{ COS1}$$
$$(-3.63) \phantom{\ln DFWAGE} (5.81) \phantom{TREND} (-3.53) \phantom{POLDUM} (-21.56)$$
$$+0.021 \text{ SIN1} + 0.011 \text{ COS2} + U$$
$$(3.12) \phantom{SIN1} (4.65)$$

$$\overline{R}^2 = 0.96; \text{ D.W.} = 1.85$$

where:

RFD, RFS, WFS = Quantity of raw milk in fluid sector (billion pounds of raw milk equivalent) (retail demand is equal to retail supply which is equal to wholesale supply);

RMD, RMS, WMS = Quantity of raw milk in manufacturing sector (billion pounds of raw milk equivalent) (retail demand is equal to retail supply which is equal to wholesale supply);

RFP, RMP = Retail fluid and manufacturing price indices (1967 = 100);

WFP = Wholesale fluid price index (1967 = 100);

WMP = Wholesale manufacturing price ($/cwt of raw milk equivalent);

P1, P2 = Class 1 and 2 price ($/cwt);

PFOOD = Retail consumer price index for all food (1967 = 100);

DPFE = Deflated producer price index for fuel and energy (1967 = 100);

DINC = Deflated U.S. personal disposable income (billion $);

DGFA, DGMA = Deflated generic fluid and manufacturing advertising expenditures (thousand $);

UNEMP = U.S. civilian unemployment rate (percent);

DMWAGE, MFWAGE = Deflated hourly wage in food manufacturing ($/hour) and farm sector (1967 = 100);

TREND = Trend variable, for retail fluid demand equals 1 (1975, quarter 1), . . . , 52 (1987, quarter 4); for other equations equals 1 (1970, quarter 1), . . . , 72 (1987, quarter 4);

DUM = Dummy variable, equal to 1 for 1981 through 1983, 0 otherwise;

POLDUM = Dummy variable, equal to 1 for quarters when Milk Diversion and Dairy Termination Programs were in effect, 0 otherwise;

QMILK = Milk production in billion pounds;

AMP, FC = Average milk price and price of 16 percent dairy ration;

COS1, SIN1 = harmonic variables representing the first wave of the cosine and sine;

COS2 = harmonic variable representing the second wave of the cosine;

U, ln = White noise, and natural logarithm, respectively; and

$\bar{R}^2$, D.W. =  Adjusted coefficient of determination, and the Durbin Watson statistic. The $t$-values are given in parentheses.

## Policy Simulation

The estimated equations presented above are used to simulate quarterly equilibrium price and quantity values from 1980 through 1987 under four promotional policy scenarios. The generic advertising variables in the retail fluid and manufactured demand equations are obtained from the Leading National Advertising (LNA) magazine. This source collects advertising data by monitoring advertising levels of major media outlets for selected times. Initially, the model was estimated with LNA data on brand advertising for manufactured dairy products. However, brand advertising is excluded in the final equations due to insignificance and/or wrong signs. The poor performance of the brand advertising variable is caused by LNA reporting total advertising expenditures for some companies with both dairy and nondairy product advertising.

The first scenario is based on actual quarterly expenditure levels from 1980 through 1987 for fluid and manufactured products. This case will be referred to as the Yes-Yes scenario. The second scenario, called the Yes-No scenario, simulates market impacts when fluid advertising is set to its historical funding levels, but it is assumed that there is no manufactured product advertising. The third scenario, No-Yes, simulates the impact of no fluid advertising given manufactured product advertising based on actual advertising levels. Finally, the fourth case, the No-No scenario, assumes no fluid and manufactured dairy product advertising. For each scenario, given the predetermined farm milk supply at the beginning of the simulation period, the retail and wholesale market equations are simulated simultaneously using the Newton method. Then, the resulting average milk price is computed and placed into the farm supply equation to determine next period's raw milk supply. This iterative procedure is carried out until the last quarter of 1987 is reached.

Comparisons of the above four scenarios provides useful insights into the impact of alternative advertising strategies. Specifically, the following information is gained by making five pairwise comparisons of the four scenarios. A comparison of the simulated Yes-Yes and No-Yes scenarios projects the impact of fluid advertising on market variables given historical values for manufactured product advertising. Contrasting the Yes-No with the No-No scenarios provides the impact of fluid advertising given no manufactured product advertising. These two comparisons are useful because they provide policymakers with information on the effectiveness of fluid advertising. On the manufactured product side, a comparison of the simulated Yes-Yes and Yes-No scenarios yields insight into the impact of manufactured product advertising on market variables given historical values for fluid advertising. Also, contrasting the No-Yes with the No-No scenarios provides the impact of manufactured product advertising given no fluid advertising. These two comparisons provide information regarding the effectiveness of manufactured product advertising. Finally, the Yes-Yes and No-No comparison measures the impact of fluid and manufactured product advertising compared with no advertising. To condense the results of the simulations, the results are presented on a quarterly average basis in Table 3.1 and the general direction of the impact of advertising on variables is listed in Table 3.2.

Table 3.1. Average quarterly endogenous variables under the four advertising scenarios and actual values[a]

|          | Scenario |         |         |         |         |
|----------|----------|---------|---------|---------|---------|
| Variable | Yes-Yes  | No-Yes  | Yes-No  | No-No   | Actual  |
| Q1       | 14.16    | 12.65   | 14.19   | 12.65   | 14.09   |
| Q2       | 16.60    | 16.78   | 15.90   | 15.92   | 16.80   |
| WMS      | 19.56    | 20.64   | 19.49   | 20.63   | 19.63   |
| QG       | 3.01     | 3.91    | 3.63    | 4.75    | 2.87    |
| QMILK    | 34.35    | 33.91   | 34.31   | 33.90   | 34.35   |
| RFP      | 74.24    | 49.41   | 74.04   | 49.40   | 74.57   |
| RMP      | 94.94    | 94.01   | 88.18   | 88.06   | 94.23   |
| WFP      | 66.71    | 52.60   | 66.27   | 52.58   | 66.42   |
| WMP      | 4.60     | 4.51    | 4.52    | 4.50    | 4.53    |
| P2       | 4.14     | 3.63    | 4.09 ·  | 3.63    | 4.02    |
| AMP      | 4.45     | 3.92    | 4.40    | 3.91    | 4.33    |

NOTE: All quantities are in billion pounds of milk equivalent. All prices are deflated by the consumer price index (1967 = 100) before averaging. The variables RFP, RMP, and WFP are price indices (1967 = 100); WMP, P2, and AMP are measured in terms of dollars per cwt of raw milk.

[a]Recall the following equilibrium conditions:

RFD = RFS = WFD = WFS ≡ Q1
RMD = RMS = WMD ≡ Q2

Table 3.2.  **The general impact of the various advertising strategies on the endogenous variables**

| Variable | Impact of fluid advertising (Yes-Yes vs. No-Yes, Yes-No vs. No-No) | Impact of manufactured product advertising (Yes-Yes vs. Yes-No, No-Yes vs. No-No) | Impact of combined advertising (Yes-Yes vs. No-No) |
|---|---|---|---|
| Q1 | + | −[a] | + |
| Q2 | −[a] | + | + |
| WMS | − | +[a] | − |
| QG | − | − | − |
| QMILK | + | +[a] | + |
| RFP | + | +[a] | + |
| RMP | +[a] | + | + |
| WFP | + | +[a] | + |
| WMP | +[a] | +[a] | + |
| P2 | + | +[a] | + |
| AMP | + | +[a] | + |

[a]Small in magnitude.

## General Impacts of Advertising on the Endogenous Variables

Some general insights regarding the impact of advertising on the endogenous variables can be inferred from Table 3.1. With respect to the impact of fluid advertising, the variables most significantly affected are: Q1, WMS, QMILK, QG, RFP, WFP, P2, and AMP. As expected, fluid advertising has a positive effect on all of these variables except WMS and QG. Since fluid advertising increases fluid demand (Q1), the retail and wholesale fluid prices (RFP and WFP) increase. Additionally, P2 and hence AMP are higher under the fluid advertising scenarios.

There are two reasons why fluid advertising causes these farm prices to increase. First, the increase in fluid demand due to advertising results in more competitive solutions (hence higher prices in all sectors). Second, even in the noncompetitive government support solutions P2 is higher with fluid advertising because there is an increase in the Class 1 price (caused by an increase in Q1) which is tied to P2 by a fixed P1 differential. With the increase in the fluid utilization rate and P2, the average milk price is higher due to fluid advertising, which causes the raw milk supply (QMILK) to increase. Hence, there is a positive farm supply response due to fluid advertising. As expected, fluid advertising has a negative effect on government purchases (QG) and the wholesale manufactured product supply (WMS). Fluid advertising is effective in reducing government purchases under the price support program because more milk is sold commercially.

The wholesale manufactured supply decreases because a greater amount of raw milk is now sold to the fluid sector.

The variables that are not significantly affected by fluid advertising are Q2, RMP, and WMP, even though the direction of the changes are as expected. Manufactured product demand (Q2) decreases slightly because more is being sold in the fluid sector. The retail and wholesale manufactured product prices (RMP and WMP) increase slightly because fluid advertising results in several more competitive solutions. However, these impacts are modest because the number of competitive regimes in the solution is very small, owing to the large milk surpluses during the early 1980s. In the government support solutions, fluid advertising has no impact on Q2, RMP, and WMP because the additional fluid demand is drawn from the government surplus and WMP is equal to the government purchase price (PG).

The variables most significantly affected by manufactured product advertising are Q2, QG, and RMP, while impacts on the rest of the variables are minimal. As expected, manufactured advertising has a positive impact on retail manufactured demand and price, and hence a negative impact on government purchases.

The reason why manufactured advertising has only a minimal effect on the other variables is due to the result that there are not many competitive regimes that enter as solutions. Hence, the increase in manufactured product demand due to advertising is simply replacing government surpluses for most periods in the simulation. Consequently the fluid sector variables (Q1, RFP, and WFP) are not affected by the increase in the manufactured product demand in the government support solutions. In the manufactured sector government support solutions, WMP simply equals PG, and the increase in Q2 is exactly offset by the decrease in QG resulting in WMS being unchanged. Notice that in the previous case of fluid advertising, the positive advertising impact on P2 was due to both an increase in the Class 1 price and an increase in the number of competitive solutions. In the current case, the positive, but insignificant impact of manufactured product advertising on P2 is due to the larger number of government support solutions. That is, since WMS is not affected by manufactured product advertising under government support regimes, Class 2 milk demand at the farm level is not affected by advertising, and hence P2 is not affected. This, together with unchanged Class 1 utilization makes AMP and QMILK unchanged in the case of government support regimes.

Finally, the comparison of the Yes-Yes with the No-No scenarios in Table 3.1 provides insights regarding the combined impact of both fluid and manufactured product advertising. All variables except WMS and QG are positively affected by combined advertising. Unlike the fluid advertising only, or manufactured advertising only cases, the combined policy has a major impact on all variables regardless of solution regime. This is because both the retail fluid and manufactured product demands are shifted by advertising. The negative impact on WMS indicates that the combined increase in retail demand for fluid and manufactured products outweighs the increase in farm supply due to the promotion program. While there is raw milk supply response due to advertising, the magnitude is relatively small.

Two important implications regarding advertising policy evaluation research may be drawn from these results. The first is the need to conduct policy analysis on both fluid and manufactured sectors simultaneously because of the interaction of the two sectors when the market is competitive. The second is the need to allow for the possibility of a competitive as well as government support solution because they yield different results.

## Specific Impacts of Advertising on Retail and Farm Markets

To gain more specific insights into the impacts of advertising on the retail and farm markets, Table 3.3 summarizes the differences between scenarios for the retail and farm sectors. In this table, the figures in the three blocks correspond to the minor impacts of various advertising strategies on specific endogenous variables discussed in previous section. The following discussion focuses on the major impacts in the rest of Table 3.3.

Table 3.3. Comparison of selected simulated quantities and prices under different scenarios[a]

| | Retail fluid | | Retail manufactured | | Farm | |
|---|---|---|---|---|---|---|
| | Q1 | RFP | Q2 | RMP | QMILK | AMP |
| Scenario | (Bil lbs) | (1967 = 100) | (Bil lbs) | (1967 = 100) | (Bil lbs) | (BP/FC) |
| Fluid advertising impact | | | | | | |
| Yes-Yes vs. No-Yes | 1.51 | 24.84 | -0.17 | 0.93 | 0.44 | 0.53 |
| | (12.02%) | (50.45%) | (-0.96%) | (1.04%) | (1.29%) | (14.10%) |
| Yes-No vs. No-No | 1.54 | 24.64 | -0.02 | 0.11 | 0.40 | 0.49 |
| | (12.27%) | (50.01%) | (-0.13%) | (0.14%) | (1.18%) | (12.82%) |
| Manufactured product advertising impact | | | | | | |
| Yes-Yes vs. Yes-No | -0.04 | 0.21 | 0.70 | 6.76 | 0.04 | 0.0 |
| | (-0.24%) | (0.31%) | (4.36%) | (7.86%) | (0.11%) | (1.10%) |
| No-Yes vs. No-No | -0.00 | 0.01 | 0.85 | 5.95 | 0.00 | 0.00 |
| | (-0.02%) | (0.02%) | (5.24%) | (6.88%) | (0.01%) | (0.08%) |
| Combined advertising impact | | | | | | |
| Yes-Yes vs. No-No | 1.51 | 24.84 | 0.68 | 6.88 | 0.44 | 0.54 |
| | (12.00%) | (50.48%) | (4.22%) | (8.02%) | (1.30%) | (14.20%) |

[a]The numbers are rounded off to the nearest second decimal point.

In the retail fluid sector, combined advertising of both fluid and manufactured products is not the most effective strategy for increasing fluid demand. This can be seen by examining the change in Q1 between the "Yes-No vs. No-No" and the "Yes-Yes vs. No-No" rows in Table 3.3. Compared to the fluid-only advertising case, the combined fluid and manufactured product advertising strategy causes the fluid sector to compete more with the manufactured sector for the predetermined raw milk supply. This makes the retail fluid price higher and fluid demand lower than the fluid-only strategy. Thus, if the primary goal is to increase fluid demand, fluid-only advertising is the most effective strategy.

In the retail manufactured product market, a similar result holds. That is, combined advertising of both fluid and manufactured products is not the most effective strategy for increasing manufactured product demand. This can be seen by examining the change in Q2 between the "No-Yes vs. No-No" and the "Yes-Yes vs. No-No" rows in Table 3.3. The result indicates that if the primary goal is to increase manufactured product demand, manufactured-only advertising is the most effective strategy.

Comparing AMP in the farm sector in the "Yes-No vs. No-No" and "No-Yes vs. No-No" rows gives the differential farm price impact between the fluid-only and manufactured-only strategies. The fluid-only scenario increases AMP substantially more than the manufactured-only strategy. Fluid-only advertising raises both fluid utilization and the Class 1 price, which causes a significant increase in the farm price. On the other hand, the manufactured-only strategy, in most periods, simply replaces government surpluses by private consumption, which has no impact on raising the farm price. However, the combined advertising strategy ("Yes-Yes vs. No-No") does increase the farm price marginally over the fluid-only strategy ("Yes-No vs. No-No"). This can be explained by the additional manufactured product advertising which slightly increases the number of competitive regimes in the solution.

These results suggest that in times of dairy surpluses, if the advertising goal is solely to increase farm prices, then investing in manufactured advertising is not an appropriate policy. However, manufactured product advertising could have a positive effect on the farm price in that it increases the probability of competitive regimes. Further, while not addressed in the model, manufactured advertising may generate goodwill to society because it causes additional reductions in government surpluses, which may be another important policy consideration.

Regarding the overall effectiveness of different advertising strategies in increasing milk and dairy product consumption, fluid advertising is more effective than manufactured product advertising. This is seen by comparing Q1, in the "Yes-No vs. No-No" row, with Q2, in the "No-Yes vs. No-No" row. Fluid-only advertising increases milk consumption by 1.54 billion pounds of raw milk equivalent, while manufactured-only advertising increases milk consumption by 0.85 billion pounds. It is interesting to note that the effect of combined fluid and manufactured advertising (the sum of Q1 and Q2 in the "Yes-Yes vs. No-No" row) is less than the sum of the above two individual impacts. This less-than-linear relationship is due to product competition, as discussed before.

## Marginal Impacts of Advertising

The above analysis has been conducted on an all-or-nothing basis. This is useful in evaluating the effectiveness of fluid advertising relative to manufactured advertising and vice versa. Another important area to investigate is the marginal impacts of the promotion program at various funding levels. To conduct the marginal analysis, the model is simulated for nine scenarios with advertising expenditure levels set at 10 percent, 25 percent, 50 percent, 75 percent, 100 percent, 125 percent, 150 percent, 175 percent, and 200 percent of the historical amount. While this is not a rigorous optimization procedure, it does shed light on the benefits and costs of the promotion program at the margin. The resulting simulated values under alternative expenditure levels are used to compute farm producer surplus, farm rates of return, and government costs of the dairy price support program. These welfare measures are presented in Table 3.4.

The generic promotion program benefits dairy farmers in terms of producer surplus. For each incremental increase in advertising expenditures, the corresponding change in producer surplus is positive. The rate of change in producer surplus, however, diminishes as expenditures increase. The change in producer surplus ranges from a high of $18 million, for the difference between the 10 percent and 25 percent expenditure levels, to slightly under $3 million, for the difference between the 175 percent and 200 percent levels.

The rate of return at the margin for each scenario gives a measure of the marginal benefits and marginal costs to dairy farmers of the promotion program. This measure is equal to the change in producer surplus (due to an incremental increase in advertising expenditures) divided by the marginal change in advertising cost. The marginal change in advertising cost is the total program assessments (15 cents per cwt) times the percentage difference associated with the nine scenarios. Marginal cost of advertising is based on the mandated assessment rather than the Leading National Advertising (LNA) estimates of fluid and manufactured product advertising expenditures. The revenue collected from the mandatory 15 cents per cwt assessment is

Table 3.4. Quarterly average change (in 1967 $) and percentage difference in producer surplus, rate of return, and government costs for alternative advertising levels

| Advertising as % of current levels | Change in farm producer surplus (million $) | Change in farm rate of return at the margin[a] | Change in government costs (million $) |
|---|---|---|---|
| 25%–10% | 18.04 (122.58%) | 10.46 | -1.66 (-115.45%) |
| 50%–25% | 13.83 (92.21%) | 4.81 | -1.26 (-90.22%) |
| 75%–50% | 8.23 (54.09%) | 2.86 | -0.74 (-54.21%) |
| 100%–75% | 5.86 (38.21%) | 2.04 | -0.53 (-39.00%) |
| 125%–100% | 4.59 (29.77%) | 1.60 | -0.41 (-30.62%) |
| 150%–125% | 3.76 (24.28%) | 1.31 | -0.33 (-25.20%) |
| 175%–150% | 3.18 (20.47%) | 1.11 | -0.28 (-21.50%) |
| 200%–175% | 2.76 (17.70%) | 0.96 | -0.25 (-18.75%) |

[a]The producer rate of return is equal to the change in producer surplus divided by the respective change in advertising expenditures.

used instead of the LNA generic advertising data. The results indicate that current funding levels should be increased because marginal benefits are greater than marginal costs (see the 100 percent–75 percent and 125 percent–100 percent scenarios). Subsequent increases in the advertising program up to about 185 percent of current expenditures would result in net benefits to dairy farmers, as the marginal gains in producer surplus are greater than the marginal costs of added assessments to farmers. However, increases in expenditures beyond this level would not be optimal to dairy farmers, as marginal costs exceed marginal benefits beyond this point.

All advertising funding levels reduce the government cost of the dairy price support program. As was the case for producer surplus, the marginal benefits of advertising to taxpayers increase at a decreasing rate with funding. For instance, taxpayers save an additional $1.7 million when funding is increased from 10 percent to 25 percent. The change in savings consistently decreases with increases in promotion, reaching a low of an additional $250,000 savings when funding is increased from 175 percent to 200 percent of actual levels.

## Summary

There are two important methodological implications of this research. The first is the need to conduct policy analysis on both fluid and manufactured sectors of the dairy market simultaneously, due to the interaction and competition for raw milk between the two sectors. Research on the fluid sector in isolation of the manufactured sector, or vice versa, may miss some important interaction effects of advertising impacting the isolated market. The second implication is the need to use a model that distinguishes between competitive and government support regimes. We have shown that the impact of alternative advertising strategies on important market variables may be quite different depending upon whether or not the market is competitive. Hence, models that assume that the market is always noncompetitive may produce misleading results.

# 4    Evaluating Advertising Using Split-Cable Scanner Data: Some Methodological Issues

HELEN H. JENSEN and JOHN R. SCHROETER

Recent changes in data collection methods have facilitated controlled market tests of household responses to food commodity promotion. The use of scanner checkout systems in stores now provides an opportunity for detailed tracking of food purchases by individual test participants. In principle, this capability can be combined with experimental control of the circulation of test advertisements to produce household purchase data sets useful for assessing the effects of advertising. While some use has been made of store-level scanner data in the evaluation of promotions (Capps 1988), evaluations based on household-level data collected in an environment characterized by experimental control of the test advertising are rare (Little 1986). Because these data bases have become available only recently and because use of them has been limited, it is worthwhile to review their nature and potential for the evaluation of commodity promotions.

The following section provides a general review of split-cable scanner data collection systems, one recently developed technique for evaluating the effectiveness of television advertising of food products. The next section describes a particular application involving a fresh beef advertising experiment in Grand Junction, Colorado. The concluding section assesses the applicability of the findings of this isolated experiment to the evaluation of livestock commodity promotion in general.

## Overview of Split-Cable Scanner Data Collection Systems

The use of the split-cable scanner technique to evaluate the effectiveness of television advertising of grocery store items has become popular recently. This technique requires the participation of several hundred subject households and a high percentage of the retail grocery outlets in a test

58

market city. All subject households are connected to a cable TV system with advertising that can be controlled on a household-by-household basis. Households can be divided between a control panel that sees none of the test advertising, and one or more experimental panels that view the advertising at different levels of intensity. In principle, the records of subject household purchases of the targeted good, during and after the test broadcast period, contain information regarding the effectiveness of the experimental advertising.

The technique utilizes a unique method for accurate compilation of these household purchase records. Each cooperating store is equipped with Universal Product Code (UPC) scanners. When the panel household member is ready to check out, an identification card is presented to the checkout clerk, a link to the service's computer is activated, and household identification information is entered. Complete purchase information (product, volume, price), all electronically read by the UPC scanner, is automatically transmitted and used to update the household's purchase record file. The recorded purchases of the targeted good, evaluated in light of the economic and demographic data collected from each panel household, thus enable an analyst to statistically separate the effect of the experimental advertising from the effects of numerous other household demand determinants.

There are three main attributes of split-cable scanner data bases that account for their appeal in assessing the effects of advertising campaigns. First, the method for generating these data bases involves a controlled experimental setting. Therefore, at least in principle, it allows the analyst a flexibility in experimental design that is unavailable in studies relying on historical demand data. For example, the monitoring period can be divided between "pretest" and "broadcast" periods in an optimal manner. The media plan for the experimental ads can be designed to enable inferences about subtle effects of ad timing and intensity of presentation. In particular, by subjecting different experimental panels to different, judiciously chosen patterns of advertising exposure, the analyst can investigate threshold effects in ad exposure, day-part timing effects, saturation levels, message decay rates, effects of changes in ad copy, and many other factors affecting advertising impact.

Second, split-cable scanner data bases enable analysis at the household level. This approach produces many more observations on consumer behavior than would be available for studies using demand data aggregated across households (for example, by store or geographic area). The household level approach is at a level consistent with traditional economic models of individual consumer behavior and provides the opportunity to control explicitly for the effects of a variety of household characteristics, other than advertising exposure, that influence demand for the targeted commodity. Thus, information on household income, size, race, residence type, age, employment status, occupation, education, and home appliance ownership are available for the analyst's use in modeling and estimating demand relationships.

Third, the purchase records that result from scanner data collection exercises can be extremely detailed, including information on the specific type of product, the price of each individual purchase, and the precise time of purchase. Given the great amount of available data, extensive aggregation is necessary. Nonetheless, it is beneficial to have the data in disaggregated form to begin with, because it allows the analyst to tailor quantity aggregates to the objectives of the particular project and to construct price indices in theoretically defensible ways.

There are disadvantages to the use of scanner data, however. One obvious problem with the split-cable scanner method is that the control for test advertising exposure is not perfect. For example, there is no assurance that experimental panel household members have actually watched the test ads. Of course, almost any practical method for the control of ad circulation would be plagued by similar problems. This data collection method also admits the possibility of systematic underreporting of purchases since participants may fail to use their panel ID cards when shopping, or they may shop in nonparticipating stores. Moreover, only purchases for at-home food consumption are recorded.

These drawbacks are relatively minor, however, compared to the most significant problem with the split-cable scanner method for evaluating TV advertising effectiveness: the design and implementation of this type of marketing experiment is very costly. Consequently, it generally will be prohibitively expensive to take significant advantage of the opportunities for experimental design. For example, only under rare circumstances would the expected benefits of promotion evaluation justify the costs of tailoring the selection and use of household panels to the needs of any one investigation. The test marketing service, therefore, rather than the client, would assemble the test panels with the intention of eventually using them in a number of experiments involving a variety of products or generic commodities. The panel selection criteria (e.g., grocery shopping habits) then would be those of the test marketing service; such criteria may or may not coincide with the specific interests of the client.

The relatively high cost of data collection may necessitate other compromises in the method of analysis as well. For example, the requirement that a high percentage of the area's grocery stores be recruited for the study normally limits available test markets to small cities. Cost considerations may overwhelm the benefits of tracking household behavior over an extended period and lead to an experiment of only a few months' duration, confining the analysis to short-term advertising effects. Finally, the incentive to economize on setup costs creates a temptation to stage more than one promotion test simultaneously. Under such circumstances, it could be difficult for the analyst to identify separately the effects of feature price, newspaper ad, and point-of-purchase promotions for the targeted good, or the indirect, contaminating effects of experimental promotions of substitute or complementing goods.

## A Sample Advertising Experiment

A recent advertising experiment for fresh beef provides an example of the use of split-cable scanner data collection systems. A market research firm, Information Resources, Inc. (IRI), used such a setup to conduct a test of television advertising for fresh beef in Grand Junction, Colorado, between October 1985 and July 1987. The resulting "behavior scan" data set was compiled using 2,500 participating households with the cooperation of stores accounting for more than 90 percent of the actual cash grocery volume in the Grand Junction area.

The television advertising campaigns that were the basis of the experiment began in January 1986, following a four-month pretest monitoring period (Figure 4.1). In phase one of the test, two experimental panels, a "heavy ad" panel and a "base ad" panel, were exposed to different intensities of the "Beef Gives Strength" campaign. A third, the control panel, received no exposure to the advertisements. The heavy ad and base ad panel exposure levels were chosen to correspond to the intensities of hypothetical national campaigns costing $30 million and $12 million per year, respectively.

In January 1987, the heavy ad and base ad panels were merged into a single ad panel, and the test advertising copy was changed to the "Real Food for Real People" campaign. During phase two of the test, the period between January and July 1987, the ad panel received exposure at a level consistent with a nationwide expenditure of $20 million per year. Again, the control panel households viewed none of the test ads. Table 4.1 shows the panel's average consumption of fresh beef during each of the test periods.

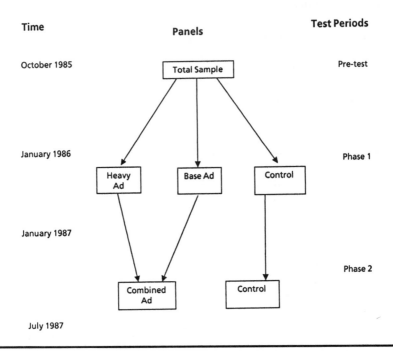

**Figure 4.1. Experimental design for beef advertising (Grand Junction, Colorado).**

**Table 4.1. Panel average consumption of fresh beef (seasonally adjusted pounds per four-week period per household) and percentage changes between periods**

|  | Control | Base ad | Heavy ad |
|---|---|---|---|
| Pretest | 5.619 | 5.582 | 5.575 |
|  | +6.763% | +5.500% | +4.861% |
| PHASE 1, ad test | 5.999 | 5.889 | 5.846 |
|  | -2.000% | -0.611% | -5.748% |
| PHASE 2, ad test | 5.879 | 5.853 | 5.510 |

SOURCE: IRI Behavior Scan Data, Grand Junction, CO (October 1985–July 1987).

## MODEL SPECIFICATION

A single-equation, linear demand model was used to explain the fresh beef purchases of panel households. The dependent variable measured the seasonally adjusted quantity of fresh beef purchased by each household in each of the 23 four-week demand periods that made up the sample. Among the independent variables were those reflecting household composition, income, demographic characteristics, age of household head, employment status of household head, occupation of household head, education, average quality of beef cuts purchased by each household, proportion of beef purchased at feature prices, beef prices, and prices of substitutes (pork and poultry).

These variables are described in detail in Schroeter (1988). Additional independent variables were introduced to capture advertising impacts and any not otherwise explained effects of the phase of the experiment. Each of these variables is defined as equal to one for observations in which the household and demand period meet the listed criteria, and as zero otherwise:

AD EFT11 = base ad panel, phase one;
AD EFT12 = base ad panel, phase two;
AD EFT21 = heavy ad panel, phase one;
AD EFT22 = heavy ad panel, phase two;
PHASE1  = control, base ad, or heavy ad panel, phase one;
PHASE2  = control, base ad, or heavy ad panel, phase two.

For example, AD EFT11 is a dummy variable equal to one for observations corresponding to base ad panel households, but only in those periods during phase one of the ad test. The coefficient of this variable will measure the difference between the beef purchases of a representative base ad panel household and an otherwise comparable control panel household during phase one of the test. It can therefore be interpreted as that portion of the effect of the base panel's exposure to experimental advertising that was realized in phase one. Likewise, the coefficient of AD EFT22 is the portion of beef demand by heavy ad panel households during phase two that can be attributed to those households' cumulative exposure to advertising in phases one and two.

If advertising has had a positive impact on the level of demand, the coefficients of the AD EFT variables should be statistically significant and positive. If an accumulation of advertising exposure over time enhances demand, the coefficients of AD EFT12 and AD EFT22 should be greater, respectively, than the coefficients of AD EFT11 and AD EFT21. If the intensity of advertising exposure at a point in time generates a lasting positive stimulus to demand, the coefficient of AD EFT21 should be greater than the coefficient of AD EFT11, and the coefficient of AD EFT22 should be greater than the coefficient of AD EFT12. On the other hand, negative or statistically insignificant estimates of these parameters will constitute evidence that the experimental TV advertising has not had the intended effect on the level of household demand for fresh beef.

PHASE1 is a dummy variable equal to one for all observations corresponding to demand periods in the first phase of the test. Its coefficient reflects any change in purchases between the pretest and phase one period that is common to households of all panels and unexplained by other independent variables (prices, for example). Similarly, the coefficient of phase two represents any panelwide differences not otherwise explained in consumption between the pretest and phase two periods.

## ESTIMATION AND RESULTS

The sample of households was limited to those who used their panel identification cards with reasonable regularity. Further curtailment was necessary because some households provided incomplete demographic information or, as in the case of one household, reported monthly beef purchases that were extreme outliers in the sample distribution. The remaining 1,788 households constituted a sample that was reasonably representative of national norms in its fresh beef purchase behavior and its demographic composition. Pooling of the time series of data for each household produced a total of 41,124 observations (23 four-week demand periods times 1,788 households).

The error components model was used for the stochastic specification of the fresh beef demand equation; that is, coefficients of the explanatory variables were treated as constants, while household-specific intercept terms were regarded as random drawings from a distribution characterizing the population at large. The method of feasible generalized least squares was applied using standard procedures for estimating the variances of the error components (Judge et al. 1982). The model performed satisfactorily, with $F$-value significant at the 0.01 percent level and estimated coefficient signs generally as expected. A Chow test verified that the hypothesis of "no behavioral differences across panels" (other than any attributable to the AD EFT variables) could not be rejected at conventional significance levels.

One important validation of the model is provided by the results concerning own- and cross-price demand elasticities. Evaluated at the sample means, the estimates of elasticities of demand for fresh beef with respect to the prices of beef, pork, and poultry are $-0.51$, 0.48, and 0.33, respectively.

These figures, all significant at the 1.5 percent level or better, are roughly consistent with estimates obtained by others (e.g., Chavas 1983).

The main objective of the estimation was the evaluation of the demand effects of the experimental television advertising. Here, there is no evidence of a positive impact on the level of demand: the point estimates of the coefficients of the AD EFT variables are all negative; one of them, the coefficient of AD EFT22, is negative with a marginal significance level of 6 percent (Table 4.2).

Table 4.2.  Results of estimation of the demand model (AD EFT and PHASE parameters only)

| Variable | Parameter estimate | Standard error | Marginal significance level (%) |
|---|---|---|---|
| AD EFT11 | -0.10 | 0.19 | 59.03 |
| AD EFT12 | -0.07 | 0.20 | 72.57 |
| AD EFT21 | -0.13 | 0.17 | 43.22 |
| AD EFT22 | -0.36 | 0.18 | 5.32 |
| PHASE1 | 0.02 | 0.14 | 90.30 |
| PHASE2 | 0.28 | 0.16 | 6.92 |

$F$-value = 97.79    Significance level for $F$-value = 0.01%   $R^2$ = 0.14

SOURCE: IRI Behavior Scan Data, Grand Junction, CO (October 1985–July 1987).

NOTE: Dependent variable = seasonally adjusted household purchases in pounds per four-week period. Mean = 5.79.

Factors related to the time periods during the experiment are indicated by the estimated effects of the phase variables. Although the coefficient of phase one was statistically insignificant, the coefficient of phase two was statistically significant and positive. During the phase two ad test period (January through July 1987), for reasons not attributable to any other explanatory factor represented in the model, household consumption was 0.28 pounds per month higher on average than in either the pretest or phase one, post-test periods. While the model offers no guidance in interpreting this difference, one possibility is that the continual growth in nonexperimental advertising (for example, the beef advertising distributed to all households through national radio and print media) began to have a significant positive impact on demand in this period.

## ALTERNATIVE FORMS FOR THE ADVERTISING EFFECT VARIABLES

In each phase of the test, the experimental advertising was distributed in a manner consistent with customary industry practices: broadcasts were concentrated within advertising "flights" of from four to six weeks, separated by hiatus periods of two weeks or more. However, the form of the AD EFT variables in the demand model implies that any effects of advertising on the level of household demand, while possibly different between the phase one and phase two periods, are constant within each phase. Thus, the model was not sufficiently general to admit the plausible hypothesis that consumer responses to advertising might differ between broadcast and hiatus periods.

A slightly modified demand model was used to investigate whether advertising effects differed between the broadcast and hiatus periods. First, the AD EFT variables were redefined:

For $j$ and $k = 1$ and 2, AD EFT$jk_{it}$ = a dummy variable equal to one for households in the corresponding panel ($j = 1$, base ad; $j = 2$, heavy ad) during broadcast periods in phase $k$, and equal to zero otherwise.

The coefficient of the redefined AD EFT11 variable, for example, represents the effect of advertising on base ad panel households during those phase one periods in which the base ad panel actually was exposed to advertising.

Second, variables AD HIAT1 and AD HIAT2 were introduced to capture behavioral differences during advertising hiatus periods. These new variables were defined as follows:

AD HIAT1$_{it}$ = a dummy variable equal to one for base ad panel households in hiatus periods and equal to zero otherwise.
AD HIAT2$_{it}$ = a dummy variable equal to one for heavy ad panel households in hiatus periods and equal to zero otherwise.

As these variables are defined, the coefficients of AD HIAT1 and AD HIAT2 will reveal, respectively, the base and heavy ad panel members' responses to hiatus periods.

The demand model was estimated with the redefined AD EFT variables and the new AD HIAT variables. The results (Table 4.3) suggest that the base ad panel's negative response to advertising during phase one was the net result of a small, but positive and marginally significant (significance level = 35 percent), response during the broadcast periods of phase one, which was more than offset by a negative and statistically significant response during the hiatus periods of phase one. However, for the base ad panel during phase two and for the heavy ad panel during phases one and two, the responses appear to be negative during broadcast periods as well as hiatuses. In fact, the heavy ad panel's response during the broadcast periods of phase two was significantly negative at the 6 percent level. Thus, while closer examination uncovered modest evidence of a small, positive test advertising effect, this effect was limited to base ad panel households and to broadcast periods during phase one. Moreover, even this small positive effect appears to have been more than offset by subsequent negative effects during hiatus periods.

**Table 4.3. Results of estimation of the demand model with redefined advertising effect variables (AD EFT and AD HIAT parameters only)**

| Variable | Parameter estimate | Standard error | Marginal significance level (%) |
|---|---|---|---|
| AD EFT11 | 0.19 | 0.20 | 35.01 |
| AD EFT12 | -0.10 | 0.20 | 61.90 |
| AD EFT21 | -0.09 | 0.17 | 60.70 |
| AD EFT22 | -0.35 | 0.19 | 5.76 |
| AD HIAT1 | -0.25 | 0.19 | 18.09 |
| AD HIAT2 | -0.30 | 0.18 | 10.74 |

SOURCE: IRI Behavior Scan Data, Grand Junction, CO (October 1985–July 1987).

NOTE: Dependent variable = seasonally adjusted household purchases in pounds per four-week period. Mean = 5.79.

## ADVERTISING EFFECTS ON EXPENDITURES MADE AT FEATURE PRICES

An alternative means of promoting fresh beef and other meats is *feature pricing,* placing a particular meat item at a "featured" price in the store display and often in newspaper ads. Using the scanner data it was possible to investigate the determinants of household use of feature-price opportunities by estimating a linear model in which the dependent variable was PROP $FT_{it}$, the proportion of household $i$'s beef budget in period $t$ that was spent at feature prices. The independent variables were the same as those for the previous analyses. The AD EFT and AD HIAT variables were as defined earlier. As an aid in interpreting the magnitudes of the estimated coefficients, note that the mean values of PROP $FT_{it}$ for the pretest, phase one, and phase two periods are 0.323, 0.285, and 0.195, respectively. The model was estimated as before, and the results are reported in Table 4.4.

Table 4.4. **Results of estimation of the "proportion on feature" model (AD EFT, AD HIAT, and PHASE parameters only)**

| Variable | Parameter estimate | Standard error | Marginal significance level (%) |
|----------|-------------------|----------------|-------------------------------|
| PHASE1   | -0.083 | 0.010 | 0.01 |
| PHASE2   | -0.141 | 0.011 | 0.01 |
| AD EFT11 | 0.078  | 0.015 | 0.01 |
| AD EFT12 | 0.005  | 0.015 | 73.86 |
| AD EFT21 | 0.051  | 0.013 | 0.01 |
| AD EFT22 | -0.005 | 0.014 | 70.74 |
| AD HIAT1 | -0.004 | 0.014 | 77.16 |
| AD HIAT2 | -0.044 | 0.014 | 0.17 |

SOURCE: IRI Behavior Scan Data, Grand Junction, CO (October 1985 – July 1987).
NOTE: Dependent variable = proportion of household beef expenditure made at feature price. Mean = 0.323 (pre-test), 0.285 (phase 1), 0.195 (phase 2).

Advertising effects on the proportion of meat purchased at feature prices are revealed by the coefficients of the AD EFT and AD HIAT variables. The strongest responses to advertising were tendencies by members of both ad panels to increase their proportionate use of feature prices during the broadcast periods of phase one. There also was some tendency, at least among heavy ad panel members, to cut back on feature-price buying during hiatus periods. In sum, advertising appears to have induced more feature-price buying, presumably an unintended effect. This finding must be interpreted with caution, however, since the analysis of the determinants of feature-price buying is preliminary. Data limitations made it impossible to control for changes through time in the number of feature prices offered by retailers or for the magnitudes of the differences between "feature" and "regular" prices. If advertising does stimulate feature-price buying, it may be because advertising, in some way, creates a consumer perception of beef as a good value. At a minimum, the results suggest an important connection between advertising and feature-price buying worthy of further study (see Capps 1988).

## Implications and Summary

In summary, split-cable scanner data offer new opportunities for examining the effects of advertising on consumer demand in an experimental setting. In practice, the experimental design is difficult to fully implement and, in some cases, may limit the interpretation of findings. In the example discussed (a fresh beef television advertising experiment in Grand Junction,

Colorado), the experimental advertising failed to increase the level of demand but did appear to influence feature-price buying patterns.

How generalizable are these conclusions about advertising's effects on beef demand? Examination of the distributions of economic and demographic characteristics within the test panels indicates that the sample was reasonably representative of national norms. The samplewide average consumption figure conformed closely to comparable statistics from the U.S. Department of Agriculture's 1985/86 Continuing Survey of Food Intakes by Individuals (1987). Moreover, results not reported here confirm the conclusions for certain demographic subgroups of the sample households (see Schroeter 1988). These observations suggest that the findings are generalizable to other populations in other areas of the country. Whether or not they are generalizable with respect to alternative advertising copy is another matter. Obviously, other messages may have been more effective or more convincingly counterproductive.

Finally, these findings must be interpreted in light of the magnitude of the task confronting would-be commodity promoters. Television advertising is likely to be most effective when it is for branded household products, particularly when the ad campaigns accompany such significant market events as the introduction of a new brand or an areawide feature-price offer. In such cases there is potential for relatively large, prompt effects, since sales can increase at the expense of the market shares of rivals' close substitute brands. These impacts should be easily discernable using split-cable scanner research means, even if cost considerations limit the experiment to a modest, affordable scope.

Using promotions in an attempt to increase total demand for a generic commodity such as fresh beef is a more ambitious undertaking, however. Success in such an endeavor requires that consumers' long-standing attitudes about familiar food products be changed. The consumption impact of such attitude changes would be realized through substitution among different products rather than among different brands of the same product. Therefore, any effects are likely to be much more subtle and take longer to manifest themselves compared to those associated with branded product advertising. The compromises in split-cable scanner experimental design necessitated by high cost make the analyst's efforts to discern these subtle effects very difficult.

# 5    Discussion: Ongoing Empirical Research on Generic Advertising

JAMES R. BLAYLOCK

The four papers on generic advertising appear to share common ground in several areas. They attempt to measure the effectiveness of generic advertising in boosting sales or, alternatively, they explore the problem of how to measure advertising in the first place. Diverse approaches to this problem in terms of methodology, statistical technique, and data are evident in the papers. The second common denominator is somewhat less obvious and not explicitly addressed in any one paper, that is, can economists be more effective if they broaden the scope of their studies and rely more heavily on the collective expertise of other disciplines? In other words, are the days of the omnipotent and omniscient economist gone? And, third, like all good research endeavors, the papers by Ghura and Schrimper, Capps and Moen, Kaiser, Liu, Mount, and Forker, and Jensen and Schroeter probably raise more questions than they answer. It is the two latter areas on which I will focus.

Before discussing each individual paper, I would like to outline briefly a simple model of the mechanics of generic promotion. Ward, Chang, and Thompson (1985) indicate that generic advertising is intended to encourage consumers to become buyers of a product on a regular basis. I shall take this as the primary goal of a generic promotion program but concede that derivative goals are possible. The first stage in the achievement of this goal is the development of an advertising message, that is, what attributes of a product should be emphasized, what is the target audience, as well as a myriad of other factors. The second stage is the translation of this advertising message into an actual advertisement, and this also entails deciding the media of transmission (e.g., television, print). These two stages shall be labeled advertising effort. The third stage is the effectiveness of the advertisement in terms of consumer recall, awareness, and whether it ultimately convinces the consumer to purchase the product. The last stage involves delineating whether the total promotion program (the sum of all advertising efforts) has increased sales (or some other tangible asset) sufficiently for the program to be justified to the group paying the bills.

Economists have traditionally viewed advertising expenditures as the sole indicator of promotion effort. Likewise, they have considered increases in product sales attributable to advertising expenditures as the barometer of a promotion program's success. The four papers in this session each break with some of these traditions, but each in a different way. My goal is to identify the advances, suggest some improvements, and delineate how the results "fit" into this simple model of promotion.

The Ghura and Schrimper paper is an interesting and novel but exploratory attempt to examine some issues that fall under stages one and two of our model: measuring promotion effort. In particular, their work studies the changing characteristics of apple newspaper advertisements and attempts to explain the amount of ad space devoted to apples. In a broader context they appear to be leading up to the perennial question: "How do we go about measuring promotion effort for inclusion as a variable in an econometric model?"

Most analysts, including myself, consider advertising expenditures in their models, usually "deflated" by some type of media cost index. Simply put this procedure implies that all ads are created equal or alternatively that all dollars spent on promotion are equally effective. No explicit recognition is given to the notion that promotion efforts may vary in content, message, and other attributes and, hence, potential effectiveness for the same level of media expenditures. Advertising executives and members of promotion organizations, among others, have made very cogent arguments why this is not the case. Even by casual observation it is clear that some ads are "better" than others and probably more effective in stimulating demand. Why one ad is more effective than another is often not clearly understood even by the Madison Avenue gurus. However, we must acknowledge that the creativity and effort on the part of all individuals involved in formulating a promotion strategy and its implementation are crucial to its success.

The above leads us to the desirability of using some measure of an ad campaign's success in econometric models to more effectively evaluate a program's success. Economists' general reluctance to incorporate some measure of each individual ad campaign's success in their models probably stems from the fact that this requires some sort of subjective evaluations, such as the level of ad recall by consumers, attitudes and beliefs toward the advertisements and products, and so on. This type of information is typically collected by way of focus groups and telephone surveys. The problem is one of incorporating this type of information into an "ad effectiveness variable" for inclusion in an econometric model. This is a difficult task with little in the way of precedence for guidance. The ad effectiveness variable, once constructed, may be used as a deflator of media expenditures or included directly into the model.

In general, if economists as a group are to have a role we must develop our models to approximate reality as closely as our best abilities allow. I believe research such as that conducted by Ghura and Schrimper is a necessary step along the path toward the development of more comprehensive and realistic econometric models. I do, however, have one more question: Why are economists so reluctant to draw upon the collective knowledge of individuals outside the profession? In the Ghura and Schrimper paper, is it not a viable strategy to simply ask those individuals who created and placed the apple newspaper ads, why certain advertising messages have changed over time, and why ad placements and size have changed. Information from this source would then provide the maintained hypotheses for testing their econometric model. While my naivete may be showing, I believe that economists, and not just those involved in analyzing promotion programs, would better serve their clientele if more effort was made to draw upon the knowledge of individuals in other professions.

Another issue related to measuring an ad campaign's effectiveness, one addressed by Capps and Moen, is which media type carries the ad, whether it be radio, TV, or print. Here again it seems plausible that the effectiveness of a producer's generic promotion program may be related to the skillful use of various media types. This is explicitly recognized in the model developed by Capps and Moen and is a step in the right direction.

Major conclusions of the Capps and Moen paper include: both radio and television advertisements increase the sales of whole milk but only television promotion increased sales of lowfat milk. These results, however, raise several interesting questions for which economists will probably have to appeal to other authorities to obtain answers. First, why is only television and not radio advertising effective in raising the demand for lowfat milk? Or, conversely, why are both media types effective in increasing whole milk demand? Secondly, why was a two-month lag identified for radio advertising and a four-month lag for television advertising? Were these phenomena caused by the ad message itself, targeting of the wrong (or right) audience, or the differing characteristics of radio vs. television audiences? And, what does this say about the optimal allocation of advertising funds across media types? Although Capps and Moen certainly can't be criticized for not providing answers to these types of questions, I think they would agree with me on one point: economists are good at identifying factors influencing some phenomenon but often not very enlightening as far as providing the whys.

For econometricians, several problems identified by Capps and Moen are worth emphasizing. The perennial problem of how to handle zero observation values in logarithmically transformed models is the first problem. They handle it by assigning the value of one to zero values, although the approach of assigning an arbitrary small value to the zeros in the data set has been taken by some econometricians. Because of the way Capps and Moen handle zero values, advertising expenditures were not placed on a per capita basis. How sensitive are model estimates to decisions of this type and does it behoove analysts to present several sets of estimates based on different assumptions? I suspect that given the large number of zeros in their data set, different results would be obtained using alternative procedures. The real test would be in the magnitude of the differences but, in any case, these issues are especially important if decision makers are going to use the model results as input into formulating advertising allocation decisions.

The second issue is the long-standing debate over the length and type of the lag structure associated with advertising. Researchers have used polynomial lags (with and without end-point restrictions), gamma lags, a Pascal formulation, etc. Which is correct (and this probably varies by application) is unknown but the sensitivity of the results to various lag formulations is well known and may suggest that researchers present results using several different type lags. At the Economic Research Service (ERS) of the U.S. Department of Agriculture, we have found that the type of distributed lag formulation is important but the length of the lag appears to have a profound effect on the increases in total sales (over a given period) that can be attributed to advertising. These types of problems are essentially empirical in nature, but it would provide valuable information to our clientele if alternative specifications were identified to give them some indication of the robustness of our results.

I would now like to turn to the Kaiser et al. paper. This work represents a comprehensive effort to examine the effects of generic advertising for dairy products at the farm, consumer, and government levels. In the framework of our simple advertising model, they attempt to shed some light on the final stage, investigating the total effects of promotion in terms of gain or loss for the producer. To accomplish this goal, an econometric model was developed that postulated a seven equation system for the dairy sector: an equation for milk prices at the farm level, two equations for wholesale supply (one each for fluid and manufactured products), two equations for manufactured supply and demand, and two equations for fluid retail supply and demand. The paper deals mainly with simulation results obtained from the model under various promotion scenarios. We certainly cannot argue with the intentions of the authors; the paper is obviously an attempt to more closely approximate reality and answer many questions all of us have had at one time or another. However, I think the important point to keep in mind is that these simulation results are only as valid as the underlying statistical model that generated them. Thus, my discussion of this paper will mainly focus on the underlying econometric model.

I preface my remarks by saying that I am well aware of the enormous complexities involved in modeling the dairy sector. At ERS we have also encountered large roadblocks with respect to econometric analysis of dairy products so I truly appreciate the research effort undertaken by the authors.

First, I would like to turn to the retail demand equations. The most obvious question that comes to mind is why are branded advertising expenditures omitted from the equations, especially for manufactured products? During late 1984 and 1985 (the start of the national dairy promotion program) branded advertising expenditures jumped dramatically and simultaneously with the huge increase in generic promotion — at least in the case of cheese. Is it not possible that the coefficient on generic advertising in the manufactured demand equation may be capturing the effect of branded promotion? This may lead to an overestimate of the effect of generic promotions. Perhaps of more concern, however, is the specification of quantity demanded on a national rather than a per capita basis. National consumption of fluid milk has increased over time and per capita consumption essentially is down.

One reason that total national consumption of fluid milk has shown increases is the steady growth in the size of the population. As population is not an explanatory variable in the model, it is probable that other variables are capturing part of its effect. I would be interested in seeing the results of the model when population is included.

In the retail manufactured demand equation, a dummy variable, equal to one for the years 1981–83, is included. The question is: What is significant about these years vis-à-vis the others? Also, in both of the retail demand equations (as well as several others) there is no intercept term. It appears that the constant term was dropped from equations in which it was not statistically significant at some given level. This is an infrequent practice. It forces the equation through the origin, implying that the value of the dependent variable is zero when all independent variables are zero. Goodness of fit measures (e.g., $R^2$) will certainly be affected as well as the standard errors of the remaining coefficients. However, the major problem I have with deleting variables on the basis of a low level of statistical significance is that it is often not applied uniformly. In the current context, the unemployment rate is statistically insignificant in the wholesale fluid supply equation but kept in the model and the constant term dropped (presumably because of low significance). The bottom line with respect to deleting variables of low significance lies in its effect on the remaining coefficients. In this regard, perhaps the authors could enlighten us.

In my view, perhaps the most significant empirical result from the Kaiser et al. paper is the finding that promotion levels for dairy products should be approximately doubled. This implies that dairy producers would be better off financially if they voluntarily increased the current 15 cents per cwt assessment of milk to about 30 cents. This is not a trivial result, especially considering the amount of money that would come directly from the bottom line of producers. Do the authors of this paper have enough confidence in this result to truly advocate a doubling of producer assessments?

I hope the authors do not view my comments to imply that I reject, out of hand, their research endeavor. I think this type of modeling effort is leading us down the path of more complete evaluation of generic programs, which is, of course, desirable. However, even with models that attempt to capture not only the effects of advertising on sales but also its effects on prices, government purchases, supply response, and other relevant factors, I would still be reluctant to rely solely on the empirical results showing anything close to a complete evaluation of a promotion program. A simple illustration shall suffice. In return for letting others use California Raisins, the raisin promotion program receives approximately $3 to $4 million a year. Modeling phenomenon such as this is difficult at best and requires extensive knowledge of the promotion program itself. However, this "extra" revenue and the free publicity given this program are certainly tangible assets that must be considered in program evaluation.

The Jensen and Schroeter paper makes use of data that help fulfill an economist's dream. That is, data developed from an experimental situation. In the case of split-cable scanner data, the experimental control is far from complete but the information collected still has a great deal of potential. Most analyses of split-cable scanner data that I have seen involve studying problems such as brand-switching. Econometric type analysis of these data sets has been somewhat limited. A study conducted by A. D. Little for the National Dairy Board (1986) analyzed data for several dairy products along similar lines as Jensen and Schroeter and also obtained results that were somewhat mixed.

I believe if economists are to obtain viable results from split-cable data sets, we must appeal to authorities in the field of marketing and business management. These disciplines appear to have the most experience with this type of data, although the entire field is fairly new. For example, I believe that the concept of reference prices has validity in this type of work although it is probably not an idea that economists will willingly embrace. The idea behind reference prices is simply that a consumer has a price in mind for a given product (derived from experience) that one is willing to pay for a product and bases a purchase decision (at least in part) on how the current price compares to the reference price. Marketing analysts appear to have had some success using this variable in their models and it does have a certain intuitive appeal.

Another field that may have something to contribute to our study of split-cable data sets is the area of biometrics. In biometrics, modeling efforts often center around the comparison of control and experimental groups. For example, a group of rats may be subdivided into control and experimental groups with the latter receiving a particular drug. The analyst's task is to detect the drug's effects in inducing certain responses within the experimental group using the control group as a base. It appears, at least to me, that this situation is analogous to the split-cable scanner type of experiment. If this is indeed true, economists may wish to focus, for example, on statistical models dealing with survival times — for example, time between stimuli (advertising) and response (increased purchases) — or growth curves and repeated measures, for example, a treatment of households' pattern of purchases over time.

Other questions that may be answered with the split-cable type data include explaining the characteristics of households most (or least) affected by advertising, does advertising induce households already purchasing the product to purchase more or is it inducing new households into the market, and how does advertising affect frequency of purchase behavior?

Jensen and Schroeter should be commended for their courage in tackling an analysis of this type of data given its complexity and the fact economists have little experience with it. On the surface, split-cable data, while extremely expensive and difficult to obtain, appears to offer a challenge to analysts and a source of valuable information to managers of promotion organizations.

A great deal of time and effort went into the development of the four papers in this session. My discussion has, without a doubt, not given them a full measure of justice but I believe that the authors have inched us toward a better understanding of the complexities of generic promotions. They have demonstrated, as do other papers in this book, that no single modeling effort will ever provide all the answers. We can only hope that the bits and pieces of research will eventually converge to form a consensus.

# 2 Incorporating Advertising in Demand Systems

# 6 Theoretical Overview of Demand Systems Incorporating Advertising Effects

## MARK G. BROWN and JONQ-YING LEE

A basic problem confronting advertising research has been maintaining theoretical plausibility while specifying models restrictive enough to be estimated. The search for model specifications involves the use of basic restrictions from theory (adding-up, homogeneity, symmetry, and negativity), specific restrictions of separability, and flexible functional forms that locally approximate general relationships.

For incorporating advertising in systems of demand equations, the problem of model specification can be illustrated by considering an $n$ good system with the level of advertising for each good as a determinant of demand. Ignoring lagged responses, the number of advertising responses would be $n^2$ without any restrictions. From the budget constraint, we can obtain $n$ adding-up restrictions associated with the advertising responses. The latter restrictions, however, do not substantially reduce the number of advertising responses to be estimated. For empirical work, additional restrictions having a theoretical appeal are needed.

We consider here some possible restrictions in the context of several basic models recommended for analyzing demographic effects. The basic models discussed are the Rotterdam model and the scaling and translating models. Advertising aspects of the Rotterdam model have been discussed elsewhere (Theil 1980; Duffy 1987; Clements and Selvanathan 1988). The present discussion of this modeling approach, therefore, is brief. The scaling and translating models developed for changes in household composition, taste, and quality (Barten 1964a; Fisher and Shell 1967; Muellbauer 1974, 1975; Gorman 1976; Pollak and Wales 1981) have received less attention with respect to analyzing advertising and are discussed in greater detail here.

In the Rotterdam and the scaling and translating models, product advertising levels are introduced in the utility function, or alternatively the indirect utility function or cost function, and can be interpreted as preference or quality shifters. The particular parameterizations for scaling and translating also allow the interpretation that advertising alters the budget constraint. The latter interpretation is similar to Stigler and Becker's (1977) interpretation of how advertising affects demand in the context of household production theory. Stigler and Becker treat advertising as an information input in the production of nonmarket commodities. In their model, a change in advertising results in changes in the shadow prices of the relevant nonmarket commodities. In the scaling and translating models, the demands for market goods, not nonmarket commodities, are considered and a change in advertising generates, in effect, price and/or income effects, depending on the particular model specification.

Alternatively, in the Rotterdam model, attention is focused on how the marginal utilities of goods are affected by their respective advertising levels. The source of restrictions in the Rotterdam model is the set of derivatives indicating how the advertising levels affect the marginal utilities; while for the scaling and translating models, the source of restrictions is the set of parameters that define the models.

The section on advertising and household production theory involves a change in the direction of discussion. Instead of considering particular specifications and restrictions, this section discusses basic variables and relationships. The discussion focuses on nontraditional demand factors, such as the opportunity cost of time and human capital, and their relationships with the impact of advertising.

## General Model Properties and the Rotterdam Model

We introduce advertising into the traditional consumer demand model and review the properties of the model; the Rotterdam model is then examined. This presentation follows Phlips's (1974) and Barten's (1977) analysis of factors other than prices and income in systems of demand equations. The discussion is limited to the role advertising plays in demand systems.

Allowing advertising to affect utility and, in turn, the bundle of market goods chosen, the consumer choice problem can, in general, be written as

$$\text{maximize } u = u(q, a)$$

$$\text{subject to } p'q = y$$

(6.1)

where $q = (q_1, \ldots, q_n)'$, $p = (p_1, \ldots, p_n)'$ and $a = (a_1, \ldots, a_n)'$ are $n \times 1$ vectors of quantities, prices, and advertising levels, respectively, for $n$ commodities, and $y$ is total expenditures or income. In the present analysis,

$a_i$ is treated as a single measure of advertising for commodity $i$, but, in general, could itself be a vector of advertising measures. For example, $a_i$ might be current and lagged advertising expenditure levels to allow for the effects of past advertising on demand. The treatment of $a_i$ as a vector would be a straightforward extension.

The demand equations obtained by solving (6.1) have the general form

$$q_i = f_i(p, a, y) \tag{6.2}$$

The indirect utility function and cost function for problem (6.1) can likewise be written as

$$u = \phi(p, a, y) \qquad \text{and} \tag{6.3}$$

$$y = c(p, a, u) \tag{6.4}$$

respectively. Equation (6.2) can be derived from (6.3) and (6.4) using Roy's identity and Shepard's lemma; i.e.,

$$q_i = - \frac{\partial \phi / \partial p_i}{\partial \phi / \partial y} \qquad \text{(Roy's identity) (6.5)}$$

$$\frac{\partial c}{\partial p_i} = h_i(p, a, u) = h[p, a, \phi(p, a, y)] = q_i \text{ (Shepard's lemma) (6.6)}$$

where $h_i$ is the compensated demand equation. The indirect utility function and cost function provide convenient ways to formulate consumer behavior focusing on the independent variables, prices, and income facing consumers. A basic property of demand systems incorporating factors such as advertising is that any demand increase(s) for some product(s) as a result of a change in the factor must be offset by demand decreases for other products, while total expenditures remain constant. Formally, the property in the present case can be written as the differentiation of the budget constraint with respect to $a_i$, that is,

$$\Sigma_j \, p_j \left( \frac{\partial q_j}{\partial a_i} \right) = 0 \qquad \text{or} \tag{6.7}$$

$$\Sigma_j \, w_j \, x_{ji} = 0 \tag{6.8}$$

where $w_j = p_j q_j / y$ and $x_{ji} = (\partial q_j / \partial a_i)(a_i / q_j)$, the elasticity of $q_j$ with respect to $a_i$. The elasticity version of the property, equation (6.8), shows that the weighted sum of advertising elasticities (with respect to advertising for a specific product) is zero where the weights are the product expenditure shares. Result (6.8) was used by Aviphant, Lee, and Brown (1988) with the Rotterdam demand subsystem in a study of fruit-beverage demand.

The effects of advertising can also be related to the compensated price responses or substitution effects (Phlips 1974; Barten 1977), that is,

$$q_a = -\left(\frac{1}{\lambda}\right) KV \tag{6.9}$$

where $q_a = (\partial q_i / \partial a_j)$ is an $n \times n$ matrix indicating how the quantities demanded are affected by advertising, $\lambda$ is the marginal utility of income $(\partial u / \partial y)$, $K = (\partial h_i / \partial p_j)$ is the $n \times n$ substitution, or Slutsky matrix, and $V = (\partial^2 u / \partial q_i \partial a_j)$ is an $n \times n$ matrix indicating how the marginal utilities are affected by advertising.

For empirical work, result (6.9) is particularly interesting as a possible source of restrictions. Theil, Duffy, and Clements and Selvanathan have used (6.9) to incorporate advertising in the Rotterdam model under the assumptions $V$ is diagonal (advertising on good $i$ does not affect the marginal utility of good $j$) and the elasticity of each good's marginal utility with respect to its advertising is constant. Formally, the Rotterdam model with advertising can be written as

$$w_i \, d \log q_i = \beta_i \, d \log Q + \Sigma_j \, \pi_{ij} \, (d \log p_j - \phi_j \, d \log a_j) \tag{6.10}$$

where $\beta_i = p_i(\partial q_i / \partial y)$, the marginal propensity to spend on good $i$; $d \log Q = \Sigma \, w_j \, d \log q_i = d \log y - \Sigma \, w_j \, d \log p_j$, the Divisia volume index; $\pi_{ij} = (p_i p_j / y)(\partial h_i / \partial p_j)$, the Slutsky coefficient for good $i$ and price $j$; and $\phi_j = (\partial^2 u / \partial q_j \partial a_j) \, / \, [a_j / (\partial u / \partial q_j)]$, the elasticity of the marginal utility of good $j$ with respect to its advertising. Note that the number of advertising parameters to be estimated in (6.10) is $n$, which is substantially less than what is implied by the unrestricted model. In Theil's specification, the number of advertising parameters is reduced further to one under the assumption $\phi = \phi_j$ for all $j$. A basic question concerning the applicability of the Rotterdam model is whether advertising on good $i$ affects the marginal utility of good $j$. For broadly defined goods with advertising messages that tend to be unrelated, the assumption that a good's advertising level does not affect another good's marginal utility may be acceptable. On the other hand, for closely related goods or for advertising messages that make comparisons between competing brands, the assumption may not be appropriate. One might also question whether the elasticity of a good's marginal utility with respect to advertising is constant.

Given the possible objections with the Rotterdam model indicated above, other approaches might be considered for analyzing the impact of advertising.

## Specific Models

Demand analysis focusing on the effects of household composition and changes in tastes and product quality suggest specific ways in which advertising might affect consumer behavior. Barten (1964b) has proposed a household utility model with equivalent adult scales used to deflate the quantities in the utility function to amounts per equivalent adult. Fisher and Shell (1967) have proposed a similar model to analyze taste and quality changes. Muellbauer (1974, 1975) and Deaton and Muellbauer (1980b) provide further analysis of both models. The basic feature of these models is that the quantities in the utility function are scaled — either multiplied or divided by parameters reflecting exogenous factors. In terms of the indirect utility function or cost function, the latter feature takes the form of interactions between prices and the exogenously determined parameters. This implies that a change in an exogenous parameter such as household composition or, in the case under consideration, advertising has an effect similar to a change in price. An alternative approach based on a specification suggested by Gorman (1976) and analyzed by Pollak and Wales (1980) introduces demographic variables in demand analysis through overhead costs. Pollak and Wales refer to the latter approach as translating and the approach first suggested by Barten as scaling. Models based on scaling and translating belong to a broader class of models discussed by Lewbel (1985). Examination of scaling and translating here focuses on the restrictive nature of the approaches. For any particular application, the restrictions of the scaling and translating approaches may or may not be considered acceptable. Lewbel's more generalized approach provides an alternative, moving toward the general model discussed earlier. We also note that the scaling and translating models discussed in this section are based on the utility maximization problem assuming an interior solution where a positive amount of each good is demanded. The analysis, however, can be extended to allow for choice between brands and closely related commodities (e.g., Deaton and Muellbauer 1980b; Muellbauer 1975; Hanemann 1984).

## SCALING

For the scaling approach, the consumer choice problem allowing for the impact of advertising can be written as

$$\text{maximize} \quad u = u(q^*)$$

$$\text{subject to} \quad p^{*\prime} q^* = y \tag{6.11}$$

where $q^* = (q_1^*, \ldots, q_n^*)$, $q_i^* = b_i q_i$; $p^* = (p_1^*, \ldots, p_n^*)$, $p_i^* = p_i / b_i$; and $b_i = b_i(a)$. In (6.11), $b_i$ is the scaling parameter and depends on advertising; $q_i^*$ is an adjusted or perceived quantity, the product between the scaling parameter $b_i$ and $q_i$; and $p_i^*$ is an adjusted or perceived price, the market price $p_i$ divided by the scaling parameter $b_i$. The scaling parameter $b_i$ is a potential source of restrictions and might be limited to a function of $a_i$, the advertising for commodity $i$, or $a_i$ plus advertising for commodities closely related to product $i$, depending on the extent that advertising between products is either complementary or competitive.

The demand equations for the choice problem (6.11) have the form

$$q_i^* = q_i^*(p^*, y) \quad \text{or} \tag{6.12}$$

$$q_i = \frac{1}{b_i} q_i^*(p^*, y) \tag{6.13}$$

and the indirect utility function and cost function for the problem have the forms

$$u = \phi(p^*, y) \quad \text{and} \tag{6.14}$$

$$y = c(p^*, u) \tag{6.15}$$

respectively.

Consider the restrictive case where advertising for product $i$ affects the perceived quantity and price for product $i$, but does not affect the perceived quantities and prices for other commodities, that is, $b_i = b_i(a_i)$, for all $i$. For this specification, the own-advertising demand elasticity (found by differentiating (6.13) with respect to $a_i$, multiplying the result by $a_i / q_i$, and using the relationship $(\partial q_i^* / \partial p_i)(p_i / b_i) = (\partial q_i^* / \partial p_i^*)(p_i / b_i^2)$ is

$$x_{ii} = -r_{ii}(e_{ii} + 1) \tag{6.16}$$

where $x_{ii}$ is the elasticity of demand with respect to advertising as defined in (6.8), $r_{ii} = (\partial b_i/\partial a_i)(a_i/b_i)$ is the elasticity of the scaling parameter $b_i$ with respect to advertising $a_i$, and $e_{ii} = (\partial q_i^*/\partial p_i)(p_i/q_i^*)$ is the elasticity of $q_i^*$ with respect to price $p_i$.

The cross-advertising demand elasticity can likewise be written as

$$x_{ij} = -r_{jj} e_{ij} \tag{6.17}$$

Considering equation (6.16) first, suppose advertising increases the utility of the product in the mind of the consumer so that $\partial u/\partial a_i > 0$ or $\partial b_i/\partial a_i > 0$ (after advertising less of the product provides the same utility as before advertising). In this case, the own-advertising demand elasticity would be positive only if the demand for $q_i^*$ is price elastic. The elasticity can be broken down into two parts: (1) $-r_{ii}$, a direct effect, which reduces demand since the product becomes more efficient in producing utility with advertising, and (2) $-r_{ii}e_{ii}$, an indirect effect, which increases demand as the effective price $p_i^*$ is reduced (the analysis here assumes non-Giffen goods). In this case, advertising can be viewed as resulting in a quantity augmenting taste change or change in quality.

An alternative possibility would be for advertising to have an impact similar to a change in family composition in the household utility model or a quantity diminishing taste change. In this case, $\partial b_i/\partial a_i < 0$; that is, after advertising more of the product is needed to produce a given level of utility. A convenient way to view this possibility is to define $b_i(a)$ in problem (6.11) to be $1/m_i(a)$ where $\partial m_i/\partial a_i > 0$, reflecting greater needs as in the equivalent adult model. Now $-r_{ii} > 0$ and reflects needs, while $-r_{ii}e_{ii} < 0$, as the effective price $p_i^*$, is increased. In this case, according to (6.16), the overall elasticity $x_{ii}$ would be positive only if the demand for $q_i^*$ is price inelastic.

The scaling model suggests that the advertising elasticity is positive when: advertising results in a quantity augmenting taste change or a quality type impact and demand is price elastic; or advertising results in a quantity diminishing taste change or a needs type impact and demand is price inelastic. The analysis does not preclude the possibility that both types of impacts occur at the same time. In this case, reference to a quantity augmenting taste change or quality type impact (quantity diminishing taste change or needs type impact) can be interpreted as dominance of that specific impact over the other type of impact.

The cross-advertising elasticity (6.17) involves only an indirect price-related effect and could be positive, negative, or neutral in sign. The sign would depend on whether the two goods $i$ and $j$ are substitutes, complements, or neutral; whether a quality or needs type impact is involved; or whether the advertising is generic or brand in nature (generic advertising would tend to promote a product category while brand advertising would promote an individual product within a category).

The advertising demand elasticities (6.16) and (6.17) by themselves show the close relationship between changes in advertising and changes in prices in the scaling model. The relationship can further be illustrated by substituting (6.16) and (6.17) into the advertising budget constraint restriction (6.8) to yield

$$\Sigma_j w_j e_{ji} = -w_i \tag{6.18}$$

which is simply the Cournot aggregation condition for a change in the price of commodity $i$.

The foregoing analysis is for the specific case where $b_i = b_i(a_i)$. For the unrestricted, more general case where $b_i = b_i(a)$, the own- and cross-advertising elasticities have the form

$$x_{ik} = -r_{ik}(e_{ii} + 1) - \Sigma_{j \neq i} e_{ij} r_{jk} = -r_{ik} - \Sigma_j e_{ij} r_{jk} \tag{6.19}$$

Now, as expression (6.19) indicates, a change in advertising has an indirect impact which, in effect, involves price changes for all goods. Also, the cross-advertising elasticity as well as the own-advertising elasticity now has a direct effect. Although signing the elasticities is more difficult with this generality, examination of extreme situations provides some insight. For example, consider under what circumstances the own-advertising effect is positive. Expression (6.19) indicates that, given a quantity augmenting taste or quality type impact ($\partial b_i / \partial a_i > 0$) and demand for $q_i^*$ is price elastic, the advertising demand effect will be positive if $\Sigma_{j \neq i} e_{ij} r_{ji} < 0$. The latter holds when there is a predominance of substitute (complementary) or neutral cross-price relationships occurring with substitute (complementary) cross-advertising parameter relationships. In this case, a substitute (complementary) cross-advertising parameter effect is defined to be negative (positive) in sign. Alternatively, given a quantity diminishing taste or needs type impact ($\partial b_i / \partial a_i < 0$) and the demand for $q_i^*$ is price inelastic, the advertising demand effect is positive when there is a predominance of complementary (substitute) or neutral cross-price relationships occurring with substitute (complementary) or neutral cross-advertising parameter relationships. For a needs type impact, the cross-advertising parameter effect is defined to be positive (negative) for a substitute (complementary) relationship. As indicated above, this definition is opposite of the substitute and complementary relationships for a quality type impact.

A comparison between the restrictive and unrestrictive versions of the scaling model, (6.16) and (6.17) versus (6.19) indicates a reduction in advertising parameter elasticities similar to the reduction previously discussed for the Rotterdam model. For the unrestricted model, there are $n^2$ advertising parameter elasticities; whereas, for the restricted model there are $n$ such elasticities. Whether or not the restrictive model is appropriate depends on the same issues about independence between goods and the competitiveness of advertising previously discussed in context of the Rotterdam model.

**TRANSLATING**

As previous results indicate, a basic feature of the scaling approach entails the indirect price changes generated by a change in advertising. Gorman (1976) and Pollak and Wales (1980, 1981) suggested an alternative approach — demographic translation — without the scaling feature. Translation introduces fixed costs which — in the present analysis, can be made functions of advertising. (See Green 1985 for a discussion of using the translation method to incorporate advertising in the almost ideal demand system.) The fixed costs can be interpreted as psychological needs or requirements.

Formally, the consumer choice problem for this approach can be written as

$$\text{maximize} \quad u = u(q^*)$$

$$\text{subject to} \quad p'q^* = y^* \tag{6.20}$$

where $q_i^*$ is now defined as $q_i^* = q_i - \gamma_i$; $y^* = y - \Sigma\, p_j\, \gamma_j$; and $\gamma_i = \gamma_i(a)$, the translation, or overhead, parameter for product $i$ through which advertising is introduced. The term $y^*$ has been referred to as supernumerary income in the context of the linear expenditure system and is income available after the overhead $\Sigma p_j \gamma_j$ has been met.

The indirect utility function and cost function for (6.20) are

$$u = \phi(p, y^*) \quad \text{and} \tag{6.21}$$

$$y = \Sigma_j\, p_j \gamma_j + c(p, u) \tag{6.22}$$

respectively.

The demand equations for (6.20) through (6.22) have the form

$$q_i = \gamma_i + q_i^*(p, y^*) \tag{6.23}$$

Differentiating (6.23) with respect to $a_k$, the advertising effects have the general form

$$\frac{\partial q_i}{\partial a_k} = \frac{\partial \gamma_i}{\partial a_k} - \frac{\partial q_i}{\partial y} \Sigma_j p_j \left( \frac{\partial \gamma_j}{\partial a_k} \right) \tag{6.24}$$

In contrast to the scaling approach where a change in advertising resulted in price changes, expression (6.24) indicates that a change in advertising in the translation model involves an income effect.

Again, consider the restrictive case where $\gamma_i = \gamma_i(a_i)$. Then the own-advertising effect is

$$\frac{\partial q_i}{\partial a_i} = \frac{\partial \gamma_i}{\partial a_i} - \frac{\partial q_i}{\partial y} p_i \left( \frac{\partial \gamma_i}{\partial a_i} \right) \tag{6.25}$$

The first term on the right-hand side of (6.25) can be viewed as a direct effect and is positive, under the assumption advertising creates needs, while the second term can be viewed as an indirect effect and depends on the income effect. Rewriting expression (6.25) as

$$\frac{\partial q_i}{\partial a_i} = \frac{\partial \gamma_i}{\partial a_i} \left[ 1 - p_i \left( \frac{\partial q_i}{\partial y} \right) \right] \tag{6.26}$$

indicates that a change in advertising positively affects demand only if the marginal propensity to consume out of income (MPC) is less than 1.

For the unrestricted, more general case where $\gamma_i = \gamma_i(a)$, the own-advertising demand effect would be positive when $0 < \text{MPC} < 1$ (MPC $<$ 0) and the cross-advertising parameter effects are negative (positive), indicating substitute (complementary) type relationships. The cross-advertising effects similarly involve direct and indirect effects through the first and second terms on the right-hand side of expression (6.24), respectively.

Comparing the restrictive and unrestrictive versions of the translating model, note that for the restrictive version there are $n$ advertising parameter responses $(\partial \gamma_i / \partial a_i; i = 1, \ldots, n)$; whereas, for the unrestrictive versions there are $n^2$ such responses $(\partial \gamma_i / \partial a_j; i = 1, \ldots, n; j = 1, \ldots, n)$. Again, we have the same reduction in the number of basic advertising parameter responses as in the Rotterdam and scaling models.

## COMBINED MODEL

To the extent that advertising affects basic needs, the translation model seems reasonable. On the other hand, scaling seems to be reasonable when advertising affects perceptions of quality or tastes. As shown, the different approaches result in basic differences, which are reflected in the indirect advertising effects: for translation, the indirect effect $[(-\partial q_i/\partial y)\ \Sigma p_j$ $(\partial \gamma_j/\partial a_i)]$ involves, in effect, a change in income; while for scaling, the indirect effect $(-\Sigma\ e_{ij}\ r_{ji})$ involves, in effect, changes in all prices. A model that explicitly allows both quality and needs type advertising effects combines the scaling and translation approaches. Combining scaling and translating has been considered by Gorman (1976), Deaton and Muellbauer (1980b), and Pollak and Wales (1980, 1981). Deaton and Muellbauer have noted that such an approach may be less likely to suffer from the excessive substitution that may occur in response to changes in advertising in the scaling model by itself. The consumer choice problem for the combined model can be written as

$$\text{maximize} \quad u = u(q^*)$$

$$\text{subject to} \quad p^{*\prime}q^* = y \tag{6.27}$$

where $p_i^* = p_i/b_i$ as in problem (6.11), $q_i^* = b_i(q_i - \gamma_i)$, $y^* = y - \Sigma\ p_j\gamma_j$, $b_i = b_i(a)$, and $\gamma_i = \gamma_i(a)$.

The indirect utility function and cost function for (6.27) are

$$u = \phi(p^*, y^*), \quad \text{and} \tag{6.28}$$

$$y = \Sigma_i\ p_i\ \gamma_i + c(p^*, u) \tag{6.29}$$

respectively.

The demand equations for (6.27) through (6.29) have the form

$$q_i = \gamma_i + \frac{1}{b_i}\ q_i^*(p^*, y^*) \tag{6.30}$$

Consider the restrictive case where $\gamma_i = \gamma_i(a_i)$ and $b_i = b_i(a_i)$. The own-advertising effect is then

$$\frac{\partial q_i}{\partial a_i} = \frac{\partial \gamma_i}{\partial a_i}\left[1 - \left(\frac{p_i}{b_i}\frac{\partial q_i}{\partial y}\right)\right] - \frac{1}{b_i}\left(\frac{\partial b_i}{\partial a_i}\right)\left[\frac{q_i^*}{b_i} + \left(\frac{\partial q_i^*}{\partial p_i}\frac{p_i}{b_i}\right)\right] \tag{6.31}$$

As expression (6.31) shows, the combined approach results in an advertising effect that involves, in effect, both income and price effects. The first term on the right-hand side of (6.31) is the same as expression (6.26) for the translation model except for the term $b_i$, while the second term is an effect similar to expression (6.16) for the scaling model.

The elasticity form for expression (6.31) is

$$x_{ii} = s_{ii} \left[ \frac{\gamma_i}{q_i} - \frac{p_i \gamma_i}{b_i y} e_i \right] - \left[ 1 - \frac{\gamma_i}{q_i} \right] r_{ii} \left[ 1 + e_{ii} \right] \tag{6.32}$$

where $s_{ii} = (\partial \gamma_i / \partial a_i)(a_i / \gamma_i)$ is the elasticity of the overhead for commodity $i$ with respect to advertising $a_i$, and $e_i$ is the elasticity of demand for $q_i$ with respect to income $y$. Notice that when $\gamma_i$ is zero, expression (6.32) becomes expression (6.16), the advertising demand elasticity for the scaling model, and with $b_i = 1$ and fixed, expression (6.32) is the elasticity equivalent of expression (6.26). Also, given $0 \leq \gamma_i \leq q_i$, then $0 \leq 1 - \gamma_i / q_i \leq 1$, and elasticity (6.32) is $1 - \gamma_i / q_i$ percent of the elasticity for the scaling case plus the elasticity for the translation model with the income effect divided by $b_i$. The value of the advertising demand elasticity is now more involved but can still be signed for general cases. For example, given quality and need type effects ($r_{ii} > 0$ and $s_{ii} > 0$), the advertising demand elasticity is positive when demand is price elastic and the income elasticity is less than $b_i / w_i$ (for $b_i \geq 1$ and given $w_i = p_i q_i / y$, $b_i / w_i > 1$). Further, demand can now be price inelastic and the overall advertising demand elasticity can be positive with a sufficiently large translation elasticity component. Likewise, the income elasticity can be larger than $b_i / w_i$ and the overall elasticity can still be positive, given demand is sufficiently price elastic.

For the unrestricted, more general case where $\gamma_i = \gamma_i(a)$ and $b_i = b_i(a)$, elasticity (6.32) becomes

$$x_{ii} = \frac{\gamma_i}{q_i} s_{ii} - e_i \sum_j \frac{p_j \gamma_j}{b_j y} \left( s_{ji} \right) - \left( 1 - \frac{\gamma_i}{q_i} \right) \left[ \left( 1 + e_{ii} \right) r_{ii} + \sum_{j \neq i} e_{ij} r_{ji} \right] \tag{6.33}$$

The result shows that, in general, the advertising effect on the demand for a commodity involves the own- and cross-price elasticities as well as an income effect involving the commodity's income elasticity and adjustment in supernumerary income $y^*$.

Specific versions of model (6.27) might also be considered. For example, consistency between $b_i$ and $\gamma_i$ might be imposed by defining $q_i^*$ in model

(6.27) as $q_i^* = b_i q_i - \gamma_i = b_i(q_i - \gamma_i/b_i)$ where $b_i = b_i(a)$ and $\gamma_i$ is fixed and not a function of $a$. In this case, the demand equation is

$$q_i = \frac{1}{b_i}\left[\gamma_i + q_i^*(p^*, y^*)\right]$$ (6.34)

where now $y^* = y - \Sigma \, p_j \gamma_j/b_j$. In this case, for a quality type impact ($\partial b_i/\partial a_i > 0$) an increase in advertising can be viewed as resulting in a decline in the overhead. Less overhead is needed with an improvement in quality. Likewise, for a needs type impact ($\partial b_i/\partial a_i < 0$) an increase in advertising can be viewed as resulting in an increase in the required overhead, as in the household composition model with overhead (Muellbauer 1974). In this framework, to achieve the result that advertising has a quality impact through $b_i$ and a needs impact through overhead, $q_i^*$ could be defined as $q_i^* = b_i(q_i - b_i\gamma_i)$.

For equation (6.34) with $b_i = b_i(a_i)$, the own-advertising elasticity is

$$x_{ii} = r_{ii}\left[e_i^*\left(\frac{p_i \gamma_i}{b_i y}\right) - e_{ii}^* - 1\right]$$ (6.35)

where $e_i^* = [\partial(b_i q_i)/\partial y][y/(b_i q_i)]$ and $e_{ii}^* = [\partial(b_i q_i)/\partial p_i][p_i/(b_i q_i)]$. Elasticity (6.35) indicates that for a quality type impact ($\partial b_i/\partial a_i > 0$), the advertising demand effect is positive given a normal good with an elastic demand. Likewise, for an inelastic demand, the advertising effect is positive given a sufficiently strong positive income effect. The situation is opposite the case previously developed for expression (6.32). For a needs type impact ($\partial b_i/\partial a_i < 0$), elasticity (6.35) is positive given an inferior good (or sufficiently weak positive income effect) and inelastic demand. The overall elasticity would also be positive when demand is elastic provided a sufficiently strong negative income effect.

## SCALING/TRANSLATING EXAMPLES

The general results for introducing advertising in demand systems by scaling and/or translating can be applied directly to particular demand specifications. Several examples are provided for illustration. The first two examples involve the linear expenditure system (Stone 1954) and the indirect addilog model (Houthakker 1960), both restrictive, first-generation type demand models. The next example involves the Rotterdam model (Barten

1964a, Theil 1965) and the final example involves the almost ideal demand system (Deaton and Muellbauer 1980a), which is a flexible functional form.

First, consider the Cobb-Douglas type utility function

$$u = \Sigma \; \beta_i \log q_i \tag{6.36}$$

with demand equations

$$q_i = \frac{\beta_i}{p_i} \, y, \qquad i = 1, \ldots, n \tag{6.37}$$

where $\beta_i$ is a parameter with $0 < \beta_i < 1$ and $\Sigma \; \beta_i = 1$.

Applying the results for combined model (6.34) to the above specifications, the direct utility function with advertising is

$$u = \Sigma_i \; \beta_i \log \left[ b_i(a) q_i - \gamma_i \right] \tag{6.38}$$

and the demand equations are

$$q_i = \frac{\gamma_i}{b_i(a)} + \frac{\beta_i}{p_i} \left[ y - \Sigma_j \, p_j \left( \frac{\gamma_j}{b_j(a)} \right) \right] \qquad i = 1, \ldots, n \tag{6.39}$$

with $q_i > \gamma_i/b_i(a)$, which is simply the linear expenditure system with overhead depending on advertising.

Second, consider the indirect addilog utility function, modified according to (6.34), that is,

$$u = \Sigma_j \; \alpha_j \left\{ \left[ y - \Sigma_j \, \frac{p_j \gamma_j}{b_j(a)} \right] \Big/ \left[ \frac{p_j}{b_j(a)} \right] \right\}^{\beta_j} \tag{6.40}$$

where $\alpha_i$ and $\beta_i$ are parameters with $\alpha_i \beta_i \geq 0$, and $\beta_i \geq -1$ with $\beta_i = -1$ for at most one commodity. Applying Roy's identity, the demand equations are

$$q_i = \frac{\gamma_i}{b_i} + \frac{\dfrac{\alpha_i \beta_i}{b_i} \left[ (y - \Sigma_j \, p_j \gamma_j / b_j) / (p_i / b_i) \right]^{\beta_i + 1}}{\Sigma_j \; \alpha_j \beta_j \left[ (y - \Sigma_j \, p_j \gamma_j / b_j) / (p_j / b_j) \right]^{\beta_j}} \qquad i = 1, \ldots, n \tag{6.41}$$

which is the basic addilog model with the overhead component $\gamma_i/b_i$ added, and $y^*$ and $p_j^*$ as defined in (6.34) replacing $y$ and $p_j$ in the basic specification.

The third example introduces advertising in the Rotterdam model by scaling under the assumption $b_i = b_i(a_i)$. In this case, the Rotterdam specification of demand can be written as

$$w_i \, d \log q_i = \beta_i \left[ d \log y - \Sigma_j \, w_j \, (d \log p_j - r_{jj} \, d \log a_j) \right]$$

$$+ \Sigma_j \, \pi_{ij} \, (d \log p_j - r_{jj} \, d \log a_j) - r_{ii} \, w_i \, d \log a_i \tag{6.42}$$

where $\beta_i = p_i(\partial q_i/\partial y)$, $r_{jj} = (\partial b_j/\partial a_j)(a_j/b_j)$, and $\pi_{ij} = (p_i p_j/y)(\partial h_i/\partial p_j)$. Incorporation of advertising in the Rotterdam model thus results in an estimable form that involves the advertising terms $r_{jj}$ and $d \log a_j$.

The last example considers the almost ideal demand system. The cost function for this model with advertising introduced through scaling is

$$\log c = \alpha_o + \Sigma_j \, \alpha_j \log \left( \frac{p_j}{b_j} \right) + \frac{1}{2} \Sigma_j \, \Sigma_k \, \pi_{jk} \log \left( \frac{p_j}{b_j} \right) \log \left( \frac{p_k}{b_k} \right)$$

$$+ u \, \beta_0 \, \Pi_j \left( \frac{p_j}{b_j} \right)^{\beta_j} \tag{6.43}$$

where the $\alpha$'s, $\beta$'s, and $\pi$'s are parameters. Applying Shepard's lemma ($w_i = \partial \log c/\log p_i$), the Hicksian demand equations for (6.43) have the form

$$w_i = \alpha_i + \Sigma_j \, \pi_{ij} \log \left( \frac{p_j}{b_j} \right) + \beta_i \, u \, \beta_0 \, \Pi_j \left( \frac{p_j}{b_j} \right)^{\beta_j} \tag{6.44}$$

[Notice that $\partial \log c/\partial \log p_j = \partial \log c/\partial \log (p_j/b_j)$.]

Solving (6.43) for $u$ and substituting into (6.44), the corresponding Marshallian demand equations have the form

$$w_i = \alpha_i + \Sigma_j \, \pi_{ij} \log \left( \frac{p_j}{b_j} \right) + \beta_i \log \left( \frac{y}{P} \right) \tag{6.45}$$

where

$$P = \alpha_0 + \Sigma \; \alpha_j \; \log\left(\frac{p_j}{b_j}\right) + \frac{1}{2} \; \Sigma_j \; \Sigma_j \; \pi_{jk} \; \log\left(\frac{p_j}{b_j}\right) \log\left(\frac{p_k}{b_k}\right)$$

Addition of fixed costs to cost function (6.43) is straightforward. For this case, the resulting demand equations involve additional nonlinearities. The cost function with fixed costs is

$$\log c^* = \log\left(\Sigma_j \; \frac{p_j \gamma_j}{b_j} + e^{\log c}\right) \tag{6.46}$$

where $\log c$ is defined by equation (6.43). Differentiating (6.46) with respect to $\log (p_j)$ yields

$$w_i = \frac{1}{c^*}\left[\frac{p_i \gamma_i}{b_i} + c\left(\frac{\partial \log c}{\partial \log p_i}\right)\right] \tag{6.47}$$

where total expenditures $y = c^*$; $c = y - \Sigma \; p_j \gamma_j / b_j$; and $\partial \log c / \partial \log p_i$ is given by expression (6.44).

Given specifications for $b_i(a)$, the foregoing models can be estimated with sufficient variation in the data. For example, $b_i$ might be specified linearly as

$$b_{it} = d_{io} + \Sigma_{j=0}^{J} \; l_{ij} \; a_{i,t-j} \qquad \text{or} \tag{6.48}$$

$$b_{it} = d_{io} + \Sigma_{j=0}^{J} \; l_{ij} \; \log a_{i,t-j} \tag{6.49}$$

where subscript $t$ stands for time and allows for the introduction of past advertising effects, and the $d$'s and $l$'s are parameters.

Nonlinear estimation methods can be employed to estimate demand equations (6.39), (6.41), (6.42), and (6.45), with the equations being nonlinear in parameters (Johnson, Hassan, and Green 1984 and Bewely 1980 provide general discussion of estimation of demand systems). Given the budget constraint, one equation should be deleted for estimation. The linear expenditure system, based on an additive utility function, is restrictive with respect to the effects of prices and income (for example, all goods have positive income effects; negative gross cross-price effects, given $\gamma_i / b_i(a) >$ 0; and positive compensated cross-price effects) and may be more suitable when analyzing the demands for aggregates of goods rather than specific products. The addilog model, based on an additive indirect utility function, is also restrictive (for example, the difference between income elasticities for two goods is constant). The results for the addilog model, however, suggest how the generalized addilog demand system (Bewely 1980), a flexible functional form, might be modified to incorporate advertising effects (namely, by adjusting prices using the $b_i$'s). The Rotterdam model (6.42) can be estimated treating $\beta_i$, $r_{jj}$ and $\pi_{ij}$ as constants over the sample and assuming a finite approximation (Theil 1965).

## Household Production Theory and Advertising

An alternative approach to incorporate the impact of advertising in demand analysis is based on household production theory (discussion of the basic theory is provided by Becker 1965; Lancaster 1966; Pollak and Wachter 1975; Stigler and Becker 1977; Deaton and Muellbauer 1980b; among others). In the traditional model of consumer behavior, market goods directly provide utility to consumers. In the household production model, market goods are inputs used in the production of nonmarket goods or commodities that give rise to utility. Other inputs used in the production of commodities include household labor and the human and nonhuman capital of the household. As suggested by Stigler and Becker, advertising can be introduced into the household production model by considering the information it provides as an input in the production of commodities. In the remainder of this section, the household production model is developed with attention to the impacts of advertising on the demands for market goods.

Consider the production of commodities $z$ from market goods $q$, household labor inputs $h$, human capital inputs or stocks of information $i$, and other capital inputs $k$. The joint production function for commodities can be written as

$$F(z, q, h, k, i) = 0 \tag{6.50}$$

One way to introduce advertising into the analysis is through the human capital inputs $i$, by considering advertising as a source of product information useful for commodity production. (The informational aspects of advertising have been widely discussed; for example, in addition to Stigler and Becker, see Stigler 1961; Nelson 1970, 1974; Ehrlich and Fisher 1982.) The information a household receives from advertising, and its stock of knowledge, depend on the household's exposure to advertising, which, in turn, depends on the level of advertising in the market, the time household members allocate to activities where they might be subject to advertising, the availability of goods important for communication (TVs, radios, newspapers, and magazines), and the educational levels of household members. Using $t$

as a subscript to denote time, the stock of information can be written as

$$i_t = i(x_t, x_{t-1}, \ldots) \tag{6.51}$$

where $x_t = (a_t, l_t, q_{t-1}, ck_t, e_t)$, where $a$ is again a vector of product advertising levels for the various goods in the market; $l$ is a vector of leisure time inputs; $c_k$ is a vector of available capital goods used for communication; and $e$ is a vector of household-member education levels ($e$ could include both formal education and learning from friends or other consumers about products). Leisure time $l$ is included in specification (6.51) based on the assumption that exposure to advertising as well as shopping around in search of product information is largely related to leisure activities; otherwise, separate time inputs for leisure, advertising exposure, and search time might be considered.

The leisure vector is also considered part of the commodity vector $z$ and, given the joint nature of production, could be part of the household labor vector $h$. The quantity vector $q_{t-1}$ is included in the specification to account for information obtained from experience with goods purchased in the past. The lagged relationship shown in (6.51) indicates the cumulative effect of advertising and learning over time. The following analysis will continue to show this relationship in the context of the impact of advertising in the short run.

Substituting equation (6.51) into equation (6.50), the joint production function at time $t$ can be written as

$$F[z_t, q_t, h_t, k_t, i(x_t, x_{t-1}, \ldots)] = 0 \tag{6.52}$$

Based on the above household production relationship, the minimum short-run cost of producing commodity vector $z$ given market good prices $p$ and wage rates $w$ (the opportunity costs associated with $h$) can be written as

$$c(z_t, p_t, w_t, k_t, x_t, x_{t-1}, \ldots) = \min p_t'q_t + w_t'h_t \tag{6.53}$$

subject to the technological constraint (6.52).

Differentiation of cost function (6.53) with respect to market prices yields the market demand equations

$$q_{it} = \frac{\partial c}{\partial p_{it}} = q_i(z_t, p_t, w_t, k_t, x_t, t_{t-1}, \ldots) \quad i = 1, 2, \ldots, n \tag{6.54}$$

where subscript $i$ denotes a specific market good.

The demand equations given by specification (6.54) are not in reduced form due to the presence of $z$, which must be determined based on the household preferences and resource constraint. The short-run optimization problem to determine $z$ can be written as

maximize     $u_t = u(z_t)$

subject to   $y_t = c(z_t, p_t, w_t, k_t, x_t, x_{t-1}, \ldots)$

$$(6.55)$$

where $u_t$ is the utility level given $z_t$, and $y_t$ is full income defined as nonlabor income plus the value of the household's time endowment.

Problem (6.55) can be solved to yield the commodity demand equations

$$z_t = z(y_t, p_t, w_t, k_t, x_t, x_{t-1}, \ldots) \tag{6.56}$$

Substituting equations (6.56) into equations (6.54), the reduced form market demand equations can be written as

$$q_{it} = q_i(y_t, p_t, w_t, k_t, x_t, x_{t-1}, \ldots) \tag{6.57}$$

A particular example of the household production model is the linear characteristics model (see Lancaster for a full discussion) where production of commodities is given by

$$z = \beta q \tag{6.58}$$

with $\beta$ defined as a matrix that transforms the market goods into commodities or characteristics. For instance, in analyzing diet and food demand, $z$ might measure nutrient, calorie, and fiber levels with a given column of $\beta$ indicating the amounts of each characteristic per unit of a particular food.

Specification (6.58) is incomplete with respect to time and human and other capital inputs and, for analyzing advertising, needs to be extended. A possible extension, suggested by Deaton and Muellbauer (1980a), would be to make the $\beta$ matrix a function of the latter omitted variables. The model then would include all the relevant variables as in the general model, equations (6.50) through (6.57).

The specification of the general household production model suggests that the impact of advertising on the demand for market goods is dependent on a number of factors sometimes overlooked by the traditional demand approach. In general, in both demand models the impact of advertising is conditional on market good prices and income, although income is defined as full income in the household production model and total expenditures on goods in the traditional model. The traditional model can include demographic factors such as advertising and household characteristics, usually based on the assumption they are preference shifters. On the other hand, through the treatment of the demands for market goods as factor demands, the household production model suggests the impact of advertising may be closely related to such variables as wage rates, availability of communication type goods, and education levels of household members. As equations (6.50) through (6.57) indicate, the wage rates or opportunity costs of time may be important with respect to the production of nonmarket commodities $z$ and the amount of time household members are exposed to advertising. For example, the increased opportunities in the labor market for women may have had an effect on exposure to some types of advertising. A specific example might be the advertising related to coupon programs that involve collecting and redeeming coupons and can be costly to a household in terms of time, especially when coupons are distributed through newspapers and magazines.

The household production model also focuses on the role of communication type goods with respect to the effectiveness of advertising. Most households probably have TVs and radios, but availability of printed material may vary across households in terms of both amount and kind. The amount and type of printed material in a household are probably related to the household's production of leisure time and entertainment as well as education. Education is an added factor in the household production model. Obviously, reading ability is a necessary requisite for exposure to advertising through printed material. Perhaps less obvious is the relationship between education and an individual's selection of reading material that results in exposure to specific types of advertising.

Although the household production model is intuitively appealing from a descriptive viewpoint, application may be difficult because of data limitations. To estimate the full model requires household-level data on the market good prices $p$ and quantities $q$, the production of commodities $z$, advertising levels $a$, full income $y$, the wage rates $w$, the education levels $e$, and the capital goods $k$ and $c_k$. The development of micro data sets on household consumption behavior will probably determine the extent the household production model is applied.

## Summary and Conclusions

Demand systems with advertising variables have two basic properties in addition to the general properties (adding-up, homogeneity, symmetry, and negativity) of any demand system. First, a change in advertising that increases the demand(s) for some good(s) must be offset by decreases in demands for other goods as total expenditures are constant. Second, the matrix of advertising demand impacts is equal to minus the inverse of the marginal utility of income times the Slutsky substitution matrix times the matrix of second-order partial derivatives of the utility function with respect to the quantities of choice and advertising variables. The latter relationship offers a means to introduce advertising in demand systems, particularly in the context of the Rotterdam model where the matrix of second-order partial derivatives has been restricted to be diagonal.

Specific methods of incorporating advertising in demand systems involve the scaling and translating modeling approaches considered by Barten (1964a and b, 1977), Gorman (1976), Muellbauer (1974, 1975), and Pollak and Wales (1981), among others. Restrictions can be introduced into the scaling and translating models through the particular parameters defining the model specifications. The scaling model suggests advertising may be more effective when demand is price elastic (inelastic) given a quantity augmenting (diminishing) type scaling impact. The latter results depend on the cross-price elasticities, as a change in advertising, in effect, generates price effects in the model. Alternatively, in the translation model the effects of advertising are felt through an overhead term or a fixed cost component. In this case, the impact of advertising on demand depends on the income effect. A positive (negative) income effect reduces (reinforces) the impact of advertising on demand, given that advertising positively affects overhead costs. Combining the scaling and translating methods offers another approach to introduce advertising in demand systems. The effects of advertising in the combined model are dependent on both the income and price elasticities as suggested by the scaling and translating models, individually.

The demand systems approach offers a consistent means to analyze advertising, particularly when advertising programs interact; for example, beef advertising may affect the demand for other meats and vice versa. Application of the demand system approaches discussed in this paper offers the potential to estimate demand systems when prices vary little or tend to be collinear, provided there is sufficient variation in advertising. The latter possibility is equivalent to the possibility of estimating price effects in the household utility model from cross-sectional data as suggested by Barten (1964b).

The household production theory approach in the context of advertising was examined in this paper. In general, household production theory leads to a much different set of market demand equations than the traditional utility maximization approach. The most obvious difference pertains to the explanatory variables included in the equations. Of course, differences in explanatory variables will depend on how one chooses to describe the household production process and what preference shifters are included in the traditional model. However, based on the specifications presented here — equations (6.2) versus (6.57) — wages, capital, leisure time, education, and past consumption are included as explanatory variables in the household production model whereas they are not in the traditional model.

Prices and advertising are included in both specifications, while the income variable is total expenditures in the traditional model and full income in the household production model. The variables omitted from the traditional model or closely related demographic variables could be included as preference shifters as has often been done on an ad hoc basis. However, such an approach tends to confound changes in technology and changes in tastes. As is often the case, model selection will probably depend on how well the model describes reality, availability of data, and fit. The scaling, translating, and household production approaches all offer interesting specifications for empirical work.

# 7 Measuring the Effects of Advertising on Demand Elasticities Using Time Series/Cross-Sectional Data

HUI-SHUNG CHANG and RICHARD GREEN

There is extensive literature associated with measuring the effects of advertising on consumer demand. Some basic problems however remain unsolved. One of these involves separating the effects of advertising from other sociodemographic variables. This issue is examined here by simultaneously incorporating advertising and demographic variables into a flexible demand system.

Two major issues are explored in empirical demand analysis: the estimation of subsystems of demand equations using combined cross-sectional and time series data, and the incorporation of advertising and demographic effects into demand subsystems. The objectives are: (1) to test the theoretical restrictions implied by demand theory, such as homogeneity and symmetry conditions, (2) to examine the relative significance of prices, total expenditure, advertising, and demographic variables in the demand for foods consumed at home, (3) to estimate demand elasticities, and (4) to measure the effects of advertising on demand elasticities.

Two sources of data are used for the estimations. The consumer expenditure (diary and interview) survey data set collected by the Bureau of Labor Statistics (BLS) provides information on household characteristics and consumption expenditures, with the exception of prices. Prices are obtained from the U.S. Department of Agriculture's food consumption, price, and expenditures series and advertising expenditures are obtained from the Broadcast Advertisers Reports/Leading National Advertisers (BAR/LNA) data series. Using this combined data set not only allows for modeling the effects of economic and noneconomic variables in consumer demand analysis but also increases the number of observations substantially.

Under classical, static demand theory, with perfect information and constant tastes, the consumer problem is formulated as one of utility maximization subject to a budget constraint. The system of Marshallian demand equations thus derived are functions of prices and income only.

However, the classical approach overlooks the sociodemographic and psychological makeup of the consumer and the possibility of taste changes over time. Moreover, since the type of data available for applied research is either time series or cross sectional, one either needs to assume demand functions are the same for all observations or to make fairly specific assumptions about how preferences vary across microunits or change over time. One way to do this, for example, is to allow certain parameters of the utility function or demand equation to depend on demographic variables or advertising, or both.

Incorporation of demographic variables into demand systems explicitly recognizes the fact that households differ in size, age composition, educational level, and other characteristics and may have different consumption patterns. Several methods have been used to model these individual differences. For example, demographic translation, demographic scaling, and household equivalence scales have been used to account for differences in household compositions. The effects of demographic variables can also be analyzed by estimating each demographic group separately. In this case, demographic variables are not included as explanatory variables; rather, the parameters are allowed to vary freely among different demographic groups. This procedure is termed "unpooled estimation" (Pollak and Wales 1980). One drawback associated with this approach is that there can be as many sets of demand systems to estimate as there are demographic characteristics.

Another procedure that is a mixture of demographic translation (or scaling) and unpooled estimation is "partially pooled" estimation. In this approach, grouping is done according to major demographic characteristics and the effects of remaining characteristics are then analyzed within each group by translating or scaling (Kokoski 1986).

Household demographic characteristics are provided in household budget surveys. Since surveys correspond to a single-price situation, an empirical analysis of demographic variations in consumer preferences within the framework of demand systems is not possible unless budget data are available for at least two time periods. This is because prices as well as income (or total expenditure) are major determinants of demand. In Pollak and Wales (1978), a complete demand system was estimated using data from only two budget studies. In Kokoski, inter-area or cross-sectional price indices were generated for 1972/73 and 1980/81 consumer expenditure diary surveys to account for price variability. Additional literature on the estimation of demand systems using budget data includes Tsujimura and Sato (1964) for Japan, and Bhattacharya (1967), Joseph (1968), and Ray (1980, 1982) for India.

In dealing with survey data, some empirical studies use grouped data for estimations. In this case, group means, rather than individual household observations, are used. Although this practice avoids large-scale computations, there is loss of information, resulting in less efficient estimates than those obtained from individual observations (Kmenta 1971). Moreover, using group means may introduce heteroscedasticity into the model structure if the number of observations in each group are not equal (Maddala 1977). In this study, individual observations are used over a period of five years.

## Theoretical Background

Under the assumptions that consumer preferences are complete, reflexive, transitive, continuous, and strongly monotonic, there exists a continuous utility function that represents these preferences. And with additional assumptions that the utility function is strictly quasiconcave and twice-differentiable, the consumer problem can be solved as a constrained maximization problem using Lagrangian techniques. The system of Marshallian demand equations thus derived are unique and have the following properties. They are homogeneous of degree zero in prices and income, the matrix of substitution effects is symmetric and negative semidefinite, and individual expenditures add up to the total expenditure exactly. These conditions, termed general restrictions, hold regardless of the form of the underlying utility function.

Demand equations and their associated properties can also be derived from a duality approach in which consumers are assumed to behave as cost minimizing agents. In duality theory, demand equations are derived using Shephard's lemma. The duality approach has the advantage of simplifying the derivation of demand functions while maintaining the essence of the demand structure (Deaton and Muellbauer 1980).

At the beginning of this section it was stated that consumer preferences were assumed to be constant in static demand theory. When this assumption is relaxed, consumer demand models can be extended to incorporate elements of dynamic consumer behavior by allowing some parameters characterizing these preferences to vary with some exogenous variables. All the general restrictions derived from the static demand theory remain, with one additional adding-up condition resulting from the exogenous variables. That is,

$$\{\partial x_i/\partial A_j\} = -1/\lambda KV \tag{7.1}$$

or in elasticity terms,

$$\Sigma_i \, w_i \, e_{i,s_j} = 0 \tag{7.2}$$

where $x$ is quantity demanded, $A$ is an exogenous variable such as advertising, $\lambda$ is the marginal utility of money, $K$ is the Slutsky substitution matrix, $V = \{\partial^2 U/\partial x_i \partial A_j\}$, and $U$ is the utility function; $w_i$ is the expenditure share for good $i$, and $e_{i,s_j}$ are cross-advertising elasticities (Basmann 1956; Aviphant, Lee, and Brown 1988). Equation (7.2) states that there is no change in total expenditure because of changes in the additional exogenous variables but rather a reallocation of the total expenditure among consumption bundles.

## The Almost Ideal Demand System Model

Preferences may differ across household units because of different household characteristics and may also change over time due to either better outside information or to "built-in" habits related to past decisions. A more general model of consumer demand should take these factors into account. The effects of demographic variables and advertising are here incorporated into the almost ideal demand system (AIDS) by translation. Persistences in consumption are not considered here because households vary from one survey to the next.

In a generalized model, one can examine not only the effects of changes in prices and income but also the impacts of additional variables such as advertising and demographics on consumer demand. The almost ideal demand system (AIDS) of Deaton and Muellbauer (1980) is generated from a consumer cost minimization problem. The system of demand equations, in share form, derived from this process is given by

$$w_{i,t} = \alpha_i + \Sigma_j r_{ij} \ln p_{j,t} + \beta_i \ln (y_t/P_t) \quad i = 1, 2, 3, \ldots, n \quad (7.3)$$

where

$$\ln P_t = \alpha_0 + \Sigma_j \alpha_j \ln p_{j,t} + 1/2 \, \Sigma_k \, \Sigma_j \ln p_{k,t} \ln p_{j,t} \quad \text{and} \quad (7.4)$$

$$\Sigma_i \beta_i = 0, \, \Sigma_i r_{ij} = 0, \text{ and } \Sigma_i \alpha_i = 1 \quad (7.5)$$

To include the effects of advertising and demographic variables, following Green, the price coefficients of the expenditure function are assumed to depend upon demographic variables and advertising expenditures. That is, the $\alpha_i$'s in equation (7.3) are assumed to conform to the following scheme:

$$\alpha_{i,t} = a_i + \Sigma_k \, b_{i,k} \, A_{i,t-k} + c_i \, D_t^h \tag{7.6}$$

where $A_{i,t-k}$ denotes advertising expenditures in time period $(t-k)$ for the $i$th commodity and $D_t^h$ represents demographic characteristics of the $h$th household at time $t$. Past advertising expenditures are included to capture the delayed effects of advertising resulting from lagged responses to advertising or brand loyalty on the part of consumers. This scheme also can be generalized to include cross-advertising effects. Other specifications for $\alpha_i$'s are also possible, such as including a stochastic error term to account for the effects of random factors on consumer preferences.

The extended demand equations of the AIDS are

$$w_{i,t} = (a_i + \Sigma_k b_{i,k} A_{i,t-k} + c_i \, D_t^h) + \Sigma_j r_{ij} \ln p_{j,t} + \beta_i \ln (y_t/P_t)$$

$$i = 1, 2, 3, \ldots, n \tag{7.7}$$

In this study, prices and advertising expenditures are assumed to be determined outside the demand system and hence are exogenous. However, advertising expenditures may influence prices, and vice versa. What is important for the subsequent estimations is that there exists no feedback from quantities on advertising and/or prices. In this case, we have a block recursive system. These assumptions are crucial for the estimations that follow. Otherwise, a much more complicated model must be developed and estimated. Based on equation (7.7), expressions for the expenditure, own-price, and cross-price elasticities are given, respectively, by

$$\eta_{i,t} = 1 + \beta_i/w_{i,t} \tag{7.8}$$

$$\epsilon_{ii,t} = -1 + \{r_{ii} - \beta_i \, [(a_i + \Sigma_k \, b_{i,k} \, A_{i,t-k} + c_i \, D_t^h) \tag{7.9}$$
$$+ \Sigma_j \, r_{ij} \ln p_{j,t}]\}/w_{i,t} \quad \text{and}$$

$$\epsilon_{ij,t} = \{r_{ij} - \beta_i \, [(a_i + \Sigma_k b_{i,k} \, A_{i,t-k} + c_i \, D_t^h)$$
$$+ \Sigma_j \, r_{ij} \ln p_{j,t}]\}/w_{i,t} \tag{7.10}$$

Expressions for own current and lagged advertising elasticities are given in equation (7.11).

$$\epsilon_{i,Ai,t-k} = [b_{i,k}(1 - \beta_i \ln p_{i,t})A_{i,t-k}]/w_{i,t} \tag{7.11}$$

where $A_{i,t-k}$ is own lagged advertising expenditure, for $k = 0, 1, 2, 3, \ldots$.

Equation (7.11) represents the percentage change in the quantity demanded of the $i$th commodity with respect to a 1 percent change in the current advertising expenditure for $k = 0$ and lagged advertising elasticities for $k \neq 0$. The cumulative or long-run effects of advertising (the intermediate or long-run multiplier) are obtained by summing the derivatives of quantity demanded with respect to current and lagged advertising expenditures (the dynamic or lagged multipliers). The long-run, own-advertising elasticities, therefore, are obtained by summing the short-run, own-advertising elasticities, evaluated at the sample means, for all periods considered.

Intuitively, the own-advertising elasticities are expected to be non-negative; otherwise, additional amounts of advertising directed toward a particular commodity would result in a reduction of the quantities demanded. However, (7.1) does not preclude a negative own-advertising effect. For $\beta_i < 0$ and $b_{i,k} > 0$, the own-advertising elasticity is always positive, assuming proper scaling on prices so that $\ln p_{i,t}$ is positive. However, for $\beta_i > 0$, the advertising elasticity is positive only if $b_{i,k}$ and $(1 - \beta_i \ln p_{i,t})$ are both positive.

Now, consider the effects of current advertising on the elasticities of demand. First, with respect to the expenditure elasticities, the effect of advertising is:

$$\partial \eta_{i,t}/\partial A_{i,t} = -(\beta_i/w_{i,t})(e_{iA_i,t}/A_{i,t}) \tag{7.12}$$

Thus, for $\beta_i < 0$, an increase in the advertising expenditure of the $i$th commodity results in the expenditure elasticity becoming more elastic or less inelastic, depending upon the signs of the advertising elasticities, which in turn depend upon the sign of the advertising coefficient $b$. The impact of advertising is, however, less clear for $\beta_i > 0$.

Second, with respect to own-price elasticities, the effect of advertising is:

$$\partial e_{ii,t}/\partial A_{i,t} = -(\beta_i b_{i,0}/w_{i,t}) - (e_{ii,t})(e_{iA_i,t}/A_{i,t}) \tag{7.13}$$

Thus, for necessary and normal goods, when advertising elasticities are positive a change in advertising expenditure will have a positive effect on own-price elasticities, making demand less elastic.

Finally, with respect to own-advertising elasticities, the effect of advertising is:

$$\partial e_{iA_i,t}/\partial A_{i,t} = (1 - e_{iA_i,t})(e_{iA_i,t}/A_{i,t}) \tag{7.14}$$

Clearly, if advertising elasticities are greater than one, the effect of advertising on advertising elasticities will be negative. That is, quantities demanded are increasing at a decreasing rate with respect to a change in advertising expenditure. This result is an indication of diminishing returns to advertising investment. On the other hand, if the advertising elasticity is negative, quantities demanded will decrease at an increasing rate. In order to estimate the magnitudes of these effects the AIDS is estimated using cross-sectional and time series data.

## Data and Estimation Procedures

Information available for the estimations includes household characteristics, household food expenditures as well as advertising and price indices for five food groups: meats, dairy products, cereal and bakery products, fruits and vegetables, and all other foods consumed at home. This is the same commodity classification used by Kokoski (1986).

Quarterly advertising expenditures were obtained from the BAR/LNA multimedia service data series collected by Broadcast Advertisers Reports, Inc. and Leading National Advertisers, Inc. The series contains quarterly advertising expenditures on various products by class, item, and company, as well as by media from 1980 to 1984. The media consist of newspapers, magazines, spot and network television, spot and network radio, and outdoor billboards. These advertising expenditures, which include both generic and brand-specific advertising, were then aggregated according to the same classifications for the food expenditures. These nominal advertising expenditures then were deflated by the cost indices for advertising expenditures to adjust for changes in media costs (Chang 1988). Since LNA tends to underreport what is actually spent on advertising, there may be problems in estimation as a result of measurement error.

Quarterly consumption expenditures for each food group are obtained from consumer expenditure diary surveys conducted by the BLS from 1980 to 1984. These data contain information on household demographic characteristics and consumption expenditures on small, frequently purchased items such as food and beverages, gas and electricity, nonprescription drugs, and the like. The quarterly price indices are obtained from *Food Consumption, Prices, and Expenditures* (Statistical Bulletin No. 749, Economic Research Service, U.S. Department of Agriculture, 1985).

For estimation purposes, the original diary survey data were split into quarters and further broken down into five regions according to their standard metropolitan statistical area (SMSA) status. These five regions include four SMSA regions and one outside SMSA and are designated as follows:

Region 1: SMSA-northeast
Region 2: SMSA-north central
Region 3: SMSA-south
Region 4: SMSA-west
Region 5: All non-SMSA areas

Household expenditure patterns are studied for each region separately in a demand system framework. The model includes the effects of prices, total expenditure, and advertising as well as the following demographic variables: household gross income, family size, family type, annual value of food stamps, and age, sex, and race of the household head.

Because of nonlinearities and the number of the parameters involved, it was not possible to estimate the model specified in (7.7). Therefore, estimations were performed with the linear approximate almost ideal demand system (LA/AIDS) in which Stone's index, $\ln P_t^* = \Sigma_i \, w_{i,t} \ln p_{i,t}$, was used to replace the price index, $\ln P$, in (7.4). Some estimation problems associated with this approximation are discussed in Blanciforti and Green (1983). In addition, there are issues on whether elasticity expressions from the AIDS or the LA/AIDS should be used. See Green and Alston (1989) for a detailed discussion of these points.

For empirical purposes, an error structure is added to the model. The error terms for the same commodity are assumed to be identically, independently, and normally distributed. That is, they are assumed to be uncorrelated over time and have the same variances. The error terms, however, are assumed to be contemporaneously correlated across equations since the error terms for different demand equations in a system at a given point in time are likely to reflect some common, unmeasurable or omitted factors. More specifically, we assume

$$E(e^n_{i,t}, e^h_{j,s}) = \sigma_{ij}, \text{ for } s = t \text{ and } n = h, \text{ and}$$

$$= 0, \text{ otherwise}$$

where $i$ refers to a given commodity, $t$ a given time period, and $h$ an individual household.

This model can be estimated consistently by Zellner's seemingly unrelated regression (SUR) method. Since the budget shares sum to one, the contemporaneous covariance matrix is singular. The model was estimated by an iterative SUR estimation technique after dropping one equation. Since iterative SUR estimators are equivalent to maximum likelihood estimators, the resultant estimators are invariant to the choice of the equation deleted as long as the error terms have a multivariate normal distribution (Judge et al. 1982). Iterative SUR estimation was employed using the computer package SHAZAM (White 1988).

## The Empirical Results and Economic Interpretations

Tests of the theoretical properties of the demand equations indicate that homogeneity conditions, symmetry conditions, as well as the joint conditions of homogeneity and symmetry hold at the 5 percent level of significance for all the regions. That is, the data fail to reject the homogeneity conditions or the symmetry conditions, or both. Since most price and advertising coefficients are not significantly different from zero, caution must be exercised in interpreting these results.

The effects of prices, total expenditure, advertising, and demographic variables on household consumption were tested by examining the significance of individual coefficients based on $t$-tests and the significance of the subsets based on partial $F$-tests. Since the estimated model involves a large number of structural parameters and the results are similar among regions, only general results are reported. Estimated coefficients for Region 2 (North Central) are presented, as an illustration, in the Appendix.

In general, the individual $t$-test results indicate that total expenditure and demographic coefficients are statistically significant while those of prices, advertising, and seasonal dummy variables are not. The statistically significant results are summarized as follows:

1. Increase in household *income* decreases consumption for meats and cereal and bakery products but increases consumption for dairy products and fruits and vegetables.
2. *Age* of the household head has an adverse effect on consumption for meats and dairy products and has a positive effect for cereal and bakery products and fruits and vegetables.
3. An increase in *family size* apparently decreases the consumption of meats, increases the consumption of dairy products and cereal and bakery products, and has no significant effect on demand for fruits and vegetables. This is true for all regions.
4. *Annual value of food stamps* does not seem to have a significant effect on the food consumption. Change in the *annual value of food stamps,* however, has a positive effect on the consumption of meats in Region 2, negative for fruits and vegetables in Region 1, but no significant effect

for other groups in other regions.

5. Households with female heads tend to consume less fruits and vegetables but more meats and dairy products compared to households with male heads.

6. There are nine *family types;* results are compared to families without children. The results show that (1) families with children under age 6 consume less meats but more dairy products, (2) families with children between 6 and 17 years of age tend to eat more cereal and bakery products but less fruits and vegetables, (3) families with children older than 17 appear to eat more fruits and vegetables, and (4) single female parents with children under age 17 tend to consume more dairy products and cereal and bakery products but less fruits and vegetables.

7. *Race* seems to have quite an impact on food consumption. Nonwhites consume more meats and less dairy products relative to their white counterparts. In addition, blacks seem to consume less cereal and bakery products but more fruits and vegetables than whites, while Asian households consume more of both cereal and bakery products and fruits and vegetables than whites.

8. There does not appear to be significant *seasonality* in food consumption, except that consumers eat less fruits and vegetables in the fourth quarter than in the third quarter for all regions, and consumers eat more dairy products in the third quarter than in any other quarter.

In testing the relevance of a certain group of variables in the regression, the partial *F*-tests indicate that demographic variables are statistically significant while prices and advertising variables, as a group, are not. This confirms the results from individual *t*-tests. A partial explanation of these test results may lie in the aggregate nature of the advertising and price series employed in the estimations. An aggregate, deflated advertising expenditure variable for the entire United States was used in the estimations for each food group. Regional price indices, as developed by Kokoski (1986), and regional advertising expenditures would provide more accurate information and their effects on consumer demand in the various regions.

To summarize, total expenditure and demographic variables (based on cross-sectional data) are significant in shaping the consumption patterns of U.S. households. Among demographic variables, family size, race, and family types are most influential. On the other hand, prices and advertising (based on time series data) show very little impact.

## ESTIMATED DEMAND ELASTICITIES

For expenditure elasticities, the results indicate that meats have food expenditure elasticities greater than one while dairy products, cereal and bakery products, fruits and vegetables, and all other foods consumed at home have food expenditure elasticities less than one. One exception is that the expenditure elasticity is 1.037 for all foods consumed at home in Region 4. In terms of magnitudes, the expenditure elasticities for meats are the largest, followed by all foods consumed at home, fruits and vegetables, cereal and bakery products, and finally, dairy products. This means consumers in general are relatively more sensitive to a change in total expenditure in terms of meat consumption than to other food groups. Among regions, the expenditure elasticities obtained for Region 4 are smaller for meats but greater for the remaining food groups compared to the other four regions.

Next, with respect to estimated own-price elasticities for the five commodities groups in five regions, some general inferences can be made. Unlike the $\beta$ coefficients for expenditure elasticities, the price coefficients are mostly statistically insignificant at the 10 percent level. This may, as already indicated, be due to aggregation problems with the price data or a result of multicollinearity problems. In any case, among few significant price coefficients, the estimated own-price elasticities for meats are $-1.123$ and $-1.111$ for Regions 2 and 3, respectively, indicating that consumers in these two regions are responsive to changes in meats price, while consumers in Region 1 are more sensitive to price changes in fruits and vegetables $(-1.169)$.

Positive own-price elasticities are obtained for all other foods consumed at home in all regions, cereal and bakery products in Region 4, dairy products in Regions 3 and 4, and meats in Region 5. In addition, some estimates are unreasonably large, for example, the own-price elasticities for dairy products are $-8.997$ for Region 1 and $-5.322$ for Region 4. What accounts for these unreasonable results besides problems with the data? We tentatively conclude that given the data at hand the LA/AIDS may not be the proper demand system to describe consumer household behavior.

Advertising elasticities obtained for current advertising expenditures and one- and two-period lagged advertising expenditures are short-run advertising elasticities. Long-run elasticities are obtained by summing the short-run elasticities. Consider own advertising elasticities. Three short-run advertising elasticities for meats are positive in all regions except for Region 5. For dairy products, they are negative for Regions 1, 2, and 4 but positive for Region 5. The estimated current advertising elasticity in Region 3 is also positive. For cereal and bakery products, the results are mixed. The estimated current advertising elasticities are negative for Regions 1, 2, and

4 but positive for Regions 4 and 5; the one-period lagged advertising elasticities are positive for Regions 2, 4, and 5 but negative for Regions 1 and 3; the two-period lagged advertising elasticities, however, are positive for all regions. For fruits and vegetables, the short-run advertising elasticities are all positive for Regions 1, 2, and 5.

For Region 1, consumers respond positively to advertising for meats and fruits and vegetables but negatively to advertising for dairy products and all other foods consumed at home. Moreover, delayed advertising effects seem to have some impact on consumption for meats and dairy products. For example, the short-run advertising elasticities for meats are 0.038, 0.046, and 0.068 for current, one-period lagged, and two-period lagged advertising elasticities, respectively. For dairy products, the corresponding figures are −0.060, −0.156, and −0.274, respectively. Consumers in Region 5 respond positively to advertising for all food groups except meats.

The long-run advertising elasticities are positive for meats in all regions, ranging from 0.054 to 0.151, except for Region 5. They are negative for dairy products in all regions ranging from −0.490 to −0.012, except for Region 5. For the remaining groups, the results are more mixed. Consumers in Region 5 respond more positively to advertising while consumers in Region 3 respond more negatively, this is also true in the short run. Once again, these results should be interpreted with caution since the estimated advertising coefficients are in general statistically insignificant. The effects of advertising on expenditure, own-price, and advertising elasticities are presented in Tables 7.1 through 7.10.

## THE EFFECTS OF ADVERTISING ON DEMAND ELASTICITIES

The effects of advertising on expenditure elasticities are negative for all other foods consumed at home and for meats in all regions except for Region 5, indicating that a change in advertising makes consumers less sensitive to changes in total food expenditure, and hence less likely to allocate additional food expenditure to meats and all other foods consumed at home. For dairy products and cereal and bakery products, the effects of advertising on expenditure elasticities are negative in Regions 1, 2, and 4 but positive in Regions 3 and 5. For fruits and vegetables, they are positive in Regions 1, 2, and 5 but negative in Regions 3 and 4. In general, the effects of advertising on expenditure elasticities are negative for most regions.

The effects of advertising on own-price elasticities are positive for meats except for Region 5; for dairy products, they are negative except for Region 3; for cereal and bakery products, they are negative for Regions 1, 2, and 4 but positive for Regions 3 and 5; for fruits and vegetables, they are positive for Regions 1, 2, and 5 but negative for Regions 3 and 4; for all other foods consumed at home, they are positive except for Region 3. For normal goods (own-price elasticities are negative), a positive effect would make own-price elasticities less negative or less elastic, assuming the sign does not change; a negative effect, on the other hand, would make own-price elasticities more negative or more elastic.

For Regions 1 and 2, the effects of advertising on advertising elasticities are positive for meats and fruits and vegetables, but negative for dairy products, cereal and bakery products, and all foods consumed at home. For Region 3, the effects of advertising on advertising elasticities are negative for fruits and vegetables and all other foods consumed at home and positive for the remaining groups. For Region 4, they are positive for meats and all other foods consumed at home and negative for the remaining groups; the opposite results are obtained for Region 5. A positive effect may be an indication of cumulative effect of advertising while a negative effect may be an indication of diminishing effectiveness of advertising. Since estimated coefficients for prices and advertising are mostly insignificant, the results should be interpreted with caution.

## Conclusions

Two sources of data were used to estimate demand for five food groups and in five different regions. The objective of this study was to examine the effects of advertising and demographic variables on consumer demand for food using combined cross-sectional and time series data.

The empirical results indicate that (1) homogeneity and symmetry conditions cannot be rejected at the 5 percent significance level, (2) demographic variables are generally statistically significant in influencing household consumption behavior for food, (3) while total expenditure is usually statistically significant, prices, advertising, and seasonal dummies are generally insignificant in explaining the variations in food consumption, (4) among the demographic variables, family size has significant effects on consumption of dairy products and cereal and bakery products, and race on consumption of meats and dairy products in all five regions, and (5) the effects of advertising on demand elasticities are marginal and vary among food groups and regions.

This paper demonstrates how advertising and demographic variables can be modeled in a demand system using combined time series and cross-sectional data. Tentative conclusions based on this analysis are (1) improved advertising and price information are needed in order to obtained precise measures of the effects of advertising on demand elasticities and (2) the

AIDS (or LA/AIDS) may not be the appropriate parametric demand system to use in explaining household food consumption behavior.

Table 7.1. Region 1. The dynamic linear approximate almost ideal demand system: Calculated own elasticities

| Food groups | Calculated own elasticities[a] | | | | | |
|---|---|---|---|---|---|---|
| | $\eta_{i,t}$ [b] | $\epsilon_{ii,t}$ | $\epsilon_{iAi,t}$ | $\epsilon_{i,Ai,t-1}$ | $\epsilon_{i,Ai,t-2}$ | $\epsilon_{i,Ai,LR}$ |
| Meats | 1.24 | -0.62 | 0.04 | 0.05 | 0.07 | 0.15 |
| Dairy products | 0.77 | -8.99 | -0.06 | -0.16 | -0.27 | -0.49 |
| Cereal and bakery products | 0.81 | -0.14 | -0.09 | -0.0004 | 0.03 | -0.07 |
| Fruits and vegetables | 0.96 | -1.17 | 0.02 | 0.01 | 0.03 | 0.07 |
| All other foods at home | 0.98 | 6.42 | -0.73 | -0.46 | -0.51 | -1.69 |

[a]Elasticities are evaluated at sample means.
[b]The own elasticities are defined as follows:

| | | |
|---|---|---|
| $\eta_{i,t}$ | = | expenditure elasticity, |
| $\epsilon_{ii,t}$ | = | own-price elasticity, and |
| $\epsilon_{iAi,t}$ | = | own-advertising elasticity. |
| $\epsilon_{i,Ai,t-1}$ | = | own-advertising elasticity, lagged one period, |
| $\epsilon_{i,Ai,t-2}$ | = | own-advertising elasticity, lagged two periods, and |
| $\epsilon_{i,Ai,LR}$ | = | long-run advertising elasticity. |

Table 7.2. Region 2. The dynamic linear approximate almost ideal demand system: Calculated own elasticities

| Food groups | Calculated own elasticities[a] | | | | | |
|---|---|---|---|---|---|---|
| | $\eta_{i,t}$ [b] | $\epsilon_{ii,t}$ | $\epsilon_{iAi,t}$ | $\epsilon_{i,Ai,t-1}$ | $\epsilon_{i,Ai,t-2}$ | $\epsilon_{i,Ai,LR}$ |
| Meats | 1.24 | -1.12 | 0.02 | 0.04 | 0.06 | 0.13 |
| Dairy products | 0.75 | -0.65 | -0.08 | -0.15 | -0.09 | -0.31 |
| Cereal and bakery products | 0.82 | -2.05 | -0.04 | -0.02 | 0.07 | -0.05 |
| Fruits and vegetables | 0.97 | -0.96 | 0.02 | 0.003 | -0.02 | 0.004 |
| All other foods at home | 0.98 | 3.95 | -0.14 | -0.24 | -0.97 | -1.35 |

[a]Elasticities are evaluated at sample means.
[b]The own elasticities are defined as follows:

| | | |
|---|---|---|
| $\eta_{i,t}$ | = | expenditure elasticity, |
| $\epsilon_{ii,t}$ | = | own-price elasticity, and |
| $\epsilon_{iAi,t}$ | = | own-advertising elasticity. |
| $\epsilon_{i,Ai,t-1}$ | = | own-advertising elasticity, lagged one period, |
| $\epsilon_{i,Ai,t-2}$ | = | own-advertising elasticity, lagged two periods, and |
| $\epsilon_{i,Ai,LR}$ | = | long-run advertising elasticity. |

**Table 7.3. Region 3. The dynamic linear approximate almost ideal demand system: Calculated own elasticities**

| Food groups | $\eta_{i,t}$ [b] | Calculated own elasticities[a] $\epsilon_{ii,t}$ | $\epsilon_{iAi,t}$ | $\epsilon_{i,Ai,t-1}$ | $\epsilon_{i,Ai,t-2}$ | $\epsilon_{i,Ai,LR}$ |
|---|---|---|---|---|---|---|
| Meats | 1.19 | -1.11 | 0.03 | 0.03 | -0.007 | 0.05 |
| Dairy products | 0.77 | -0.42 | 0.001 | 0.07 | -0.08 | -0.01 |
| Cereal and bakery products | 0.86 | -0.98 | 0.04 | -0.09 | 0.05 | -0.008 |
| Fruits and vegetables | 0.97 | -0.52 | -0.02 | 0.01 | -0.03 | 0.07 |
| All other foods at home | 0.98 | 1.88 | -0.81 | -0.83 | 0.51 | -1.13 |

[a]Elasticities are evaluated at sample means.
[b]The own elasticities are defined as follows:

| | | |
|---|---|---|
| $\eta_{i,t}$ | = | expenditure elasticity, |
| $\epsilon_{ii,t}$ | = | own-price elasticity, and |
| $\epsilon_{iAi,t}$ | = | own-advertising elasticity. |
| $\epsilon_{i,Ai,t-1}$ | = | own-advertising elasticity, lagged one period, |
| $\epsilon_{i,Ai,t-2}$ | = | own-advertising elasticity, lagged two periods, and |
| $\epsilon_{i,Ai,LR}$ | = | long-run advertising elasticity. |

**Table 7.4. Region 4. The dynamic linear approximate almost ideal demand system: Calculated own elasticities**

| Food groups | $\eta_{i,t}$ [b] | Calculated own elasticities[a] $\epsilon_{ii,t}$ | $\epsilon_{iAi,t}$ | $\epsilon_{i,Ai,t-1}$ | $\epsilon_{i,Ai,t-2}$ | $\epsilon_{i,Ai,LR}$ |
|---|---|---|---|---|---|---|
| Meats | 1.15 | -0.24 | 0.01 | 0.05 | 0.03 | 0.09 |
| Dairy products | 0.81 | -5.32 | -0.07 | -0.14 | -0.11 | -0.32 |
| Cereal and bakery products | 0.86 | 1.91 | -0.06 | 0.05 | -0.05 | -0.009 |
| Fruits and vegetables | 0.98 | -0.77 | -0.02 | -0.05 | -0.05 | -0.16 |
| All other foods at home | 1.04 | 1.91 | 0.41 | 0.25 | 0.43 | 1.09 |

[a]Elasticities are evaluated at sample means.
[b]The own elasticities are defined as follows:

| | | |
|---|---|---|
| $\eta_{i,t}$ | = | expenditure elasticity, |
| $\epsilon_{ii,t}$ | = | own-price elasticity, and |
| $\epsilon_{iAi,t}$ | = | own-advertising elasticity. |
| $\epsilon_{i,Ai,t-1}$ | = | own-advertising elasticity, lagged one period, |
| $\epsilon_{i,Ai,t-2}$ | = | own-advertising elasticity, lagged two periods, and |
| $\epsilon_{i,Ai,LR}$ | = | long-run advertising elasticity. |

**Table 7.5. Region 5. The dynamic linear approximate almost ideal demand system: Calculated own elasticities**

| | Calculated own elasticities[a] | | | | | |
|---|---|---|---|---|---|---|
| Food groups | $\eta_{i,t}$ [b] | $\epsilon_{ii,t}$ | $\epsilon_{iAi,t}$ | $\epsilon_{i,Ai,t-1}$ | $\epsilon_{i,Ai,t-2}$ | $\epsilon_{i,Ai,LR}$ |
| Meats | 1.26 | 0.06 | -0.19 | -0.19 | -0.15 | -0.53 |
| Dairy products | 0.79 | 10.25 | 0.24 | 0.19 | 0.82 | 0.51 |
| Cereal and bakery products | 0.84 | -0.15 | 0.91 | 0.59 | 0.46 | 1.95 |
| Fruits and vegetables | 0.91 | -5.01 | 0.55 | 0.11 | 0.32 | 0.97 |
| All other foods at home | 0.97 | 18.20 | -0.69 | 2.38 | 1.24 | 2.93 |

[a]Elasticities are evaluated at sample means.
[b]The own elasticities are defined as follows:

$\eta_{i,t}$ = expenditure elasticity,
$\epsilon_{ii,t}$ = own-price elasticity, and
$\epsilon_{iAi,t}$ = own-advertising elasticity.
$\epsilon_{i,Ai,t-1}$ = own-advertising elasticity, lagged one period,
$\epsilon_{i,Ai,t-2}$ = own-advertising elasticity, lagged two periods, and
$\epsilon_{i,Ai,LR}$ = long-run advertising elasticity.


**Table 7.6. Region 1. The dynamic linear approximate almost ideal demand system: Effects of advertising on elasticities**

| | The effects of advertising on elasticities[a] | | |
|---|---|---|---|
| Food groups | $\partial \eta_{i,t}/\partial A_{i,t}$ [b] | $\partial \epsilon_{ii,t}/\partial A_{i,t}$ [c] | $\partial \epsilon_{iA,t}/\partial A_{i,t}$ [d] |
| Meats | -0.00003 | 0.0003 | 0.00011 |
| Dairy products | -0.00004 | -0.00256 | -0.00018 |
| Cereal and bakery products | -0.00001 | -0.00038 | -0.00007 |
| Fruits and vegetables | 0.000002 | 0.00027 | 0.00004 |
| All other foods at home | -0.000004 | 0.00051 | -0.00028 |

[a]The effects of advertising on elasticities are evaluated at sample means.
[b] $\partial \eta_{i,t}/\partial A_{i,t}$ = current advertising effects on own-expenditure elasticity.
[c] $\partial \epsilon_{ii,t}/\partial A_{i,t}$ = current advertising effects on own-price elasticity.
[d] $\partial \epsilon_{iA,t}/\partial A_{i,t}$ = current advertising effects on own-advertising elasticity.

**Table 7.7. Region 2. The dynamic linear approximate almost ideal demand system: Effects of advertising on elasticities**

| Food groups | The effects of advertising on elasticities[a] | | |
|---|---|---|---|
| | $\partial \eta_{i,t}/\partial A_{i,t}$ [b] | $\partial \epsilon_{ii,t}/\partial A_{i,t}$ [c] | $\partial \epsilon_{iA,t}/\partial A_{i,t}$ [d] |
| Meats | -0.00002 | 0.00022 | 0.00006 |
| Dairy products | -0.00005 | -0.00148 | 0.00023 |
| Cereal and bakery products | -0.000005 | -0.00023 | -0.00003 |
| Fruits and vegetables | -0.000001 | 0.00024 | 0.00004 |
| All other foods at home | -0.0000005 | 0.00004 | -0.00003 |

[a]The effects of advertising on elasticities are evaluated at sample means.
[b] $\partial \eta_{i,t}/\partial A_{i,t}$ = current advertising effects on own-expenditure elasticity.
[c] $\partial \epsilon_{ii,t}/\partial A_{i,t}$ = current advertising effects on own-price elasticity.
[d] $\partial \epsilon_{iA,t}/\partial A_{i,t}$ = current advertising effects on own-advertising elasticity.


**Table 7.8. Region 3. The dynamic linear approximate almost ideal demand system: Effects of advertising on elasticities**

| Food groups | The effects of advertising on elasticities[a] | | |
|---|---|---|---|
| | $\partial \eta_{i,t}/\partial A_{i,t}$ [b] | $\partial \epsilon_{ii,t}/\partial A_{i,t}$ [c] | $\partial \epsilon_{iA,t}/\partial A_{i,t}$ [d] |
| Meats | -0.00002 | 0.00033 | 0.00010 |
| Dairy products | 0.0000007 | 0.00002 | 0.000003 |
| Cereal and bakery products | 0.000004 | 0.00021 | 0.00003 |
| Fruits and vegetables | -0.000001 | -0.00025 | -0.00005 |
| All other foods at home | -0.000004 | -0.00018 | -0.00032 |

[a]The effects of advertising on elasticities are evaluated at sample means.
[b] $\partial \eta_{i,t}/\partial A_{i,t}$ = current advertising effects on own-expenditure elasticity.
[c] $\partial \epsilon_{ii,t}/\partial A_{i,t}$ = current advertising effects on own-price elasticity.
[d] $\partial \epsilon_{iA,t}/\partial A_{i,t}$ = current advertising effects on own-advertising elasticity.

**Table 7.9. Region 4. The dynamic linear approximate almost ideal demand system: Effects of advertising on elasticities**

| Food groups | The effects of advertising on elasticities[a] | | |
|---|---|---|---|
| | $\partial\eta_{i,t}/\partial A_{i,t}$ [b] | $\partial\epsilon_{ii,t}/\partial A_{i,t}$ [c] | $\partial\epsilon_{iA,t}/\partial A_{i,t}$ [d] |
| Meats | -0.000005 | 0.00010 | 0.00004 |
| Dairy products | -0.00004 | -0.00232 | -0.00022 |
| Cereal and bakery products | -0.000006 | -0.00020 | -0.00005 |
| Fruits and vegetables | -0.0000007 | -0.00019 | -0.00004 |
| All other foods at home | -0.000003 | -0.00008 | 0.00005 |

[a]The effects of advertising on elasticities are evaluated at sample means.
[b] $\partial\eta_{i,t}/\partial A_{i,t}$ = current advertising effects on own-expenditure elasticity.
[c] $\partial\epsilon_{ii,t}/\partial A_{i,t}$ = current advertising effects on own-price elasticity.
[d] $\partial\epsilon_{iA,t}/\partial A_{i,t}$ = current advertising effects on own-advertising elasticity.


**Table 7.10. Region 5. The dynamic linear approximate almost ideal demand system: Effects of advertising on elasticities**

| Food groups | The effects of advertising on elasticities[a] | | |
|---|---|---|---|
| | $\partial\eta_{i,t}/\partial A_{i,t}$ [b] | $\partial\epsilon_{ii,t}/\partial A_{i,t}$ [c] | $\partial\epsilon_{iA,t}/\partial A_{i,t}$ [d] |
| Meats | 0.00013 | -0.00110 | -0.00059 |
| Dairy products | 0.00014 | -0.00269 | 0.00050 |
| Cereal and bakery products | 0.00009 | -0.00345 | 0.00005 |
| Fruits and vegetables | 0.00009 | 0.01008 | 0.00044 |
| All other foods at home | -0.000005 | 0.00222 | -0.00024 |

[a]The effects of advertising on elasticities are evaluated at sample means.
[b] $\partial\eta_{i,t}/\partial A_{i,t}$ = current advertising effects on own-expenditure elasticity.
[c] $\partial\epsilon_{ii,t}/\partial A_{i,t}$ = current advertising effects on own-price elasticity.
[d] $\partial\epsilon_{iA,t}/\partial A_{i,t}$ = current advertising effects on own-advertising elasticity.

**Appendix: Estimated coefficient of the dynamic LA/AIDS for Region 2**

| Variable | Meats | | Dairy products | | Cereal and bakery | | Fruits and vegetables | |
|---|---|---|---|---|---|---|---|---|
| | Coef. | S.E. | Coef. | S.E. | Coef. | S.E. | Coef. | S.E. |
| STONES | 6.926[a] | 0.469 | -3.461[a] | 0.271 | -2.498[a] | 0.266 | -0.510 | 0.323 |
| LOPM | 0.108 | 0.162 | -0.810 | 1.009 | 0.570 | 0.959 | -0.465 | 1.164 |
| LOPD | -0.198 | 0.697 | 0.635 | 4.044 | 0.139 | 0.353 | 0.150 | 0.414 |
| LOPCB | 0.331 | 0.494 | -0.804 | 3.084 | -0.143 | 0.292 | 0.481 | 0.400 |
| LOPFV | -0.054 | 0.147 | -0.207 | 0.004 | 1.412 | 0.995 | 0.002 | 0.113 |
| LOPO | -0.767 | 0.769 | 0.288 | 0.370 | -0.111 | 0.399 | -0.749 | 0.534 |
| INCOME | -1.123[a] | 0.261 | 0.187 | 0.150 | 0.185 | 0.148 | 0.476[a] | 0.180 |
| AGE | -0.398[a] | 0.165 | -0.860 | 0.957 | 4.311[a] | 0.938 | 1.063[a] | 0.114 |
| SIZE | -1.335[a] | 0.307 | 0.977[a] | 0.177 | 0.570[a] | 0.174 | -0.207 | 0.211 |
| STAMPS | 1.270[a] | 0.693 | -0.126 | 0.400 | 0.197 | 0.393 | -0.741 | 0.478 |
| S1 | 1.094 | 0.751 | 0.674 | 0.434 | 0.176 | 0.425 | -1.900[a] | 0.517 |
| R2 | -0.423[a] | 0.109 | 1.124[a] | 0.634 | 0.532 | 0.622 | 0.481 | 0.758 |
| R3 | -0.140 | 0.106 | 0.487 | 0.614 | 1.481[a] | 0.602 | -1.521[a] | 0.732 |
| R4 | -0.307 | 1.129 | 1.359[a] | 0.653 | 0.182 | 0.640 | -2.114[a] | 0.778 |
| R5 | 0.569 | 1.673 | 0.149 | 0.967 | -0.390 | 0.948 | -0.134 | 0.115 |
| R6 | 0.936 | 2.609 | 0.401 | 1.509 | -0.260 | 1.479 | -0.233 | 0.179 |
| R7 | -0.320[a] | 0.133 | 2.125[a] | 0.774 | 2.225[a] | 0.759 | 2.568[a] | 0.922 |
| R8 | -2.665[a] | 0.928 | 0.353 | 0.536 | 0.424 | 0.526 | 0.562 | 0.639 |
| I1 | 1.112[a] | 0.082 | -3.927[a] | 0.476 | -1.301[a] | 0.467 | 0.938[a] | 0.568 |
| I2 | 1.057[a] | 0.333 | -0.345[a] | 0.192 | -0.477 | 1.891 | -0.224 | 2.299 |
| I3 | 0.659[a] | 0.360 | -0.241 | 0.208 | 0.417 | 2.045 | 0.450[a] | 0.243 |
| ADPI-0 | 0.309 | 0.389 | -0.254 | 0.204 | -0.345 | 0.599 | 0.589 | 1.104 |
| ADPI-1 | 0.593 | 0.475 | -0.485 | 0.332 | 0.172 | 0.561 | 0.110 | 0.961 |
| ADPI-2 | 0.889[a] | 0.477 | -0.311 | 0.308 | 0.618 | 0.548 | -0.618 | 1.206 |
| D2 | 0.227[a] | 0.113 | -0.783 | 0.619 | 0.282 | 0.679 | -0.287 | 0.785 |
| D4 | 1.662[a] | 0.968 | -0.937 | 0.613 | 0.420 | 0.624 | -1.841[a] | 0.697 |
| D1 | 2.035[a] | 0.995 | -1.354[a] | 0.632 | 0.834 | 0.631 | -0.613 | 0.846 |

Variable definition:

STONES = total food at home expenditure in logarithm.

LOPM-LOPO = prices in logarithm for meats, dairy products, cereal and bakery products, fruits and vegetables, and all others, respectively.

INCOME = household income.

AGE = age of the household head.

SIZE = family size.

STAMPS = value of food stamps.

S1 = dummy variable for sex, zero for female and 1 for male.

R2 – R8 = dummy variables for family types, relative to husband/wife households.

I1 – I3 = dummy variables for races, relative to whites.

D1 – D4 = dummy variables for seasonality, relative to summer quarter.

ADPI 0-2 = current, one-period and two-period lags own-advertising expenditures, respectively.

[a]Indicates that the estimated coefficients are at least 1.645 times greater than the corresponding standard errors.

# 8   A Preliminary Look at Advertising Beef, Pork, Chicken, Turkey, Eggs, Milk, Butter, Cheese, and Margarine in Canada

ELLEN W. GODDARD and BRIAN COZZARIN

Generic advertising has become a major part of the marketing activities of most commodity groups in Canada during the last two decades. Marketing activities for a number of commodities are directed by national supply management marketing boards (feather and dairy industries). At the same time demand for most food commodities has been affected by concerns about health and changes in style of living. Advertising has been seen by commodity groups as a way of fighting back against the negative attitudes of consumers toward their products.

Generic advertising expenditure in Canada has reached such a significant level that most commodity groups are now facing some pressure from their members to evaluate the effectiveness of their investment. In evaluating advertising effectiveness there are two complementary tools that can be used. The first is market research: consumer awareness of and attitudes toward the advertisement are monitored. This type of evaluation is critical in providing advertisers with timely information about the effects of their promotions. The second approach uses aggregate time-series data to quantify the link between advertising and sales in a framework that includes other economic factors affecting the purchase decision. Analyzing time-series data is necessary to calculate return on investment.

The research reported in this study concerns the aggregate evaluation of national advertising campaigns for beef, pork, chicken, turkey, eggs, butter, cheese, margarine, and fluid milk in Canada over the period 1967 to 1986. It should be noted that not all commodity boards have been conducting national advertising campaigns over the entire sample period. In fact most started in the late 1970s, with national beef and pork promotion programs beginning in the early 1980s. Fluid milk advertising is conducted by provincial marketing boards rather than by a national agency. For this study, advertising by the Ontario milk marketing board is used as a proxy for national milk advertising. Ontario has had the largest and longest running advertising campaign for fluid milk. The impact of fluid milk advertising will likely be overestimated slightly because of the problem with the data.

A conceptual framework to empirically evaluate the impact of national advertising campaigns is described and the estimated results are presented in this chapter.

## Conceptual Framework

It has become accepted practice for economists to analyze the impact of advertising by including advertising expenditure levels as explanatory variables in demand functions. The rationale for such a specification is that advertising operates as a taste change parameter in underlying utility functions. The debate about whether it is appropriate or not to include advertising in utility functions continues to rage and is not addressed here. Instead, different methods for including advertising in indirect utility functions are developed.

Following the development of Jorgenson and Lau (1975), who examined different ways of incorporating time into utility functions, two possible methods for incorporating advertising are as follows:

Indirect utility function with preferences shifted by advertising:

$$V = f\left(\frac{P_i}{M}, A_i\right) \qquad i = 1, \ldots, n \text{ number of goods,}$$

where $V$ = maximum level of utility

$P_i$ = prices

$M$ = total expenditure

$A_i$ = advertising expenditure

Indirect utility function with advertising operating as an augmenting factor:

$$V = f\left(\frac{A_i P_i}{M}\right) \qquad i = 1, \ldots, n \text{ goods}$$

The difference in the approaches is the role that advertising plays in affecting consumer preferences. In simple terms, the first method results in advertising operating as a demand curve shifter, while in the second method advertising operates to change the slope of the demand equations.

In empiricizing the model above it is necessary to specify a functional form for the indirect utility function. The selection of the functional form to be used in any particular analysis is problematic because the global properties of the different "flexible functional forms" are not known. Popular models are the translog model developed by Christensen, Jorgenson, and Lau (1975) and the almost ideal demand system (AIDS) model developed by Deaton and Muellbauer (1980).

A translog indirect utility function without advertising variables results in budget share equations of the following form:

$$W_i = \frac{a_i + \Sigma_j \, b_{ij} \, \ln P_j}{\Sigma_j \, a_j + \Sigma_j \, \Sigma_i \, b_{ij} \, \ln P_j} \tag{8.1}$$

where $P_j^* = P_j/Y$.

With advertising incorporated as an independent shifter then the underlying indirect utility function is as follows:

$$
\begin{aligned}
\ln V = a_0 &+ \Sigma_i^n \, a_i \, \ln P_i^* + 1/2 \, \Sigma_i \, \Sigma_j \, b_{ij} \, \ln P_i^* \, \ln P_j^* \\
&+ \Sigma_{i=1}^n \, e_i \, \ln A_i + 1/2 \, \Sigma_i \, \Sigma_j \, d_{ij} \, \ln A_i \, \ln A_j \\
&+ \Sigma_i \, \Sigma_j \, f_{ij} \, \ln P_i \, \ln A_i \qquad i, j = 1, \ldots, n
\end{aligned}
\tag{8.2}
$$

where $A_i$ = advertising expenditure on good $i$.

Budget share equations derived from the above indirect utility function are

$$W_i = \frac{a_i + \Sigma_j \, b_{ij} \, \ln P_j^* + \Sigma_j \, f_{ij} \, \ln A_j}{\Sigma_j \, a_i + \Sigma_j \, \Sigma_i \, b_{ij} \, \ln P_j^* + \Sigma_j \, \Sigma_i \, f_{ij} \, \ln A_j} \qquad i, j = 1, \ldots, n \tag{8.3}$$

If advertising is incorporated as an augmenting parameter then the indirect utility function is

$$\ln V = a_0 + \Sigma_i \, a_i \, (\ln P_i^* + \ln A_i) + 1/2 \, \Sigma_i \, \Sigma_j \, b_{ij} \, (\ln P_i^* + \ln A_i) \cdot$$
$$(\ln P_j^* + \ln A_j) \qquad i, j = 1, \dots, n \qquad (8.4)$$

Budget share equations can then be expressed as

$$W_i = \frac{a_i + \Sigma_j \, b_{ij} \, (\ln P_j^* + \ln A_i)}{\Sigma_j \, a_i + \Sigma_j \, \Sigma_i \, b_{ij} \, (\ln P_j^* + \ln A_i)} \qquad i, j = 1, \dots, n \qquad (8.5)$$

or as

$$W_i = \frac{a_i + \Sigma_j \, b_{ij} \, (\ln P_j + f_{ij} \, \ln A_i)}{\Sigma_j \, a_i + \Sigma_j \, \Sigma_i \, b_{ij} \, (\ln P_j^* + f_{ij} \, \ln A_i)} \qquad i, j = 1, \dots, n \qquad (8.6)$$

if we allow a less than one-to-one relationship between price and advertising. An alternate specification to the above would be to only allow variability by advertising program (e.g., $f_j \ln A_j$ instead of $f_{ij} \ln A_j$) rather than by advertising program and good.

For an AIDS model, without including advertising the basic budget share equations are expressed as

$$W_i = a_i + \Sigma \gamma_{ij} \ln p_j + b_i \ln (X/P) \qquad (8.7)$$

where $W_i = \dfrac{p_i X_i}{\Sigma_i p_i X_i}$

$p_j$ = price of individual goods

$X$ = total expenditures

$P$ = price index that can be approximated by the Stone's index,
$\ln P^* = \Sigma_i \, W_i \ln p_i$

The above budget share equations are derived from a cost function:

$$\ln c(u,p) = a(p) + ub(p) \tag{8.8}$$

where

$$a(p) = a_0 + \Sigma_i \, a_i \, \ln p_i + 1/2 \, \Sigma_i \, \Sigma_j \, \gamma_{ij} \, \ln p_i \, \ln p_j \tag{8.9}$$

and

$$b(p) = b_0 \, \pi \, p_i^{b_i} \tag{8.10}$$

Incorporating advertising into an AIDS model is undertaken by modifying the $a(p)$ function. If advertising is incorporated as an independent shifter, then

$$
\begin{aligned}
a(p) = a_0 &+ \Sigma_i \, a_i \, \ln p_i + 1/2 \, \Sigma_i \, \Sigma_j \, \gamma_{ij} \, \ln p_i \, \ln p_j \\
&+ \Sigma_i \, e_i \, \ln A_i + 1/2 \, \Sigma_i \, \Sigma_j \, d_{ij} \, \ln A_i \, \ln A_j \\
&+ \Sigma_i \, \Sigma_j \, f_{ij} \, \ln p_i \, \ln A_j
\end{aligned}
\tag{8.11}
$$

and budget share equations are derived as

$$W_i = a_i + \Sigma_j \, \gamma_{ij} \, \ln p_j + \Sigma f_{ij} \, \ln A_j + b_i \, \ln (X/P) \tag{8.12}$$

If advertising is incorporated as an augmenting factor, then

$$
\begin{aligned}
a(p) = a_0 &+ \Sigma_i \, a_i \, (\ln p_i + \ln A_i) + 1/2 \, \Sigma_i \, \Sigma_j \, \gamma_{ij} \, \cdot \\
&(\ln p_i + \ln A_i) \, (\ln p_i + \ln A_j)
\end{aligned}
\tag{8.13}
$$

and budget share equations are derived as

$$W_i = a_i + \Sigma_j \, \gamma_{ij} \, (\ln p_i + \ln A_j) + b_i \, \ln (X/P) \tag{8.14}$$

Neither model is nested in the other, but it is possible to estimate each and compare the explanatory power. It should be noted that in both the translog and AIDS models when advertising is used as an augmenting parameter (with coefficient on advertising equal to one), cross-price and cross-advertising elasticities will be the same.

The models are also tested in a dynamic form following the method of Manser (1976) for the translog model. From Henning (1986) it has been shown that the AIDS model can not be "dynamized" in the same way as a translog model. For an AIDS model to be consistent, dynamic elements can be included by either incorporating all lagged quantities (or expenditure shares) into each equation or incorporating lagged aggregate quantity or total expenditure into each equation.

## Estimated Model

The above description refers to three models: one without advertising; one with advertising as a shifter; and one with advertising as an augmenting factor for each specification. All three systems of expenditure share equations will be estimated and the results examined. Each system of expenditure share equations must, by definition, sum to one. Thus, only $n - 1$ of the equations are independent and can be estimated. The demand properties (commonly known as adding up, homogeneity, and Slutsky symmetry) can be shown to be satisfied for the AIDS model if the following conditions are met. Budget shares will sum to one if $\Sigma_i \, a_i = 1$, $\Sigma_i \, \gamma_{ij} = 0$, and $\Sigma_i \, b_i = 0$ (and $\Sigma_i \, f_{ij} = 0$ for the relevant model). The homogeneity condition holds if $\Sigma_i \, \gamma_{ij} = 0$. The symmetry restriction holds if $\gamma_{ij} = \gamma_{ji}$. All of the above restrictions are imposed on the estimated models. The translog model will satisfy demand properties if $b_{ij} = b_{ji}$; homogeneity is satisfied if $\Sigma_i \, a_i = -1$.

The expenditure share systems of equations are estimated using an iterative seemingly unrelated regression (SUR) estimation procedure to allow for dependence among error terms and cross-equation coefficient constraints. The systems of expenditure share equations will each be assumed to have additive disturbances. The vector of disturbances, in each case, is assumed to be identically and independently joint-normally distributed with mean vector zero and nonsingular covariance matrices.

## Data

Annual data from 1967 to 1986 were used for the study. Data on disappearance of commodities were obtained from Statistics Canada catalogs and Agriculture Canada data banks. Prices, price indices, and population data were also obtained from Statistics Canada publications. Data on advertising expenditure levels were reported by individual commodity groups for advertising at a national level. For the purposes of this study, most brand and provincial level advertising was excluded. Explanatory variables were all scaled to equal 1.0 in 1977, the midpoint of the sample, to facilitate convergence of the nonlinear demand systems. Parameter estimates are not invariant to such a rescaling. However, it has been shown by Christensen and Manser (1977) that price, expenditure, and substitution elasticities are all invariant to such a multiplicative scaling of the data in the case of translog models. Similar properties hold for the AIDS model.

## Results

The results of the various different estimations in terms of values of the log of the likelihood function are presented in Table 8.1. In both the AIDS and the translog models the restriction of excluding advertising as a shift parameter could not be accepted. The alternate method of including advertising as an augmenting parameter reduced the explanatory power of the model considerably when there was an implicit one-to-one relationship between advertising and price (see Tables 8.1 and 8.2). The model was also estimated with augmenting parameters with the coefficients on advertising constrained to a variety of different values to examine the explanatory power of the augmenting model (e.g., equation [8.6]). From the data presented in Table 8.1 it is clear that with both the translog and AIDS models, explanatory power increases as we move the augmenting coefficient to levels much smaller than one. From the data in Table 8.2, the AIDS model gives evidence of autocorrelation problems when the augmenting parameter is constrained to a small number. The translog model was also estimated in a dynamic form to test if dynamic responses were significant. The AIDS model was not estimated in a dynamic form because of degrees of freedom problems.

**Table 8.1 Model specification**

| Model | Log of likelihood | | Number of restrictions | Calculated test statistic |
|---|---|---|---|---|
| AIDS | | | | |
| Base | 853.885 | | | |
| | | | | |
| With advertising | | | | |
| Model 1 | 1053.13 | | 45 | 398.49 |
| Model 2 | 748.518 | (all $f_{ij} = 1$) | | |
| Model 2(a) | 856.003 | (all $f_{ij} = .001$) | | |
| | | | | |
| Translog | | | | |
| Base | 1081.26 | | | |
| | | | | |
| With advertising | | | | |
| Model 1 | 1143.75 | | 45 | 124.98 |
| Model 2 | 764.938 | (all $f_{ij} = 1$) | | |
| Model 2(a) | 762.413 | ($f_{ij} = .5$) | | |
| Model 2(b) | 763.741 | ($f_{ij} = 2$) | | |
| Model 2(c) | 884.343 | ($f_{ij} = .01$) | | |
| Model 2(d) | 1050.71 | ($f_{ij} = .001$) | | |
| Model 3 (dynamic) | 1288.53 | ($f_j$ estimated) | | |

**Table 8.2. Fit of estimated demand system models with advertising**

| AIDS | Model 1 | | Model 2 | | Model 2(a) | |
|---|---|---|---|---|---|---|
| | $R^2$ | D.W. statistic | $R^2$ | D.W. statistic | $R^2$ | D.W. statistic |
| Beef | .98 | 1.97 | .62 | 1.24 | .92 | 1.22 |
| Pork | .99 | 3.02 | .89 | 2.69 | .99 | 1.05 |
| Chicken | .98 | 2.75 | .96 | 2.22 | .94 | 1.29 |
| Turkey | .94 | 2.51 | .62 | 2.14 | .81 | 1.62 |
| Eggs | .99 | 1.45 | .91 | 2.01 | .98 | 1.62 |
| Butter | .99 | 1.94 | .91 | 1.22 | .96 | .73 |
| Fluid milk | .99 | 2.53 | .95 | 1.40 | .98 | .99 |
| Cheese | .99 | 2.47 | .93 | 1.11 | .99 | 2.16 |

| TRANSLOG | Model 1 | | Model 2 | | Model 2(a) | |
|---|---|---|---|---|---|---|
| | $R^2$ | D.W. statistic | $R^2$ | D.W. statistic | $R^2$ | D.W. statistic |
| Beef | .99 | 2.66 | .48 | 1.17 | .99 | 2.47 |
| Pork | .98 | 2.53 | .72 | 1.39 | .99 | 1.99 |
| Chicken | .98 | 2.27 | .97 | 2.08 | .96 | 1.83 |
| Turkey | .95 | 2.92 | .64 | 2.13 | .86 | 1.85 |
| Eggs | .99 | 2.20 | .88 | 1.73 | .99 | 2.42 |
| Butter | .99 | 2.85 | .90 | 1.59 | .99 | 2.32 |
| Fluid milk | .99 | 2.34 | .91 | 1.34 | .98 | 1.64 |
| Cheese | .99 | 2.46 | .97 | 1.57 | .99 | 1.69 |

To further examine the results, estimated price and expenditure elasticities from the various models are reported in Tables 8.3 and 8.4. Incorporating advertising as a demand shifter into an AIDS and a translog model produces results that are at odds with each other and with economic theory. For example, in each case certain own-price elasticities exhibit the wrong sign. From the elasticities reported for AIDS and translog model 2 (augmenting), it is clear that constraining the response to price and advertising to be the same imposes enormous restrictions on the model. The fit is poor and all the own-price and expenditure elasticities are approximately one, with the cross-price elasticities all extremely small (in fact, unrealistically small given other estimates of cross-price elasticities reported in the literature). A completely different set of demand elasticities results from the estimates of the AIDS model with the augmenting parameter constrained to .001. While more of the own-price relationships exhibit theoretically correct signs, more of the expenditure elasticities are negative, a fact that is somewhat surprising given *a priori* expectations. Similar variability is evidenced in the estimated substitution and advertising elasticities reported in Tables 8.5, 8.6, 8.7, and 8.8.

Table 8.3. Price and expenditure elasticities for translog model evaluated at 1977 data points

| | Beef | Pork | Chicken | Turkey | Eggs | Butter | Fluid milk | Cheese | Margarine | Expenditure |
|---|---|---|---|---|---|---|---|---|---|---|
| **Model 1** | | | | | | | | | | |
| Beef | -1.21 | -.13 | -.19 | -.07 | -.14 | -.12 | -.12 | -.16 | -.06 | 2.19 |
| Pork | .49 | .25 | -.03 | -.43 | .52 | -.24 | .04 | .17 | .16 | -.94 |
| Chicken | -.25 | -.12 | -.19 | .20 | -.09 | .22 | -.20 | -.17 | -.12 | .71 |
| Turkey | -1.29 | -.78 | .21 | .56 | -.88 | -.53 | .41 | -.78 | -.29 | 3.37 |
| Eggs | 1.14 | .53 | .17 | -.36 | .56 | .12 | -.24 | .59 | .16 | -2.67 |
| Butter | .59 | -.22 | .68 | -.27 | .09 | 1.80 | -1.09 | -.15 | .26 | -1.60 |
| Fluid milk | .34 | -.03 | -.16 | .35 | -.68 | -.33 | .64 | -.09 | -.07 | .03 |
| Cheese | .10 | .003 | -.13 | -.23 | -.19 | -.11 | .13 | -.14 | -.04 | .52 |
| Margarine | .32 | .18 | -.22 | -.17 | .08 | .12 | -.14 | -.06 | -.16 | .06 |
| **Model 2** | | | | | | | | | | |
| Beef | -1.01 | .0008 | .0009 | .0004 | .001 | .001 | -.002 | .003 | -.001 | 1.01 |
| Pork | .006 | -.99 | .010 | .005 | -.002 | -.007 | -.02 | -.01 | -.003 | 1.02 |
| Chicken | .001 | .006 | -1.00 | -.008 | .002 | -.0005 | -.003 | -.007 | -.007 | 1.01 |
| Turkey | .006 | .008 | -.02 | -.96 | -.006 | -.027 | .005 | -.011 | .003 | 1.01 |
| Eggs | .009 | -.002 | .004 | -.004 | -1.00 | .003 | -.007 | -.004 | -.010 | 1.01 |
| Butter | .037 | -.005 | .005 | -.022 | .007 | -.96 | .004 | .002 | -.016 | .95 |
| Fluid milk | .012 | -.008 | .002 | .005 | -.002 | .003 | -.97 | .003 | .010 | .95 |
| Cheese | .017 | -.004 | -.006 | -.004 | -.001 | -.002 | -.002 | -1.00 | .005 | 1.00 |
| Margarine | .0006 | -.003 | -.018 | .004 | -.012 | .020 | .018 | .016 | -.97 | .99 |
| **Model 3** | | | | | | | | | | |
| Beef | -1.08 | -.07 | -.11 | -.04 | -.06 | -.04 | -.10 | -.12 | -.05 | 1.88 |
| Pork | -.04 | -.10 | -.08 | -.07 | .10 | -.04 | -.01 | -.10 | .0000 | .31 |
| Chicken | .04 | -.04 | -.32 | .17 | -.17 | -.04 | .05 | .01 | .07 | .19 |
| Turkey | .007 | -.16 | .36 | -.20 | -.37 | -.45 | .07 | .03 | .08 | .64 |
| Eggs | .59 | .25 | -.19 | -.20 | .16 | .05 | .19 | .01 | .005 | -.87 |
| Butter | .39 | -.03 | -.04 | -.38 | .03 | -1.07 | .53 | .84 | -.0002 | -.27 |
| Fluid milk | -.16 | -.02 | .01 | .03 | .25 | .04 | -.59 | -.28 | .02 | .70 |
| Cheese | .08 | -.07 | .002 | .026 | .33 | -.18 | -.06 | -.36 | -.05 | .29 |
| Margarine | -.48 | -.03 | .09 | .09 | -.06 | .02 | -.23 | -.10 | -.30 | 1.01 |

Table 8.4. Price and expenditure elasticities for AIDS model evaluated at 1977 data points

| | Beef | Pork | Chicken | Turkey | Eggs | Butter | Fluid milk | Cheese | Margarine | Expenditure |
|---|---|---|---|---|---|---|---|---|---|---|
| **Model 1** | | | | | | | | | | |
| Beef | -1.05 | -.09 | -.17 | -.07 | -.09 | -.03 | -.19 | -.22 | -.04 | 1.94 |
| Pork | .11 | .11 | -.16 | -.17 | -.01 | .06 | -.36 | .08 | .09 | .24 |
| Chicken | -.15 | -.12 | -.22 | .34 | -.22 | -.19 | .05 | .14 | -.14 | .51 |
| Turkey | -.37 | -.30 | .72 | -.35 | -.27 | .18 | -.41 | -.25 | -.01 | 1.05 |
| Eggs | .15 | .003 | -.31 | -.15 | .17 | -.45 | .40 | .17 | -.06 | .08 |
| Butter | .42 | .08 | -.45 | .22 | -.70 | -1.03 | 1.11 | -.14 | -.02 | .39 |
| Fluid milk | -.19 | -.26 | .10 | -.17 | .29 | .63 | -.47 | .04 | -.06 | .09 |
| Cheese | .37 | .11 | .25 | -.02 | .15 | -.004 | .11 | -.15 | .01 | -.82 |
| Margarine | -.17 | .10 | -.45 | -.02 | -.17 | -.07 | -.24 | -.20 | -.08 | 1.29 |
| **Model 2** | | | | | | | | | | |
| Beef | -1.01 | .002 | -.002 | .0009 | .002 | .004 | .001 | .0002 | .001 | 1.8 |
| Pork | -.0009 | -.99 | -.010 | .0008 | -.001 | -.003 | -.011 | -.015 | -.004 | 1.03 |
| Chicken | .002 | -.003 | -.95 | .007 | .004 | -.013 | -.021 | .004 | -.009 | .98 |
| Turkey | .0003 | .003 | .014 | -.95 | .0008 | -.043 | -.022 | -.007 | .001 | 1.00 |
| Eggs | .0004 | -.001 | .002 | -.0006 | -.99 | -.005 | -.011 | -.013 | -.007 | 1.03 |
| Butter | .003 | -.003 | -.032 | -.038 | -.005 | -.97 | -.002 | .005 | -.008 | 1.02 |
| Fluid milk | .009 | -.005 | -.028 | -.011 | -.006 | .00009 | -.97 | .003 | .006 | .99 |
| Cheese | .026 | -.003 | .007 | -.0004 | -.002 | .006 | .006 | -.99 | .009 | .95 |
| Margarine | .008 | -.005 | -.027 | .061 | -.009 | -.009 | .014 | .020 | -.99 | 1.00 |
| **Model 2(a)** | | | | | | | | | | |
| Beef | -1.13 | -.15 | -.24 | -.10 | -.14 | -.11 | -.15 | -.30 | -.10 | 2.40 |
| Pork | -.03 | -.02 | -.03 | -.09 | .09 | .01 | .03 | -.10 | .04 | .09 |
| Chicken | .35 | .04 | -.26 | .19 | -.08 | .11 | -.02 | .47 | -.01 | -.79 |
| Turkey | -.10 | -.14 | .34 | -.06 | -.18 | -.16 | -.11 | .06 | .07 | .29 |
| Eggs | .37 | .15 | -.14 | -.08 | .09 | -.05 | .25 | .11 | .05 | -.75 |
| Butter | .15 | .04 | .18 | -.11 | -.10 | -.31 | -.03 | .30 | .17 | -.29 |
| Fluid milk | -.19 | -.03 | -.19 | -.08 | .08 | -.08 | -.13 | -.36 | .004 | .99 |
| Cheese | .22 | -.01 | .40 | .06 | .06 | .15 | -.13 | -.09 | .04 | -.70 |
| Margarine | -.17 | .06 | -.11 | .09 | .03 | .20 | .08 | .03 | -.29 | .08 |

Table 8.5. Substitution elasticities for translog model evaluated at 1977 data points

| | Beef | Pork | Chicken | Turkey | Eggs | Butter | Fluid milk | Cheese | Margarine |
|---|---|---|---|---|---|---|---|---|---|
| **Model 1** | | | | | | | | | |
| Beef | -.41 | .11 | .17 | .59 | -.21 | -.34 | .75 | .75 | .52 |
| Pork | | 3.26 | -1.28 | -9.48 | 6.06 | -5.31 | -.39 | .58 | 3.09 |
| Chicken | | | -1.26 | 5.54 | -.89 | 5.56 | -1.65 | -.82 | -2.67 |
| Turkey | | | | 16.89 | -11.01 | -7.20 | 8.37 | -3.80 | -4.07 |
| Eggs | | | | | 6.69 | -.03 | -5.54 | 2.71 | 1.45 |
| Butter | | | | | | 37.40 | -14.72 | -3.00 | 2.61 |
| Fluid milk | | | | | | | 5.00 | -.81 | -1.67 |
| Cheese | | | | | | | | -.72 | -.52 |
| Margarine | | | | | | | | | -4.05 |
| **Model 3** | | | | | | | | | |
| Beef | -.45 | .23 | .39 | .65 | .38 | .57 | .35 | .47 | -.01 |
| Pork | | -1.40 | -.56 | -1.99 | 3.30 | -.72 | .30 | -.82 | .48 |
| Chicken | | | -3.10 | 4.32 | -2.78 | -.70 | .81 | .31 | 1.98 |
| Turkey | | | | -4.25 | -5.61 | -9.37 | 1.50 | .92 | 2.90 |
| Eggs | | | | | 1.83 | .29 | 1.41 | -.78 | -.75 |
| Butter | | | | | | -23.71 | 6.13 | 7.43 | -.27 |
| Fluid milk | | | | | | | -6.35 | -1.91 | 1.20 |
| Cheese | | | | | | | | -3.04 | -1.07 |
| Margarine | | | | | | | | | -7.05 |

Table 8.6. Substitution elasticities for AIDS model evaluated at 1977 data points

| | Beef | Pork | Chicken | Turkey | Eggs | Butter | Fluid milk | Cheese | Margarine |
|---|---|---|---|---|---|---|---|---|---|
| **Model 1** | | | | | | | | | |
| Beef | -.31 | .47 | .19 | .26 | .40 | 1.30 | -.32 | -.03 | .92 |
| Pork | | 2.02 | -1.43 | -3.80 | .13 | 1.63 | -4.13 | 1.01 | 2.86 |
| Chicken | | | -1.79 | 8.55 | -3.17 | -3.69 | 1.16 | 1.78 | -3.34 |
| Turkey | | | | -7.18 | -3.43 | 4.90 | -3.97 | -1.18 | .86 |
| Eggs | | | | | 2.89 | -9.73 | 4.91 | 1.66 | -1.50 |
| Butter | | | | | | -21.95 | 13.83 | -.92 | -.13 |
| Fluid milk | | | | | | | -5.61 | .50 | -1.63 |
| Cheese | | | | | | | | -2.22 | -.54 |
| Margarine | | | | | | | | | -.86 |
| **Model 2(a)** | | | | | | | | | |
| Beef | -.04 | .03 | -.03 | .05 | .05 | .03 | .58 | -.22 | -.30 |
| Pork | | -.28 | -.20 | -1.99 | 1.70 | .30 | .49 | -.81 | 1.13 |
| Chicken | | | -3.40 | 3.62 | -2.14 | 1.61 | -1.01 | 3.39 | -1.00 |
| Turkey | | | | -1.15 | -2.79 | -3.04 | -1.05 | .84 | 2.17 |
| Eggs | | | | | .85 | -1.86 | 2.33 | .24 | .58 |
| Butter | | | | | | -6.87 | -.64 | 2.41 | 4.25 |
| Fluid milk | | | | | | | -.58 | -2.28 | 1.10 |
| Cheese | | | | | | | | -1.47 | .30 |
| Margarine | | | | | | | | | -7.78 |

**Table 8.7. Advertising elasticities for translog model evaluated at 1986 data points**

| | Beef | Pork | Chicken | Turkey | Eggs | Butter | Fluid milk | Cheese | Margarine |
|---|---|---|---|---|---|---|---|---|---|
| **Model 1** | | | | | | | | | |
| Beef | -.0008 | -.003 | -.002 | .004 | -.006 | -.002 | .017 | .001 | .004 |
| Pork | -.008 | .011 | .004 | -.011 | .012 | .014 | .014 | .0004 | .008 |
| Chicken | .007 | .003 | .014 | .030 | -.008 | -.015 | .028 | -.0002 | -.010 |
| Turkey | .003 | -.023 | .057 | .006 | -.014 | -.008 | -.083 | .008 | -.030 |
| Eggs | -.0004 | .023 | -.008 | -.003 | .025 | .013 | .075 | .011 | .017 |
| Butter | .003 | .023 | -.035 | -.002 | .010 | .004 | .080 | -.019 | .004 |
| Fluid milk | .011 | -.004 | .019 | -.072 | .040 | .045 | -.316 | .011 | -.013 |
| Cheese | -.00007 | -.002 | -.004 | .006 | -.003 | -.008 | .019 | -.008 | .005 |
| Margarine | .005 | .007 | -.043 | -.040 | .013 | -.0009 | -.011 | .009 | -.026 |
| **Model 3** | | | | | | | | | |
| Beef | -.001 | -.002 | -.004 | -.002 | -.005 | -.008 | -.009 | .001 | -.0007 |
| Pork | -.001 | -.0002 | -.003 | -.002 | -.005 | -.009 | .031 | .0007 | -.002 |
| Chicken | -.0007 | -.002 | .007 | -.005 | -.006 | -.009 | .026 | -.00007 | -.003 |
| Turkey | -.0008 | -.003 | .005 | -.016 | -.006 | -.007 | .045 | -.001 | -.004 |
| Eggs | .004 | -.002 | -.005 | .0007 | -.002 | -.009 | .112 | -.002 | -.003 |
| Butter | .002 | -.002 | -.002 | .004 | -.005 | -.009 | .196 | -.014 | -.002 |
| Fluid milk | -.001 | -.002 | .0005 | -.005 | -.005 | -.011 | .22 | .004 | -.003 |
| Cheese | -.0007 | -.002 | -.003 | -.003 | -.005 | -.009 | -.022 | -.007 | -.001 |
| Margarine | -.003 | -.002 | .0008 | -.005 | -.006 | -.009 | .037 | .002 | -.018 |

**Table 8.8. Advertising elasticities for AIDS model evaluated at 1986 data points**

| | Beef | Pork | Chicken | Turkey | Eggs | Butter | Fluid milk | Cheese | Margarine |
|---|---|---|---|---|---|---|---|---|---|
| Model 1 | | | | | | | | | |
| Beef | -.003 | -.0001 | .0007 | .00002 | .0008 | .002 | -.002 | .001 | .001 |
| Pork | -.001 | -.003 | .01 | -.01 | .004 | -.008 | 0 | 0 | .02 |
| Chicken | .003 | .004 | .003 | .007 | -.0005 | .0004 | -.014 | .002 | -.012 |
| Turkey | .0002 | -.012 | .023 | .060 | -.012 | -.057 | .107 | .007 | -.117 |
| Eggs | .009 | .006 | -.002 | -.011 | -.004 | .009 | -.039 | .011 | .021 |
| Butter | .023 | -.011 | .001 | -.059 | .009 | .023 | -.068 | -.007 | .088 |
| Fluid milk | -.018 | -.015 | -.035 | .083 | -.031 | -.050 | .177 | -.013 | -.098 |
| Cheese | .003 | .00002 | .002 | .002 | .003 | -.002 | -.005 | -.002 | -.0009 |
| Margarine | .011 | .036 | -.048 | -.152 | .029 | .109 | -.165 | -.004 | .183 |
| Model 2(a) | | | | | | | | | |
| Beef | -.0001 | -.0001 | -.0002 | -.0001 | -.0001 | -.0001 | -.0001 | -.0003 | -.0001 |
| Pork | -.00003 | .0011 | 0 | -.0001 | .0001 | 0 | .0001 | -.00008 | .00004 |
| Chicken | .0003 | .00001 | .0006 | .0001 | -.0001 | .0001 | -.0001 | .0004 | -.00001 |
| Turkey | -.0001 | -.0001 | .0004 | .0010 | -.0002 | -.0002 | -.0001 | .00008 | .00007 |
| Eggs | .0005 | .0002 | -.0001 | -.0001 | .0015 | -.0001 | .0003 | .0002 | .0001 |
| Butter | .0002 | .00003 | .0003 | -.0001 | -.0001 | .0008 | -.0001 | .0004 | .0002 |
| Fluid milk | -.0003 | -.00004 | -.0003 | -.0001 | .0001 | -.0001 | .0012 | .0005 | .000005 |
| Cheese | .0002 | -.00002 | .0004 | .00005 | .00002 | .0001 | -.0001 | -.0002 | .00003 |
| Margarine | -.0002 | .00006 | -.00009 | .00009 | .00001 | .0002 | .00007 | .00005 | .0008 |

The results of the dynamic translog specification are not a significant improvement over other models specified. The own-price elasticity of eggs is consistently of a conceptually implausible sign. Many of the own-advertising elasticities are negative, also a counter-intuitive result.

The selection of a set of goods to examine cross-price and advertising effects is essentially arbitrary. The underlying assumption is that there is weak separability between goods within the group and any goods outside the group. In the research reported here the hypothesis is that beef, pork, chicken, turkey, eggs, butter, fluid milk, cheese, and margarine are weakly separable from all other goods consumed but not from each other. In fact there may be an underlying rationale for the hypothesis that some of these goods are weakly separable from others in the group. An initial way of examining this is to break the group down and reestimate the model. To examine this, the group of nine goods was subdivided into two groups: (1) beef, pork, chicken and turkey; and (2) eggs, butter, fluid milk, cheese and margarine. As always, the selection was arbitrary (a rationalization might be the location of the goods in the grocery store). It is worthwhile noting that a very simple test for weak separability of these two groups of goods was conducted by constraining cross-price and advertising effects to zero in the nine-good estimation. For a number of different model specifications using likelihood ratio criterion, weak separability could not be accepted.

Different trends of model specifications were estimated for each of the subgroups, with the results reported in Table 8.9. It should be noted that this significantly reduces the number of parameters to be estimated in the models by eliminating approximately half of the cross-price and advertising effects. The results in terms of goodness of fit are reported in Table 8.10. The results in terms of price and expenditure elasticities and advertising elasticities are reported in Tables 8.11 and 8.12.

For the meats, the price and expenditure elasticities are similar to the translog model 3 with the exception of the turkey own-price elasticity. The strongest substitution relationship in each case is between chicken and turkey. However, very different results are obtained for the other subgroup than for any of the other estimated models; for example, there is a large positive expenditure elasticity for butter when all other estimates were small or negative.

Further testing is required to specify the most appropriate model to capture the price and advertising responses for these goods.

**Table 8.9. Model specification tests**

| | Subgroup 1 | | | Subgroup 2 | | |
|---|---|---|---|---|---|---|
| | Log of likelihood function | Calculated test statistic | Chi-square 5% | Log of likelihood function | Calculated test statistic | Chi-square 5% |
| Translog | 272.967 | | | 328.770 | | |
| With advertising | | | | | | |
| Model 1 | 297.946 | 49.96 | 26 | 346.986 | 36.43 | 36.42 |
| Model 2 (all $f_{ij} = 1$) | 244.195 | | | 285.302 | | |
| 2d (all $f_{ij} = .001$) | 272.954 | | | 328.552 | | |
| 2e ($f_j$ estimated) | 284.856 | | | 335.341 | | |
| Dynamic | | | | | | |
| Model 3 ($f_j$ estimated) | 319.889 | Convergence not achieved after 100 iterations | | 398.528 | | |

**Table 8.10. Fit of estimated demand systems**

| | Subgroup 1 | | | Subgroup 2 | |
|---|---|---|---|---|---|
| | $R^2$ | D.W. statistic | | $R^2$ | D.W. statistic |
| Beef | .91 | 1.64 | Eggs | .96 | 3.05 |
| Pork | .99 | 1.32 | Butter | .97 | 2.13 |
| Chicken | .96 | 1.47 | Fluid milk | .99 | 1.72 |
| | | | Cheese | .98 | 1.79 |

**Table 8.11. Price and expenditure elasticities evaluated at 1977 data points**

| Commodity | Beef | Pork | Chicken | Turkey | Commodity | Eggs | Butter | Fluid milk | Cheese | Margarine |
|---|---|---|---|---|---|---|---|---|---|---|
| Beef | -.94 | -.10 | -.15 | -.06 | Eggs | -.07 | -.53 | -.29 | .30 | -.19 |
| Pork | -.12 | -.19 | -.11 | -.02 | Butter | -.90 | -.52 | -.36 | -.37 | -.17 |
| Chicken | .02 | -.05 | -.34 | .20 | Fluid milk | -.18 | .04 | -.37 | -.09 | -.08 |
| Turkey | -.51 | -.09 | .34 | -.76 | Cheese | .10 | -.01 | -.20 | -1.19 | .13 |
| Expenditure | 1.25 | .44 | .17 | 1.02 | Margarine | -.14 | .13 | .02 | .73 | -.66 |
| | | | | | Expenditure | .78 | 2.32 | .68 | 1.17 | -.08 |

**Table 8.12. Advertising elasticities evaluated at 1986 data points**

| Commodity | Beef | Pork | Chicken | Turkey | Commodity | Eggs | Butter | Fluid milk | Cheese | Margarine |
|---|---|---|---|---|---|---|---|---|---|---|
| Beef | -.004 | -.002 | -.002 | -.003 | Eggs | .009 | .019 | .066 | -.016 | -.129 |
| Pork | -.006 | -.002 | .001 | -.001 | Butter | .018 | .009 | .069 | -.020 | -.123 |
| Chicken | -.005 | -.002 | .053 | .007 | Fluid milk | .014 | .013 | .012 | -.018 | -.087 |
| Turkey | -.010 | -.002 | .032 | .008 | Cheese | .013 | .014 | .061 | -.019 | -.009 |
| | | | | | Margarine | .014 | .013 | .047 | -.013 | .069 |

## Conclusions

A comparison of price, expenditure, and advertising elasticities generated in this and earlier studies is presented in Table 8.13. The critical differences between the earlier studies and this one are as follows:

1. This study is annual, while earlier ones are quarterly.
2. Earlier studies were on beverages (fluid milk, soft drinks, fruit juices) and fats and oils (butter, margarine, shortening, vegetable oils).
3. Earlier studies were over the time period 1972–1986, while the current one is over the period 1967–1986.

**Table 8.13. Comparison of results**

| | Uncompensated price and expenditure elasticities | | | Advertising elasticities | |
|---|---|---|---|---|---|
| | Butter | Margarine | Expenditure | Butter | Margarine |
| Goddard (1989) | | | | | |
| Butter | -.82 | -.36 | 1.17 | .011 | -.001 |
| Margarine | -.26 | -.43 | .69 | -.02 | .0012 |
| Goddard and Amuah (1989) | | | | | |
| Butter | -.72 | -.29 | 1.18 | .01 | -.06 |
| Margarine | -.26 | -.60 | .84 | -.81 | .04 |
| Present study | | | | | |
| 9-good: Butter | -1.07 | -.0002 | -.27 | -.009 | -.002 |
| Margarine | .02 | -.30 | 1.01 | -.009 | -.018 |
| 5-good: Butter | -.90 | -.17 | .78 | .009 | -.123 |
| Margarine | -.14 | -.66 | -.08 | .013 | .069 |
| Goddard et al. (1989) | | | | | |
| Fluid milk | -.293 | | .434 | .002 | |
| Present study | | | | | |
| 9-good: Fluid milk | -.59 | | .70 | .22 | |
| 5-good: Fluid milk | -.37 | | .68 | .012 | |

It is, perhaps, refreshing that there seems to be a common thread between the studies. For example, butter and margarine are gross complements (net substitutes) in both this (five-good) and the earlier study (Goddard and Amuah). The nine-good model reported in this study has the most strikingly different results. Advertising elasticities are roughly similar for butter and margarine between this (five-good) and the earlier study with the exception of the cross-advertising elasticity of demand for margarine with respect to butter price. For milk there is also some similarity between the results reported in this study (five-good) and the earlier study.

The questions remaining to be answered are

1. Have dynamic responses been accounted for in a realistic manner?
2. Are consumer responses greater to lagged advertising than to current advertising?

The results reported to date are far from final results on the impact of generic advertising on demand for a number of goods in the Canadian economy. The results to date are sensitive to functional form (i.e., AIDS or translog) and to method of incorporating advertising. The results suggest that enormous care should be taken in model specification. One of the problems in analysis of this sort is that degrees of freedom vanish as the number of goods increases. This suggests that part of the instability in results may be due to inefficient parameter estimation. In fact, in estimating the models with advertising as a shift variable (model 1), convergence was only achieved when the convergence criterion was relaxed. This may explain some of the differences between the two models.

# 9    A Rotterdam Model Incorporating Advertising Effects: The Case of Canadian Fats and Oils

THOMAS L. COX

This paper presents a Rotterdam type demand systems approach to measuring the impacts of advertising on commodity demand.

A household production framework is used to motivate an advertising induced augmentation model of structural change in Canadian fats and oils consumption during 1978–86. This framework generates restrictions on the advertising parameters (slopes) that are implied by demand theory under the augmentation/structural change hypotheses. As with the demand systems framework generally, these restrictions can increase degrees of freedom, increase the precision of parameter estimates (i.e., if the restrictions are true), and provide a theoretically consistent means of specifying own- and cross-commodity advertising as well as price effects. In addition, these procedures provide an inductive basis for testing alternative hypotheses concerning advertising induced structural change in consumption.

Rigorous and thorough incorporation of factors generally considered to exhibit dynamic impacts (such as advertising) into demand systems can be quite problematical. All of the single-equation subtleties in measuring the shape and length of the lag distribution as well as choosing an appropriate functional form for the advertising/sales response are compounded in a demand system with nonlinear cross-equation restrictions on the advertising slopes as well as the familiar demand theory restrictions. Quite a bit of work remains concerning these issues. In particular, a more systematic and concerted effort on the incorporation of cross-commodity, dynamic advertising sales response in the presence of strong seasonal consumption patterns is warranted. What follows is one approach to addressing these issues.

The paper proceeds with a brief literature review of demand systems incorporating advertising to motivate the Rotterdam specification used. Next, the conceptual framework is presented from a household production viewpoint. This provides a framework for developing a model and investigat-

139

ing explicit hypotheses concerning the impacts of advertising on commodity consumption. The empirical specification follows with a discussion of the data, the advertising stocks/dynamic specification, the seasonally adjusted Rotterdam model, and the econometric specification. Results of the estimations and hypotheses tests are then presented and discussed, followed by conclusions, caveats, and suggestions for further research.

## Literature Review: Demand Systems with Advertising

The single-equation advertising sales response literature is both diverse and in-depth. (See the 1985 Proceedings of *Research on Effectiveness of Agricultural Commodity Promotion* as well as the 1983 NC-117 Monograph, *Advertising and the Food System;* and Connor and Ward 1989.) The extant literature on demand systems incorporating advertising, however, is relatively sparse. Two general conceptual approaches characterize the literature on advertising in demand systems: adding advertising effects to duality based demand systems using the translog indirect utility or Almost Ideal Demand System (AIDS); or incorporating advertising into the Rotterdam Demand System following Theil (1980a). Examples of the first approach using translog indirect utility specification include: Amuah (1985); Goddard (1988, 1989); Goddard and Amuah (1988); Goddard and Tielu (1988). AIDS specifications incorporating advertising are found in the work of Green (1985). Examples of the second approach using a Rotterdam specification include Duffy (1987), Aviphant, Lee, and Brown (1988), Clements and Selvanathan (1988). An alternative Rotterdam type approach will be explored in this paper.

Because most popular demand function specifications such as the Rotterdam model have counterparts in explicit algebraic utility functions (Barnett 1979, 1981; Mountain 1988; Theil 1980b), the Rotterdam approach is equivalent to choosing an algebraic representation for consumers' preferences. While the Rotterdam model has been criticized for a lack of flexibility in modeling demand relations, this demand system is flexible in the sense of not imposing a priori restrictions on the local Allen elasticities of substitution (AES). The apparent lack of flexibility arises from the local consistency with the theory; or somewhat equivalently, Rotterdam models become inflexible if they are forced to be globally consistent. Barnett (1979, 1981) has shown that the Rotterdam model applied to aggregate per capita consumption data can be viewed as a Taylor series approximation (with reminder terms of at least second order) to a very useful demand system. Recent work by Mountain extends these arguments further by proving that the discrete Rotterdam formulation can be derived from the individual consumer as valid linear approximation in variable space with an order of approximation no lower than other flexible functional forms such as the translog, generalized Leontief, AIDS, and others.

Both approaches impose a priori structure on the preferences and yield implicit or explicit restrictions required to "solve" the structural change identification problem (Diamond, McFadden, and Rodriguez 1978; Cox 1989). In contrast to the highly nonlinear demand functions that derive from the nonhomothetic translog indirect utility specification, however, the commonly estimated demand functions that derive from AIDS and (absolute price) Rotterdam frameworks are linear in parameters. This greatly facilitates the incorporation of nonlinear dynamics and structural change hypotheses in the demand systems with advertising/sales response. Work by Wohlgenant (1982) suggests, moreover, that Rotterdam type models are fairly robust relative to AIDS and translog demand systems in their ability to flexibly model structural change in red meat demand. Because Rotterdam demand systems have been shown to provide reasonable and robust approximations (Barnett 1979, 1981; Theil 1980b; Wohlgenant 1982; Mountain 1988) and are easy to implement empirically (particularly for incorporating the impacts of preference shift variables such as generic advertising), this approach is taken. In a sense, the fairly robust, linear in demand parameters Rotterdam specification allows the analyst to concentrate the available nonlinear estimation capacity on unraveling the dynamics of the advertising/sales response.

## The Conceptual Framework

The conceptual framework for this analysis assumes that advertising potentially influences the marginal utility of commodity consumption. Following Cox (1989), advertising effects are conceptualized as "augmentations" that can increase or decrease the marginal utility of a commodity through informational and/or persuasive messages. The household production model provides a very general and convenient conceptual framework for incorporating these types of augmentations in a demand systems context.

Assume that consumers behave as if they optimize a well behaved utility function represented as

$$\text{MAX } U(Z_1, \ldots, Z_Q) \qquad (9.1a)$$
$$Z > 0$$

subject to:

$$Z_i = Z_i(X_i, A, B) \qquad i = 1, \ldots, Q \tag{9.1b}$$

$$M = \Sigma_i P_i X_i \tag{9.1c}$$

where the $P_i$ are the prices of market goods, $M$ is income (or group expenditure in the context of the second stage of a two-stage budgeting process under weak separability), and where the household production functions $(Z_i)$ specify how purchased market goods $(X_i)$ are affected by the vector of advertising measures $(A)$ and other exogenous factors $(B)$ such as seasonality, trends, and demographics. The $Z_i$ functions are interpreted as "effective" quantity levels, which are functions of the observed quantities $X_i$ "augmented" in a positive or negative manner by the advertising vector $(A)$. This is exactly the structural change hypothesis, where advertising is hypothesized to shift the marginal rates of substitution between commodities (one would hope) in favor of the commodity being advertised. To make this more explicit, substitute the household production functions into the utility function. The optimization problem in (9.1) becomes

$$\text{MAX } U\{Z_1(X_1, A, B), \ldots, Z_Q(X_Q, A, B)\} \qquad \text{s.t. (9.1c)} \tag{9.2a}$$
$$X > 0$$

or, in "reduced form,"

$$\text{MAX } U(X_1, \ldots, X_Q; A, B) \qquad \text{s.t. (9.1c)} \tag{9.2b}$$
$$X > 0$$

where the vectors A and B are interpreted as exogenous demand (preference) shifters (Deaton and Muellbauer 1980, Chapter 10). Assuming usual regularity conditions (i.e., well-behaved preferences, an interior solution, etc.), the demand functions associated with the maximization of (9.2b) subject to the budget constraint (9.1c) can be represented as

$$X_i = f(P_1, \ldots, P_Q, M, A, B) \qquad i = 1, \ldots, Q \tag{9.3}$$

To further focus this conceptual model, more explicit formulation of the household production functions $(Z_i)$ (or, equivalently, the generalized augmentation hypothesis) in (9.1b) is required. Pollak and Wales (1980, 1981) summarize two popular special cases of this approach as translating and scaling. Both of these special cases of the augmentation hypothesis generate implied restrictions of the demand system impacts of advertising. These restrictions are derived next, and then used below to analyze the impacts of advertising in a demand systems context.

## ADDITIVE AUGMENTATIONS (TRANSLATING)

In the case of translating, the household production functions (or, equivalently, the additively augmented, "effective" quantities) are specified as

$$Z_i = X_i - T_i(A) \tag{9.4}$$

where $T_i(A)$ represents some function of the advertising variables that additively augment the observed $X_i$. Noting that (9.4) implies $X_i = Z_i + T_i(A)$ and substituting this relation into the budget constraint (9.1c) yields the associated commodity demand functions under the translating (additive augmentation) hypothesis as

$$X_i(P_1, \ldots, P_Q, M, A, B) = Z_i(P/[M - \Sigma_j P_j T_j(A)], B) + T_i(A) \tag{9.5}$$

where $P = (P_1, \ldots, P_Q)$, and $P/[M - \Sigma_j P_j T_j(A)]$ is the vector of (adjusted income) normalized prices (this normalized price vector basically imposes homogeneity on the price and income terms of the Marshallian demand curve). $X_i(.)$ represents the classical, Marshallian demand specification of observed quantities, and $Z_i(.)$ represents the Marshallian demand for "effective" or additively augmented (translated) quantities.

Note that this additive form of the augmentation hypothesis implies that the demand impacts of the advertising induced preference shifts act like income effects and generates moderately nonlinear specifications that are empirically convenient. To further clarify this point, assume that the augmentations are of the form $T_i(A) = T_i(A_i)$, that is, determined by the own- (versus cross-) advertising factors. (This does not imply that cross-commodity advertising effects are zero as these effects are captured, *ceteris paribus* by $j$ ($j = 1, \ldots, 0$) separate commodity stocks in each equation. Hence, cross-commodity advertising influences the $T_i(A_i)$ *ceteris paribus* rather than directly in this specification). The advertising slopes implied by this translating hypothesis then take the form

$$\frac{\partial X_i}{\partial A_j} = \delta_{ij} \frac{\partial T_i(A)}{\partial A_j} + \frac{\partial Z_i}{\partial M} \left\{ \frac{[M - \Sigma_j P_j T_j(A)]}{T_j} \right\} \frac{\partial T_j}{\partial A_j} = \left( \delta_{ij} - P_j \frac{\partial X_i}{\partial M} \right) \frac{\partial T_i}{\partial A_j} \tag{9.6}$$

where $\delta_{ij}$ is the Kronecker delta and $P_j(\partial X_i/\partial M)$ is the marginal budget share. This implication of the additive augmentation (translating) hypothesis will be used below to generate empirical restrictions for hypotheses testing within a demand systems framework.

## MULTIPLICATIVE AUGMENTATIONS (SCALING)

In the case of scaling, the household production functions (or, equivalently, the multiplicatively augmented, "effective" quantities) are specified as

$$Z_i = X_i/S_i(A) \tag{9.7}$$

Noting that (9.7) implies $X_i = Z_i S_i(A)$ and substituting this relation into the budget constraint (1c) yields the associated commodity demand functions under the scaling (multiplicative augmentation) hypothesis as

$$X_i(P_1, \ldots, P_Q, M, A, B) = Z_i(PS/M, B)S_i(A) \tag{9.8}$$

where $PS/M = \{P_i S_i(A)/M\}$ is the vector of scaled and normalized prices, $X_i(\cdot)$ represents the classical Marshallian demand specification for the observed quantities, and $Z_i(\cdot)$ represents the Marshallian demand for "effective" or multiplicatively augmented (scaled) quantities.

Note that this multiplicative form of the augmentation hypothesis implies that the demand impacts of advertising induced preference shifts basically act like price effects and generates multiplicative specifications. To further clarify this point, assume that the multiplicative augmentations are of the form $S_i(A) = S_i(A_i)$, that is, are determined by the own- (versus cross-) advertising factors. The advertising slopes implied by this scaling hypothesis then take the form

$$\frac{\partial X_i}{\partial A_j} = \delta_{ij}\left[\frac{\partial S_i(A)}{\partial A_i}\right]Z_i + S_i(A)\frac{\partial Z_i}{\partial [P_j S_j(A)/M]}\left[\frac{\partial(P_j S_j(A)/M)}{\partial S_j}\right]\frac{\partial S_j(A)}{\partial A_j}$$

$$= \frac{\partial S_j(A)}{\partial A_j}\left[\frac{1}{S_j(A)}\right]\left(\frac{\partial X_i^c}{\partial P_j}P_j - P_j X_j\frac{\partial X_i}{\partial M} + \delta_{ij}X_i\right) \tag{9.9}$$

where $\delta_{ij}$ is the Kronecker delta, $\partial X_i^c/\partial P_j$ is the (Slutsky) compensated price slope, and $(\partial X_i/\partial M)$ is the marginal propensity to consume. This implication of the multiplicative augmentation (scaling) hypothesis will also be used below to generate empirical restrictions for testing within a demand systems framework.

Examples of this type of scaling approach (either explicitly or implicitly) are numerous in the advertising/sales response literature. The "pure repackaging" model of Fisher and Shell (1968) explicitly formulates this type of advertising augmentation as disembodied taste change; that is, a change in tastes independent of any change in commodity quality but attributable to an information gain concerning the product (also see Deaton and Muellbauer 1980, Chapter 10). Further extensions and refinements of this model to advertising/sales analysis include Dixit and Norman (1978), and Nichols (1985).

## The Empirical Specification

### THE DATA

Quarterly data on the Canadian fats and oils sector from 1973 to 1986 were used for the empirical analysis. Total retail packaged sales (metric tons, catalog 32-006) and the corresponding price indices (1981 = 100, catalog 62-010) of butter, margarine, shortening, and salad oils were obtained from Statistics Canada. Monthly data were aggregated to quarters where necessary. The consumption data were then converted to kilograms per capita using population data from Statistics Canada (catalog 91-201). Nominal prices are derived by rescaling the price indices to the first quarter of 1981 = 100 and applying the following base period prices: butter ($3.94/kg), margarine ($2.387/kg), shortening ($2.11/kg), and salad oils ($2.67/kg).

The butter and shortening base period prices are weighted averages from Table 11 of Statistics Canada Catalogue 63-010. Following Statistics Canada suggestions, the industry leader price for margarine and salad oil was utilized. In 1981, Kraft's Parkay brand of margarine was the market leader and sold for $2.17 per two-lb tubs, or $1.085/lb, 2.206 lb/kg = @2.387/kg. Proctor and Gamble's Crisco was the leading salad oil in 1981, and sold for $2.43/liter (Ambler Food Pricing Services of Toronto). Converting salad oil density at $0.91kg/100cm^3$ yields $2.43/liter, 1 liter/0.93kg = $2.67/kg. I wish to express thanks to Ellen Goddard and Brian Cozzarin of the University of Guelph for providing these data.

The advertising data are from two sources. Monthly media advertising expenditures (aggregated across TV, newspaper, and magazine) for margarine, shortening, and salad oils are from Elliot Research and Media Measurement Institute, Toronto. These aggregate advertising expenditures are primarily brand specific in nature. While Elliot advertising measures for butter are available, generic butter advertising purchased by the Dairy

Bureau of Canada (DBC) from 1978 to present are used in this analysis because they are believed to be more appropriate. All advertising expenditures are converted to a one-hundred-thousand person, quarterly basis using the Canadian population figures above.

Figures 9.1–9.3 summarize the butter and margarine data and provide additional motivation for the deseasonalized Rotterdam model derived and estimated below. Figure 9.1 contrasts butter and margarine per capita sales with pre- and post-1978:3 linear trends. Note strong fourth quarter peaks (seasonality) and the apparent structural shift in the linear butter and margarine consumption trends pre- and post-1978, when the (DBC) started its explicit butter advertising. In addition, note that the margarine peaks are generally lower (and butter peaks generally higher) after 1978. The casual inference is that these gains in butter consumption have likely come at the expense of margarine, at least over part of the 1978–86 period. Figure 9.2, showing per capita margarine consumption and advertising, suggests that the margarine industry reacted quite vigorously to the DBC butter campaign, as advertising levels were considerably above the average trend in the 1978–84 period. The flatness in the seasonal margarine consumption peaks, despite the increased level of margarine advertising, reinforces the casual inference that the DBC butter advertising was doing something right. In contrast, however, Figure 9.3 (comparing butter consumption with DBC butter advertising trends) indicates increasing butter advertising and decreasing butter consumption on average over the 1978–86 period.

These casual observations, which are not *ceteris paribus* to other potentially relevant factors, suggest that DBC butter advertising has reduced but not reversed the downward butter consumption trends, and has likely done so at the expense of margarine. The research task is to partial out the effects of prices, expenditures, and cross-commodity advertising in order to isolate the *ceteris paribus* impacts of the own- and cross-advertising effects. Unfortunately, an aggregate index measuring health/diet concerns with respect to fat intake is unavailable; hence, a likely very relevant factor is not being held *ceteris paribus* in what follows.

## ADVERTISING DYNAMICS

Considerable conceptual and empirical results support the existence of delayed peak in the advertising/sales response (Bass and Clarke 1972; Clarke 1976; Jastram 1976; Little 1979; Simon and Arndt 1981). While the research analyst is generally forced to impose some prior structure on the advertising sales response surface, some latitude can be exercised. In particular, the presence of a lagged peak or geometric decay in the advertising/sales

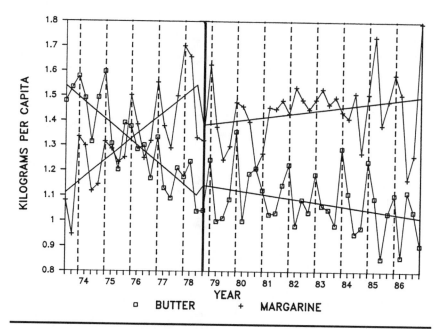

**Figure 9.1.** Total retail sales per capita, 1973–86;
pre- and post-1978:3 consumption trends.

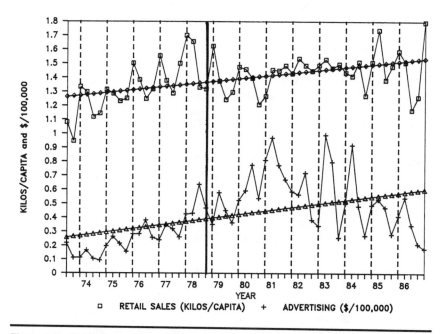

**Figure 9.2.** Margarine sales and advertising per capita for Canada, 1973–86.

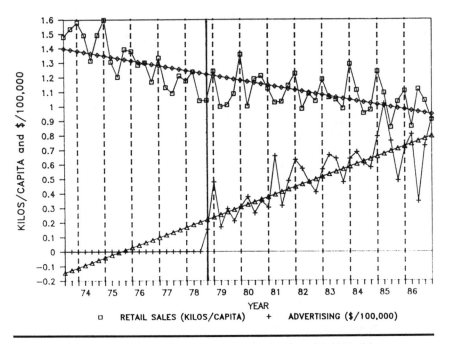

**Figure 9.3. Butter sales and advertising per capita for Canada, 1973–86.**

response surface can be evaluated with dynamic stocks specifications that "flexibly" allow for either type of response to be supported by the data. Several members from the family of restricted infinite distributed lag (rational, Pascal, gamma, geometric polynomial, and exponential lag) specifications are among the available options that can be used to evaluate these hypotheses (Judge et al. 1980).

The carryover effects of advertising on commodity demand are commonly viewed as a stock (versus flow) concept in the agricultural economics, advertising/sales response literature (e.g., Kinnucan and Forker 1986). Advertising stocks of goodwill are then treated similarly to capital stocks. Popular specifications of carryover effects in the agricultural economics literature include low order (usually linear or quadratic) polynomial distributed lags (Thompson and Eiler 1977; Ward and Davis 1978; Ward and Myers 1979; Ward and Dixon 1987), lagged quantity variables using the partial adjustment or habit formation hypothesis (Amuah 1985; Goddard 1988b, 1989; Goddard and Amuah 1988; Goddard and Tielu 1988), moving average or moving sums of advertising (Aviphant, Lee, and Brown 1988), and the Pascal distribution (Kinnucan and Forker 1986). (Somewhat surprisingly, the Duffy, and Clements and Salavanthan applications of Theil's Rotterdam system with advertising do not incorporate advertising dynamics.) In contrast to the extant literature, a second order (quadratic) exponential lag specification of advertising stocks was chosen for its flexibility and parameter parsimony.

Given the monthly, bimonthly, and quarterly based econometric evidence (e.g., Clarke 1976) that most of the cumulative effects of advertising are likely to occur within nine months for mature, frequently purchased, and low-priced products like butter, margarine, shortening, and salad oils, five lags are used to specify advertising stock of the $i$th commodity as:

$$K_i = \Sigma_{j=0}^5 W_{i,t-j} A_{i,t-j} \tag{9.10}$$

$$W_{i,t-j} = [\exp(D_{0i} + D_{1i} j + D_{2i} j^2)] \tag{9.11}$$

The weight on the last lag ($j = 5$) is restricted to be zero (following Thompson and Eiler 1977; Ward and Davis 1978; Ward and Myers 1979; Ward and Dixon 1978), that is, $W_{i,t-5} = 0$. Similarly, the weight on current period ($j = 0$) advertising expenditures is restricted to be 1, that is, $W_{i,t} = 1$, a normalization that fixes the scale of measurement for the advertising stock $K_i$. These end-point restrictions reduce the dynamic specification to a single parameter. Incorporating five lags, noting that $\exp(0) = 1$, and taking $\exp(-20) \approx 0$ for purposes of approximation, yields the following specification of the lag weights:

$$D_{0i} = 0$$

$$D_{1i} = -4.0 - D_{2i} 5$$

$$W_{i,t-j} = [\exp(D_{0i} + D_{1i} j + D_{2i} j^2)]$$

$$= [\exp(-4.0 j + D_{2i} (j^2 - 5 j))] \tag{9.12}$$

While this specification is essentially arbitrary, as are all specifications of unobserved dynamic response functions, it does allow for either geometric decay or a lagged peak in the response surface of interest. (Several issues concerning truncation of remainder terms are essentially ignored in this treatment. See Judge et al. 1980, pp. 694–96, for more details.) Figure 9.4 demonstrates the flexibility of this specification for various levels of the quadratic term.

## THE ROTTERDAM SPECIFICATION WITH SEASONAL ADJUSTMENT

Given the pronounced seasonality and consumption trends characterizing the data to be analyzed (Figures 9.1–9.3), and following previous advertising sales analyses using quarterly data (e.g., Ward and Myers 1979; Kinnucan 1983), four quarterly dummy variables $(D_j, j = 1$ to $4$, and constraining the dummy variable coefficients within each demand equation to sum to zero) and a trend term are specified as the other exogenous shift factors $(B)$ in (9.3) above.

It is unclear how best to proceed in specifying the Rotterdam model with quarterly data. Duffy 1987 (p. 1055, footnote 5) acknowledges these difficulties and proceeds to estimate an annual model (without dynamics) after the ad hoc addition of quarterly dummy variables to the Theil Rotterdam, with advertising specification resulting in those dummy variables being almost the only significant variables in the estimated equations. If most of the advertising/sales response literature is correct, *that is the importance of these dynamic advertising effects,* then aggregation to an annual level is clearly offensive. Taking the advertising variables as the stock measures defined above, the directly specified demand functions in (9.3) are now represented as

$$X_i = f(P_1, \ldots, P_Q, M, K_1, \ldots, K_Q, D_1, D_2, D_3, D_4, \text{TREND}) \quad (9.13)$$

In quarterly or monthly data, the dependent variable of a distributed lag formulation may exhibit seasonality that is not captured by seasonal changes in the regressors (Judge et al. 1980). One can either seasonally adjust the data or include seasonal dummy or seasonal harmonic variables as commonly done in the agricultural economics literature (Thompson and Eiler 1977; Ward and Davis 1978; Ward and Myers 1979; Kinnucan and Forker 1986; Ward and Dixon 1987). Deseasonalizing the data can generate high order moving average error terms and generally distort the lag function estimates in distributed lag models. Wallis (1974), however, demonstrates that this prospect is less likely if one deseasonalizes both the dependent and independent variables with the same seasonal adjustment. Alternatively, one can specify a variable lag formulation using seasonal (dummy) interaction terms in the distributed lag formulation, but this is seldom done in the extant agricultural economics literature.

Following Wallis, both the dependent variables and the regressors are deseasonalized by taking fourth differences. Note that the quarterly/seasonal dummy variables disappear (are zeroed out) by this seasonal adjustment. Similarly, the common trend specification $t_i(\text{TREND})$ becomes $t_i(\text{TREND} - \text{TREND} - 4) = -4t_i$, essentially a constant (i.e., an intercept

term) in a fourth difference model. A deseasonalized Rotterdam approximation to this reduced form demand curve incorporating the trend and
quarterly seasonal dummy variables can be represented in a differential form
as

$$w_i^* d \ln X_i = i_0 + \Sigma_q G_{iq} d \ln P_q + B_i(d \ln X) + \Sigma_q A_{iq} dK_q + v_i \qquad (9.14)$$

where
$w_i^* = (w_{i,t} + w_{i,t-4})/2$ are the Divisia budget shares;
$w_i$ are the budget shares of the $i$th commodity;
$d \ln x_i = (\ln X_i, t - \ln X_{i,t-4})$;
$d \ln P_q = (\ln P_{q,t} - \ln P_{q,t-4})$;
$d \ln X = \Sigma_i w_i^* d \ln X_i$ is the Divisia quantity index of consumption;
$G_{iq} = (\partial X_i^c/\partial P_q)(P_q P_i/M) = E_{ij}^* w_i$ (where $E_{ij}^*$ are the compensated
    price elasticities);
$B_i = P_i(\partial X_i/\partial M) = E_{iM} w_i$ (where $P_i(\partial X_i/\partial M)$ is the marginal budget
    share and $E_{iM}$ is income, or expenditure, elasticity);
$dK_q = (K_{q,t} - K_{q,t-4})$ is the fourth difference in advertising stocks;
$A_{iq} = (\partial X_i/\partial K_q)(P_i/M)$ are the unrestricted, advertising stocks induced
    demand responses.

Given this fourth-order log differential approximation to the reduced form
seasonal demand function in (9.13), the "intercept" terms $i_0 = -4t_i P_i/M$ are
interpreted as measures of structural change not accounted for by the rest
of the model.

Note that the advertising stocks specification is in difference rather than
log differential form. We use this specification for a variety of reasons. First,
given the presence of zero levels of butter advertising by the CDB prior to
the third quarter of 1978, the log differential specification requires some ad
hoc "fixup" since the log of zero does not exist. Second, deseasonalized, log
differential stocks add considerable nonlinearity to an already nonlinear
specification.

To see this note that

$$d \ln K_q = \ln (K_{q,t}) - \ln (K_{q,t-4})$$

$$= \ln \{\Sigma_{j=0}^{5} W_{i,t-j} A_{i,t-j}\} - \ln \{\Sigma_{j=0}^{5} W_{i,t-j} A_{i,t-j-4}\} \qquad (9.15)$$

In contrast, the deseasonalized, fourth difference stock specification in
(14) derives as

$$dK_q = (K_{q,t} - K_{q,t-4})$$

$$= \{\Sigma_{j=0}^{5} \, W_{i,t-j} \, A_{i,t-j}\} - \{\Sigma_{j=0}^{5} \, W_{i,t-j} \, A_{i,t-j-4}\} \tag{9.15}$$

$$= \Sigma_{j=0}^{5} \, W_{i,t-j} \, (A_{i,t-j} - A_{i,t-j-4}) \tag{9.16}$$

which is considerably less nonlinear than in (9.15).

Given the convergence difficulties encountered in the econometric estimation of (9.14), to be discussed further below, and the potential log of zero problems, this was considered a reasonable way to proceed.

## THE RESTRICTIONS IMPLIED BY THE THEORY

The familiar restrictions from demand theory for this specification are $\Sigma_i B_i = 1$ (adding up); $\Sigma_q G_{iq} = 0$ (homogeneity of compensated price slopes); and $G_{iq} = G_{qi}$ (Slutsky symmetry). In order for the system to add up, the following must also hold: $\Sigma_i i_0 = 0$, and $\Sigma_i A_{iq} = 0$. In addition, demand theory implies the Tintner-Ichimura relations on the advertising stock slopes (Phlips 1974, pp. 181–83; Theil 1980a):

$$A_K = -(1/\lambda)G_P^* V = \{-(1/\lambda)(\Sigma_q G_{iq} V_{qr})\} \tag{9.17}$$

where $A_K$ is the $(Q \times Q)$ matrix with elements $A_{iq} = (\partial X_i / \partial K_q)$, $\lambda$ is the marginal utility of income, $G_P$ is the $(Q \times Q)$ symmetric, negative semi-definite, Slutsky matrix of compensated price effects (slopes) with elements $G_{iq}$, and $V$ is the $(Q \times Q)$ matrix of second-order cross-partial derivatives of the utility function with elements $V_{qr} = \partial^2 U / (\partial X_q \partial K_r)$.

If correctly specified, compensated own- and cross-price effects are important for maintaining a theoretically consistent *ceteris paribus* context within which to measure advertising/stocks impacts, the analyst may want to impose the curvature restrictions on the Slutsky matrix, $G_P$. At the cost of additional nonlinearity, this is relatively straightforward.

Note that Cholesky decomposition of a symmetric, negative definite matrix yields $G_P^* = P'P$ where $P = (P_{iq})$ is upper triangular. For $Q = 4$ (and, assuming homogeneity, that is, $\Sigma_q G_{iq} = 0$), this yields the following nonlinear restrictions on the $G_{iq}$ price terms of (9.14):

$$G_{11} = -P_{11}P_{11} \qquad G_{12} = -P_{11}P_{12} \qquad G_{13} = -P_{11}P_{13}$$
$$G_{22} = -P_{12}P_{12} -P_{22}P_{22} \qquad G_{23} = -P_{12}P_{13} -P_{22}P_{23}$$
$$G_{33} = -P_{13}P_{13} -P_{23}P_{23} -P_{33}P_{33}$$

As indicated by (9.17) demand system restrictions on the effects of preference shift factors such as advertising are implied by the theory. While these restrictions are usually not developed nor utilized in most of the applied literature, they can be tested for and, if found true, aid in the estimation of demand systems incorporating these shift factors. The Rotterdam/advertising work following Theil exploits this relation (see Duffy 1987; Aviphant, Lee, and Brown 1988; Clements and Selvanathan 1988). On the other hand, (9.17) also indicates that the demand analytics of these shift factors require the additional knowledge of how these shift factors influence the curvature of the preference function (that is, via the $V_{qr}$ elements, the second-order cross-partial derivatives of $U(.)$). In other words, knowledge or assumptions about these second-order curvature properties imposes the structure necessary to identify the nature of these preference shifts. This information is either implicitly or explicitly imposed in the specification and estimation of commodity demand functions incorporating preference shift factors. The translating and scaling augmentation hypotheses provide some of this a priori structure in the present context of a deseasonalized Rotterdam type demand system.

To further clarify this point for the translating hypothesis, denote $T_q^* = (\partial T_q/\partial K_q)(P_i/M)$ $(q = 1, \ldots , Q)$ as the translated advertising/stock parameters to be estimated, and multiply (9.6) by $P_i/M$ to yield the following restrictions on the advertising/stock parameters $A_{iq}$ in (9.14):

$$A_{iq} = (\delta_{iq} - B_i)T_q^* \qquad (9.18)$$

where $\delta_{iq}$ is the Kronecker delta, and $B_i$ is the estimated marginal budget share from (9.14). Hence, (9.18) yields a set of a modestly nonlinear, cross-equation restrictions amenable to empirical hypothesis testing against the unrestricted specification of the $A_{iq}$. Note that for all $i \neq q$, $T_q^* > 0$ (i.e., positive translating parameters) and $B_i > 0$ (i.e., no inferior goods) implies $A_{iq} < 0$ (i.e., negative cross-commodity advertising effects). Conversely, for all $I = q$, positive own-advertising effects ($A_{ii} > 0$) implies either $T_i^* > 0$ and $B_i < 1$, or, $B_i > 1$, that $T_i^* < 0$. Similarly for scaling, denote $S_q^* = (\partial S_j(A)/\partial K_q)/K_q$, $(q = 1, \ldots , Q)$ as the scaled advertising stock parameters to be estimated, and multiply (9.9) by $P_i/M$ to yield the following restrictions on the advertising/stock parameters $A_{iq}$ in (9.14):

$$A_{iq} = \{G_{iq} - \delta B_i + \delta_{iq} w_i\} S_q^*$$                                    (9.19)

where, as above in (9.18), $\delta_{iq}$ is the Kronecker delta, $B_i$ is the estimated marginal budget share from (9.14), and $G_{iq}$ is the estimated compensated price response from (9.14). In contrast to (9.18), note that the scaling augmentation hypothesis in (9.19) yields a set of more nonlinear, cross-equation restrictions involving the $G_{iq}$ terms. These restrictions are likewise amenable to empirical hypothesis testing against the unrestricted specification of the $A_{iq}$.

Equations (9.18) and (9.19) summarize the empirical restrictions jointly implied by demand theory and the translating or scaling augmentation hypothesis in the context of the deseasonalized Rotterdam demand system incorporating advertising stocks in (9.14). These restrictions are empirically testable and, noting that the derivative of the budget constraint with respect to $K_q$ implies that $\Sigma_i A_{iq} = 0$ if adding-up is to be satisfied, generate $Q$ versus $Q^2 - Q$ advertising response parameters to estimate in the restricted demand system. Hence, at the cost of adding nonlinearity to the demand system, these cross-equation restrictions can provide an inductive basis for evaluating alternative hypotheses on the nature of advertising induced structural change, reduce the parameter space and, if true, increase the precision of the resulting estimates.


## ECONOMETRIC SPECIFICATION

Substitution of (9.10), (9.11), and (9.12) into (9.14) yields a seemingly unrelated, nonlinear demand system with an "unrestricted" advertising/stocks specification. (In addition to the second-order exponential (with end-point restrictions) specification of advertising stocks, the restrictions from demand theory (adding up, homogeneity, and Slutsky symmetry) are imposed throughout as maintained hypotheses. Hence, "unrestricted" in this context relates to (9.17) in the sense of no *explicit hypotheses* on the impact of the advertising stocks on consumption or marginal utility.) The nonlinear restrictions to impose negative semi-definiteness on the matrix of Slutsky price effects (following Barten 1977) are also evaluated with this specification. The additional substitution of (9.18) or (9.19) for the advertising/stock effects, $A_{iq}$, yields nonlinear nested specifications of the additive (translating) or multiplicative (scaling) advertising/stock augmentation hypotheses, respectively. Nonlinear seemingly unrelated regression (SUR) was performed using SAS's SYSNLIN software. Following Chavas and Segerson (1987), consistent estimates of the cross-equation residual covariance matrix were obtained. These procedures yield estimates that are consistent, asymptotically efficient, and invariant to the omitted equation using noniterated SUR, i.e., the results are asymptotically equivalent to those from maximum likelihood. This facilitates empirical estimation, as iterated SUR (for example ITSUR in SAS's SYSNLIN) can be expensive in very nonlinear demand systems such as those incorporating cross-commodity advertising dynamics and explicitly augmentation hypotheses.

Gallant and Jorgenson (1979) test procedures are used to test all hypotheses. Basically this test involves using the same consistent estimate of the cross-equation covariance matrix of residuals to estimate both the unrestricted and restricted models. The Gallant and Jorgenson test statistic is computed as $T_0 = nS^{**} - nS^*$ where $S^{**}$ and $S^*$ are the weighted error sum of squares evaluated at convergence for the restricted and unrestricted models, respectively. This test statistic is asymptotically distributed as chi-square with degrees of freedom equal to the difference in the number of parameters in the unrestricted and restricted models.

## Results

The "unrestricted" advertising model was estimated first with the 1973–86 data. I used the standard second stage Rotterdam specification based on first rather than fourth differences. Positive, compensated own-price effects for margarine and shortening (salad oils is the omitted equation throughout), negative (and significant) own-advertising stocks effects for butter and margarine resulted, and were considered unacceptable. The somewhat ad hoc addition of trend terms, with and without quarterly dummy variables, yielded essentially the same results. Similar to Duffy (1987), the addition of quarterly dummy variables resulted in the loss of almost all significance in the price and advertising effects. Imposing negative semi-definiteness yielded theoretically plausible price effects, but failed to change the negative own-commodity advertising/stocks effects. With few exceptions, the imposition of the negative semidefiniteness restrictions also resulted in the imposition of Pss = 0, and Pss = Pmm = Pms = 0 in order to get convergence in the estimation routines. Note that the corresponding price effects are not zero under these additional restrictions, but rather Gss = −Pbs(Pbs), Gmm = −Pbm(Pbm), and Gms = −Pbm(Pbs). Complementary research by Chang and Kinnucan (Chapter 10 of this book) suggested structural change in consumption patterns around 1978, corresponding to the start of the DBC's explicit butter advertising campaign. Figure 9.1 provides further casual evidence for such change. Accordingly, I decided to focus on the 1978:3–1986:4 period to minimize these issues.

Table 9.1 summarizes the parameter estimates for the unrestricted advertising/stocks specification, with and without negative semidefiniteness imposed (hereafter referred to as UAWOC and UAWC, respectively), as well as the scaled and translated advertising stocks specification with negative semidefiniteness imposed (hereafter referred to as SAWC and TAWC, respectively). Table 9.2 summarizes the corresponding elasticities for selected parameters of interest that are statistically significant in Table 9.1.

Starting with the summary statistics on the second page of Table 9.1, note the minimum root mean square errors (RMSE) across specifications and commodities are: butter (UAWC), margarine (SAWC), and shortening (UAWOC). Hence, no specification is clearly superior across all commodities in terms of RMSE criterion. Given that the dependent variables are divisia share weighted fourth differences of logarithms, the individual equation $R$-squares are quite reasonable. The Durbin-Watson "$D$" statistics indicate that all equations except for shortening (SAWC and TAWC specifications) do not have significant first order autocorrelation problems.

The system weighted sums of squared errors (weighted with the same consistent, cross-equation covariance matrix) are the basis for the Gallant and Jorgenson tests discussed above. The computed test statistic for the test of the curvature restrictions given the unrestricted advertising model is 14.4 (i.e., 60.1758 − 45.7664). It is unclear, however, how many degrees of freedom (d.f.) are needed to evaluate the chi-square critical value: there are six nonlinear restrictions imposed by negative semidefiniteness, and three additional restrictions (Pss = Pmm = Pms = 0) were required to obtain convergence. Critical values at the 95 percent and 99 percent significance levels are (12.6, 15.1) for six d.f. and (16.9, 21.7) for nine d.f., respectively. Given the importance of theoretically consistent compensated price effects for the specification and, hence, testing of the augmentation hypotheses (particularly scaling), the curvature results are imposed as maintained hypotheses for the tests that follow. When comparing the UAWOC and UAWC elasticities in Table 9.2, note that aside from the price and shortening expenditure elasticities, all other elasticities are quite similar with or without negative semidefiniteness imposed.

The calculated Gallant and Jorgenson test statistics for the null hypotheses of scaling (SAWC) or translating (TAWC) versus the unrestricted advertising results (UAWC) are 20.33 (i.e., 80.5065 − 60.1758) and 23.86 (i.e., 84.0371 − 60.1758), respectively. Recalling that these hypotheses generate $Q$ versus $Q^2 - Q$ advertising/stocks parameters, each null hypothesis has 8 degrees of freedom. Critical chi-square values at the 95 percent and 99 percent significance levels are (15.5, 20.1). Hence, while scaling performs somewhat better than translating (also compare weighted sums of squares in Table 9.1), both hypotheses are rejected in favor of the unrestricted advertising model for these data. (Similar results from the full

1972–86 period, however, indicate a failure to reject scaling and marginal rejections of translating.)

Table 9.1.  **Alternative parameter estimates of the Canadian fats and oils sector, 1978:3–1986:4 using deseasonalized (4th difference) Rotterdam specification**[a]

| | Unrestricted without curvature | With curvature imposed: Pss = Pmm = Pms = 0[b] | | |
| --- | --- | --- | --- | --- |
| | | Unrestricted advertising | Scaled advertising | Translated advertising |
| Intercepts ($i_0 = -4t_i P_i / M$) | | | | |
| b0 | 0.0106 * | 0.0125 * | 0.0054 | 0.0081 |
| m0 | -.0035 | -.0091 | -.0012 | -.0046 |
| s0 | -.0153 *** | -.0107 *** | -.0040 | -.0071 ** |
| Conditional income effects ($B_i$) | | | | |
| Bb | 0.4878 **** | 0.4640 **** | 0.4726 **** | 0.4751 **** |
| Bm | 0.2262 *** | 0.2263 *** | 0.2760 **** | 0.2754 **** |
| Bs | 0.0487 | 0.0982 ** | 0.0919 ** | 0.0761 ** |
| Conditional, compensated price effects ($G_{iq}$)[c] | | | | |
| Gbb | -.0285 | Pbb  0.4057 **** | 0.1330 * | 0.3685 **** |
| Gbm | 0.0804 | Pbm  -.2886 ** | -.1329 | -.2995 ** |
| Gbs | -.0552 | Pbs  -.3608 ** | -.2138 *** | -.2378 * |
| Gmm | 0.0578 | Pmm  - | - | - |
| Gms | -.0988 | Pms  - | - | - |
| Gss | 0.5841 *** | Pss  - | - | - |
| Advertising stock effects ($A_{iq}$, $S_i$, or $T_i$) | | | | |
| Abb | -9.13E-04 *** | -9.23E-04 *** | Sb  -.0044 ** | Tb  -.0009 * |
| Abm | 1.87E-04 | 2.22E-04 | Sm  -.0019 * | Tm  -.0053 * |
| Abs | -4.53E-08 | -4.10E-07 | Ss  0.0000 | Ts  0.0000 |
| Abo | 2.15E-05 | 1.26E-05 | So  -.0089 | To  -.0001 |
| Amb | 4.99E-04 ** | 6.16E-04 ** | - | - |
| Amm | -4.73E-04 ** | -3.09E-04 * | - | - |
| Ams | -8.54E-08 | -5.42E-07 | - | - |
| Amo | -5.39E-06 | -3.85E-06 | - | - |
| Asb | -4.17E-05 | 2.42E-04 * | - | - |
| Asm | 1.36E-04 | -1.19E-04 | - | - |
| Ass | 2.08E-07 | 1.34E-06 | - | - |
| Aso | -2.00E-06 | -6.30E-06 | - | - |

**Table 9.1. (cont.)**

| | Unrestricted without curvature | With curvature imposed: $Pss = Pmm = Pms = 0$[b] | | |
| --- | --- | --- | --- | --- |
| | | Unrestricted advertising | Scaled advertising | Translated advertising |

*Dynamic stocks quadratic term ($D2_i$)*

| | | | | |
| --- | --- | --- | --- | --- |
| D2b | -1.0600 **** | -1.1052 **** | -1.0048 **** | -1.1814 **** |
| D2m | -.1683 | -.9151 *** | _d | _d |
| D2s | -2.7826 *** | -2.4008 *** | -2.8311 ** | -2.7482 ** |
| D2o | -1.9505 **** | -2.0899 **** | -1.6332 **** | -1.5102 **** |

*Root mean square errors*

| | | | | |
| --- | --- | --- | --- | --- |
| Butter | 0.0217 | 0.0205 | 0.0215 | 0.0252 |
| Margarine | 0.0217 | 0.0223 | 0.0216 | 0.0225 |
| Shortening | 0.0123 | 0.0154 | 0.0168 | 0.0179 |

*R-squares*

| | | | | |
| --- | --- | --- | --- | --- |
| Butter | 0.8134 | 0.8239 | 0.7717 | 0.6851 |
| Margarine | 0.6786 | 0.6389 | 0.6016 | 0.5665 |
| Shortening | 0.7541 | 0.5863 | 0.4224 | 0.3427 |

*Durbin-Watson "$D$" statistic*

| | | | | |
| --- | --- | --- | --- | --- |
| Butter | 2.7050 | 2.4690 | 2.6050 | 2.0200 |
| Margarine | 2.1080 | 2.0360 | 2.0370 | 1.7730 |
| Shortening | 1.7770 | 1.9100 | 1.4950 | 1.3140 |

*Objective function (weighted sum of squared errors) for system*

| | | | | |
| --- | --- | --- | --- | --- |
| Obj | 1.8307 | 2.4070 | 3.2203 | 3.3615 |
| Obj·n | 45.7664 | 60.1758 | 80.5065 | 84.0371 |

SOURCE: Computations by the authors using SAS PROC SYSNLIN, Marquardt algorithm with convergence criterion of 0.001.

[a] These results have adding-up, Slutsky symmetry, and homogeneity imposed. ****, ***, **, and * indicate statistical significance at the alpha = 0.001, 0.01, 0.05, and 0.10 level, respectively.

[b] These restrictions were imposed in addition to concavity as the result of hypotheses tests of Pss = 0, and Pmm = Pms = 0. The demand system became singular when Pss approached zero. Setting Pss = 0 and dropping it as parameter to estimate then yielded Pmm and Pms approaching zero and singularity. The results presented here are converged parameter estimates with Pss = Pmm = Pms = 0 imposed.

[c] The $S_{ij}$ are functions of the $P_{ij}$ via the Cholesky decomposition. Note in particular that Pss = Pmm = Psm = 0 does not imply that the corresponding Gss, Gmm, or Gms equal zero.

[d] The additional restriction that Dm2 = 0 was imposed when the model failed to converge after iterating to Dm2 = 0. This implies that the lag response in margarine advertising occurs within one quarter (see Figure 9.4 for the implied lag shape due to this restriction).

**Table 9.2 Selected elasticity estimates associated with statistically significant parameters from Table 9.1, evaluated at the 1978:3–1986:4 means**

|  | Expenditure elasticities | | | |
|---|---|---|---|---|
|  | Butter | Margarine | Shortening | Salad oils |
| Unrestricted w/o curvature: | 1.2938 | 0.7774 | 0.2505 | 1.7263 |
| Unrestricted w/ curvature: | 1.2306 | 0.7777 | 0.5047 | 1.5390 |
| Scaling w/ curvature: | 1.2534 | 0.9486 | 0.4722 | 1.1607 |
| Translating w/ curvature: | 1.2601 | 0.9465 | 0.3911 | 1.2614 |

|  | Price elasticities | | | |
|---|---|---|---|---|
| Model | Compensated | | Uncompensated | |
| Quantity | Butter | Margarine | Butter | Margarine |
| Unrestricted w/o curvature: |  |  |  |  |
| Butter | -0.0755 | 0.2762 | -0.5634 | -0.1002 |
| Margarine | 0.2132 | 0.1986 | -0.0799 | -0.0276 |
| Unrestricted w/ curvature: |  |  |  |  |
| Butter | -0.4364 | 0.4024 | -0.9004 | 0.0443 |
| Margarine | 0.3105 | -0.2863 | 0.0173 | -0.5126 |
| Scaling w/ curvature: |  |  |  |  |
| Butter | -0.0469 | 0.0608 | -0.5159 | -0.3039 |
| Margarine | 0.0469 | -0.0607 | -0.3108 | -0.3368 |
| Translating w/ curvature: |  |  |  |  |
| Butter | -0.3601 | 0.3793 | -0.8352 | 0.0126 |
| Margarine | 0.2927 | -0.3083 | -0.0642 | -0.5837 |

|  | Advertising elasticities | | | |
|---|---|---|---|---|
| Model | Stocks | | Current period | |
| Quantity | Butter | Margarine | Butter | Margarine |
| Unrestricted w/o curvature: |  |  |  |  |
| Butter | -0.3259 | 0.0568 | -0.1203 | 0.0264 |
| Margarine | 0.2818 | -0.1022 | 0.0852 | -0.0869 |
| Unrestricted w/ curvature: |  |  |  |  |
| Butter | -0.2870 | 0.0274 | -0.1216 | 0.0315 |
| Margarine | 0.2034 | -0.0901 | 0.1051 | -0.0566 |
| Scaling w/ curvature: |  |  |  |  |
| Butter | -0.2281 | 0.0321 | -0.1088 | 0.0315 |
| Margarine | 0.1414 | -0.0670 | 0.0674 | -0.0658 |
| Translating w/ curvature: |  |  |  |  |
| Butter | -0.2036 | 0.0365 | -0.0611 | 0.0359 |
| Margarine | 0.1384 | -0.0722 | 0.0415 | -0.0709 |

SOURCE: Computations by the authors.

Moving on to the parameter estimates and associated elasticities, recall that the intercept terms $i_0 = -4t_i P_i/M$. Thus, the results on the first page of Table 9.1 indicate negative (positive) *ceteris paribus* trends in butter (margarine) consumption much as Figure 9.1 suggested. With few exceptions (e.g., unrestricted advertising without curvature (UAWOC) shortening results), the estimated conditional income effects are statistically significant and quite robust across the alternative specifications. The corresponding conditional expenditure elasticities are found in Table 9.2. The unrestricted advertising expenditure elasticities (UAWOC and UAWC) are quite comparable to each other as are the augmentation restricted results (SAWC and TAWC). The margarine and butter results are particularly robust across model specifications.

The UAWOC conditional, compensated price effects in Table 9.1 are generally not statistically significant (exception: shortening own-price effect), and the margarine and shortening own-price effects have the wrong sign and will not be discussed further. Imposition of the curvature restrictions in the unrestricted advertising specification, UAWC, yielded more plausible results as evidenced by the conditional, compensated, and uncompensated price elasticities in Table 9.2. The correspondence between the UAWC (unrestricted) and TAWC (translating) compensated price elasticities is quite close. The considerably smaller SAWC (scaling) price elasticities reflect the fact that advertising is explicitly hypothesized to scale, and in this case reduce the price effects. Butter and margarine (as well as the shortening and salad oils results not shown due to space limitations) are estimated to have moderately inelastic compensated own-price responses (butter $(-0.4)$ and margarine $(-0.3)$ from the UAWC and TAWC specifications) and somewhat more elastic Marshallian own-price response (butter $(-0.5$ to $-0.9)$ and margarine $(-0.5$ to $-0.6)$ from the UAWC and TAWC specifications). In addition, butter and margarine are indicated to be net substitutes by all models, and gross substitutes by all models (with curvature restrictions) except SAWC (scaling).

Moving to the estimated advertising parameters in Table 9.1, note that with one exception (UAWC: Asb, the cross-commodity impact of butter advertising stocks on shortening consumption), the only statistically significant parameters concern butter and margarine stocks. The statistically significant advertising stocks parameters of Table 9.1 are summarized as advertising elasticities in Table 9.2. (The stocks measure reflects the percentage changes in current consumption due to a 1 percent change in the stock of advertising goodwill, *ceteris paribus*. These stocks are computed from equations (9.10), (9.11), and (9.12) using the dynamic stocks quadratic terms from Table 9.1. In contrast, the current period elasticity (which via (9.12) has a weight of one) reflects the percentage change in current consumption due to a 1 percent change in current advertising, *ceteris paribus.* Hence, these measures are not discounted for future consumption induced by current advertising. These elasticities are moderately robust with respect to magnitudes across equations with some exceptions (e.g., TWAC current period, own-advertising elasticity for butter). Unfortunately, they are also quite robust with respect to signs that are exactly opposite to most researchers' prior expectations, i.e., negative own- and positive cross-advertising effects for butter and margarine. Similar results were obtained using 1972–86 data, first (vs. fourth) difference specifications with/without trend terms, with/without quarterly dummy variables, and with/without imposing the curvature restrictions. Either this general demand systems approach is seriously flawed, or these data are trying to tell us something!

Aside from these somewhat negative results, the estimated dynamics in the advertising stocks are quite interesting. The estimated magnitudes are fairly robust across the alternative specifications: butter −1.1, margarine 0.0 (exception: UAWC, −0.9), shortening −2.4 to −2.8, and salad oils −1.5 to −2.1. Referring to Figure 9.4, these results indicate that the dynamic specification used is capable of identifying geometric decay (i.e., when the quadratic term is 0.0 as in the case of margarine) as well as lagged peaks in the advertising/sales response. Thus, for example, butter advertising was found to attain its peak impact within two to three months, to decay and cease by the third quarter. Margarine decays immediately and virtually ceases within one quarter. Shortening and salad oils, in contrast, have very small initial advertising impacts, which increase rapidly, peak within four to six months, then decay quite rapidly and cease by the third quarter.

While the assumed functional form is unquestionably imposing quite a bit of structure on the shape of these estimated advertising/sales response surfaces, this type of approach appears promising. Given the competitive response by the margarine industry evidenced by Figure 9.2 during much of the period analyzed, researchable questions concerning the advertising media mix arise. Quick hitting competitive messages and/or vigorous price/promotions via print media might yield relatively rapid advertising/sales decay. Also, the degree of price competition between brands could induce relatively quick advertising decay; i.e., if there was little brand loyalty and lots of price induced switching between brands. In contrast, if there was a clearly dominant brand in a category such as Crisco in shortening and salad oils, then one might expect this stronger brand loyalty (and perhaps a different media mix and message) to be manifest as a relatively longer delayed peak in the advertising sales response. Further research might explore the feasibility of disentangling competitive, cross-commodity advertising sales response by type of media.

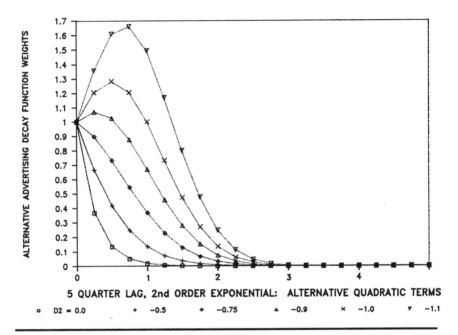

Figure 9.4. Hypothetical advertising stocks decay functions.

## Summary and Conclusions

A household production framework is used to motivate an advertising induced, commodity augmentation model of structural change. Dynamic cross-commodity advertising effects are estimated with quarterly data (1978–86) under unrestricted, additive (translating), and multiplicative (scaling) augmentation hypotheses using a fourth difference (seasonally adjusted) Rotterdam demand specification. Both of the latter hypotheses are nonlinear nested within an unrestricted model, hence amenable to nonlinear hypotheses tests. Both hypotheses are rejected by these data in the results presented. Results from the 1972–86 period, however, indicate failure to reject scaling and marginal rejections of translating. A second-order exponential with five lags is used for the specification of advertising stocks of butter, margarine, shortening, and salad oils. This dynamic stock specification flexibly allows for a geometric or lagged peak decay function, an issue of considerable conceptual and empirical interest in the literature. The fairly robust results indicate a lagged peak advertising sales response for butter (two to three months), shortening (four to six months), and salad oils (four to six months), but a rapid (within one quarter) geometric decay for margarine. Each of these dynamic stock measures is estimated in each equation to allow for theoretically consistent cross-commodity advertising effects.

The procedures used are unable to find a positive impact of DBC butter advertising on butter consumption over the time period analyzed. Similar results were found across several alternative specifications of log-differential Rotterdam type demand systems (with second-order exponential stocks) prior to the results presented. Given similar difficulties with these data using translog and AIDS specifications, I consider these results to be relatively robust. Thus, despite the casual inferences based on Figures 9.1–9.3 that would support the conclusion that the DBC butter program successfully offset a declining trend in butter consumption, the *ceteris paribus* demand system results suggest that, on average across the 1978–86 period, butter advertising and consumption are inversely related.

Considering that a key *ceteris paribus* factor, health/diet induced concerns about cholesterol from animal fats such as butter, is not explicitly accounted for in this research (the intercept/trends term for butter was found to be negative, however), these results may not be unrealistic. *If* a very large stock of negative messages or "bad will" based on moderately reputable sources (correctly or incorrectly, such as medical journals and family physicians) has accumulated over time, *and if* your goodwill messages are unable to overcome this countervailing bad will on a sustained basis as new research and other band wagon effects occur, then it seems quite reasonable that certain messages could have an effect just the opposite of their intention and desired effect. That is, targeted advertising might induce recall of the product category (table spreads/fats), but is unable to surmount the negativity that, rightly or wrongly, is associated with the product. Hence, the recall merely serves to reinforce the "bad will." As a result, despite what Figures 9.1–9.3 might suggest as obviously successful dimensions to the DBC butter advertising over the 1978–86 period, those successful dimensions do not average out in a positive fashion when holding *ceteris paribus* an admittedly limited set of relevant factors via a demand system.

A primary motivation for the systems approach concerns correct specification of the *ceteris paribus* demand context within which to isolate the impacts of advertising. In particular, the demand systems approach provides a theoretically consistent way to specify own- and cross-commodity advertising effects in addition to the more familiar own- and cross-price and income effects. While the familiar homogeneity restriction can be imposed in a single-equation framework, adding-up and, more importantly, Slutsky symmetry require a systems context. Since the Slutsky restrictions are required for demand functions to be integrable back to an expenditure function, which in turn can be used to construct a consistent utility function, the cross-equation Slutsky relationships give a complete list of the restrictions imposed by the utility maximization hypothesis (Varian 1978, pp. 100–101). Thus, Slutsky symmetry is the crucial implication of demand theory. This suggests that disciplinary progress through inductively based research on the issues of advertising's impacts on commodity demands requires a systems framework.

On the other hand, inductively based disciplinary research is only one of several types of legitimate and appropriate knowledge generating activities we pursue. Quite often a recalcitrant reality fails to confirm our theoretical formulations. For example, ad hoc single-equation formulations may outperform theoretically consistent formulations in terms of predictive power and intuitively plausible results. Since much of our research on generic commodity advertising concerns evaluation of its effectiveness for either marketing board management and/or congressional oversight purposes, the predictive power of competing formulations is important. Unfortunately, relatively accurate, single-equation predictive models can also give very biased estimates of dynamic response in general (see Anderson and Blundell 1982), and of the nature, shape, and duration of the advertising/sales response in particular. Multiple, competing maintained hypotheses (i.e., implicit structure), with very different implications concerning advertising effectiveness, can be found to rationalize the data equally well using conventional goodness of fit tests. To me it seems that we require considerable detail and attention to the testing of the often highly nonlinear, competing dynamic specifications.

Aside from *explicitly* imposing necessary a priori structure on the objective (utility, indirect utility, expenditure) or demand functions, the benefits of deriving structural inferences on the advertising effects motivated from the general conceptual model are primarily to generate inductive insights concerning a complex measurement problem. Thus, the derivation of additional structure (implied restrictions) about advertising effects using a theoretically consistent demand system can reduce data needs, facilitate hypothesis testing, and, hopefully, increase statistical precision concerning these effects. This dimension of advertising/consumption response methodology is largely unexplored in the empirical literature. Hence, at the cost of being more explicit about the structure imposed on a problem to make it empirically tractable, we may be able to gain inductive insights and more precision in our estimates by exploring these types of restrictions more fully.

# 10 Performance of the AIDS Model for Advertising Evaluation: Results Based on Canadian Data

HUI-SHUNG CHANG and HENRY W. KINNUCAN

Empirical demand relationships form the cornerstone of modern economic evaluation of generic advertising programs for food commodities (e.g., Goddard and Amuah 1989; Kinnucan and Forker 1986; Liu and Forker 1988; Ward and Dixon 1989). As such it is desirable that these demand relationships be grounded in theory. Recent developments in consumer demand theory have led to functional forms for demand equations that are estimative and yet retain desirable theoretical properties. One such set of equations is the Almost Ideal Demand System (Blanciforti and Green 1983). This chapter reports the results of using the AIDS specification for evaluating Canada's butter advertising program. The advertising campaign is also evaluated using a nonsystem (ad hoc) model for comparison purposes.

The analysis is similar to that discussed by Cox in Chapter 10 in that butter is considered in the context of the fats and oils grouping and quarterly time series data are used. An important difference, however, is that the empirical results presented in this study are based on a longer time period (1973–86 versus 1978–86 used by Cox).

Other related work includes a demand systems analysis of fats and oils advertising based on a translog indirect utility function (Goddard and Amuah 1989), a study of the impact of Dairy Bureau of Canada butter advertising on the demand structure for Canadian fats and oils (Chang and Kinnucan 1990), and a study of the relative impacts of advertising, health information, and economic factors on Canadian butter consumption patterns (Chang and Kinnucan 1991). This study adds to the literature by focusing on the methodological issue of how results might be affected by functional form selection. Specifically, we seek to determine whether inferences drawn from an empirical demand system based on neoclassical demand theory are consistent with inferences drawn from a nonsystem specification. The findings should shed light on the strengths and shortcomings of each approach for program evaluation and policy analysis.

A brief discussion of the relevant economic literature on advertising precedes the presentation of the AIDS and nonsystem models, data, and the respective empirical results. The chapter closes with a summary of our findings and some concluding comments about using theory-based systems for advertising evaluation.

## The Economics of Advertising

Studies on the economics of advertising focus mainly on two aspects: (1) determination of the optimal scale of advertising expenditures, and (2) measurement of the effectiveness of advertising and the effects of advertising on the structure, conduct, and performance of the market. In this section, the impact of advertising on consumer demand and on the market is briefly reviewed.

Classical static demand theory assumes perfect information and constant tastes. However, consumers frequently possess less-than-perfect information; moreover, tastes may change as consumers receive better information or experience changes in their environments, such as their sociodemographic backgrounds. Therefore, in addition to prices and income, one should also take into account the composition and dynamics of the consumers preference fields.

Variable preferences, or changing tastes, imply an alteration in the form of the ordinal utility function or indifference map. In this case, parameters of the utility function are postulated to depend on some state variables such as consumers' stock of knowledge as well as internal and external factors. As state variable changes, so do the parameters of the utility function, which result in changes in the preferences and behavior of consumers. A system of Marshallian demand equations can be derived from the constrained utility maximization problem. The resulting comparative dynamics include the effects of a change in prices, income, and state variables on quantities demanded. That is,

$$x_y = \{\partial x/\partial y\} \tag{10.1}$$

$$X_p = K - x_y x' \quad \text{and} \tag{10.2}$$

$$X_s = \{\partial x/\partial s\} = -1/\lambda KV \tag{10.3}$$

The first two equations indicate consumers' responses to a change in prices and income. The third equation indicates how consumers' behavior is affected by a change in the state variables. $\lambda$ is the marginal utility of money, $K$ is the Slutsky substitution matrix, and $V = \{\partial^2 U/\partial x \partial s\}$. Rewriting equation (10.3) in scalar notation, one obtains

$$\partial x_i/\partial s_j = -1/\lambda \; \Sigma_k K_{ik}\{\partial^2 U/\partial x_k \partial s_j\} \tag{10.4}$$

Equation (10.4) says that the effect of the additional exogenous variable, such as advertising, on demand for good $i$ depends on three things: the effect of advertising for good $i$ on the marginal utility of all the goods in the system, the substitutability between good $i$ and any other good in the system, and the marginal utility of money. This expression implies that advertising's effect is multifaceted, and its effect on demand, which may be positive or negative, has to be determined empirically.

Alternatively, equation (10.4) can be written in elasticity terms,

$$\Sigma_i w_i \, e_{i,sj} = 0 \tag{10.5}$$

where $w_i$'s are expenditure shares and $e_{i,sj}$'s are cross-advertising elasticities for good $i$ with respect to a change in the advertising $j$. Equation (10.5) implies that advertising causes no changes other than a reallocation of budget shares, given that only good $j$ is advertised. Equation (10.5) also serves as an additional restriction on demand equations resulting from the presence of advertising and can be tested or imposed similarly to homogeneity and symmetry restrictions.

The effects of advertising on consumer behavior can also be analyzed through a duality approach in which consumers minimize their total expenditures subject to a predetermined utility level. The duality approach has the advantage of simplifying the derivation of demand equations while preserving the structure of consumer behavior. To account for taste changes, a static expenditure function can be extended to include the dynamic effects of state variables by making parameters of the expenditure function dependent on state variables — a procedure similar to that applied to utility functions discussed earlier. All the restrictions implied by the extended utility maximization problem carry over.

Now, let us see how advertising works in the market. Advertising is intended to shift the demand curve outward; however, the slopes of demand curves may also change. The question is: Under what conditions would advertising make demand more or less elastic? Two schools of thought have emerged with respect to this question (e.g., Albion and Farris 1981). One school views advertising as a form of persuasion that creates product differentiation, thereby making the demand curve less elastic and leading to higher prices. The other school maintains that advertising provides additional information to consumers,which enhances competition, making demand curves more elastic and leading to lower prices.

Economists also possess divergent views on the relationship between advertising and consumers' utility functions and hence their behavior. For example, some hold that advertising changes consumer tastes directly as a shift variable (e.g., Basmann 1956; Dixit and Norman 1978) while others argue that advertising changes tastes indirectly by providing external information (Phlips 1983; Nelson 1974). Still others think of advertising in terms of its impact on household consumption technologies (Stigler and Becker 1977) or perceptions of product quality (Kotowitz and Mathewson 1979).

## The LA/AIDS Model

The AIDS model of Deaton and Muellbauer (1980) is generated from a cost or expenditure function of Gorman polar form; therefore, it aggregates consistently across individuals. Moreover, it is of flexible functional form, allowing testing of theoretical restrictions on demand equations. The AIDS model in share form for a group of $n$ commodities can be written as

$$w_i = \alpha_i + \Sigma_j \, r_{ij} \ln p_j + \beta_i \ln (y/P) \qquad i = 1, 2, \ldots, n \qquad (10.6)$$

where $\ln P$ is defined as

$$\ln P = \alpha_0 + \Sigma_j \, \alpha_j \ln p_j + \tfrac{1}{2}\Sigma_i\Sigma_j \, r_{ij} \ln p_i \ln p_j \qquad (10.7)$$

To introduce advertising effects, the $\alpha_i$'s in equation (10.6) are postulated to depend on advertising (Green 1985),

$$\alpha_i = a_i + \Sigma_j\Sigma_k \, b_{j,k} A_{j,t\text{-}k} \qquad (10.8)$$

where $A_{j,t\text{-}k}$ denotes own-advertising expenditures for $i = j$ and competitors' advertising expenditures for $i \neq j$. $A_{j,t\text{-}k}$ denotes current advertising expenditures for $k = 0$ and lagged advertising for $k \neq 0$. Alternatively, $A_{j,t\text{-}k}$ may represent a stock of goodwill or stock of knowledge created by advertising to account for the carryover effects of advertising. In this case, a function needs to be specified showing how stocks of goodwill or knowledge accumulate (Nerlove and Arrow 1962; Kinnucan and Forker 1986).

To avoid nonlinearities, one common practice is to estimate a linear approximating version of the AIDS model. That is, instead of estimating the complete AIDS model specified in equation (10.6), its linear approximation is employed by replacing ln $P$ with ln $P^*$. ln $P^*$ is the Stone index defined as ln $P^* = \Sigma_i w_i$ ln $p_i$. Estimation problems associated with this approximation are discussed in Blanciforti and Green 1983. With the incorporation of advertising effects, the linear approximation of the AIDS model (LA/AIDS) is

$$w_i = (a_i + \Sigma_j \Sigma_k b_{jk} A_{j,t-k}) + \Sigma_j r_{ij} \ln p_j + \beta_i \ln (y/P^*) \qquad (10.9)$$

In equation (10.9), $w_i$ is the $i$th budget share; $r_{ij}$ is the income-compensated price effect; $b_{j,k}$ ($i = j$) is the own-advertising effect; $b_{j,k}$ ($i \neq j$) is the cross-advertising effect; and $\beta_i$ represents the change in the $i$th budget share with respect to a percentage change in the real total group expenditure, holding prices and advertising expenditures constant.

In applying equation (10.9) to the Canadian fats and oils market, several assumptions are made. First, we assume that fats and oils products are separable as a group from other food and nonfood items. Second, advertising is postulated to provide and change the state of information or stocks of knowledge consumers have about a product, such as its availability, price, and characteristics. This, in turn, changes the information-dependent parameters of the utility function and results in changes in preferences and behavior of consumers.

## DATA AND ESTIMATION PROCEDURES

Data available for estimation are quantities consumed of butter, margarine, shortening oils, and salad oils and associated price indices and advertising expenditures. The observation period covers the second quarter of 1973 through the third quarter of 1986. Advertising expenditures for margarine, shortening oils, and salad oils were mostly branded advertising compiled by Elliot Research and Media Measurement Institute, Toronto. Advertising expenditures for butter, beginning the third quarter of 1978, represent generic advertising paid for by the Dairy Bureau of Canada. Data on sales of fats and oils were obtained from monthly data compiled from Statistics Canada catalog 32-006. These data comprise both domestic and industrial use of fats and oils. Population, prices, and price indices were obtained from Statistics Canada catalogs 91-201 and 62-010, respectively.

The error terms for each equation are assumed to be identically, independently, and normally distributed but contemporaneously correlated across equations. The linear approximation of the AIDS was estimated by iterative seemingly unrelated regression (SUR) after excluding the salad oil equation. The coefficients were estimated with symmetry and homogeneity conditions imposed and all the elasticities were derived based on the complete AIDS model.

## RESULTS

Estimated price coefficients in general are significant but a number of them do not have the expected sign (Table 10.1). For example, the own-price coefficients, which should have the same sign as the income-compensated own-price effects in the AIDS model, are all positive, violating the law of demand. The preponderance of negative signs for cross-price effects suggests goods in the fats and oils grouping are complements rather than substitutes, a counterintuitive (but not implausible) result. The lack of significance of the cross-price effects for butter and margarine suggests these two goods are independent, contradicting other empirical findings (e.g., Goddard and Amuah 1989; Chang and Kinnucan 1990, 1991).

The estimated expenditure coefficients have conflicting signs and are not significant at usual probability levels. Note that because the income elasticity is obtained by multiplying the expenditure elasticity by its marginal budget share elasticity with respect to a change in income (Barten 1977), the insignificance of the expenditure coefficients implies insignificance of the corresponding income elasticities as well. Thus, according to these estimates, the demand for fats and oil products in Canada is not influenced by income.

Estimated advertising coefficients in general are not significant. Two exceptions are the advertising coefficients for butter lagged two and lagged three periods. Taken together, an $F$-test indicates the current and lagged coefficients of butter advertising are significant at the 5 percent level. The implied long-run advertising elasticity, however, is negative ($-0.02347$).

Less acceptable is the suggestion that butter advertising, which is generic in type, caused the demand for butter to decrease. Nonetheless, demand theory as developed above (see equation (10.4)) does not require the own-advertising effect to be positive; therefore, these results are not implausible. Moreover, since the direction of causality from advertising to sales was not established in this study, the results suggest only a negative correlation, not cause and effect, between sales and advertising.

A matrix of price elasticities shows an own-price elasticity for butter of $-0.74$, indicating butter is a normal good and the demand is price inelastic (Table 10.2). Own-price elasticity estimates for the remaining three products, however, are positive. The preponderance of negative signs for the off-diagonal elements indicates fats and oils products interact as gross comple-

**Table 10.1 Estimated coefficients for the LA/AIDS model**

| Variable | Butter | Margarine | Shortening |
|---|---|---|---|
| RADM | -0.33425E-06 | -0.10077E-05 | 0.79855E-06 |
| | (-0.35)[a] | (-1.26) | (1.12) |
| RADBD | b | -0.00930 | 0.00295 |
| | | (-1.33) | (0.46) |
| RADS | 0.41429E-05 | -0.18176E-05 | -0.69269E-06 |
| | (1.42) | (-0.80) | (-0.42) |
| RADO | -0.22525E-05 | 0.51158E-06 | 0.20757E-05 |
| | (-0.90) | (0.26) | (1.42) |
| RADB | -0.11825E-06 | b | b |
| | (-0.22) | | |
| RADB1 | 0.13020E-06 | b | b |
| | (0.24) | | |
| RADB2 | -0.87363E-06 | b | b |
| | (-1.66) | | |
| RADB3 | -0.14824E-05 | b | b |
| | (-2.98) | | |
| RADB4 | 0.81823E-06 | b | b |
| | (1.63) | | |
| RADB5 | 0.76687E-06 | b | b |
| | (1.41) | | |
| RADB6 | 0.37847E-06 | b | b |
| | (0.70) | | |
| RADB7 | -0.20305E-07 | b | b |
| | (-0.036) | | |
| RADB8 | -0.10172E-05 | b | b |
| | (-1.55) | | |
| D1 | -0.02575 | 0.02786 | -0.02141 |
| | (-1.91) | (2.59) | (-2.56) |
| D2 | -0.01595 | 0.78182E-03 | 0.00312 |
| | (-1.05) | (0.06) | (0.34) |
| D3 | -0.01210 | -0.00803 | 0.01003 |
| | (-0.91) | (-0.77) | (1.32) |
| RPB | 0.09589 | 0.013343 | -0.08248 |
| | (2.14) | (0.39) | (-2.51) |
| RPM | 0.01334 | 0.32244 | -0.12312 |
| | (0.39) | (5.96) | (-2.41) |
| RPS | -0.08248 | -0.12312 | 0.20440 |
| | (-2.52) | (-2.42) | (2.79) |
| RPO | -0.02676 | -0.21266 | 0.00120 |
| | (-1.30) | (-4.46) | (0.02) |
| TEXP | -0.02761 | 0.03771 | -0.04679 |
| | (-0.29) | (0.49) | (-0.82) |
| CONSTANT | 0.44889 | 0.15755 | 0.33665 |
| | (2.08) | (0.93) | (2.68) |

[a]Figures in parentheses are $t$-values.
[b]Variable does not appear in the equation.

ments in the consumer allocation process. As noted above, margarine and butter are shown to be independent goods.

Table 10.2  Calculated price elasticities for the LA/AIDS model[a]

| Variable | Butter | Margarine | Shortening | Salad oil |
|---|---|---|---|---|
| Butter | -0.74288 | 0.04464[b] | -0.17379 | -0.06299 |
| Margarine | -0.01766[b] | 0.13020 | -0.48435 | -0.76357 |
| Shortening | -0.28001 | -0.53172 | 0.02524 | 0.00553 |
| Salad oils | -0.53694[b] | -2.65449 | -0.12370[b] | 1.87268 |

[a]All elasticities are evaluated at sample means.
[b]Not significant.

Seasonality appears to be a factor in fats and oils consumption. Specifically, consumption of butter and shortening oils is smaller and consumption of margarine is greater in the first quarter than in the fourth.

The counterintuitive results obtained from the LA/AIDS model may be an indication of model misspecification. First, the LA/AIDS may not be a good approximation to the original AIDS model, given the structure of the Canadian fats and oils market. Second, consumption of fats and oils may consist of too small a portion in the consumer's budget to be compatible with a multistage budgeting process. That is, the weak separability assumption implicit in the demand subsystems approach may not be realistic given the disaggregated nature of the fats and oils grouping.

## The Nonsystems Approach

The nonsystems demand model is specified as follows:

$$QB = a1 + m1*RADM + s1*RADS + o1*RADO + x1*D1 + y1*D2$$
$$+ z1*D3 + c11*RPB + c12*RPM + k1*TEXP + bp1*ADBB$$
$$+ \Sigma_k b_k * RADB_{t-k} \tag{10.10}$$

$$QM = a2 + m2*RADM + s2*RADS + o2*RADO + x2*D1 + y2*D2$$
$$+ z2*D3 + c21*RPB + c22*RPM + k2*TEXP + mp2*ADMM$$
$$+ b2*RADBD \tag{10.11}$$

$$QS = a3 + m3*RADM + s3*RADS + o3*RADO + x3*D1 + y3*D2$$
$$+ z3*D3 + c33*RPS + k3*TEXP + sp3*ADSS + b3*RADBD$$
$$\text{and} \tag{10.12}$$

$$QO = a4 + m4*RADM + s4*RADS + o4*RADO + x4*D1 + y4*D2$$
$$+ z4*D3 + c44*RPO + k4*TEXP + op4*ADOO + b4*RADBD$$
$$(10.13)$$

Equations (10.10)–(10.13) are per capita demand, in pounds, for butter (QB), margarine (QM), shortening oils (QS), and salad oils (QO), respectively. Symbols in capital letters are variables which are defined in the Appendix; symbols in lower case are parameters to be estimated. Prices are expressed in natural logarithms.

Notice that equations (10.10)–(10.13), unlike the LA/AIDS model, contain different sets of prices. This avoids multicollinearity among prices and focuses attention on the competition between butter and margarine. In both the butter and margarine equations, prices for butter and margarine are included, whereas only the own-price is included for shortening and salad oils.

The butter equation also differs from the other equations in that an eight-quarter lag is specified for butter advertising. This lag period was selected based on previous research relating to generic advertising of manufactured dairy products (Kinnucan and Fearon 1986). In addition, a dummy variable defining the period of Dairy Bureau of Canada generic butter advertising is specified in the margarine, shortening, and salad oil equations. This specification has the advantage of simplicity in that it provides a direct means of testing whether the commencement of generic butter advertising 1978 had an impact on the related fats and oils products.

Finally, the nonsystem model differs from the AIDS specification in that no restriction is imposed and the dependent variable is measured as the level of consumption in the nonsystem model.

## DATA AND ESTIMATION PROCEDURES

The data used to estimate the nonsystem model are identical to the data used to estimate the LA/AIDS model. Based on preliminary tests showing no autocorrelation or heteroscedasticity in any of the equations, the error structure for the four equations as a system was assumed to be identically, independently, and normally distributed. The error terms, however, are assumed to be correlated across equations because demand for these commodities are likely to be influenced by unknown factors common to them all. The four equations were then estimated by iterative SUR. Unless otherwise stated, statistical significance is determined using a simple $t$-test and a 5 percent probability level.

## RESULTS

The estimates for the expenditure coefficients are all positive and significant (Table 10.3). The associated expenditure elasticities (reported in Table 10.4) are 0.90, 1.15, 0.72, and 1.22 for butter, margarine, shortening oils, and salad oils, respectively.

**Table 10.3 Estimated coefficients for the nonsystem model**

| Variable | Butter | Margarine | Shortening | Salad oil |
|---|---|---|---|---|
| RADM | -0.11935E-05 | 0.82676E-05 | 0.26151E-05 | -0.27446E-05 |
| | (-0.17)[a] | (0.78) | (0.46) | (-0.50) |
| RADBD | b | -0.31063 | 0.04935 | 0.28534 |
| | | (-4.77) | (0.88) | (5.07) |
| RADS | 0.21493E-04 | -0.44221E-04 | 0.31679E-04 | 0.22200E-04 |
| | (0.96) | (-1.79) | (0.78) | (1.41) |
| RADO | -0.79384E-05 | 0.76536E-05 | 0.17034E-04 | -0.16183E-04 |
| | (-0.41) | (0.35) | (1.17) | (-0.59) |
| RADB | -0.29718E-05 | b | b | b |
| | (-1.78) | | | |
| RADB1 | -0.15132E-05 | b | b | b |
| | (-1.23) | | | |
| RADB2 | 0.30595E-06 | b | b | b |
| | (0.26) | | | |
| ADB3 | -0.10708E-05 | b | b | b |
| | (-1.08) | | | |
| RADB4 | 0.11670E-05 | b | b | b |
| | (1.15) | | | |
| RADB5 | 0.543010E-06 | b | b | b |
| | (0.46) | | | |
| RADB6 | 0.11927E-05 | b | b | b |
| | (1.02) | | | |
| RADB7 | 0.50826E-05 | b | b | b |
| | (3.89) | | | |
| RADB8 | 0.25211E-05 | b | b | b |
| | (1.81) | | | |
| D1 | -0.18650 | 0.17747 | -0.24525 | 0.25415 |
| | (-1.84) | (1.53) | (-3.04) | (3.23) |
| D2 | -0.08315 | -0.14861 | 0.02581 | 0.20948 |
| | (-0.71) | (-1.13) | (0.28) | (2.38) |
| D3 | -0.09430 | -0.15664 | 0.07425 | 0.16774 |
| | (-0.91) | (-1.35) | (0.94) | (2.18) |
| RPB | -3.5891 | 4.0121 | b | b |
| | (-2.84) | (3.31) | | |
| RPM | 0.72223 | -1.0325 | b | b |
| | (2.06) | (-2.90) | | |
| RPS | b | b | -0.33291 | b |
| | | | (-2.04) | |

**Table 10.3 (cont.)**

| Variable | Butter | Margarine | Shortening | Salad oil |
|---|---|---|---|---|
| RPO | b | b | b | -0.33394<br>(-1.59) |
| TEXP | 2.2495<br>(3.10) | 3.6115<br>(4.40) | 1.6285<br>(2.90) | 1.4704<br>(2.67) |
| ADBB | 0.16978E-05<br>(3.02) | b | b | b |
| ADMM | b | -0.74526E-05<br>(-1.03) | b | b |
| ADSS | b | b | -0.26266E-04<br>(-0.74) | b |
| ADOO | b | b | b | -0.21628E-05<br>(-0.07) |
| CONSTANT | 0.10179<br>(0.06) | -6.9879<br>(-3.55) | -1.3398<br>(-1.09) | -2.3155<br>(-1.92) |

[a]Figures in parentheses are $t$-values.
[b]Variable does not appear in the equation.

Estimated own-price coefficients are all negative and significant. In terms of own-price elasticities, we obtained a value of $-1.42$ for butter, $-0.36$ for margarine, $-0.17$ for shortening oils, and $-0.28$ for salad oils (Table 10.4). Contrary to the LA/AIDS estimates, these elasticities indicate all goods in the fats and oils grouping are normal. Moreover, demand for butter is shown to be price elastic while demand for the other three products is price inelastic. An elastic demand implies the existence of close substitutes. Practical reasoning suggests margarine represents such a substitute for butter.

**Table 10.4  Own-price expenditure and own-advertising elasticities for the nonsystems model[a]**

| | Own-price<br>elasticity | Expenditure<br>elasticity | Own-advertising<br>elasticity |
|---|---|---|---|
| Butter | -1.42253 | 0.89682 | 0.02280 |
| Margarine | -0.35663 | 1.15318 | 0.00575[b] |
| Shortening | -0.17198 | 0.72086 | 0.00587[b] |
| Salad oil | -0.28364 | 1.22074 | -0.07388[b] |

[a]All elasticities are evaluated at sample means.
[b]Not significant.

Estimated cross-price effects are significant and positive in sign (Table

10.3). The associated cross-price elasticities are 0.299 for butter with respect to the price of margarine and 1.28 for margarine with respect to the price of butter. These results indicate margarine is a close substitute for butter but butter is a relatively weak substitute for margarine. This result is consistent with the fact that butter in Canada is almost twice as expensive as margarine, implying a larger relative price effect when the price of butter increases than when the price of margarine increases. The cross-price elasticity estimates are also consistent with the notion that butter demand is price elastic while margarine demand is price inelastic. The corresponding income-compensated cross-price elasticities are 0.59 and 1.90.

Estimated coefficients of the advertising expenditure variables are not significant in the case of margarine, shortening, and salad oils. A number of the individual advertising coefficients for butter are not significant. An $F$-test, however, indicates that the long run effect of butter advertising (the sum of current and lagged coefficients) is significant at the 1 percent level. The estimated long-run effect, moreover, is positive. The associated long-run advertising elasticity of 0.0228 compares well with estimates obtained in other studies of generic advertising of food commodities (Kinnucan and Forker 1986; Ward and Dixon 1989). The lack of significance of advertising variable for goods other than butter suggests that advertising for these products, mostly the branded type, is not effective at expanding market share for the respective product categories. This result is acceptable on the ground that branded advertising is designed to expand the market shares of individual firms, not product categories.

The estimated coefficient of the binary variable to indicate the period of butter advertising (RADBD) is significant for margarine and salad oils but not shortening. The signs of the RADBD coefficients indicate the commencement of butter advertising in 1978 by the Dairy Bureau of Canada is associated with a decrease in the per capita consumption of margarine but an increase in per capita consumption of salad oils.

Estimated coefficients of the cross-product terms of price and advertising are positive and significant for butter but insignificant for the remaining three products. A positive coefficient for the interaction term means that advertising makes demand less price elastic. The positive coefficient for butter, therefore, implies that advertising has made the demand for butter less price elastic.

According to the two schools of thought, informative advertising makes demand more price elastic while persuasive advertising makes demand less price elastic. But are we willing to conclude that the butter advertising campaign was persuasive rather than informative? Probably not, since there may be other explanations for obtaining such a result.

## Conclusions

Results suggest inferences about the economic impacts of commodity advertising programs are sensitive to the functional specification of the empirical demand relations. The (linear approximate) AIDS specification indicated (1) the demand curves for all commodities in the fats and oils grouping except butter are upward sloping, (2) the demand for fats and oils products in Canada is not influenced by income, (3) margarine and butter are neither complementary nor substitute goods, and (4) advertising has no impact on the market shares of the respective product categories in the fats and oils grouping.

The nonsystem specification, by contrast, indicated (1) the demand curves for all products in the fats and oils grouping are downward sloping, (2) the demand for fats and oils products in Canada *is* influenced by income, (3) margarine and butter are substitutes, and (4) advertising increased the demand for butter but not the other fats and oils products.

A basic difference between the AIDS and nonsystem specifications is the definition of the dependent variable. In the AIDS model the dependent variable is specified in share form whereas in the nonsystem model the dependent variable is specified as the *level* of consumption. This difference may explain the inability of the AIDS model in our application to produce results consistent with economic logic. In any case, the results suggest caution must be exercised in using the AIDS specification for commodity advertising evaluation purposes.

One interpretation of the poor performance of the AIDS specification is that the underlying theory is inadequate for explaining consumer response to information. A more detailed theory may be necessary, perhaps one based on theories of buyer behavior advanced in the marketing literature. (For references and an application of such a theory to commodity advertising, see Kinnucan and Venkateswaran 1990.) But clearly more research is needed to determine whether existing demand systems specifications are suitable for commodity advertising evaluation.

# Appendix

## Description of variables used in the econometric equations

| Variable | Definition |
| --- | --- |
| QB | Per capita consumption of butter |
| QM | Per capita consumption of margarine |
| QS | Per capita consumption of shortening oil |
| QO | Per capita consumption of salad oil |
| RADM | Real[a] advertising expenditure for margarine |
| RADS | Real advertising expenditure for shortening oil |
| RADO | Real advertising expenditure for salad oil |
| RADB | Real advertising expenditure for butter |
| $RADB_{t-k}$ | RADB lagged $k$ periods, $k = 1,2, \ldots ,8$ |
| D1 | Seasonal dummy variable, 1 for the first quarter; 0, otherwise |
| D2 | Seasonal dummy variable, 1 for the second quarter; 0, otherwise |
| D3 | Seasonal dummy variable, 1 for the third quarter; 0, otherwise |
| RADBD | Dummy variable for the introduction of butter advertising, 1 for 1978:3 to 1986:3; 0, otherwise |
| RPB | Real price of butter per pound, in logarithms |
| RPM | Real price of margarine per pound, in logarithms |
| RPS | Real price of shortening oil per pound, in logarithms |
| RPO | Real price of salad oil per pound, in logarithms |
| TEXP | Total group expenditure for fats and oils, in logarithms |
| ADBB | Cross-product term of advertising and price for butter |
| ADMM | Cross-product term of advertising and price for margarine |
| ADSS | Cross-product term of advertising and price for shortening oil |
| ADOO | Cross-product term of advertising and price for salad oil |
| CONSTANT | A vector of ones |

[a]"Real" means the variable in question is deflated by the Consumer Price Index (1981 = 100).

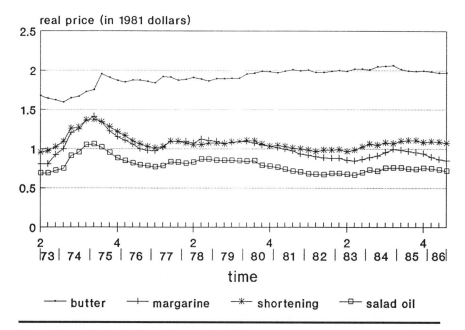

**Figure 10.1. Prices for Canadian fats and oils.**

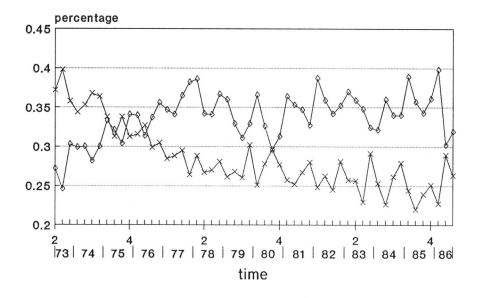

**Figure 10.2. Quantity shares for butter and margarine.**

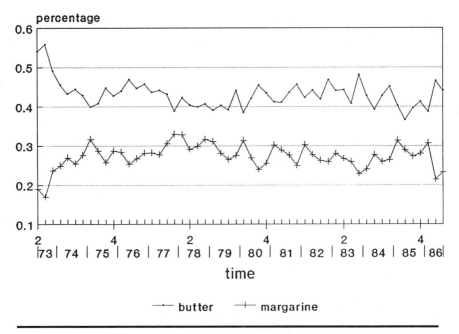

Figure 10.3. Expenditure shares for butter and margarine.

# 11 Discussion: Incorporating Advertising into Demand Systems

## DERMOT HAYES

The literature pertaining to the development and estimation of demand systems is vast. Any sampling of this literature will convince the reader that some of the brightest agricultural and general economists have spent time incorporating the microeconomic theory of the consumer into tractable models that allow us to estimate the parameters of the consumer preference function. These systems have faults, but they incorporate much of what has been learned by economists since the profession adopted scientific methods. Given today's computer technology, it is possible for any literate person to estimate an ad hoc relationship between quantities and prices. The economist, however, knows something about how the relationship should look and is able to improve upon the ad hoc estimates by imposing this prior structure on the parameters, thereby increasing the efficiency and precision of the results. If we can provide any answers about the usefulness of generic advertising, the obvious place to begin is with the demand systems approach that is the focus of this session.

A second motivation for using these systems lies in the limited data set that we have for this purpose. Given that we can run the experiment only once, it is important to avoid the temptation to search among the distribution of possible parameters to find the results that best appeal to the intuition. Unless we can artificially restrict this search, we would be better off guessing the results in advance. In an excellent article, Leamer (1983) discusses this problem. He argues that, unless we restrict this searching process, we can draw several conclusions from any particular experiment. Demand systems greatly limit our ability to search among alternative models, functional forms, and explanatory variables; and as such, demand systems limit the number of whimsical decisions made, thereby improving the robustness, if not the intuitive appeal, of the results.

A third reason for using a demand system approach is the possibility that consumers have reached a saturation level of consumption. If this theory is true, producers can only increase consumption of their product at the expense of the market share of producers of similar products. Given that the government has begun to use its legislative power to enforce compliance with some of these programs, we must be able to evaluate the cross-advertising effects. If it were shown that pork advertisements are effective only at the expense of chicken and beef consumption, it would be difficult to justify the use of centralized governmental power in what would be a zero sum game.

## Research Needs to be Addressed

There are at least three important research needs that should be addressed in this session. The first need is to conduct research to determine how we should incorporate advertising into a demand system. The second is to determine how to measure cross-advertising effects. Finally, and most importantly, we need to determine whether advertising pays. Considering the available literature, the contributing authors for this session have done an excellent job of addressing the first two needs. Given the available data, I would argue that the third need cannot be met. Consequently, I will include in my final comments a brief overview of the experimental design that would make it possible to determine whether advertising is effective.

### BROWN AND LEE

The paper by Brown and Lee (Chapter 6) begins with a good review of the literature on the use of the Rotterdam model to measure advertising effects. One noticeable omission is the paper by Mountain (1988) referenced in Cox. Brown and Lee cite the standard Ichimura (1951) and Tintner (1952) result relating the effect of advertising on demand to the advertising-induced changes in marginal utilities. This result seems to be the most intuitive way to theoretically incorporate the effect of advertising. Unfortunately, any attempt to measure changes in marginal utility will necessitate the assumption of a cardinal utility function. Possibly for this reason, none of the authors in this session pursues the Ichimura-Tintner result any further. If one were to assume cardinal utility, it would be possible to measure the advertising-induced change in marginal utility by noticing that consumers maintain consumption in the face of higher prices. Here, the condition equating marginal utility to price could be used. Much of the research on risk analysis in agricultural production has been made possible by specifying the functional form of the utility function (i.e., assuming cardinal utility).

Consequently, this condition offers an interesting way to incorporate these effects into models other than the Rotterdam model. Unfortunately, none of the participants in this session chose this approach.

Interestingly, all of the participants chose to use scaling and/or translating to incorporate advertising. Intuitively, scaling assumes that the effect of advertising is to lower the consumer's perception of the per-unit price. Alternatively, one could argue that scaling increases the perceived product *quantity*. Both arguments imply that advertising increases the perceived product value. Slogans such as "10 percent more per carton" or "45 cents off" immediately spring to mind as perfect applications of the scaling principle. However, most generic advertisements are not of this type; rather, many attempt to increase perceived product *quality* or attempt to increase the utility derived from product consumption by positioning it as a product consumed by the rich and healthy. It is not immediately clear that this type of advertising can be viewed as similar to changes in the perceived value of the product. For example, one can imagine a situation in which a health-conscious individual would increase pork consumption in response to the "other white meat" campaign. Yet this same individual might not increase pork consumption in response to price decreases as long as he or she felt that additional pork consumption would be detrimental to their health.

The assumption that motivates translating is that advertisements increase the minimum or price- and income-independent quantity consumed. For example, some milk advertisements emphasize the importance of calcium in the diet. If these advertisements successfully convince consumers that there is a certain minimum level of milk consumption required for good health, then the translating assumption is valid. From personal observation, many consumers feel that they should consume certain minimum quantities of the basic food products. If generic advertisements serve to increase or to slow the rate of decrease of this subsistence level, then translating is a suitable way to incorporate this effect.

Brown and Lee show how each of these terms can be incorporated into the consumer's utility maximization problem and how to derive the relationships between the price and income elasticities and the advertising elasticities. This original research is important in that it provides a theoretical underpinning for predicting the effect of advertising on estimated elasticities. The authors also provide an excellent intuitive discussion of both the scaling and translating effects, individually and combined, on the demand parameters.

Brown and Lee also discuss advertising as a source of information that enhances commodity production in the household production function. The results in this section of the paper are somewhat incomplete; the final form of the proposed demand equations contains a variable that reflects the stock of information at time $t$. Although this variable could reflect information about leisure-time inputs and available capital goods, it is unlikely that sufficient data would be available to satisfactorily estimate the required relationships. The applied economist would be forced to ignore many of the complexities of the process and to include advertising as a shift variable in the demand equation in the same manner as that used for translating. This section, however, is useful in that it makes obvious the difficulties of this approach.

Overall, the paper provides an excellent overview of the known theory on incorporating advertising into demand systems. The authors chose to build on the existing theory rather than to develop new methods of incorporating advertising effects that were specifically designed for generic promotions. Unfortunately, much of the existing literature has been developed for the more traditional type of branded advertising. While it is possible that generic advertising acts in the same way that branded advertising does, it is not guaranteed. Perhaps all that is required is a good motivation of the scaling and translating effects, with intuition and examples based on generic promotional campaigns.

A second minor criticism is that the authors ignore some of the practical difficulties of estimating demand systems. For example, it is difficult to find enough data to estimate a demand system over the entire range of consumption items. If we are to retain enough commodity-specific detail to enable the analysis of a specific campaign, we would be forced to include only a subgroup of possible expenditure items. It is not clear that the budget constraint is binding in this case. Advertising beef, pork, and poultry might increase expenditures on meats. Many of the theoretical restrictions used in the paper (e.g., homogeneity and adding-up) are based on the assumption of a binding budget constraint. If one were to use these results on a subsystem, one would actually impose a zero sum game. If this were truly the case, we already know that the campaigns are not effective from the perspective of the government.

## CHANG AND GREEN

This paper incorporates demographic variables and advertising into an almost ideal demand system (AIDS). As the authors note, this is similar to translating, where the price- and income-dependent component of consumption is the intercept term in the AIDS share equation. The idea here is that certain demographic features may influence this base year share and, by allowing this intercept term to vary with advertising expenditures, the effects of advertising can be incorporated.

I am not sure that one can pick up changes in the own- and cross-price elasticities in this specific case. In the original AIDS paper, Deaton and Muellbauer (1980) do not show how to calculate elasticities from the estimated parameters. It is possible to do this in at least two ways, depending upon whether one uses Stone's price index or the "correct" price index specified in the paper. Chang and Green (Chapter 7) have chosen to use the latter approach to calculate the elasticities and to use Stone's price index to estimate the parameters. The elasticity formulas derived using Stone's price index are

$$\varepsilon_{ii} = -1 + \gamma_{ii}/w_i - \beta_i$$

and

$$\varepsilon_{ij} = \gamma_{ij}/w_i - \beta_i(w_j/w_i)$$

Obviously, none of these formulas depends on the intercept term; consequently, they are independent of the translating effects of advertising. Chang and Green are fully aware of this debate. I understand that Richard Green has done more research in this area.

The authors estimate a cross-sectional time-series model of the U.S. food expenditure system. The cross-sectional information comes from the Bureau of Labor Statistics (BLS) expenditure surveys from 1980 to 1984. My understanding is that the BLS used different survey techniques for these surveys; I am not sure that the surveys are all compatible.

Unfortunately, advertising expenditures do not vary across regions in the data. Consequently, advertising is introduced only by the intercept shifter through time. The authors are to be commended for the amount of work involved in manipulating and cleaning this enormous data set. Unfortunately, most of the cross-sectional analysis does not address the immediate needs of this conference. This type of analysis would be useful if some advertising agencies were to randomly assign advertising time across regions.

I am unsure how the different demographic variables varied through time. For cross-sectional time series, one needs data on each explanatory variable in each observation. In the current version of the paper, it is not clear how this was achieved. I realize that the paper is already long; however, I would suggest that the section on data and estimation procedure be expanded greatly. For example, each AIDS equation has 20 estimated parameters, yet the $R^2$s reported are all less than 0.17. Also, it is not clear how the authors corrected for autocorrelation or imposed the theoretical restrictions.

The paper is obviously part of a much greater project. I would suggest that the authors ignore the cross-sectional effects and concentrate on explaining the time-series results in more detail. For example, one would expect to see one intercept shifter for each of the 20 quarterly observations and advertising expenditures.

## GODDARD AND COZZARIN

This paper (Chapter 8) presents results for both scaling (augmenting) and translating (shifting) for both the AIDS and the translog system. Again, the authors are to be commended for the enormous amount of empirical work undertaken.

The study uses 20 annual observations on prices and quantities of 9 annual product categories, which means that there may be some problem with degrees of freedom. For example, in the AIDS model with the translating parameters (equation 8.12), there are 8 prices, 8 advertising effects, and the intercept and expenditure terms. The authors have imposed symmetry, homogeneity, and adding-up on the system, reducing the required degrees of freedom to estimate the entire system from $n + 2n^2 = 136$ to $(2n - 1)(1/2n + 1) + 36 = 111$. The number of observations within the entire system is 160. The ratio of estimated parameters (111) to the number of observations (160) may not be sufficient to justify the use of asymptotic properties of the estimations.

In general, the results from the augmenting approach look good, but those from the translating approach are more problematic. The authors point out that the effects of scaling are intimately linked with the effects of price changes. This link leads to a restriction between the price and advertising terms. When this restriction is imposed, however, all of the own-price elasticities approach $-1$, while the expenditure elasticities approach 1. This interesting result may indicate that scaling is an overly restrictive assumption.

The authors present results that indicate that margarine and butter are complements, which is somewhat counterintuitive. Complementarity is a very common result in this type of model; mostly, it is ignored. A limited amount of information can be drawn from price and consumption data. Quite often, own-price and income effects can explain much of the observed behavior in consumption. Complementarity may be observed because of problems with either the data or the assumptions that underlie the model. For example, we typically assume that prices are given, which is similar to assuming that the supply curve is perfectly elastic. If this is not true, our parameter estimates will exhibit simultaneous equations bias. If supply shocks cause the quantities supplied (and consumed) to move together and if we ignore them on the demand side, we may attribute this unexplained positive correlation between quantities consumed to complementarity. I would encourage the authors to present the standard errors of their elasticities so that the reader can judge the robustness of this result.

Overall, the paper is very well written and well developed. It is surprising that the authors could fit so much useful information into such a short paper.

## COX

The paper by Tom Cox (Chapter 9) is perhaps the most ambitious of the five papers in this section. He examines both scaling and translating within the context of a household production model and develops and estimates a Rotterdam model capable of estimating dynamic advertising effects. The paper's importance lies in the excellent discussion of the econometric procedures used and in the up-to-date review of the literature. There is an enormous amount of technical detail in the paper, and the timeliness of the work and the quality of the thinking make the paper very worthwhile reading. Interestingly, he rejects translating and accepts scaling; however, the results do not strongly support either approach.

## CHANG AND KINNUCAN

This paper (Chapter 10) uses the same data set that Cox uses and the same methodology that Chang and Green use. Chang and Kinnucan show that a structural change has occurred in the Canadian butter market but do not find any significant positive advertising effect. They then estimate a nonsystem model and find such an effect. Using the latter results, they calculate a rate of return to producers from advertising.

The results are a little unsettling for two reasons. First, the nonsystem model has different prices in each equation; obviously, the results would be different had they included the same set of prices in each equation. One wonders how they selected among alternative models.

Second, the reason given for rejecting the AIDS specification was the estimated positive own-price elasticities. This is the same data, albeit over different time periods, used by Goddard and Amuah (1989) and by Cox in his paper included in this book. Neither of these studies indicated the presence of positive own-price elasticities. The authors indicate that the AIDS model performed poorly due to the multicolinearity of prices. One solution to this problem would be to normalize all prices so that they all equalled 1 in the base year. The normalization should be done before the logarithmic transformation but after the shares have been calculated. If severe multicolinearity existed after normalization, one might consider combining both shares and arguing that the evidence suggests that it is the same commodity.

Overall, the authors are to be applauded for the enormous amount of time, work, and thought that went into this paper.

## Final Comments

The authors of the papers presented in this section have accepted a very difficult task in applying the formal theoretical results of demand analysis to the analysis of commodity promotions. All five papers are good applications of the relevant literature to a specific problem.

The results of the four empirical papers are somewhat disappointing. The interested reader will learn how to incorporate and measure advertising effects but will not learn whether advertising pays. The problem lies in the very poor data the authors have used, yet this is the best data available. A useful analogy can be made to the work of plant scientists. If these scientists were interested in determining the effectiveness of a new fertilizer, they would randomly apply different levels of fertilizer to randomly selected plots. There is an enormous literature in experimental design of this sort. Suppose, however, that the fertilizer manufacturer decided that this procedure was too expensive and that the new experiment would consist of applying the same amount of fertilizer to each plot. Anyone but an economist would give up at this point, knowing that one could never separate out the effects of weather, husbandry practices, and soil quality, regardless of how many years the experiment was rerun.

The situation just described is similar to that which led to this session. The problem in both cases is also similar — effectiveness cannot be measured given the available data. The answer to the problem is to randomly select certain cities or regions and to advertise a commodity at different levels in each region. The analysis would then be straightforward. If retail store sales figures indicated that more of the commodity was being sold in the heavily advertised regions, then we could measure the effectiveness of the campaign. We could measure the cross-advertising effects in a similar manner. This approach would be expensive, but we could determine whether producers' money is being wasted in a zero sum game. It is not in the interests of advertising agencies to make possible an objective evaluation of their methods. If we could convincingly prove that advertising did not pay money, producers would stop advertising. As long as economists are prepared to work with the data that are available, producers will continue to fund these campaigns. Perhaps the obligation lies with economists to demand well-constructed experiments before they analyze the results.

Using the fertilizer analogy, had the plant scientists accepted the impossible task of evaluating fertilizer response, they might be holding a conference focusing on the physical and chemical aspects of nutrient uptake. Their results would be of interest to other scientists but not to producers. If one assumes that the number of commercial-sized farms in the United States is approximately half a million and that approximately $500 million is spent per year on advertising programs, the per-farm cost is $1,000. With the same money, the farmers and their spouses could visit the attractions here in Orlando. I am not yet convinced that producers are better off by funding our participation at this conference than by taking a winter vacation themselves.

# 3 Effectiveness of Brand versus Generic Advertising

# 12 Advertising of Fresh and Processed Potato Products

EUGENE JONES and YANG CHOI

Evaluation of commodity advertising and promotion has focused primarily on major commodity programs such as beef, citrus, dairy, and poultry. Minor commodities such as apples, grapes, and potatoes have received limited attention from agricultural economists and other researchers because of, among other factors, sparse data and limited funds for program evaluation. By addressing generic and brand advertising of fresh and processed potato products, this paper attempts to provide insights on a minor commodity program.

Although the sales response of potatoes to generic promotion has not been evaluated by the National Potato Promotion Board (NPPB), several surveys of consumer attitudes toward potatoes have been conducted. These surveys show that generic advertising has generated an improved and positive image for potatoes. Inferences about sales response have been drawn from studies of major commodities. For example, the NPPB concluded recently that generic advertising and promotion of potatoes must be effective because an empirical study of dairy promotion for August 1984 through December 1985 showed that "an increase of $18.1 million in generic promotion . . . [led to] an increase in consumer purchases of 181.1 million pounds of fluid milk" (Mercer 1986). While such broad-based inference drawing may help program administrators sell producers on continued funding of the potato check-off program in the short run, the long-run viability of potato promotion probably is dependent on direct assessment of the economic returns to producers.

Evidence suggests that potato producers already may be questioning the economic validity of promotion programs administrators' inferences. For example, potato producers have increased their refund requests from a low of 9.3 percent in 1982, to a high of 18.4 percent in 1987. (Refunds averaged 10 percent annually during the 1973–83 period when the assessment fee was 1 cent per hundredweight. Since the fee increased to 2 cents in 1983, refunds have averaged 18 percent.) Refunds, of course, occur even with successful promotion because benefits accrue to contributing and noncontributing producers. However, the primary objective of this paper is to determine whether there are increased potato sales and producers' returns from generic and branded advertising, irrespective of how the benefits are distributed.

## Potato Advertising and Consumption

Unlike major commodity programs that generate up to $200 million in revenues (Frank 1985; Liu and Forker 1988) the potato check-off program currently generates an average of $5.7 million (fiscal years 1987 and 1988). Approximately 75 percent of net revenues are used for media advertising, nutrition education, and other promotion, intended to increase demand and the value perception of fresh potatoes and processed potato products. Relative to brand advertising expenditures for potato products, generic expenditures are reasonably small, amounting to $3.7 million in 1987 compared to $46 million for branded expenditures. Potato chips are the most heavily advertised processed product, with expenditures averaging $38.4 million annually for the 1985–87 period. Advertising expenditures for frozen and dehydrated potatoes during the same period averaged $12.1 million and $2.8 million, respectively. Advertising expenditures for potato products appear to be related to retail sales and their distribution channels. For example, advertising expenditures for frozen potatoes are relatively low, which is probably due to their dominant distribution (80 percent) through institutional establishments. Larger advertising expenditures for chips are probably related to the distribution of over 75 percent of the product through retail stores.

The level of advertising expenditures and the distribution channels for potato products appear to be significant factors influencing their retail values. For example, per capita consumption of frozen potatoes amounted to 45 pounds in 1987, with a retail value of $2.8 billion. By contrast, consumption of chips totaled 18 pounds, with a retail value of $3.8 billion. Such differences in values are not easily explained by production costs and the conversion ratios of raw potatoes into the two processed products. A plausible hypothesis is that two large potato chip firms, with over 50 percent of the market, have market power and the ability to influence retail value. Per capita consumption of dehydrated potatoes totaled 10.5 pounds in 1987, with an estimated retail value of $1 billion. Finally, per capita consumption of fresh potatoes amounted to 52 pounds, with an estimated retail value of $3.3 billion.

Although brand advertising expenditures for potatoes are much larger than generic expenditures, a dollar-for-dollar comparison is not completely accurate. Most generic advertising messages are placed in national magazines targeted to women. More specifically, the target audience of generic advertising are "women between the ages of 25 and 54, well-educated, [and] living in households with annual income levels above $30,000" (NPPB September 1987). Other desirable characteristics of these households are the presence of children and a weekly consumption of potatoes of 3 pounds or less. Presence of children are desirable because advertising which influences the potato-eating habits of existing households is hypothesized to have positive effects on households of the next generation. Households consuming less than 3 pounds of potatoes per week are targeted because they are considered "light users" and therefore have tremendous potential for increased consumption.

Branded advertising for potatoes occurs mainly in the broadcast media of radio and television. These media are more expensive in terms of cost per advertising message, but may be more effective for creating the desired product image. The NPPB does limited radio advertising and no television advertising. These media are not used because advertising funds are considered too limited to commit to relatively low message exposure. The exposure is lower than that deemed necessary to change consumers' perception of potatoes. Indeed the first strategy of the potato board was to change the "starchy" and "fattening" image of potatoes to a positive low calorie image. After consumer surveys showed that this objective was reasonably accomplished, the primary strategy became one of conveying to consumers the high nutritional value of potatoes. Most recently, the strategy has become one of conveying to consumers that potatoes are not only low in calories and an excellent source of nutrition, but they are also convenient to eat. This latter strategy was adopted as the board recognized that a positive product image does not necessarily lead to increased sales. Many competing products also have positive images.

## Potato Advertising Data

Unlike major commodity programs that generate funds for tracking monthly or quarterly changes in advertising expenditures and consumption, the limited funds generated by the potato program do not permit the NPPB tracking monthly or quarterly changes in advertising and consumption. Program evaluation of potatoes requires the use of annual data collected by public agencies. The use of annual data to evaluate a commodity program is inconsistent with empirical studies which suggest that monthly data are needed to estimate the intertemporal effects of advertising over time

(Kinnucan 1982, 1983, and 1985). However, since 90 percent of the effects of advertising on low-priced products occurs within one year (Clarke 1976), the use of annual data with no lag structure should provide reasonable estimates of the effects of potato advertising.

Potato advertising, as measured by the NPPB, consists of consumer media advertising, nutrition education, trade show promotion, point-of-purchase materials, and other forms of promotion. Leading National Advertisers (LNA), a common source of advertising data, reports only media advertising expenditures. For potatoes, LNA's reported expenditures for generic advertising differ substantially from those reported by NPPB. For example, LNA reports potato advertising expenditures of $1.6 million for 1987, while the NPPB reports expenditures of $3.6 million. Since the advertising expenditures as reported by NPPB are measures of total promotion, these expenditures seem more relevant for specifying the generic advertising variable. Branded expenditures, as used in this study, are media advertising as reported by LNA. Relative to generic expenditures, branded expenditures probably are biased downward.

Federal data sources are used for most of the nonadvertising variables. Retail price data on chips, dehydrated, fresh, and frozen potatoes were collected from the Food Department of the Bureau of Labor Statistics (BLS). When data series were incomplete, interpolation and other statistical methods were used for missing observations. Away-from-home consumption and income data were readily available from the Department of Commerce. Potato consumption data were collected from the U.S. Department of Agriculture and these data are available only on an annual basis. Indeed, annual consumption data proved to be the limiting factor in using monthly data to evaluate potato promotion. Monthly data on all other variables were available. This data availability suggests that the dynamic effects of potato advertising could be measured if the NPPB or other agencies tracked monthly changes in potato sales.

## Theoretical Model of Advertising

Traditional demand theory maintains that consumers attempt to maximize their utility subject to an income constraint. Advertising, within this framework, influences consumer tastes and preferences and ultimately the utility derived from goods and services (Galbraith 1958). The new approach to consumer demand theory (Lancaster 1966; Stigler and Becker 1967) postulates an indirect effect of advertising on demand for goods through its direct effect on the "implicit" price of characteristics or commodities. Since consumers purchase market goods to produce desired characteristics or commodities, advertising can influence the implicit or shadow price of characteristics and thereby influence the demand for goods that are used to produce characteristics (Stigler and Becker 1967). Thus, if $m$ is a market good and advertising increases the characteristic productivity of $m$ more than the price of $m$, utility maximizers will purchase and consume more of $m$ (Nichols 1985). Advertising that informs consumers of an unknown characteristic of a good can serve to increase the perceived or actual value of the good. For example, the generic advertising message that one 5 oz potato contains more potassium (750 mg) than a medium banana (450 mg) could increase the characteristic productivity of the potato if such information was not previously known. Even higher productivity may be realized if this message is coupled with the message that doctors recommend potassium-rich foods to reduce the risk of stroke.

The characteristic productivity aspect of consumer demand theory relates to the fact that consumers are assumed to produce commodities or characteristics from market goods, their own time, human capital, advertising, and other inputs (Stigler and Becker 1967). Holding all other inputs constant, an increase in advertising is assumed to provide knowledge or information about product characteristics and thereby increase consumer demand for the product because of a perceived greater output of the characteristic from a given input of the advertised product.

Relative to potatoes, advertising that informs consumers that "potatoes have complex carbohydrates, fiber, and vitamin C" should lower the shadow prices of these characteristics and lead to increased consumption of potatoes. As such, advertising is an exogenous variable that impacts consumer demand. And although conceptual differences are often made between generic and brand advertising, there is little theoretical or empirical basis for distinguishing their exogenous effects on demand. Additionally, demand theory provides little guidance as to the measurement form (dollar expenditures, frequency of message, media use, etc.) of either generic or brand advertising. Wu, Kesecker, and Meinhold (1985) observed, perhaps correctly, that total advertising expenditures may be an inappropriate proxy for advertising effectiveness, especially when advertising strategies and media use change over time. Theory suggests that the advertising variable, irrespective of how measured, should be adjusted to reflect changes in its magnitude or proportion.

While both generic and brand advertising are intended to influence product demand, it is generally postulated that brand advertisers emphasize increased market shares while generic advertisers (commodity groups) focus on increased total sales (Connor et al. 1985). Concurrent brand and generic advertising can be both complementary and competitive (Ward, Chang, and Thompson 1985). Further, recent evidence suggests that consumers' evaluation of generic advertising messages is a function of the products included. For example, consumers give a higher ranking to nutritional messages about potatoes when these messages apply to fresh potatoes alone than when these messages apply to fresh and processed potato products (NPPB 1987). The competitive nature of generic advertising is reflected in attempts by some states in the Pacific Northwest to gain brand identity for potatoes by stressing their superiority, while the NPPB attempts to emphasize the overall quality of potatoes.

Advertising is just one of many factors that influence product demand. Consumer taste, income, population, product price, household size and its age distribution are other important factors. If advertising is a primary source of a household's information, it can be instrumental in determining consumers' purchases of goods like food products (Nelson 1974). Advertising is viewed as crucial to the survival of firms producing branded products (Connor et al. 1985). Moreover, current and growing interest among commodity groups for generic advertising would suggest that these groups also view advertising as a survival strategy. (In addition to the more than $350 million annually that is currently being spent on generic promotion, many commodity groups are initiating and/or expanding their promotion efforts.) Advertising efforts, whether brand or generic, are expected to have positive impacts on sales. Total industry sales should be influenced positively by generic advertising, whereas firm sales, as a minimum, should be impacted positively by branded advertising.

While generic advertising may serve to increase demand for potatoes, it is important to emphasize that there are no supply controls to allow producers to capture the long-run benefits of their advertising efforts. Observations on production for the past two decades show potato acreage remaining reasonably constant and total production increasing at an annual rate of less than 2 percent, suggesting minimum, if any, response to demand changes. Producers of processed or branded potato products, it should be noted, can control their supply and product flow. These marketing attributes provide advertisers of branded products with the sufficient conditions to capture the long-run benefits of their advertising efforts.

## Econometric Model

Empirical studies of farm commodity promotion suggest a functional form that can capture diminishing marginal effects of advertising on sales (Clement 1963; Kinnucan 1982, 1983; Ward and Myers 1979). Some commonly used functions are the double logarithmic, semilogarithmic, logarithmic reciprocal, and the reciprocal. From among these functions, economists usually choose one based on the data fit, reasonableness of estimates, and conformity to economic theory. Of the aforementioned functional forms, the double logarithmic with the advertising variables in inverse form provided the most consistent estimates. Hence, the sales-advertising relationship for each of the four products is evaluated using the double logarithmic. Mathematically, the four equations are written as

$$\ln (FC) = \beta 0 + \beta 1 \ln (PF) + \beta 2 \ln (RICE) + \beta 3 \ln (WOMEN) \\ + \beta 4 \ln (INCOME) + \beta 5(1/GAE) + \mu 1 \tag{12.1}$$

$$\ln (RC) = \alpha 0 + \alpha 1 \ln (PR) + \alpha 2 \ln (PF) + \alpha 3 \ln (WOMEN) \\ + \alpha 4 \ln(INCOME) + \alpha 5(1/ADR) + \alpha 6(1/GAE) + \mu 2 \tag{12.2}$$

$$\ln (CC) = \tau 0 + \tau 1 \ln (PC) + \tau 2 \ln (COOKIE) + \tau 3 \ln (UN) \\ + \tau 4 \ln (INCOME) + \tau 5(1/ADC) + \tau 6(1/GAE) + \mu 3 \tag{12.3}$$

$$\ln (DC) = \delta 0 + \delta 1 \ln (PD) + \delta 2 \ln (PF) + \delta 3 \ln (WOMEN) \\ + \delta 4(1/ADD) + \delta 5(TREND) + \mu 4 \tag{12.4}$$

where

| | | |
|---|---|---|
| ln | = | natural logarithm; |
| FC | = | consumption of fresh potato sales in pounds per capita; |
| RC | = | consumption of frozen potato sales in pounds per capita; |
| CC | = | consumption of chips in pounds per capita; |
| DC | = | consumption of dehydrated potatoes in pounds per capita; |
| PF | = | retail price of fresh potatoes, deflated by the CPI; |
| PR | = | retail price of frozen potatoes, deflated by the CPI; |
| PC | = | retail price of potato chips, deflated by the CPI; |
| RICE | = | retail price of long-grain rice, deflated by the CPI; |
| WOMEN | = | women in labor force as a percentage of total labor force; |
| INCOME | = | disposable personal income in real dollars (1967) per capita; |
| GAE | = | generic advertising expenditures on fresh, frozen, and dehydrated potatoes, deflated by CPI; |
| ADR | = | branded advertising expenditures on frozen potatoes, deflated by CPI; |
| ADC | = | branded advertising expenditures on potato chips, deflated by CPI; |

ADD     =  branded advertising expenditures on dehydrated potatoes, deflated by CPI;

COOKIE  =  retail price of chocolate chip cookies, deflated by the CPI;

UN      =  annual unemployment rate; and

TREND   =  a trend variable with 1970 = 1.

Annual data for the 1970–87 period are used in each equation. Expenditures on generic advertising of potatoes did not start until 1973; therefore, there are no expenditures for the first three observations. High correlation was apparent among many of the variables (income and women in the labor force, for example), so ridge regression was used to address this problem. Each diagonal element of the $X'X$ matrix was multiplied by $(1 + d)$, where $d$ is a small number with values starting at 0.01, until the regression parameters were stable. In all equations, this number was between 0.1 and 0.4. The variable, women in the labor force, in all but the chip equation is intended to capture the increasing demand for convenience emanating from a growing percentage of households with two wage earners. Since potato chips are predominately a snack food, the convenience factor, as captured by increasing percentages of women in the labor force, should not be a factor influencing chip consumption.

## Empirical Results

As shown in equation 12.1, Table 12.1, generic advertising (GA) has a positive and statistically significant effect on fresh potato consumption (FC). This positive effect is a recent phenomenon as previous studies have shown generic advertising of fresh potatoes to be statistically insignificant (Jones and Ward 1984; Jones 1987). The elasticity estimate of 0.017, Table 12.2, suggests that a 10 percent increase in generic advertising leads to a 0.17 percentage change in per capita consumption. Using the elasticity parameter to calculate sales change (see Thompson and Eiler, 1975, for a similarity between rigorous methods of calculating), estimated annual sales from generic advertising of fresh potatoes are $15.1 million. With producers' returns averaging 35 percent of retail sales, an estimated $5.3 million accrue to producers from generic advertising of fresh potatoes. Relative to annual expenditures of $3 to $4 million on advertising, these returns provide a favorable benefit-cost ratio even if there are no returns to other advertised potato products.

**Table 12.1  Empirical results[a]**

ln (FC)  =  3.524 − .0799 ln (PF) + .0443 ln (RICE) − .0032 ln (WOMEN)
        (12.65)[a]    (−.411)    (1.735)          (−3.1092)[a]

    +  .0296 ln (INCOME) − .0749 (1/GAE)
       (1.186)              (−2.3130)[a]

    $R^2$ adj. = .590    Rho = −.246

ln (RC)  =  −1.0614 + .0037 ln (PR) − .2086 ln (PF) + .0215 ln (WOMEN)
        (−1.247)   (.0329)      (−1.108)        (6.809)[a]

    +  .5614 ln (INCOME) − .0904 (1/GAE) − .0953 (1/ADR)
       (6.479)[a]           (−1.995)[a]      (−5.104)[a]

    $R^2$ adj. = .722    Rho = .202

ln (CC)  =  1.631 − .0541 ln (PC) + .0153 ln (COOKIE) − .005 ln (UN)
        (4.02)[a]   (−1.97)[a]    (.627)             (−.1505)

    +  .1340 ln (INCOME) + .0262 (1/GAE) − .5238 (1/ADC)
       (2.771)[a]           (1.250)         (−2.559)[a]

    $R^2$ adj. = .668    Rho = −.1030

ln (DC)  =  1.929 − .0830 ln (PD) + .4512 ln (PF) + .0005 ln (WOMEN)
        (3.571)[a]   (−2.087)[a]   (1.942)[a]     (2.616)[a]

    +  .0383 ln (INCOME) − .0039 (TREND) − .1068 (1/ADD)
       (1.975)[a]           (−.6976)        (−2.074)[a]

    $R^2$ adj. = .761    Rho = −.097

[a]Indicates significance at the 0.05 level or better. Numbers in parentheses are $t$-ratios.

Another important phenomenon revealed in equation 12.1 is the positive, though statistically insignificant, income parameter. This parameter suggests that fresh potatoes may no longer be perceived as an inferior good. However, the demand for convenience, as reflected in the parameter estimate for women in the labor force (WOMEN), continues to have a negative impact on fresh potato consumption. Neither the own price (PF) nor the substitute commodity price (RICE) has a statistically significant impact on fresh consumption, probably reflecting the fact that potatoes are a small part of the consumer budget.

Equation 12.2 shows that both branded and generic advertising are

**Table 12.2  Potato sales and producers' returns[a]**

| | ln (FC) | ln (RC) | ln (CC) | ln (DC) |
|---|---|---|---|---|
| | | Dependent variable | | |
| Branded advertising elasticity[b] | . . . | .0157 | .0205 | .069 |
| Change in pounds per capita | . . . | .6204 | .3498 | .9369 |
| Price per pound | . . . | $.2221 | $.8608 | $.7172 |
| Per capita sales change | . . . | $.1378 | $.3011 | $.6719 |
| Total sales change | . . . | $29.4 | $64.3 | $143.4 |
| Producer share | . . . | $5.3 | $11.6 | $25.8 |
| Generic advertising elasticity | .0171 | .0222 | . . . | . . . |
| Change in pounds per capita | .8869 | .8773 | . . . | . . . |
| Price per pound | $.0794 | $.2221 | . . . | . . . |
| Per capita sales change | $.0706 | $.1948 | . . . | . . . |
| Total sales change | $15.1 | $41.6 | . . . | . . . |
| Producer share | $5.4 | $7.5 | . . . | . . . |

[a]Total sale changes are derived as follows: The elasticity parameter is multiplied times average per capita consumption (1970–87) to derive changes in pounds per capita; this figure is then multiplied times price per pound to derive per capita sales change; per capita sales change times average 1970–87 population of 213.5 million gives total sales change in millions of dollars; finally, the producer share is 18 percent of total sales for processed products and 35 percent of total sales for fresh potatoes.

[b]Note that the absolute values of the elasticity are reported in this table.

effective in increasing sales of frozen potatoes, though statistically branded advertising is more significant. Each 10 percent increase in branded advertising is shown to generate a 0.157 percentage change in frozen consumption; a change of the same magnitude in generic expenditures generates a 0.22 percentage change in sales. Relative to the 1970–87 sample period, branded advertising expenditures are shown to have generated $29.4 million in frozen sales. By contrast, generic advertising has expanded sales by $41.6 million. With producers receiving an estimated $0.18 from each $1.00 of frozen potato sales, the producer shares from branded and generic advertising expenditures are respectively $5.3 and $7.5 million. (It is assumed in this paper that producers of potatoes for chips and dehydrated products also receive $0.18.) This $7.5 million together with the $5.4 million from generic promotion of fresh potatoes yields producers' returns of more than $3.00 for each $1.00 of expenditure.

Frozen potato consumption, just as fresh consumption, is not impacted by its own price (PR) and its substitute commodity price (PF). However, income growth and increasing proportion of women in the labor force have positive and statistically significant impacts on frozen consumption. The income (INCOME) parameter probably captures the income elasticity of away-from-home food consumption, as 80 percent of all frozen potatoes are consumed away from home. Moreover, since over 60 percent of all frozen potatoes are consumed at fast-food establishments, the significance of the women (WOMEN) parameter surely reflects a growing demand for labor-saving convenience meals. Indeed away-from-home consumption of frozen potatoes increased more than 100 percent during the 1970–87 sample period, while at-home consumption increased less than 2 percent. Since one firm has a predominate share of the at-home frozen potato market, most frozen potato advertising is directed at reinforcing brand identity and expanding the proportion of households purchasing frozen potatoes.

Equation 12.3 shows that branded advertising has a positive and statistically significant impact on chip consumption, while generic advertising has a negative but statistically insignificant impact. Since chips often are advertised jointly with fresh and frozen potatoes, perhaps the negative parameter for generic advertising suggests a shift to fresh and frozen products. Each 10 percent increase in branded advertising is seen to generate a 0.205 percentage increase in potato chip sales. At this rate of change, annual chip sales resulting from branded advertising are estimated at $64.3 million. Assuming an $0.18 producer share, estimated producer returns amount to $11.57 million. No estimates are derived for annual reductions in sales resulting from generic advertising because the parameter is statistically insignificant.

Unlike the insignificant own-price effects for fresh and frozen potatoes, the price of chips (PC) has a statistically significant impact on chips consumption. However, a price increase for the substitute commodity, chocolate chip cookies, does not have a statistically significant impact on chips consumption. Also, statistically speaking, chips consumption is not impacted by changes in the unemployment rate. Because chips are a snack food, it was hypothesized that much of their consumption occurs during workers' snack breaks. The empirical results refute this hypothesis. Income does have a positive and statistically significant impact on consumption.

Equation 12.4 shows that branded advertising has a positive and statistically significant impact on dehydrated potato consumption. Since an insignificant amount of generic expenditures are allocated to promote dehydrated potatoes, generic advertising is not included in this equation. The low level of generic advertising expenditures for dehydrated potatoes is due partly to the chosen advertising media. Because most generic advertising of potatoes occurs in print media, it is more difficult to illustrate the "freshness" of dehydrated potatoes. Each 10 percent increase in branded expenditures leads to a 0.69 percentage increase in dehydrated potato consumption. For the sample period of this study, estimated sales resulting from branded advertising amount to $143.4 million annually. At $0.18 per

$1.00 return to producers, annual producer shares amount to $25.8 million.

As with frozen potatoes, the parameter estimates for income (INCOME) and women in the labor force (WOMEN) suggest that dehydrated potatoes are both a convenience food and an income-elastic, away-from-home food product. Both variables have positive and statistically significant impacts on dehydrated consumption. Also, both the own price (PD) and the substitute commodity price (PF) are seen to be statistically significant factors influencing dehydrated potato sales. Both variables have the hypothesized signs and the parameter estimates suggest that fresh and dehydrated potatoes are substitute commodities. A trend variable was included to try and capture some of the unexplained variance, but it proved to be insignificant.

## Summary and Conclusions

The results reported in this paper indicate that branded and generic advertising are generally effective in increasing potato sales. Generic advertising has positive and statistically significant impacts on frozen and fresh potato sales. The positive effect on fresh potato sales is a very recent phenomenon and it is the product which has been the primary focus of the industry's promotion efforts. Reversing the declining consumption of fresh potatoes lends credence to the argument advanced by Lavidge and Steiner (1961) that people respond to advertising through a series of steps (p. 61). Negative attitudes existed about potatoes and it seems that the NPPB's approach to reverse consumption trends by first changing consumers' attitudes and the image of the potato may be a useful approach for other commodity groups to emulate. Also, much of the success of potato promotion probably is due to factual and health-related information provided about potatoes. For example, *Time* magazine (October 12, 1987) gives the NPPB favorable coverage for its advertising strategy of providing factual and nutritional information to consumers.

While the results reported here show positive returns to advertising, much more refined data are needed to evaluate such factors as optimal levels of expenditures, optimal product and/or media mix, profit-maximizing levels of expenditures, advertising lag structures, and carryover effects. Although tentative results suggest that the potato board should not promote potato chips, new product developments that diminish some of the negatives associated with chips may allow for effective chips promotion. With only one major firm involved in dehydrated potato advertising, it is difficult to assess whether there are major advantages to a separate generic advertising effort. That is, current brand advertising of dehydrated potatoes should have the effect of expanding sales since there is little reason to reinforce brand identity. To a lesser extent, frozen potatoes are also advertised largely by a single firm with more than 50 percent of the retail market. Since consumption of fresh potatoes is responding to generic promotion, perhaps a larger and more extensive advertising effort on fresh potatoes would yield higher marginal returns.

In addition to the traditional approach used in this paper, more rigorous models should be developed to incorporate advertising directly into the demand system. The traditional approach seems less capable of integrating the linkages of information and demand in an advanced consumer society. An alternative approach for incorporating information is the characteristic demand framework as developed by Lancaster (1966) and Stigler and Becker (1967). Conceptually, it seems that the characteristics framework can provide plausible and direct estimates when advertising changes preferences and/or tastes over goods. This conceptual framework needs to be operationalized to provide a fully integrated theory of consumer choice based on characteristic concepts. A tentative model that incorporates potato advertising has been developed (Choi 1988), but still needs some refinements. With these refinements, a plausible hypothesis is that the characteristic demand approach will provide reasonable estimates of the advertising parameters.

# 13 Commodity versus Brand Advertising: A Case Study of the Florida Orange Juice Industry

## JONQ-YING LEE and MARK G. BROWN

Recent studies have sparked some controversy about the effectiveness of advertising programs in expanding the domestic demand for orange juice (OJ). Research conducted by the Florida Department of Citrus (FDOC) Economic Research Department (ERD) staff suggests that FDOC-funded Florida quality commodity advertising has been effective in expanding U.S. retail demand for OJ. However, FDOC research indicates that brand advertising is not statistically important in expanding U.S. retail OJ demand, but is a contributing factor to the increasing brand dominance of the OJ category. Research conducted by Ward (1988a, 1988b) suggests that commodity advertising has been important in expanding OJ demand. Moreover, Ward's research suggests that brand advertising has been effective in increasing OJ consumption, which would appear to contradict FDOC research findings.

The research controversy regarding the effect of brand and commodity advertising has created uncertainty with respect to the roles of commodity and brand advertising in the OJ category. This uncertainty has raised some concerns within the Florida citrus industry, since the industry supports both commodity and brand advertising programs. Traditionally, brand advertising has been viewed as a means to increase or maintain a particular brand's market share within a product category, while commodity advertising has been viewed as a means to expand category demand (Ward and Chang 1985). If brand advertising increases market shares of branded products within the OJ category without expanding category demand, one would have to question the merit of an industry-sponsored brand advertising effort since the primary marketing goal of the industry is to expand OJ demand. However, if brand advertising also helps expand the demand of the OJ category, one would have to question the relative importance of brand advertising and an industry-sponsored commodity advertising program, particularly when the OJ category is becoming more dominated by brands with heavy advertising support.

This paper examines the recent studies on the impacts of OJ advertising programs on the demand for OJ. It attempts to resolve the controversy regarding the effects of brand advertising on domestic retail OJ demand. A detailed discussion of the rationale behind the models used to measure the effects of advertising is provided.

## Measuring Advertising Effectiveness

One can ask a variety of questions relating to the general problem of measuring advertising effectiveness. The particular question addressed determines, to a large extent, the design and methodology used in the research study. There is considerable discussion in the literature concerning the appropriate response variable to use when measuring advertising effectiveness. Although there is consensus that the objective of advertising should be to increase demand, many researchers argue that sales increases attributable to advertising expenditures cannot be directly measured for various reasons. Therefore, they prefer to use variables such as advertising awareness, advertising and product recall, and consumer attitude toward the product as proxies for sales. In addition, there is no one method for properly measuring the effectiveness of advertising expenditures. The methodology chosen depends on (1) the specific questions asked; (2) the nature of the data available; (3) to some extent, what the researcher believes the demand structure should be; and (4) the amount of time and money one is willing to spend on measuring the response rates.

Two major types of advertising impacts have been discussed in the marketing literature. The first type states that several exposures may be required before an individual decides to buy. The second one states that current advertising expenditures do not have their full impact on sales in the current accounting period; instead, their impact on sales is assumed to extend well into the future. An idea related to both types of impacts is that if an established advertising program ceases, sales will not drop immediately to the level that would have existed without the program. The usual assumption is that the total effect of a dollar's worth of advertising is spread out over several time periods. This is called the decay or carryover effect.

Zielske (1959) demonstrated that advertising will be quickly forgotten if the consumer is not continuously exposed to it. Without repeated exposures to advertising, the number of recalls decreases over time. Furthermore, Ostheimer (1970) found that each additional advertisement produces a smaller effect than the prior one. Appel (1966) found that advertising changes in effectiveness with the passage of time. There was a slight increase in score, which was attributed to learning, followed by a fairly regular decline, which was attributed to exhaustion of the advertising message. In addition, Greenberg and Suttoni (1973) found that commercials for infrequently purchased products (e.g., an automobile, a camera, etc.) may wear out more slowly than those for everyday products (e.g., milk, OJ, beef, etc.). This empirical evidence indicates that the decay effect of advertising depends on the way the product is advertised and the nature of the product itself.

## Review of Advertising Effort in the OJ Category

Historically, advertising support of the OJ category has been dominated by FDOC-supported commodity advertising rather than brand advertising. A major factor contributing to the importance of FDOC-supported commodity advertising relative to brand advertising was a lack of intensive brand competition, particularly at the national level. Prior to 1983, there were only two national brands, with one brand specializing in the chilled orange juice (COJ) segment and the other brand specializing in the frozen concentrated orange juice (FCOJ) segment. However, in 1983 a third national brand, Citrus Hill, was introduced and brand competition intensified considerably. As a result, brand advertising increased dramatically, overtaking FDOC-supported advertising as the dominant form of advertising in the OJ category.

During the fiscal year 1980–81, FDOC commodity advertising expenditures in support of the OJ category totaled $9.1 million or 53.9 percent of the total advertising dollars devoted to the OJ category. On the other hand, brand advertising expenditures totaled an estimated $7.8 million, accounting for the remaining 46.1 percent of all OJ advertising expenditures. By 1986–87, brand advertising had increased to $52.9 million and accounted for 83.2 percent of the total advertising expenditures. FDOC advertising declined in 1986–87 to $10.7 million, accounting for 16.8 percent of the total advertising expenditures.

Beginning in the 1983–84 fiscal year, industry brand advertising expenditures have partially been supported by an FDOC brand advertising rebate (BAR) program. Following the implementation of the BAR program in late 1983, program expenditures have grown significantly, increasing from $1.6 million in 1983–84 to $4.9 million in 1984–85, $7.8 million in 1985–86, and $9.9 million in 1986–87. Although BAR program support of the total brand advertising effort continues to be relatively small, its importance in supporting brand advertising has clearly grown.

While OJ advertising expenditures reached new record levels, retail grocery store sales of OJ decreased from 884 million single strength equivalent (SSE) gallons in 1985–86 to 858 million SSE gallons in 1986–87. Likewise, retail OJ revenue also decreased from $2,871 million (current dollars) in 1985–86 to $2,866 million in 1986–87.

## Review of OJ Advertising Research

A series of studies designed to evaluate the effects of OJ advertising expenditures on OJ consumption was completed between 1973 and 1977. The first studies were conducted by Richardson (1973) and Ward (1973). The data were quarterly observations for July 1966 through June 1972. Brand and commodity advertising expenditures were included in the models, and the effects of each were assumed to be independent. In another study, Ward (1975) analyzed the interaction between commodity and brand expenditures. The latter study was limited because the decay effects for brand and commodity advertising were constrained to be equal, and inflationary effects were not accounted for. Lee (1977) updated Ward's 1975 study, relaxing the constraint on the decay effects for commodity and brand advertising and adjusting advertising expenditures for inflation. The results from these studies were similar and are summarized as follows: (1) both commodity and brand advertising have positive influences on OJ sales; (2) both commodity and brand advertising have carryover effects on sales beyond the quarter during which the money is actually spent; and (3) the optimum mix between brand and commodity expenditures depends on the total level of advertising effort. In general, as the total effort decreases, a larger percent should be allocated to commodity programs.

Ward (1974) also conducted a study to evaluate the impact of an FDOC OJ advertising rebate program implemented in 1973. The effectiveness of the program, as measured by increased consumer sales, was evaluated using both Nielsen and MRCA data. Results indicated there were no major gains from the rebate program.

More recently, Ward has conducted additional research on the effectiveness of OJ advertising. Using Nielsen bimonthly data for the period from September/October 1978 through December/January 1987–88, Ward estimated the impacts of commodity and brand advertising on OJ consumption with a polynomial distributed lag model. In his model, Ward included separate lag structures for commodity and brand advertising. The dependent variable, per capita OJ consumption, was considered a function of the price of OJ, real per capita income, seasonality, and both the real commodity and brand advertising expenditures for OJ.

In his analysis, Ward imposed restrictions on the lag structures for both commodity and brand advertising variables. The brand advertising impact on OJ consumption was restricted to dissipate gradually. The commodity advertising impact was restricted to dissipate gradually and equal zero before the advertising dollars were spent. Ward's results are shown in Table 13.1.

**Table 13.1  Estimated orange juice advertising impacts by Ward (1988a)**

| Lag | Commodity advertising | | Brand advertising | |
|-----|-------------|-------------|-------------|-------------|
|     | Coefficient | t-statistic | Coefficient | t-statistic |
| 0   | 0.0034 | 2.4789 | 0.0077 | 2.5756 |
| 1   | 0.0040 | 3.2470 | 0.0066 | 2.5756 |
| 2   | 0.0042 | 2.7816 | 0.0055 | 2.5756 |
| 3   | 0.0042 | 2.3304 | 0.0044 | 2.5756 |
| 4   | 0.0039 | 2.0447 | 0.0033 | 2.5756 |
| 5   | 0.0034 | 1.8593 | 0.0022 | 2.5756 |
| 6   | 0.0025 | 1.7318 | 0.0011 | 2.5756 |
| 7   | 0.0014 | 1.6395 | | |
| Sum | 0.0270 | | 0.0310 | |

The results from Ward's study show that both commodity and brand advertising have had a positive impact on total OJ consumption. However, the commodity and brand effects differ in both their immediate and long-term responses. The coefficient estimates shown in Table 13.1 indicate that commodity advertising has a lagged impact on OJ consumption, the peak impact occurring during the third bimonthly period after the advertising expenditures are made and the remaining advertising impacts declining for the next four bimonthly periods. The brand advertising coefficient estimates show that brand advertising has its greatest impact on OJ consumption in the initial period, with a long-term effect similar to that for commodity advertising. The brand advertising effects for all remaining periods after the initial period decline. Based on Ward's analysis, over the periods from 1984 through 1987, generic advertising resulted in a 7.95 percent increase in consumption above the level predicted under the assumption of a minimal level of advertising. In comparison, brand advertising generated a 17.5 percent increase in overall orange juice sales for the same periods. In addition, according Ward, the estimated brand advertising effect in 1986–87 equalled 124.7 million SSE gallons (total sales for the season were 858 million SSE gallons). Further analysis shows that for 1986–87 expenditure levels: (1) the marginal return for commodity advertising was about three times the marginal return for brand advertising; and (2) the optimal share of commodity advertising was about 46 percent of total advertising expenditures (in 1986–87, the estimated share for commodity advertising expenditures was about 20 percent).

The analyses conducted by Ward indicate that the expenditures allocated to industry-supported brand advertising programs could have been more efficiently used in commodity advertising programs to enhance the overall demand for OJ. However, it needs to be pointed out that increasing OJ consumption is only one of the many objectives of industry-supported brand advertising programs. Other objectives include program participation and quality of advertising effort.

Since Ward's study does not explicitly address the occurrence in 1986–87 of record high advertising expenditures and decreased sales (in terms of quantity sold and retail revenue), and given that our research suggests that the recent increases in brand advertising have not been helpful in expanding OJ demand, we considered alternative econometric models to study how advertising has impacted OJ consumption patterns. Specifically, we conducted a series of additional studies using a variety of empirical specifications.

One study was based on a single-equation econometric model incorporating a distributed lag structure for the effects of advertising. Past experiences indicate that research results are sensitive to the lag structure specified (i.e., the length and the degree of lag). Basically, our models do not take into consideration the degree of the lag; they differ from Ward's model in several ways.

Our research is based on the fact that OJ, especially COJ, which generally has a shelf-life of less than a month, is a perishable commodity. Hence, it is often bought and consumed within four weeks. Because OJ is not a new product, it is unlikely to have experienced any significant demand gain from education through OJ advertising. Therefore, under the assumption that purchases are positively related to recalls, it is doubtful that the advertising effect could have peaked beyond the period during which advertising occurred. Since the data used in our analysis are bimonthly, a decreasing decay structure for the advertising impacts was used. The advertising impacts were specified in the context of the Houthakker and Taylor (1970) habit persistence model. In this model, current per capita OJ consumption is considered a function of lagged per capita OJ consumption, the real price of OJ, real per capita income, seasonality (a dummy variable for summer months), real commodity and brand advertising expenditures for OJ, and real advertising expenditures for all other fruit juices and drinks.

In addition to the difference in the lag structures for advertising expenditures, our measuring unit for advertising is different from the one used in Ward's model. Real per capita advertising expenditures were used as the measuring unit for advertising in Ward's model, while real total advertising expenditures were used in our models. In addition, advertising expenditures for other juices/drinks were included in the analysis. Results for our model are shown in Table 13.2.

**Table 13.2. Estimates of advertising response parameters for OJ (December/January 1975 through August/September 1986)**

| Advertising expenditures | Dependent variables[a] | | | |
|---|---|---|---|---|
| | FCOJ | COJ | CSSOJ | ALL OJ |
| Other juices | -.9132 | .4097 | -.1654 | 1.2563 |
| | (0.461) | (0.276) | (1.545) | (0.348) |
| Brand OJ | -1.6595 | -2.0156 | -.0768 | .8130 |
| | (0.593) | (1.050) | (.505) | (0.191) |
| All OJ | 18.8129 | 5.6790 | .4555 | 21.9572 |
| | (4.085) | (1.895) | (1.769) | (2.985) |
| $\phi$[b] | 0.7231 | 0.9109 | 0.8565 | 0.7840 |
| | (0.0600) | (0.0521) | (0.0510) | (0.0650) |

[a]Dependent variables are the quantities of orange juice demanded per 1,000 persons. Numbers in parentheses are $t$-ratios.
[b]These are the estimated habit persistence parameters for the Houthakker and Taylor model.

The results for the aforementioned demand model indicate that (1) a $1 million increase in real advertising expenditures for other fruit juices/drinks would decrease the sales of canned single-strength OJ (CSSOJ) by 0.17 gallons per 1,000 persons for a bimonthly period; (2) a $1 million increase in real commodity advertising expenditure would increase the sales of FCOJ, COJ, CSSOJ, and all OJ, respectively, by 18.81, 5.68, 0.46, and 21.96 gallons per 1,000 persons for a bimonthly period; and (3) a change in real brand advertising expenditures would not appreciably impact the sales of OJ in any form. For each form of OJ, the decay impact can be derived by multiplying the current impact by the habit persistence parameter estimate. The sum of the current impact and decay impacts gives the cumulative impact.

## A NOTE ON THE DISTRIBUTED LAG STRUCTURE
## IN MEASURING THE EFFECTIVENESS OF OJ ADVERTISING

Both analyses discussed above used distributed lag modeling techniques to measure the impact of current and lagged advertising on the consumption of OJ. In Ward's model, a finite distributed lag model was used. In our model, an infinite distributed lag model was used. Both approaches suffer from the lack of exact knowledge about the lag structure.

One of the ways to circumvent the imposition of restrictions on advertising parameters is to estimate the cumulative effect of advertising. In this approach, one includes lagged advertising variables as explanatory variables in the regression, regardless of the resulting signs or the $t$-ratios of each individual estimate for the current and lagged advertising variables. The researcher only tests whether the sum of these estimates is statistically different from zero or positive. Using a similar model to Ward's (except there is a difference in the lag structure for the advertising variables), we tested the cumulative impacts of advertising. Results are presented in Table 13.3.

**Table 13.3 Estimated cumulative advertising impact[a]**

|  | Advertising expenditures for | | |
|---|---|---|---|
|  | Brand OJ | All OJ | All other juices |
| Current | -7.0899 | 13.4920 | 2.2453 |
|  | (4.9243)[b] | (9.1088) | (2.1021) |
| Lag (1) | 9.2374 | 0.2434 | -0.2303 |
|  | (6.3963) | (10.5910) | (3.4592) |
| Lag (2) | -6.0898 | 16.1110 | 0.6034 |
|  | (6.8675) | (9.7352) | (3.3825) |
| Lag (3) | 4.5352 | -3.7503 | 2.3267 |
|  | (5.2991) | (9.3552) | (2.3675) |
| Sum | 0.5929 | 26.0950 | 3.7383 |
|  | (4.1164) | (11.9680) | (2.2131) |

[a]The first-order autocorrelation coefficient estimate equals 0.5232 with a $t$-ratio of 4.0464.
[b]The number in parentheses is the standard error of estimate.

The estimates presented in Table 13.3 show that the cumulative impacts of OJ commodity and other juice advertising on the demand for OJ are positive, while the brand advertising impact was not different from zero. However, the above results still suffer from the lack of a priori knowledge about the lag length and are by no means conclusive.

## DEMAND SYSTEM APPROACH

One problem with the above analyses is they are all based on the single-equation approach to measure the impact of advertising. In addition, these models do not provide any information about why brand advertising did not have a positive impact on the demand for the OJ category. Increasing competition from other juices and juice-based beverages may limit the effect of OJ advertising expenditures. For example, advertising expenditures for noncitrus juices and noncitrus fruit juice–based beverages have increased from $39.79 million in 1982 to $83.46 million in 1987. Also, the quantity share of apple juice (a close substitute of OJ, see Lee 1984; Brown and Lee 1985) in the fruit-juice beverage market has increased from 8.26 percent in 1980 to 13.23 percent in 1987. The competition currently taking place in the juice and juice-beverage markets was not considered in the above analyses. One of the ways to handle this problem is to use a demand system approach.

In general, there are two approaches to estimate advertising effects in demand systems (Brown and Lee 1989). The first approach is to use a system of Marshallian or Hicksian demand equations. The second approach is based on household production theory (Becker 1965; Stigler and Becker 1977). Application of either of these approaches to study a particular commodity can further be based on the two-stage or multistage budget allocation assumption, which results in a demand subsystem (e.g., the Rotterdam subdemand model derived by Theil [1976] or the linear expenditure subdemand system discussed by Powell [1974]).

In this study, the Rotterdam subdemand model was estimated using an additional general demand restriction, i.e., the adding-up restriction (Phlips 1974) for advertising variables (a change in advertising expenditures will lead to a shift in the expenditure pattern, but not total outlay, see Aviphant, Lee, and Brown 1988). The elasticity estimates for the advertising variables in the Rotterdam model are presented in Table 13.4.

Table 13.4. Advertising elasticity estimates for the demand for orange juice, July 1983 through August 1986[a]

| Advertising expenditures for | Demand for | | | |
|---|---|---|---|---|
| | Three major brand OJ | Other brand | Private label OJ | All other fruit juices |
| | Advertising elasticities | | | |
| Three major brand OJ | .0331 | -.0161 | -.0367 | .0197 |
| | (1.6083) | (1.5724) | (2.0859) | (.8653) |
| Other brand OJ | .0321 | .0389 | -.0413 | -.0297 |
| | (1.0131) | (2.4754) | (1.5260) | (.8492) |
| All orange juices | -.0011 | -.0003 | .0098 | -.0084 |
| | (.1335) | (.0781) | (1.4287) | (.9642) |
| All other fruit juices/drinks | .0036 | -.0015 | -.0094 | .0073 |
| | (.8391) | (.7172) | (2.5178) | (1.5191) |

[a]Numbers in parentheses are $t$-ratios.

The results in Table 13.4 indicate that (1) all own-advertising expenditure elasticity estimates are statistically different from zero, with OJ commodity advertising expenditures increasing the sales of private-label OJ; and (2) all cross-advertising expenditure elasticity estimates are either statistically not different from zero or negative and statistically different from zero. The latter result indicates that advertising activities for one OJ category has negative impacts on the sales of OJ outside the category.

The estimated cross-advertising expenditure elasticities indicate that; (1) if real advertising expenditures for the three major brands of OJ were increased by 1 percent, the demand for nonmajor brands and private-label OJ would be decreased by .0161 percent and .0367 percent, respectively; (2) if real advertising expenditures for the non-major brands of OJ were increased by 1 percent, the demand for private-label OJ would be decreased by 0.0413 percent; (3) if real advertising expenditures for other fruit juices/drinks were increased by 1 percent, the demand for private-label OJ would be decreased by 0.0094 percent; and (4) if real commodity advertising expenditures were increased by 1 percent, the demand for private-label OJ would be increased by 0.0098 percent, and the demand for three major brands of OJ, nonmajor brands of OJ, and all other fruit juices and drinks would not be affected.

## HOUSEHOLD PRODUCTION THEORY APPROACH

In household production theory, one considers the consumer as a firm. The firm produces an output vector $z$ from a vector of material inputs $q$; a vector of labor inputs $t_0$; a vector of capital inputs $k_0$; the consumer's stock of knowledge about the production process, where the stock of knowledge is a function of certain capital items $k_1$ allowing the consumer to view, read, or hear the advertising messages; and the consumer's leisure time $t_1$. The objective is to minimize short-run cost $m = pq + wt_0$, subject to the constraint imposed by the technology given $z$, $t$ (both $t_0$ and $t_1$) and $k$ (both $k_0$ and $k_1$), where $p$ and $w$ are vectors of market good prices and wage rates, respectively. The optimization problem is

$$C(z,w,p;k) = \min_q \{p'q + wt_0 : h(q,k,t,s,z) \geq 0\} \tag{13.1}$$

where $h$ is a joint production function.

The primary advantage of utilizing the cost function to characterize the household's transformation of $q$ into $z$ is that it provides a direct means of imputing values to the nonmarket vector $z$. The shadow values (Deaton and Muellbauer 1980) of the $z_i$ are defined by

$$\pi_i = \partial C / \partial z_i \qquad i = 1, \ldots, g \tag{13.2}$$

Because of the lack of a good measurement of $z$ for different fruit-juice beverages, advertising expenditure levels for different types of fruit-juice beverages were used as proxies for $z$. Since aggregate data were used, variables $w$ and $k$ were deleted from equation (13.1). With this assumption, the $z$ vector in equation (13.1) was replaced by a vector of advertising expenditures, $a$; that is, the expression becomes $C(a,p)$. In addition, because no *a priori* information was available to suggest an explicit functional form for the cost function in expression (13.1), a translog specification was adopted. Formally, the translog cost function can be written as

$$\ln C = \alpha_0 + \Sigma_i^n \alpha_i \ln p_i + \Sigma_j^n \beta_j \ln a_j \tag{13.3}$$

$$+ 1/2 \Sigma_i^n \Sigma_j^n \alpha_{ij} \ln p_i \ln p_j + 1/2 \Sigma_i^n \Sigma_j^n \beta_{ij} \ln a_i \ln a_j$$

$$+ 1/2 \Sigma_i^n \Sigma_j^n \phi_{ij} \ln p_i \ln a_j$$

The numbers of parameters to be estimated can be reduced by imposing theoretically derived restrictions. The symmetry condition is

$$\alpha_{ij} = \alpha_{ji} \tag{13.4}$$

and states that elasticities of substitution between juice $i$ and juice $j$ are symmetric. The linear homogeneity conditions are

$$\Sigma \alpha_i = 1; \; \Sigma_j \alpha_{ij} = 0 \text{ for all } i, \quad \text{and} \quad \Sigma_i \phi_{ij} = 0 \text{ for all } j \tag{13.5}$$

These expressions imply homogeneity of degree one in prices but do not impose homogeneity on the household production function. Without loss of generality, symmetry in the $\beta_{ij}$'s is imposed by requiring $\beta_{ij} = \beta_{ji}$.

Budget share equations can be derived by differentiating equation (13.3) with respect to each of the input prices and applying Shephard's lemma:

$$(\partial \ln C / \partial \ln p_i) = w_i = \alpha_i + \Sigma_j \alpha_{ij} \ln p_j + \Sigma_j \phi_{ij} \ln a_j$$
$$i = 1, \ldots, n \tag{13.6}$$

where $w_i = p_i q_i / C$ is the proportion of total juice cost spent on juice group $i$. The $\phi_{ij}$ parameters show the effect of changes in $a$ on the factor shares. If $\phi_{ij}$ equals zero for all $i$ and $j$, the household production structure is homothetic, meaning that, at constant factor prices, factor shares are not affected by the variety composition or level consumed.

The shadow prices of the elements of $a$ can be obtained by recognizing

$$\pi_i = (\partial C/\partial a_i) = (\partial \ln C/\partial \ln a_i)(C/a_i) \qquad i = 1, \ldots, n \qquad (13.7)$$

Estimation may then be accomplished by the joint treatment of (13.3) and the $(n - 1)$ share equations. If either the iterated seemingly unrelated least squares method or the full information maximum likelihood method is employed as the estimation method, upon convergence, maximum likelihood parameter estimates, invariant to the share equation dropped, will be obtained.

Three juice groups — national-brand OJ (0.2871), private-label OJ (0.3521), and all other single-flavored fruit juices (0.3608) with average budget shares in parentheses — were analyzed. Using the three juice groups, the translog cost function had 24 parameters after imposing restrictions (13.4) and (13.5). The advertising expenditure variables analyzed were media expenditures for brand advertising for OJ ($a_1$), commodity advertising for OJ ($a_2$), and advertising for all other fruit juices and drinks ($a_3$). The cost function in conjunction with the two share equations were estimated using the full information maximum likelihood method.

The estimated budget share equations for the household production model are

$$w_1 = .3518 - .2468 \ln p_1 + .1200 \ln p_2 + .1268 \ln p_3 + .0003 \ln a_1$$
$$\quad (.1013) \ (.0605) \qquad (.0522) \qquad (.0485) \qquad (.0056)$$

$$+ .0029 \ln a_2 - .0083 \ln a_3$$
$$\quad (.0091) \qquad (.0056)$$

$$w_2 = .3745 + .1200 \ln p_1 - .3867 \ln p_2 + .2667 \ln p_3 - .0018 \ln a_1$$
$$\quad (.0951) \ (.0522) \qquad (.0678) \qquad (.0481) \qquad (.0047)$$

$$- .0098 \ln a_2 - .0061 \ln a_3$$
$$\quad (.0075) \qquad (.0052)$$

$$w_3 = .2737 + .1268 \ln p_1 + .2667 \ln p_2 - .3935 \ln p_3 + .0015 \ln a_1$$
$$\quad (.1172) \ (.0485) \qquad (.0481) \qquad (.0651) \qquad (.0055)$$

$$+ .0069 \ln a_2 + .0143 \ln a_3$$
$$\quad (.0105) \qquad (.0062)$$

where subscripts 1, 2, and 3 for $w$ and $p$ represent national-brand OJ, private-label OJ, and all other fruit juices, respectively, and numbers in parentheses are the coefficient standard errors.

The above equations show that all market shares are negatively related to the levels of their own prices and positively related to the levels of cross prices. The expenditure share of national-brand OJ is positively related to both brand and commodity advertising expenditures for OJ and negatively related to advertising expenditures for other fruit juices. However, $\hat{\phi}_{11}$ and $\hat{\phi}_{12}$ are not significantly different from zero at conventional levels. The expenditure share of private-label OJ is negatively related to all types of advertising expenditures, but all $\hat{\phi}_{2j}$'s are not significantly different from zero. The expenditure share of other fruit juices is positively related to all types of advertising expenditures. Again, $\hat{\phi}_{31}$ and $\hat{\phi}_{32}$ are not significantly different from zero. This result shows that advertising expenditure for other fruit juices had a positive impact on the expenditure share for other fruit juices and a negative impact on the expenditures for national-brand OJ. The estimated impacts of both brand and commodity OJ advertising expenditures on the expenditure shares of the three juices studied were not significant.

Table 13.5 presents the mean shadow prices of the advertising variables $a_i$, $i \leq 3$. These shadow prices can be interpreted as the change in total cost with respect to an additional unit increase in advertising expenditure. The result indicates that all three types of advertising expenditures had positive impacts on total cost. However, the shadow price estimate for brand advertising expenditures for OJ is not significantly different from zero. This may indicate that brand advertising is concerned with persuading people to switch from one "brand" of a commodity to another; therefore, there was no significant effect on total juice expenditure. The results presented in Table 13.5 indicate that a consumer's juice expenditure would be increased by $0.6856 and $0.2700 if OJ commodity advertising expenditure and other fruit juice advertising expenditures were increased by $1.00, respectively.

**Table 13.5. Mean shadow prices ($\pi_i$)**

| Media advertising expenditure | Shadow price | Standard error[a] |
|---|---|---|
| National brand orange juice | .1037 | .2603 |
| Florida orange juice | .6856 | .5286 |
| Other fruit juices | .2700 | .1763 |

[a]Calculated standard error.

Note that the study referred to above did not include capital and labor in the analysis. This is the equivalent of saying that consumers do not need time and proper equipment (e.g., television, newspapers, magazines, etc.) to receive advertising messages (if the capital and labor inputs remained at constant levels over the period analyzed, their effect might also be assumed to be included in the intercept). Therefore, the analysis lacks the very essence of the household production theory. More work needs to be done to include these variables in the analysis.

## Summary

As mentioned previously, the methods and the models used in advertising research and, therefore, the results obtained, depend to some extent on what the researcher believes the demand structure should be. Ward has assumed that the decay effect can peak during a time period other than the one when advertising expenditures were spent; therefore, he chose a polynomial lag model and allowed the data to determine the lag structure. On the other hand, given that estimation results are sensitive to model specification, we have assumed the decay effect decreases monotonically over time. Hence, we chose the Houthakker and Taylor (1970) model and did not experiment with the data to determine the advertising lag structure. As a result, the alternative modeling approaches have yielded different conclusions using almost identical data. Ward concluded that brand advertising had a positive impact on the total demand for OJ, while we concluded it did not. However, both analyses suggest that the BAR expenditures were misallocated.

The demand system approaches we used are not perfect even though both approaches provided similar results, i.e., commodity advertising for OJ had a positive impact on OJ category demand and brand advertising had significant impacts on maintaining particular brands' market shares within the OJ category; however, in both approaches, the decay effects of advertising were not explored. In addition, the household production theory approach used in the analysis assumed the household capital and labor inputs had no impact on the household stock of knowledge for the products of interest. The latter suggests a need to further research the decay nature of advertising in demand systems and household capital and labor effects in the household production theory approach.

Based on the above discussions, our conclusion is that nothing is complete nor conclusive in recent advertising impact studies. There is still a lot to be learned and explored, for example, the decay effect of advertising in the context of translation and scaling discussed by Brown and Lee in Chapter 6. The latter suggests that advertising may not only affect the intercept of the demand curve (shift the demand curve to the right) but may also affect the responsiveness of demand to changes in prices and income. Some research has been done in this area, but more work is needed.

The Houthakker and Taylor model estimated in this study suggests that consumers' habits play an important role in the consumption of OJ, with a decrease in the habit effect resulting in a decrease in the advertising effect. Given that most food products are purchased and consumed during a relatively short time period, and as past research indicates, television-commercial recall decays rapidly, the conclusion that the advertising effect can last for more than a year, as Ward's study suggested, or forever, as our model indicated, needs further research. Another interesting topic to be studied is whether our model confused the habit and advertising effects.

Previous studies (Ward 1975; Lee 1977) suggest that commodity and brand advertising had complementary effects on the demand for OJ. However, above studies assumed commodity and brand advertising had independent effects on the demand for OJ and did not address the interaction between these two types of advertising. More specific econometric models need to be developed to address this problem.

Most of the studies discussed above used deflated advertising expenditures as the measuring unit for advertising effort. Since the unit price of advertising depends heavily on the practices of advertising agencies, deflated advertising expenditures may not actually reflect the physical units purchased with a given amount of advertising dollars. Therefore, other measuring units (e.g., gross rating points, the number of pages of printed material, the total commercial time during prime-time television programs, etc.) should be considered as candidates for measuring advertising effort in future studies.

From published studies one learns that commodity and brand advertising efforts or promotions for agricultural products have positive impacts on the promoted products. Given that the at-home food expenditure share of total consumer expenditures has been decreasing during the last decade and that most advertising research has been based on consumer panel data focusing on at-home food expenditures, research on whether commodity advertising activities have positive impacts on away-from-home food expenditures (a growing segment of the food industry) is also needed. In addition, in order to understand the competitive nature of agricultural commodity advertising within the food category and against nonfood categories, systems of demand equations are needed.

The FDOC not only promotes OJ through consumer advertising but also through other media. For example, FDOC field representatives visit retail chain-store headquarters to synchronize store promotional activities and consumers advertising (e.g., point-of-sale displays, coupon promotions, use of Florida logos and shelf location of citrus products in stores, etc.). FDOC nutritionists visit school districts to promote the nutritional values of OJ. Given that consumer advertising accounts for less than 60 percent of total promotional activities, other promotional activities should be incorporated in future advertising studies.

Initially, the variance in the results of the present study and Ward's 1975 study stresses the need to develop more accurate and acceptable methods to measure the impact of advertising. If the results of our study and Ward's study were used in a public hearing to represent rival interest groups, one would have a difficult time in deciding which study is correct.

# 14 Discussion: Generic and Brand Advertising

## RONALD W. WARD

Three broad issues relating to the joint use of generic and brand advertising need addressing:

1. What theoretical framework do we have to draw from when dealing with generic and brand advertising?
2. What methodologies are appropriate for measuring the effects of generic and brand advertising?
3. What empirical evidence exists to show the relative effects of both types of advertising?

Let me briefly comment on the first two issues, and then I will reserve time to provide additional insight into the empirical results for orange juice. The Jones and Choi and Lee and Brown papers provide needed empirical results. Jones and Choi deal with the potato market which does not provide a long history of advertising evaluation; whereas, Lee and Brown provide additional empirical results to an industry that has been studied on a continuous basis for several years.

## Theoretical Framework

What do we know about the theoretical framework? The Jones and Choi paper draws on the work by Stigler and Becker (1967), Nichols (1985), and subsequent work by Chang (1988). That is, advertising enters the demand model via the advertiser's ability to influence consumer perceptions and understanding of product characteristics. One can take the Nichols framework and directly show the theoretical roles of both generic and brand advertising. Chang has worked on this in his 1988 dissertation.

There is little in the theoretical literature that precludes either generic or brand advertising from entering the aggregate demand model. Accepting that premise, then the issue becomes: Would one expect the advertising effectiveness between generic and brand to differ? Advertising effectiveness should be related to (1) the potential *characteristic space* for a commodity (i.e., how much differentiation can occur?), (2) the current *state of knowledge* and product use, and (3) what is *being conveyed* with both types of advertising. The list below identifies specific product and market attributes that will directly impact both generic and brand advertising elasticities:

* Product nutritional and health attributes
* Current state of consumer knowledge
* Current consumer perceptions
* Importance to consumer's diet
* Consumption saturation
* Shelf life
* Product identity throughout the marketing channels
* Product forms — differentiability
* Number of uses
* Nature of product forms
* Frequency of use
* Storability
* Production seasonality, quality variation, and availability
* Production differentiation
* Geographical production and distribution
* Number of substitutes
* Foreign versus domestic markets
* Consumption customs among potential markets
* Product value

There are several working hypotheses related to the differences in generic versus brand advertising, including:

1.  The effectiveness of generic and brand advertising should show little difference for those goods that have limited ability for differentiation, i.e., cooperative goods. A cooperative good is one for which total sales increase equally with either type of advertising. Similarly, brand advertising cannot increase the share of one brand within the goods category.
2.  Joint generic and brand advertising can both provide the consumer with information and influence perceptions, thus impacting the aggregate demand for the product category. Typically, in industries with both generic and brand programs, the generic message is more informative

but less focused to specific target audiences and attributes. The brand message is direct and often provides comparative messages.

3.  A strong generic program may force brand advertisers to redirect their efforts to claims that are more difficult to verify. That is, new efforts to achieve differentiation may be compounded by the generic emphasis on overall quality, standardization, and uniformity.

4.  There may be overlapping in the message content between generic and brand advertising. In such cases, some types of joint ventures may be appropriate.

As I read the literature and work with the theoretical models, I see little to preclude the incorporation of both types of advertising in the aggregate analysis. Clearly the objectives are different.

The fundamental difference between generic and brand advertising lies within two broad areas. The most obvious difference is the source of funding. The funding source has a direct and sometimes limiting effect on what can and cannot be communicated in the advertising message. Brand messages are typically more focused on specific attributes and often entail direct comparison among brands within the product group and between product groups. Product information may be relegated to a lesser role because of the strong need to provide contrast and changes in perceptions. However, there is nothing fundamental to brand advertising that precludes emphasizing the overall product attributes, as generic advertising does. Yet, generic advertising typically precludes brand identification.

Second, generic vs. brand advertising differs in that "conjecture variation" is important to the brand but not necessarily to the generic. That is, each firm must always be cognizant of a competing brand's reaction to a brand message. If the potential for strong brand reprisal is possible, one could argue that this alone forces brands to more closely attune their programs to the generic message. The limits to brand advertising elasticity depend on the direct response by consumers along with the reaction by competing brands. These limits in turn are directly influenced by the product attributes, market characteristics, and market structure.

Accepting this, then the impact becomes an empirical question. Let me now turn to the empirical results, and in particular the orange juice model.

## The OJ Advertising Debate

Lee and Brown present an interesting empirical exercise and in some cases report results in direct conflict with my own analysis. There is little question that different empirical methodologies can yield differing results.

Yet, it does concern me when separate analyses lead to directly opposite conclusions. Let me take a few minutes to add some additional clarification (or confusion) to the modeling.

The basis question is: Does brand advertising of the orange juice market influence the total demand for orange juice? This is a separate issue from the brand advertising potential for shifting shares. There is little question that when products can be differentiated, market shares can be shifted (or at least maintained) through brand advertising. The issue is its impact on the total market. The Florida Department of Citrus (FDOC) interest in the brand effect relates to an advertising rebate program that allocates a sizeable share of generic funds to brand rebate programs. These programs were designed and implemented by FDOC. There has been concern among the FDOC staff that too large of a share of generic funds were being diverted to brand rebate programs. Hence, the question of effectiveness of both generic and brand advertising of citrus is of paramount importance to achieving an optimal allocation of generic funds.

Figure 14.1 provides data on total orange juice advertising efforts for the periods from February 1978 through December 1987. The major increases in brand activity starting in 1983 is clearly evident. The FDOC conclusions are that this brand advertising had no impact on the aggregate demand for orange juice while the generic advertising impact is strong. They used a habit persistence model to capture the lag effects for both generic and brand advertising. Their model points to a strong generic effect and an insignificant brand effect. They then draw the conclusion that a $1 million increase in generic advertising will increase sales by 21.96 gallons per 1000 persons per bimonthly period. Assuming retail prices of $3.50 per gallon single strength equivalent, this translates into sales increases in excess of $60 million for the $1 million increases in advertising. This rate of return seems quite high if not implausible given our experiences with other commodities.

Lee and Brown's habit persistence model was estimated in the traditional way except that they included a seasonal dummy variable. One can argue that seasonal dummies also reflect some type of habit persistence and, hence, should not be included in the model since this effect is already imbedded in the lagged dependent variable. Using the exact data that my original model was estimated with, I reestimated the habit persistence model with and without the seasonal dummy variables. This model did not include the advertising from other juices but, as Lee and Brown argue, this is partially captured with a lagged dependent variable. (An appendix containing the econometric model and estimated coefficients is available from the author upon request.)

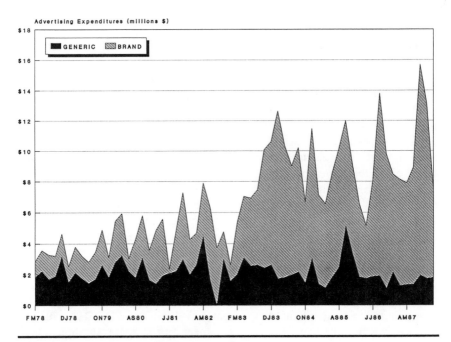

**Figure 14.1. Bimonthly orange juice advertising.**

Here are the results from four basis models:

1.  Model A — Habit Persistence with Seasonal Dummy
2.  Model B — Habit Persistence without Seasonal Dummy
3.  Model C — Polynomial Model with Seasonal Dummies
4.  Model D — Polynomial Model with Seasonal Dummies Removed

Model A (Figure 14.2) shows the lag structure using the *habit persistence model* and the seasonal adjustment. Note that any lag structure to the advertising is assumed identical for generic and brand. The lines are with seasonal adjustments and the bar values are for the habit persistence without seasonal adjustments. From this model one draws the conclusion outlined in Lee and Brown's paper.

Now, removing the seasonal adjuster in the *habit persistence model* (Model B), a dramatically different conclusion is evident. In the model without the seasonal shifter, brand advertising is significant and substantially larger than that shown for generic advertising. My conclusion from their *habit persistence model* with the seasonal factor is that part of their seasonal

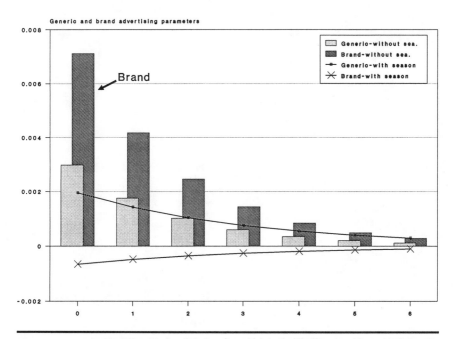

**Figure 14.2.** Orange juice advertising analysis using habit persistence with and without seasonal adjustment.

adjuster, along with the lagged demand variable, has compromised the brand parameter. Part of this may be attributable to some seasonality in the advertising activities and in part to statistical problems associated with having two similar measures of habit persistence in the same model. In addition, problems associated with a lagged dependent variable cannot be ignored.

Now let us compare the *revised habit persistence model* (Model B) to the results from the *polynomial lag model* (Model C). In Figure 14.3 I have plotted the generic and brand lagged structure derived from the polynomial model (see Ward 1988a, 1988b). The bar values represent the results based on using a polynomial lag structure, while the lines use habit persistence with seasonality removed. The differences in generic and brand advertising are clear, giving a larger initial brand impact with subsequent declines for the polynomial model. The generic effect is initially not as large but has a less rapidly decaying carryover effect relative to the brand. Again as Lee and Brown noted, these models are based on restricted polynomial lags. To this figure I have added the results from the *habit persistence model* after removing the seasonal shifter.

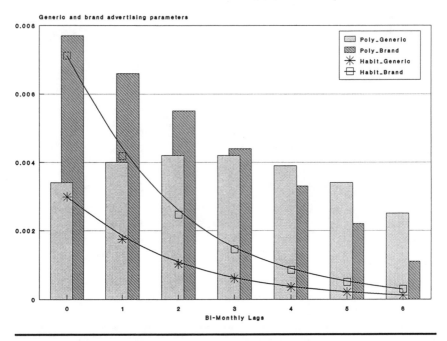

**Figure 14.3.** Orange juice advertising analysis using habit persistence compared with polynomial models.

Several conclusions are apparent:

1. The initial brand effects in the two models are almost identical, with brand advertising being significant. This is in complete contrast with the initial results using the seasonality factor. (Model A).
2. The generic effects are also nearly equal in Figure 14.3.
3. The relative generic and brand effects from both models are almost equal.
4. The lagged lengths used in the polynomial model correspond closely with those evident from the unrestricted habit persistence model.
5. Brand advertising is statistically significant in both models as is generic.

To be complete, I also deleted the seasonal dummies from the polynomial model in order to show any sensitivity to the removal of seasonality. In Figure 14.4, I have plotted the original generic and brand carryover effects along with those measured with the model where the seasonal dummies are removed from my original estimates. As evident in this graph, the seasonal dummies have little effect on the polynomial

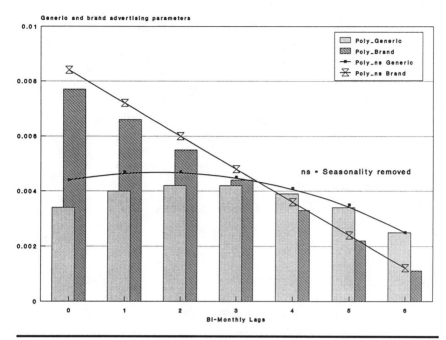

**Figure 14.4.** Orange juice advertising analysis using polynomial lag models with and without seasonality.

model's advertising parameters. The estimates for both current and lagged generic and brand advertising differ little with or without the seasonality in the polynomial models.

What are my conclusions from this exercise?

1.  First, there will never be complete agreement and this provides the stimulant necessary for progress. Nevertheless, it is still apparent to me that brand advertising has a strong positive impact on the total orange juice market and is somewhat greater than that measured for generic.
2.  Second, brand advertising in the OJ market has caused brand shifting, primarily from private label to brands. Whether this is good or bad is another issue. One can set forth all kinds for arguments relating to the benefits and cost from increased competition to the industry, and of course to the consumer. In any case, the brand switching has little to do with the effect on the total market.
3.  Third, as Lee and Brown point out, there are clear differences in the marginal returns from both types of advertising, with the marginal rates being tied primarily to the substantial differences in the levels of generic

and brand advertising. My analysis of the level of use of both types of citrus advertising is that at current expenditure levels the marginal returns to both are approaching one (see Ward 1988b). This is clearly different from the profound conclusion from Lee and Brown that the marginal return to brand for the industry is near zero or insignificant.

Given the dominance of a few brand advertisers in the industry and the large brand expenditure levels (Figure 14.1), I simply fail to see any logical argument for expecting the demand for a product like orange juice to be totally invariant to brand advertising. The attributes of the product are such that it is closer to a cooperative good than a predatory good. Recall that for a predatory good, brand advertising simply shifts shares but does not change the total demand (see, e.g., Ward et al. 1985). I doubt that the industry is willing to put orange juice into the class of predatory goods.

## Jones and Choi Potato Model

The potato analysis is a much more complex modeling effort. Generic and brand advertising enter the demand for potatoes, while simultaneously recognizing the structural effects on the industry. I was involved in this modeling, thus it is hardly fair for me to critique it. The reasonableness of the results is what is important. Jones and Choi's analysis points to an impact of generic advertising on fresh potatoes and a positive brand impact on processed potatoes, primarily potato chips. Given that brand advertising is almost exclusively limited to the processed potato sector, it is not at all surprising to see the importance of the brand effort. Likewise, the generic message (while not restricted to fresh) has had a fresh orientation. The results seem consistent with prior hypotheses and expectations.

The generic and brand advertising of potatoes is fundamentally different from orange juice. In the citrus industry, both the generic and brand messages are primarily for the same product, i.e., frozen and ready-to-serve orange juice. Whereas, generic and brand potato advertising is directed to almost two distinctly different products. One would expect to see considerably more differences in the effectiveness of generic and brand advertising in potatoes compared with orange juice.

## Conclusions

Most of the past empirical analyses of advertising responses have been directed toward achieving segmented markets. We are now struggling with a relatively new set of issues where both collective and private advertising exist. Industrial organization literature provides some insights into the potential market power issues relating to the competing brand effects. We are, however, still some considerable distance away from developing a clear conceptual framework for dealing with both generic and brand advertising in the same set. Much can be learned by first having a good understanding of the industry, its product characteristics, and consumption history. Likewise, one must always know the limitations of the data. Measurement error and model specification as illustrated above can lead to profoundly different conclusions. "Rules of reasonableness" must always be a part of the evaluation process. If our results make little sense in terms of "reasonableness" to an industry, then I doubt that our research efforts will ever have much impact.

# 4 Attitudes in Advertising Research

# 15 Evaluating the Effectiveness of Generic Pork Advertising: The First Fifteen Months

SUE HOOVER, MARVIN HAYENGA, and STANLEY R. JOHNSON

With the proliferation of farm commodity organizations and their associated promotion programs during the late 1970s and 1980s, generic advertising has become an increasingly important component of the marketing of agricultural products. Since 1982, newly enacted federal check-off legislation, including programs for dairy, tobacco, beef, and pork,[1] has substantially increased the collection of check-off funds from producers and growers for use in commodity promotion. Media advertising expenditures in particular have increased. Because increasing resources are being channeled into government-authorized, producer-supported advertising of farm products, there is considerable interest in measuring the effectiveness of generic advertising.

Effective advertising either encourages consumers to pay more per unit for a given quantity of a product, or increases the quantity of a product consumers wish to purchase at a given price, holding constant other factors expected to affect consumer choice. Therefore, from the commodity organization's standpoint, the primary considerations in evaluating the effectiveness of generic advertising are: (1) the advertising impact on consumer attitudes toward and demand for the product; and (2) the producer benefits derived from advertising-induced increases in product demand.

The literature provides a variety of empirical studies measuring the impact of farm commodity advertising on demand. Almost exclusively, econometric models estimated with aggregate time series or pooled time series and cross-sectional data have been used to measure advertising impact on sales. The major findings of these studies can be summarized as follows:

1. Advertising has a positive and statistically significant effect on sales (e.g., Nerlove and Waugh 1961; Ward and Dixon 1987; Ward and Myers 1979).

235

2. The effects of advertising expenditures accumulate (carryover) and dissipate (decay) over time (e.g., Ward 1976).
3. Advertising has a diminishing marginal effect on sales (Kinnucan 1985).

With the exception of a recent beef advertising evaluation (CARD 1988), studies have seldom used experimental data to measure the economic impact of generic advertising. Few studies have incorporated supply response and cross-commodity effects into advertising evaluation (see CARD 1988 for an example). Although the marketing and operations research literatures offer a variety of methodologies for characterizing consumer response to advertising (e.g., Bagozzi 1983; Fishbein 1967), the impact of generic advertising on message recall, consumer awareness, and attitudes has not been thoroughly analyzed. In studies addressing these issues, Jensen and Kesavan (1987) applied a multistage information-decision process model to evaluate the effect of calcium advertising on dairy product consumption, and Thompson and Eiler (1975) analyzed the impact of advertising awareness on milk usage.

The objectives of this paper are to use experimental data on fresh pork advertising to analyze the effectiveness of generic advertising after a relatively short period of experience. In accomplishing this objective, we will (1) demonstrate the usefulness of advertising tracking and consumer attitude survey instruments for evaluating generic advertising; (2) use a simple consumption model to measure consumer response to advertising media; (3) use a sequential model of the consumer decision making process to estimate the recall, attribute perception, and consumption responses to media advertising; and (4) use a dynamic livestock industry model, incorporating supply response and cross-commodity impacts to evaluate the aggregate producer organization payoff from generic advertising. These are not newly developed approaches for evaluating generic advertising but are being applied to a relatively new media advertising program for which no previous economic research exists.

## Overview of Fresh Pork Advertising and Promotion

A mandatory check-off for pork producers, effective in November 1986, provided funding for an expanded pork promotion program. The National Pork Producers Council (NPPC) through agreement with the National Pork Board, an independent body charged with administering the check-off, is using check-off funds to conduct a broad promotional campaign intended to reposition fresh pork in the marketplace. Consumer attitude research has revealed that pork — unlike chicken — is not widely perceived as possessing the product attributes that today are considered most important when selecting foods. NPPC's "Pork—The Other White Meat" campaign is designed to inform consumers that pork is a white meat and it is nutritious, convenient, versatile, and good tasting.

A substantial share of the check-off funds earmarked for promotion are being used to promote pork through print and television advertising. Since February 1987 print advertising has been used throughout the United States, and television commercials have been used to reinforce the print message in key markets identified as good prospects for large increases in pork consumption. In 1987, $7.5 million, or approximately 30 percent of the check-off funds collected, was spent on advertising, and $8.3 million was budgeted for advertising in 1988.

## Experimental Data

The NPPC staff, in conjunction with advertising agency and market research consultants, designed an experiment to test advertising. Data from the experiment were collected for the "Pork Attitude and Perception Study" (PAPS) by a private market research firm, Rozmarin and Associates, Inc., of Omaha, Nebraska.

Six cities receiving three different levels of advertising exposure were selected as test markets. Because print advertising and other forms of NPPC's Other White Meat promotion programs occurred nationwide, it was not possible to designate control markets without exposure to the Other White Meat message. (The cost and difficulty of suppressing print advertising in test markets were considered too high by NPPC staff.) Instead, two cities that did not receive television advertising were used as "control" markets. The four experimental markets consisted of two urban markets receiving 200 gross rating points (GRPs) of television advertising per week, or the equivalent of a $13 million per year national advertising campaign, and two urban markets receiving 100 GRPs of television advertising per week, or the equivalent of a $6 million per year national campaign.

The six test markets by type of media buy were:

heavy television (200 GRPs per week) and magazines — Cleveland and Sacramento;
base television (100 GRPs per week) and magazines — Pittsburgh and Denver;
magazines only — Baltimore and San Diego.

About 20 percent of the U.S. population is located in markets that receive the base level of television advertising and print. The remaining 80 percent of the population (except for the two heavy television test markets) is located in markets exposed to only print advertising, costing approximately $2.8 million per year.

## SURVEY PROCEDURE

Three telephone surveys of randomly selected households were conducted in each of the six test markets for the PAPS. To establish a benchmark of consumer beliefs about fresh pork, a pretest survey of 1200 households (200 interviews from each test market) was conducted during February 1987 before the Other White Meat television advertising began. A second survey of 1800 households (300 interviews from each test market) was completed in October 1987 after the first year's advertising, and a third survey of 1800 households was made in May 1988 at the midpoint of the second year advertising program.

A screening procedure was used to identify and interview a quota of primary target audience consumers — women between the ages of 25 and 54 with children living at home. Interviews were also conducted with other females and males in the 25 to 54 age category if they were the primary food buyers for their households. Therefore, the sample represents only primary food buyers between 25 and 54 years old.

## DATA

The same basic questionnaire was administered in all three surveys. Data on the survey respondent's advertising exposure and message recall, beliefs about fresh pork attributes, and socioeconomic characteristics were available from the survey. The socioeconomic data included: age, employment status, marital status, education, household size, household income, geographic location, and the presence of children under 18 in the household. The data on beliefs about fresh pork were obtained from questions requesting the respondent to rate fresh pork on six characteristics.

As with most advertising tracking studies, the data in the PAPS were limited in measuring actual fresh pork consumption. Consumption data were collected by asking the number of times in the past two weeks each respondent had served fresh pork. These data may not reflect actual pork consumption in terms of either the number of servings or the quantity consumed. They are instead estimates of the respondent's "perceived" frequency of consumption.[2] They should be considered indicators of fresh pork consumption levels, or of the respondent's overall attitude toward fresh pork.

## Evaluation of Short-Term Impacts of Fresh Pork Advertising

To evaluate the advertising's impact on consumer attitudes and consumption behavior after the first 15 months of the campaign, data from the PAPS were analyzed using several approaches. The key questions addressed by these analyses were:

1. Does television advertising, when used in conjunction with print advertising and other promotion, affect fresh pork consumption and consumer beliefs about fresh pork?
2. Does a higher level of television advertising have more of an effect on fresh pork consumption and consumer beliefs than a low level of television advertising?
3. Which socioeconomic and demographic characteristics are the most important determinants of beliefs about and consumption of fresh pork?

### THE EXPLORATORY MODEL

An exploratory model was specified to investigate the relationship between advertising exposure, demographic characteristics, and perceived frequency of fresh pork consumption. The model conditions for household characteristics the observed effects of advertising and explores the relationship between household characteristics and frequency of fresh pork consumption. The choice of explanatory variables and the functional form was based on economic theory and the data available. The advertising exposure variables measure consumption behavior differences between households that were exposed to the advertising treatments. Thus, the regression model allowed estimation of the incremental consumption effects of television plus print advertising over just print advertising alone, and of a heavy level of television advertising over a base level of television advertising. The cumulative impact of television advertising over time was also estimated.

The exploratory specification was a single equation and linear with an additive error term:

$$
\begin{aligned}
FPCON_i = f(&AGE_i, HHSIZE_i, ONEHEAD_i, KIDS_i, INC1_i, INC2_i, \\
&INC3_i, INC4_i, COLLEGE_i, WH\_COL_i, NOT\_EMP_i, \\
&TWO\_ERN2_i, WCOAST_i, ECOAST_i, HTVEFF2_i, \\
&BTVEFF2_i, PRTEFF2_i, HTVEFF3_i, BTVEFF3_i, \\
&PRTEFF3_i) + e_i \qquad\qquad\qquad\qquad\qquad (15.1)
\end{aligned}
$$

where:

$i = 1, \ldots, n$ is the number of household observations;

FPCON is perceived frequency of consumption of fresh pork for the household during the previous two-week period, measured at the midpoint of the categories provided for responses (0, 1-2, 3-4, 5-6, 7-8, 9+);

AGE is age of primary food shopper in the household, measured at the midpoint of 10-year increments from 25 to 54;

HHSIZE is number of members in the household;

ONEHEAD is a dummy variable equal to 1 if the household has only one head and zero otherwise;

KIDS is dummy variable equal to 1 if there are children under 18 in the household and zero otherwise;

INC1, INC2, INC3, INC4 are dummy variables equal to 1 if the household reported annual income falls within the indicated ranges, and zero otherwise:

INC1: $15,000 to $29,999
INC2: $30,000 to $44,999
INC3: greater than $45,000
INC4: don't know or no response;

COLLEGE is a dummy variable equal to 1 if the primary food shopper in the household had some college classes or technical training, and zero otherwise;

WH_COL is a dummy variable equal to 1 if the household had a head employed in a professional, technical, managerial, or other white collar occupation, and zero otherwise;

NOT_EMP is a dummy variable equal to 1 if all the head(s) of the household were not employed, and zero otherwise;

TWO_ERN is a dummy variable equal to 1 if the household had two heads of household employed, and zero otherwise;

WCOAST, ECOAST are dummy variables equal to 1 if the household was in a city located on the East or West Coast, respectively, and zero otherwise;

HTVEFF2, BVTEFF2, PRTEFF2, HTVEFF3, BTVEFF3, PRTEFF3 are dummy variables equal to 1 for households in the indicated media

markets surveys, and zero otherwise:
HTVEFF2: heavy TV and print market, second survey
BTVEFF2: base TV and print market, second survey
PRTEFF2: print market, second survey
HTVEFF3: heavy TV and print market, third survey
BTVEFF3: base TV and print market, third survey
PRTEFF3: print market, third survey;
$e$ is the additive disturbance, assumed independently, identically, and normally distributed.

## RESULTS

The data from households in the media markets and for all surveys were merged. Estimation of the model was by ordinary least squares (OLS) using a sample of 4,440 households from the surveys. The results are reported in Table 15.1. The $R^2$ value indicates that the conditioning variables explained approximately 5.2 percent of the variation in the consumption indicator. This figure is "low," but not out of line with $R^2$ values obtained in similar analyses.

### Sociodemographic Effects on Fresh Pork Consumption

The results indicated that several sociodemographic characteristics were significant in explaining frequency of fresh pork consumption: age of the household's primary food buyer, household size, and education of the primary shopper and occupation of the household's primary wage earner. Of particular interest, frequency of fresh pork consumption was lower among households located in coastal regions of the country than among households located elsewhere. The 1985 Continuing Survey of Food Intakes by Individual (CSFII) report shows the "percentage of individuals using pork at least once in four consecutive days" to be highest in the southern United States, followed by the Midwest, West, and northeastern regions of the country. Higher relative prices for fresh pork in the coastal regions and the availability of substitute products, such as fresh seafood, may have been reflected in the location variable. The remaining sociodemographic variables did not significantly affect the consumption indicator.

### Advertising Effects on Fresh Pork Consumption

The remaining variables in the model reflect advertising effects. It is

Table 15.1  Advertising and other factors influencing perceived frequency of household fresh pork consumption: Estimated ordinary least squares coefficients

| Variable | Estimated coefficient | $t$-statistic |
|---|---|---|
| INTERCEPT | 1.28[a] | 7.92 |
| AGE | -0.005[a] | -1.77 |
| HHSIZE | 0.11[b] | 4.50 |
| ONEHEAD | 0.02 | 0.36 |
| KIDS | 0.004 | 0.07 |
| INC1 | 0.05 | 0.55 |
| INC2 | 0.04 | 0.46 |
| INC3 | 0.05 | 0.49 |
| INC4 | -0.17[a] | -1.70 |
| COLLEGE | -0.16[b] | -3.35 |
| WH_COL | -0.24[b] | -4.95 |
| NOT_EMP | 0.03 | 0.36 |
| TWO_ERN | 0.08[a] | 1.64 |
| WCOAST | -0.31[b] | -5.43 |
| ECOAST | -0.32[b] | -4.16 |
| HTVEFF2 | 0.19[b] | 2.73 |
| BTVEFF2 | 0.06 | 0.73 |
| PRTEFF2 | -0.03 | -0.43 |
| HTVEFF3 | 0.35[b] | 5.17 |
| BTVEFF3 | 0.18[b] | 2.41 |
| PRTEFF3 | 0.20[b] | 2.69 |
| $R^2$ | 0.052 | |
| $F$-Value | 12.041 | |

[a]Statistically significant at .10 level.
[b]Statistically significant at .05 level.

important to note that these variables measure the effects of potential exposure to advertising, not the effect of actual exposure to the print or television advertising.

It is also important to remember that advertising is only part of NPPC's Other White Meat promotional campaign. About 75 percent of NPPC's annual marketing expenditures was for advertising, and the other 25 percent was for promotion other than advertising, such as food service merchandising, cooperative advertising with retailers, merchandising seminars, and consumer information programs. Although expenditures for these other types of nationwide promotion were available, assessments of their relative importance in the test markets was not available. The information on households collected with the PAPS survey instrument did not clearly differentiate those households whose behavior might have been influenced by exposure to advertising, or indirectly by other forms of promotion using the Other White Meat theme.

In the second survey, the effect of heavy television exposure was positive and significant; the base television effect was positive but insignificant. In the third survey, the effects of exposure to heavy television, base television, and print only were positive and significant. The positive and significant heavy television effect in the second survey, for example, implies that a household exposed to heavy television and print advertising for nine months typically consumed fresh pork more frequently than a comparable household surveyed before advertising or the Other White Meat promotion began. The other advertising effects are interpreted similarly.

Of course, these differences in consumption frequency do not accurately represent the impact of the advertising, because the advertising variables also are proxies for effects of other time-varying consumption determinants, such as changes in the price of fresh pork relative to substitutes. (In the period of time between the preadvertising and second survey: fresh pork prices—the national average retail per-pound-price of a center-cut pork chop—had increased 8 percent; beef and veal prices had increased 5 percent; and poultry prices had decreased 4 percent. And between the second and third surveys: fresh pork prices decreased 5 percent; beef and veal prices increased another 4 percent; and poultry prices decreased 2 percent.) Furthermore, the effect of the advertising reflected in the qualitative variables may be over- or understated. For instance, although the base television and print only coefficients in the second survey were insignificant, it is possible that higher pork prices at the time of the second survey may have overwhelmed the positive advertising effect from the first nine months of advertising.

Given the six-market experimental design, it was not possible to measure the effect of print advertising over time because the test markets receiving television advertising and the print only test markets were all potentially influenced by other forces. However, significant differences in consumption between the test markets at the same point in time can be attributed to the television advertising and differences in those markets. For example, the heavy television effect in the second survey minus the print effect in the second survey (HTVEFF2 − PRTEFF2) can be interpreted as that portion of advertising's effect on frequency of consumption attributable to the households' exposure to a heavy level of television advertising, given their exposure to print advertising and other promotion. See Table 15.2 for the values of these differences.

The differences between the heavy television plus print and the print only effects were significant in both the second and third surveys. These results suggest that when a heavy level of television advertising was used with print advertising, the television advertising had an incremental impact on the frequency of consumption. Evidence was not conclusive on the

**Table 15.2 Calculation of conditional advertising effects using coefficients estimated in exploratory model**

| Effect | Estimated parameters[a] | | | Value |
|---|---|---|---|---|
| Heavy TV effect/print in second survey | HTVEFF2 (0.19) | − | PRTEFF2 (-0.03) | 0.22[b] |
| Base TV effect/print in second survey | BTVEFF2 (0.06) | − | PRTEFF2 (-0.03) | 0.09 |
| Heavy TV effect/base TV and print in second survey | HTVEFF2 (0.19) | − | BTVEFF2 (0.06) | 0.13 |
| Heavy TV effect/print in third survey | HTVEFF3 (0.35) | − | PRTEFF3 (0.20) | 0.15[b] |
| Base TV effect/print in third survey | BTVEFF3 (0.18) | − | PRTEFF3 (0.20) | -0.02 |
| Heavy TV effect/base TV in print in third survey | HTVEFF3 (0.35) | − | BTVEFF3 (0.18) | 0.17[b] |
| Heavy TV effect/print difference between second and third surveys | (0.15) | − | (0.22) | -0.07 |
| Base TV effect/print difference between second and third surveys | (-0.02) | − | (0.09) | (-0.11) |
| Heavy TV effect/base TV and print difference between second and third surveys | (0.17) | − | (0.13) | (0.04) |

[a]Estimated coefficients from Table 15.1.
[b]Statistically significant at .10 level.

incremental impact of a base level of television advertising used with print advertising. The base television plus print effect was slightly larger than the print only effect in the second survey but was smaller in the third survey, although neither of the differences was significant. The differences between the heavy television plus print effect were positive in both the second and third surveys, but the difference was significant only in the third survey. Therefore, from the first 15 months of experience, there appeared to be no significant impact from adding a base level of television advertising to print advertising; but there was a significant positive impact when a heavy level of television advertising was added to print advertising.

To investigate whether the effects of television advertising became more pronounced after households were exposed to the advertising for a longer time, the differences between the heavy television and the base television effects were compared in the second and third surveys. These values are also shown in Table 15.2. Since the differences were not significantly larger in the third survey period, there did not appear to be an incremental effect from a longer period of exposure.

## A STANDARDIZED SAMPLE DEMOGRAPHIC COMPOSITION MODEL

An alternative statistical procedure used to analyze the experimental data standardized the sample for demographic composition across time and sorted the preadvertising and postadvertising differences in reported frequency of fresh pork consumption. The exploratory model (equation 15.1), respecified to include only the sociodemographic explanatory variables, was used to estimate city-specific sets of coefficients for households in each survey. The preadvertising consumption relationships were used to determine the "expected" household consumption frequency, assuming no advertising, for households in the second and third surveys. The predicted values of consumption frequency for households in the second and third surveys were obtained from the model estimation. The difference between the "expected" and predicted consumption frequency can be attributed to the impact of the advertising program. These differences were regressed on advertising exposure variables as described in the previous section.

The results from this analysis (not reported) indicated that both heavy and base television advertising, when used with print, had a significant incremental impact over print advertising alone in the second and third survey periods. Furthermore, the incremental impact of the two levels of television were similar. However, the incremental impacts were significantly less in the third survey than in the second.

## A MULTISTAGE MODEL OF ADVERTISING EFFECTIVENESS

A multistage model of consumer behavior reflecting the stimulus-organism-response concept of consumer behavior, postulates that advertising communication (the stimulus) impacts on the consumer behavior in a hierarchical fashion (Bagozzi 1983; Jensen and Kesavan 1987). In this conceptual framework, after a consumer is exposed to an advertising stimulus, he or she processes the informational content of the message (the cognitive state) and develops an attitude toward the product (the affective state). In the final stage, a consumption decision is made. This hierarchy of effect is related to the consumers' prior learning and degree of involvement with a product or service, including perceived importance of the decision and the degree of actual or perceived risk involved. When prior learning has taken place, as would be the case for most food products, the effect of advertising stimuli is related to the type of message conveyed.

One type of advertising message provides factual information to help consumers understand product characteristics. This attribute-specific advertising message affects consumption by changing consumers' subjective distributions of beliefs about the product, thereby changing their preference for the advertised product. In other words, the consumer updates existing affective and cognitive states. This type of informational message may be especially valuable for those food product attributes that cannot be determined easily by consumer experience; for example, product safety, nutritive value, alternative uses.

Alternatively, by virtue of its mere existence rather than its factual content, advertising may "signal" product quality, thereby, providing information in an indirect form (Nelson 1974). Or, advertising may encourage repeat purchases of the product by using methods that keep the product "top of the mind" with consumers. In this case, the advertising might stimulate recall and recognition of learned psychological reactions (Bagozzi 1983). In contrast to the message carrying information about product characteristics, which impacts indirectly on consumption through its effect on beliefs and attribute perception, these nonattribute-specific messages impact directly on the consumption behavior.

## MULTISTAGE MODEL

An ad hoc model of the consumer decision making process was used in this analysis (Jensen and Kesavan 1987). The model measures responses relating directly to the stated objective of the Other White Meat promotion, that is, to inform consumers that fresh pork possesses those product attributes considered important in food selection. This approach also takes into account actual exposure to the advertising.

The model incorporates advertising in the following way. In the first stage, consumers are exposed to the Other White Meat advertising stimulus. Whether consumers actually process the message is measured by their reported recall of the advertising message. Reported message recall is assumed to be determined by sociodemographic characteristics and the intensity and duration of the advertising exposure. In the second stage, the advertising information and the consumers' sociodemographic characteristics (predisposition) determine how fresh pork attributes are perceived. In the final stage, the decision to consume fresh pork reflects both the attribute-specific advertising information through favorable attribute perception, and the direct effect of the reminder and nonattribute-specific information.

To implement the model, the following relationships can be estimated: effects of sociodemographic characteristics and advertising exposure on reported recall, effects of sociodemographic characteristics and reported advertising recall on attribute perception; and effects of sociodemographic characteristics, reported recall, and attribute perception on consumption.

The three-equation model is:

$$M^* = f(Z_1, \text{AD\_EXP}) + e_1 \tag{15.2}$$
$$A^* = g(Z_2, M) + e_2 \tag{15.3}$$
$$C^* = h(Z_3, M, A) + e_3 \tag{15.4}$$

where:

$M^*$ is a binary response variable equal to 1 if the respondent reported recalling the "Other White Meat" message unaided, and zero otherwise;

AD\_EXP is a set of dummy variables indicating the intensity of advertising to which the respondent was exposed. Specifically, HTVEFF2, BTVEFF2, PRTEFF2, HTVEFF3, BTVEFF3, PRTEFF3 are dummy variables equal to 1 for households in the indicated media market survey, and zero otherwise;

> HTVEFF2: heavy TV and print market, second survey
> BTVEFF2: base TV and print market, second survey
> PRTEFF2: print market, second survey
> HTVEFF3: heavy TV and print market, third survey
> BTVEFF3: base TV and print market, third survey
> PRTEFF3: print market, third survey;

$A^*$ is a binary response variable equal to 1 if the respondent's perception of fresh pork attributes was favorable, and zero otherwise;

$M$ is the inverse Mills ratio derived from equation 15.2, and used to evaluate the effect of selection through the recall of the advertising message;[3]

$C^*$ is a binary response variable equal to 1 if the respondent had served fresh pork at home during the two weeks prior to the survey, and zero otherwise;

$A$ is the inverse Mills ratio derived from equation 15.3;

$Z_1, Z_2$, and $Z_3$ are sets of household characteristics; and

$e_1, e_2, e_3$ are disturbance terms with appropriate distributions.

## Measuring Reported Message Recall, Consumer Attitudes, and Consumption

Information on reported message recall ($M^*$) and consumption ($C^*$) was available directly from the PAPS. However, to measure consumer perception of fresh pork attributes ($A^*$) using the data available, an index was constructed as follows:

$$A_j = \Sigma B_{jk}/n \tag{15.5}$$

where:

$j = 1, \ldots, m$ is the number of consumers;
$k = 1, \ldots, n$ is the number of attribute ratings;
$A_j$ is consumer $j$'s perception of fresh pork attributes; and
$B_{jk}$ is the belief of individual $j$ regarding fresh pork attribute $k$.

Because only six attribute ratings were incorporated in the PAPS surveys, the available data placed limitations on the calculation of the attribute perception index for fresh pork. Survey respondents were asked to rate fresh pork, using a 1-to-5 scale, on the following characteristics: nutritive value, cholesterol content, calories per serving, taste or flavor, ease of preparation, and versatility ($B_j$'s).

If the respondent's attribute perception index measurement ($A_j$) was 3.0 (the mid-range rating) or greater, the respondent's perception of fresh pork attributes was categorized as "favorable," with $A^*$ set equal to 1. If $A_j$ measured less than 3.0, the respondent's attitude was categorized as "unfavorable," with $A^*$ set equal to 0.

## ESTIMATION OF THE MODEL

Equations 15.2, 15.3, and 15.4 form a recursive system in consumption, attribute perception, and reported recall. An estimation procedure was used to control a selectivity problem in the data. This selectivity problem results from the conditional structure of the hypothesized recursive system. For example, it is presumed in equation (15.2) that the respondents who did not recall the message, in fact, had been exposed to it. This, of course, is not necessarily true. Some respondents did not report recall because they were not exposed to the ad. For example, some respondents may not have watched television when the ads were run. A two-stage estimation procedure, adjusting equations (15.3) and (15.4) for this selectivity problem, used the inverse Mills ratio as a correction factor and yielded consistent results for the parameters of the model (Maddala 1983; Lee 1981). A maximum likelihood probit estimation was carried out on each equation.[4] The inverse Mills ratio of the $M^*$ variable represents reported recall in the attribute perception and consumption equations. Similarly, the favorable attribute perception was carried through to the consumption equation by the inverse Mills ratio of the $A^*$ variable. The entire sample of 4,440 households was used in the estimation.

## EMPIRICAL RESULTS

The estimation results are reported in Table 15.3. The appropriate likelihood ratio test indicated that for each of the three equations the independent variables as a group explain a significant share of the variation in the dependent variable.

**Table 15.3 Influence on advertising message recall, perception of fresh pork attributes, and fresh pork consumption: estimated probit coefficients**

| Variable | Message recall | Attribute perception | Consumption |
|---|---|---|---|
| Intercept | -1.04[b] | -0.22 | -0.18 |
|  | (-6.44) | (-1.45) | (-1.12) |
| Household size | -0.04 | 0.03 | 0.12[b] |
|  | (-1.44) | (1.06) | (5.17) |
| One head of household | -0.20[b] | -0.28[b] | -0.09 |
|  | (-3.18) | (-4.80) | (-1.54) |
| Children under 18 in | -0.03 | -0.05 | 0.05 |
| household | (-0.24) | (1.85) | (0.92) |
| Age (primary food shopper) | -0.001 | 0.01 | -0.01 |
|  | (-0.24) | (1.85) | (-1.44) |
| Total household income: |  |  |  |
| $15,000–$29,999 | 0.17 | 0.09 | 0.05 |
|  | (1.79) | (1.06) | (0.62) |
| $30,000–$44,999 | 0.27[b] | 0.11 | 0.18[b] |
|  | (2.80) | (1.25) | (2.00) |
| $45,000 or more | 0.30[b] | 0.14 | 0.15 |
|  | (3.10) | (1.51) | (1.58) |
| No response | 0.12 | -0.01 | -0.09 |
|  | (1.09) | (-0.13) | (-0.87) |
| Two employed head of | -0.08 | -0.13[b] | 0.10[a] |
| household | (-1.59) | (-2.66) | (1.92) |
| No employed head of | 0.07 | 0.11 | 0.02 |
| household | (0.77) | (1.23) | (0.25) |
| White collar occupation | 0.06 | -0.06 | -0.17[b] |
| (primary wage earner) | (1.21) | (-1.30) | (-3.64) |

**Table 15.3 (cont.)**

| Variable | Message recall | Attribute perception | Comsumption |
|---|---|---|---|
| Post high school education | 0.28[b] | 0.03 | -0.19[b] |
| (primary shopper) | (5.84) | (0.54) | (-4.06) |
| Location: | | | |
| Cleveland | | 0.28[b] | 0.40[b] |
| | | (4.24) | (5.86) |
| Sacramento | | 0.16[a] | 0.13[a] |
| | | (2.45) | (1.92) |
| Pittsburgh | | 0.32[b] | 0.35[b] |
| | | (4.83) | (5.15) |
| Denver | | 0.38[b] | 0.32[b] |
| | | (5.66) | (4.63) |
| Baltimore | | -0.09 | -0.07 |
| | | (-1.33) | (-0.95) |
| | | | |
| Time: | | | |
| October, 1987 | | | 0.02 |
| | | | (0.44) |
| May, 1988 | | | 0.13[a] |
| | | | (2.16) |
| | | | |
| Advertising exposure: | | | |
| as of October, 1987 — | | | |
| Heavy TV and print | 0.80[b] | | |
| | (11.83) | | |
| Base TV and print | 0.57[b] | | |
| | (7.90) | | |
| Print only | 0.10 | | |
| | (1.30) | | |
| as of May, 1988 — | | | |
| Heavy TV and print | 0.98 | | |
| | (14.59) | | |
| Base TV and print | 0.81 | | |
| | (12.08) | | |
| Print only | -0.02 | | |
| | (-0.31) | | |
| | | | |
| Recalled ad message | | 0.30[b] | 0.13[b] |
| (Inverse Mills ratio) | | (11.59) | (4.98) |
| Attribute perception | | | 0.40[b] |
| (Inverse Mills ratio) | | | (16.23) |
| Likelihood ratio test ($X^2$) | 522.08 | 269.63 | 571.06 |
| | (df = 18) | (df = 18) | (df = 21) |

[a]Statistically significant at .05 level.
[b]Statistically significant at .10 level.

**Reported Message Recall (Unaided)**

The results from the estimated reported message recall equation (15.2) imply the following: The probability of reported message recall was higher for a respondent in a higher income household than in a lower income household. Post high school education of the primary shopper increased the probability of reported message recall. A respondent in a household with only one head was less likely to report recalling the advertising message than a respondent in a two-head household. Other sociodemographic variables did not affect the probability of reported recall.

Respondents in the second and third surveys who lived in cities that received the television plus print advertising treatment had significantly higher probabilities of reported message recall than respondents in the preadvertising survey. The probability of reported recall by a respondent exposed to television plus print advertising was greater in the third survey than in the second, implying that advertising effects are cumulative. However, at the given print advertising level, heavy television produced a greater short-term effect on recall and less incremental effect from continued exposure, while base television produced less initial effect and more incremental effect from longer exposure. Exposure to print only advertising did not significantly affect a respondent's probability of unaided message recall in either the second or third surveys. (However, the effect of print was significant when the recall variable was redefined.) To investigate whether the results of the estimation were sensitive to the definition of the recall variable, the model was reestimated. The probability of aided plus unaided recall of the Other White Meat message was used in place of unaided recall as the dependent variable in the reported recall equation. The results of the second estimation were generally consistent with those reported here except that the print advertising treatment had a significant effect on probability of recall. Unlike the base television advertising treatments, the significance of the print treatment decreased between the second and third surveys.

**Attribute Perception**

The results from estimation of the attribute perception equation (15.3) indicated that respondents in households with only one head or two wage earners had a lower probability of favorable fresh pork attribute perception than others in households with two heads or one wage earner. Dummy variables to account for differences in perception among the six cities were included in this equation. A respondent living in Cleveland, Sacramento, Pittsburgh, or Denver had a significantly higher probability of favorable attribute perception than a respondent living in San Diego. Of greatest importance, recall of the advertising message had a positive and statistically significant effect on the probability that his or her perception of fresh pork attributes was favorable.

### Consumption

Estimation of the consumption equation (15.4) indicated that the probability of fresh pork consumption at home within the past two weeks tended to increase with household size. A respondent in a two-income household had a lower probability of fresh pork consumption than a respondent in a single-income household. A respondent living in Cleveland, Sacramento, Pittsburgh, or Denver was less likely to consume fresh pork than a respondent living in San Diego. For respondents in households where the primary wage earner had post high school education or white collar employment, the probability of fresh pork consumption was reduced. Dummy variables to control for differences across time were included in this equation. A respondent in the third survey had a higher probability of consumption than a respondent in the preadvertising survey. Again, these variables may be picking up the effects of the nationwide print advertising and promotional programs in addition to other time-varying factors, such as prices, which would have influenced the probability of fresh pork consumption. Given the design of the experiment, it was impossible to sort the effects of the print advertising from other factors.

More important, whether the respondent reported recalling the white meat message and whether his/her perception of fresh pork attributes was favorable had a positive effect on the probability of fresh pork consumption in the previous two weeks. These results provide evidence that the fresh pork advertising message played a role in affecting reported consumption frequency both directly and indirectly through consumer beliefs about pork.

The model was also estimated for three separate groups of consumers: nutrition-conscious consumers, taste-conscious consumers, and other consumers. The respondents were classified as nutrition-conscious consumers or taste-conscious consumers if they indicated that factor as the most important consideration when purchasing meat. A likelihood ratio test indicated that there was no significant difference between results from the model estimated using the complete sample versus the model estimated separately for the three sample segments.

## Long-Term Pork Industry Advertising Response Simulations

In addition to the above approaches evaluating short-term advertising effects, the long-term effects of advertising on key industry performance indicators were assessed using Iowa State University's Center for Agricultural and Rural Development (CARD) econometric models of the livestock sector. The models developed at CARD use supply and demand concepts to simultaneously determine the equilibrium levels of production, consumption, and prices for beef, pork, and chicken (documentation of those models is available from CARD).

## EXPERIMENTAL EVALUATION OF PORK ADVERTISING

The impacts of the generic pork promotion were evaluated using the livestock industry models to simulate the effects of a continuous advertising campaign on the pork industry. Industry performance indicators were compared under the simulations with advertising and baseline simulation without advertising. Of particular interest in the analysis are advertising's influence on market indicators such as pork prices, supply, consumption, and producer profits. The simulations were made for a 15-year period, using quarterly time series data from 1967 to 1986. The estimation allowed for the cross-commodity influence of beef and chicken on pork.

Advertising effects were introduced in the model in the form of intercept shifts in the price-dependent pork demand equations. Advertising was assumed to gradually increase demand in each of the first eight quarters of the advertising campaign and then to have no net incremental effects in the remaining quarters of the simulation period. Carryover effects from advertising in the previous quarters were taken into account so that at the end of the second year of advertising, demand had shifted by 3.3 percent (or 5.4 cents per pound). For the remainder of the simulation period, advertising expenditures were assumed at the level necessary to maintain the 3.3 percent increase in demand. Carryover effects were assumed to counter any natural decay effect and the effect of advertising competitive meat products.

The size of the demand shock to the model was identified by linking the sample data available from the PAPS to changes in aggregate pork consumption. Recall of the advertising message was used to estimate the impact of the advertising on the frequency of fresh pork consumption for households in each of the three media test markets. Population weights were applied to the test market findings to estimate the percentage change in aggregate consumption frequency attributable to the national advertising campaign. The percentage change in aggregate frequency of consumption was assumed to be equivalent to the percentage change in aggregate consumption. Roughly, a 3 percent change in the aggregate consumption level occurred after households were exposed to the Other White Meat campaign for 15 months. The effect of the advertising was arbitrarily assumed to continue to increase marginally after 15 months until it reached 3.3 percent after two years of advertising.

The 3.3 percent impact in two years is only a rough approximation of the likely impact of NPPC's generic advertising and promotion nationally applied after two years. However, the important "patterns" of response to a successful pork advertising program are illustrated by the simulations.

## SIMULATION RESULTS

The demand shift for pork gradually increased the retail price of pork during the initial two years of the advertising as shown in Figure 15.1. Prices peaked at 3.4 percent above the baseline simulation (or preadvertising) level and gradually retreated toward the baseline level, finally leveling off slightly above the baseline level in year eight.

The advertising demand shock was transmitted to pork producers through an increase in market hog price. Farm-level price changes (in percentage change from baseline values) are plotted in Figure 15.2. As illustrated in Figure 15.3, pork supplies started to increase in year one, peaked at 3 percent above the baseline level in year three, and leveled off at about 2 percent above the baseline in year five. The increased pork supplies put downward pressure on pork prices. The leveling off at 2 percent above the baseline probably would have occurred closer to zero if the assumption had been dropped that the net shift in demand could be sustained at 3.3 percent.

Consumers reacted to the higher pork prices by substituting beef and chicken in their diets, which led to increased beef and chicken retail and farm level prices (Figure 15.2). Beef and chicken producers responded to higher prices by increasing their production. Consumption increased correspondingly. The retail price increase for pork was affected by the relative shifts in beef and chicken demand and supply, and their subsequent feedback to the pork sector.

As shown in Figure 15.4, profits for feeder pig finishers peaked at the end of the second year of the advertising campaign. However, as pork, beef, and chicken producers responded to higher prices by increasing production, profits began to decline. Eventually, as expected in a competitive industry, per head profit for pork producers leveled off near the baseline value.

Changes in market share and market value of pork are plotted in Figure 15.5. These indicators are directly correlated with supplies. Market share and value increased initially, but then decreased somewhat and leveled off above baselines values.

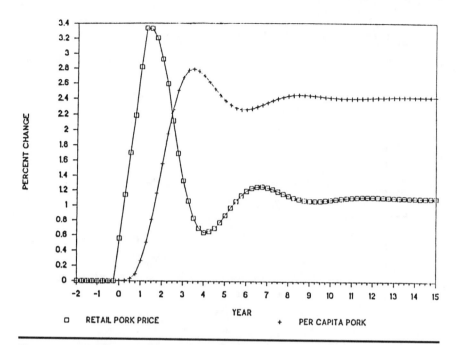

**Figure 15.1. Retail pork price and per capita pork consumption response.**

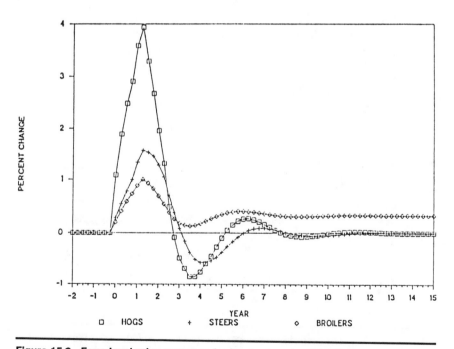

**Figure 15.2. Farm-level price response for hogs, steers, and broilers.**

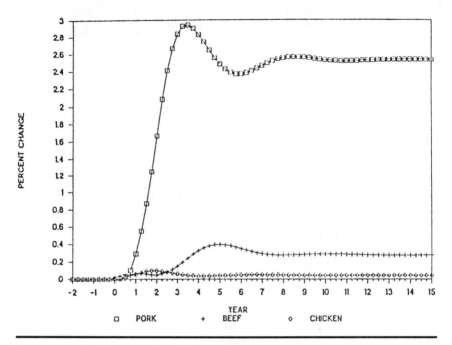

Figure 15.3.  Pork, beef, and chicken supplies.

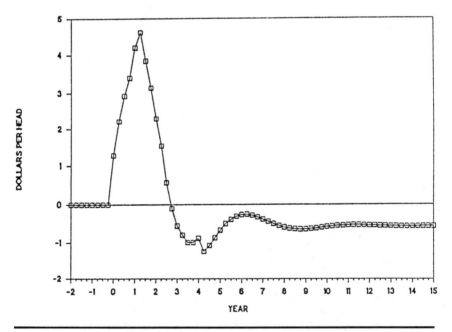

Figure 15.4.  Producer profit in dollars per head from finishing feeder pigs (changes from baseline).

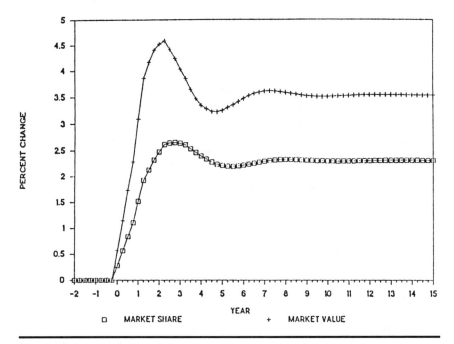

**Figure 15.5. Pork retail market share and market value.**

These livestock industry model simulations illustrate that the effectiveness of advertising campaigns should not be judged on the basis of short-run indicators alone. Also, the only way to consistently generate above-normal returns in the competitive livestock and meat sector is to continually "shock" the system with stimuli that beneficially shift industry demand or cost curves.

## Conclusions

Several analytical approaches were used to evaluate the effectiveness of generic advertising for the pork industry. Data from the first 15 months of a controlled experiment were used to measure the short-term impacts of advertising treatments on an indicator of household fresh pork consumption. The design of the advertising test did not allow direct estimation of the effect of print advertising treatment on the consumption indicator. The analysis provided information only on the incremental impact of two levels of television advertising used in conjunction with print advertising.

Two alternative modeling approaches were used to estimate consumption behavior differences between households exposed to different television advertising treatments. After 9 and 15 months of advertising, the heavy level of television had a significant incremental effect over just print advertising in both models. In one model, the advertising exposure generated from 9 or 15 months of base level television plus print treatment had no incremental impact over the print advertising treatment. However, in another model, the base television effects were similar to the heavy television effects for households sampled after both 9 and 15 months of advertising treatment.

Advertising effects were more clearly identified in a multistage model characterizing consumer response to advertising as a recall-perception-consumption process. The results indicated that print advertising alone had no significant effect on unaided consumer recall of the advertising message after either 9 or 15 months. (When an expanded measure of recall — aided plus unaided — was used in the estimation, print did have a significant effect.) Both the heavy and base levels of television plus print treatments had significant effects on recall. Recall of the message significantly affected consumer perceptions of fresh pork attributes. Recall and favorable attribute perception both affected the indicator of fresh pork consumption.

The findings with respect to television advertising's short-term impact on the consumption indicator were mixed. The heavy television treatment appears to be effective in all three modeling approaches. The effectiveness of the base level television treatment is less clear. It appears to affect consumption through its significant effects on message recall; but statistical analysis did not always reveal consumption behavior differences among households located in base television media markets versus those in print only media markets.

The long-term effects of advertising on key industry performance indicators were evaluated using econometric models of the livestock sector. The simulation results indicated that when supply-response and cross-commodity impacts are taken into account, even if advertising causes demand to shift, expected producer returns temporarily increase but long-run returns are not appreciably different from returns where no advertising had occurred. However, the analysis suggests there are some positive long-run advertising impacts such as increased market share, potential for using advertising to smooth out price variability faced by producers, and the like.

The implications of this research should be of value to commodity organization staffs for planning the evaluation of future advertising campaigns. In evaluations, careful consideration should be given to producer supply response, cross-commodity effects, and confounding influences. Just as promotional campaigns should not be designed to achieve short-run goals alone, neither should their effectiveness be evaluated based only on short-run impacts. Justification for producer support of advertising should be broadened from the current rate-of-return criterion. Profitability measures can be influenced only in the short run in an industry without supply control.

## Notes

1. Dairy and Tobacco Adjustment Act, U.S. Code P.L. 98-180, 97 Stat. 1128, 1983; Beef Promotion, Research and Consumer Information Act, U.S. Code P.L. 99-198, 99 Stat. 1854, 1985; and Pork Promotion, Research and Consumer Information Act, U.S. Code P.L. 99-198, 99 Stat. 1354, Sections 1613-1630, 1985.

2. The validity of using the Pork Attitude and Perception Study (PAPS) frequency of consumption figures as indicators of actual consumption is questionable. However, since the USDA does not report consumption data in a strictly comparable form, evaluating the reliability of the PAPS information based on its correlation with USDA data is troublesome. For comparative purposes, the most suitable USDA consumption figure is "the percentage of individuals using pork at least once in the previous 24 hours" from the 1985 Continuing Survey of Food Intakes by Individuals (CSFII). CSFII data are available for both men, aged 19 to 50, and women, aged 19 to 50.

When the CSFII figures are transformed to reflect a 14-day period and a 75 percent female sample, an average two-week pork consumption frequency of 3.1 is obtained. The figures found in Table 15.1 indicate a much lower two-week consumption frequency. However, this inconsistency does not provide clearcut evidence that the PAPS data are unreliable for the following reasons: (1) "pork" in the USDA report includes fresh pork, as well as ham, bacon, smoked, pickled and cured pork, except frankfurters, sausages, and luncheon meats; (2) per capita pork consumption fell between 1987 when the first PAPS survey was done and 1985 when the CSFII data were collected.

3. The inverse Mills ratio is $\phi(M^*)/\Phi(M^*)$ if $M^* = 1$ and is $\phi(M^*)/[1 - \Phi(M^*)]$ if $M^* = 0$, where $\phi(M^*)$ is the normal probability density function and $\Phi(M^*)$ is the cumulative density function for $M$.

4. The probit model determines the probability of an observation belonging to one of two mutually exclusive groups (e.g., recall or no recall of the advertising message). The dependent variable is defined as a dichotomous random variable which takes the value of 1 if the event occurs and 0 if it does not. Using the specific case of recall versus no recall of the advertising message, the probabilities are defined by:

$$Pr(M_i = 1) = F(Z_i, EXP_i)$$
$$Pr(M_i = 0) = 1 - F(Z_i, EXP_i)$$

where

$Pr(M_i = 1)$ is the probability of advertising message recall by individual $i$;

$Pr(M_i = 0)$ is the probability of no advertising message recall by individual $i$;

$Z_i$ is sociodemographic characteristics of individual $i$;

$EXP_i$ is type of advertising exposure to which individual $i$ was exposed; and

$F$ is normal cumulative density function.

# 16 Health Concerns and Changing Consumer Attitudes toward Characteristics of Dairy Products: A Selected Analysis of the Attitude, Usage, and Trends Survey Data (AUTS), 1976-1988

## CAMERON S. THRAEN and DAVID E. HAHN

Milk and dairy products play an important role in the diets of most consumers. These products make up one of the four basic food groups that every school girl or boy learns about beginning in the first grade. On a product pound basis the average American consumer used approximately 236 pounds of fluid milk, 4.6 pounds of butter, 24 pounds of cheese, and 18.3 pounds of ice cream in 1987. The per capita utilization of milk, whether as fluid or as a manufactured dairy product, has changed over the last twenty years (Table 16.1). Consumption of fluid milk with a 3.5 percent fat content has declined in favor of those milk products with lower or no-fat content. Per capita use of butter has remained approximately constant, while cheese and ice cream use have climbed significantly. In fact, while the American consumers have shown a definite preference shift away from higher fat content fluid milk, they have also increased the use of higher fat cheeses and ice creams.

The changing composition of consumer use of dairy products has lead to an increased interest in the relationship between consumers' attitudes toward health related issues and their perception of the health influencing characteristics of dairy products. The shift in preference toward lowfat or skim milk appears to reflect the consumer's awareness of diet related health issues. This is reflected as an interest in a lower fat, lower cholesterol lifestyle, yet the increased use of higher fat products such as cheese and ice cream is not entirely consistent with this assessment. Recent research, which has carefully examined the determinants of changing consumption levels, has concluded that relative prices, income levels, and to some extent advertising may explain most of the shift in consumer use patterns (Haidacher and Blaylock 1989).

The importance of a product's characteristics as perceived by consumers has been investigated theoretically and empirically in the economics literature. Ladd presents a thorough review of this field (Ladd 1979). A

Table 16.1. Per capita use of fluid milk and milk products 1965–1988

| Product | 1965 | 1966 | 1967 | 1968 | 1969 | 1970 | 1971 | 1972 | 1973 | 1974 | 1975 | 1976 | 1977 | 1978 | 1979 | 1980 | 1981 | 1982 | 1983 | 1984 | 1985 | 1986 | 1987 | 1988 |
|---|---|---|---|---|---|---|---|---|---|---|---|---|---|---|---|---|---|---|---|---|---|---|---|---|
| Fluid milk[a] | 286 | 286 | 278 | 277 | 275 | 272 | 269 | 270 | 266 | 257 | 262 | 258 | 254 | 252 | 247 | 244 | 239 | 236 | 239 | 238 | 232 | 229 | 227 | 226 |
| Whole milk | 246 | 245 | 234 | 227 | 220 | 214 | 205 | 200 | 191 | 180 | 178 | 170 | 161 | 156 | 150 | 143 | 137 | 133 | 132 | 128 | 120 | 115 | 111 | 108 |
| Lowfat milk | | | | | | | | | | | | | | | | | | | | | | | | |
| Lowfat (1–2%) | 39 | 41 | 44 | 49 | 54 | 57 | 63 | 69 | 74 | 76 | 83 | 88 | 92 | 95 | 97 | 100 | 101 | 102 | 105 | 109 | 112 | 114 | 115 | 118 |
| Skim (<1%) | 11 | 14 | 18 | 22 | 27 | 30 | 35 | 40 | 44 | 46 | 54 | 58 | 62 | 65 | 68 | 71 | 74 | 75 | 77 | 80 | 83 | 86 | 88 | 91 |
| Cheese | 14 | 14 | 14 | 15 | 15 | 16 | 17 | 18 | 18 | 19 | 19 | 20 | 20 | 21 | 21 | 22 | 22 | 24 | 24 | 25 | 26 | 27 | 29 | 30 |
| Any cheese | 9 | 9 | 10 | 10 | 10 | 11 | 12 | 13 | 13 | 14 | 14 | 15 | 16 | 17 | 17 | 17 | 18 | 20 | 20 | 21 | 22 | 23 | 25 | 26 |
| Cottage cheese | 5 | 5 | 4 | 5 | 5 | 5 | 5 | 5 | 5 | 5 | 5 | 5 | 4 | 4 | 4 | 5 | 4 | 4 | 4 | 4 | 4 | 4 | 4 | 4 |
| Frozen products | 28 | 28 | 28 | 29 | 29 | 28 | 28 | 28 | 27 | 27 | 28 | 27 | 27 | 27 | 26 | 26 | 26 | 26 | 27 | 27 | 27 | 28 | 28 | 29 |
| Ice cream | 18 | 18 | 17 | 18 | 18 | 17 | 17 | 17 | 17 | 17 | 18 | 17 | 17 | 17 | 17 | 17 | 17 | 17 | 17 | 18 | 18 | 18 | 19 | 19 |
| Butter | 6 | 5 | 5 | 5 | 5 | 5 | 5 | 5 | 5 | 4 | 4 | 4 | 4 | 4 | 4 | 4 | 4 | 4 | 5 | 5 | 5 | 5 | 5 | 5 |
| Commercial sources[b] | 6.4 | 5.7 | 5.5 | 5.7 | 5.4 | 5.3 | 5.1 | 4.9 | 4.8 | 4.5 | 4.7 | 4.3 | 3.9 | 4.0 | 4.1 | 3.9 | 3.8 | 3.9 | 3.8 | 3.8 | 4.0 | 4.3 | 4.5 | 4.9 |

SOURCES: *Dairy and Outlook Situation*, Economic Research Service, various publications, U.S. Department of Agriculture.
[a] Includes lowfat and skim milk, buttermilk, flavored milk and drink, yogurt; does not include filled milk items.
[b] Commercial source does not include butter consumed on farms or USDA donations.

primary issue in that research has been the relationship between changing product characteristics and the effect upon effective demand. The identification of those characteristics that are influential in determining the strength of consumer demand has been the topic of other research inquiries (Aronson, Eiler, and Forker 1973; Eiler and Thompson 1974; Eiler and Cook 1977).

The principal objective of this study is to explore changing consumer preferences toward milk and dairy product characteristics, particularly those pertaining to health concerns. By carefully examining survey data wherein consumers report scale indices on health attributes of dairy products over the time period 1976 through 1988 it may be possible to ascertain whether or not consumer attitudes have changed in a manner consistent with an increased awareness of health issues and concerns. Data used in the study are from the Market and Economic Research Division, United Dairy Industry Association, Consumer Attitude and Usage Trends Survey (AUTS). A cross-sectional time series containing approximately 20,000 sample observations over the period 1976–1988 forms the basis for the analysis. While the survey contains information on many dairy products and survey question responses and the complete study investigates a large number of these relationships, this paper focuses on two products: regular whole milk and lowfat skim milk. Consumers' use of these products clearly reflects the issues involved in health concerns and shifts in consumption patterns.

## Consumer Choice and Demand Theory

The economic theory of demand has evolved along a couple of lines of inquiry. Traditional demand theory postulates the existence of a utility function dependent upon the bundle of goods and the individual's resource endowment. The consumer maximizes his or her welfare by allocating this resource endowment across the goods bundle such that the utility function reaches a maximum value. From this basic setup, a number of demand concepts can be derived. The most obvious is the existence of a quantity dependent demand function. Likewise, price dependent functions can also be derived. The latter approach focuses on consumer goods characteristics models CGCM (Ladd). Consider a paraphrasing of a CGCM developed by Ladd and Suvannunt (1976). The individual consumer is assumed to maximize a utility function defined over a vector of microgoods or characteristics. These microgoods are generally not available in the market but must be purchased in the form of a composite good. For example, a consumer may desire the microgoods safety, locomotion, durability, energy efficiency, status, reliability, etc., for which direct markets do not exist. The consumer acquires these microgoods in the form of the composite good, an automobile. In fact the consumer may own a number of automobiles that, in aggregate, supply different amounts of each of these microgoods.

Producers of products can compete in the market by altering the level of microgoods provided by the commodity in question. For example, by increasing the level of quality in a product, e.g., "new and improved," without altering the product price, producers can expect to change the level of product sales.

This leads to the idea that the demand for a commodity can be expressed as a function of the price of the product, other substitute/complement product prices, income, and the levels of characteristics or microgoods embodied in the commodity. What is lacking is any indication of what these microgoods might be. In traditional demand analysis we can observe through a type of revealed preference just what commodities the consumer demands. This information is recorded in markets with public reporting of transactions. Identification of microgoods is not as easy as simply observing market data. What microgoods are being demanded, for example, in a basket of food items? Or a consumer's purchase of durables over a period of time?

Another issue that must be addressed is the role that sociological, psychological, and demographic variables (SPD) play in the demand function. It is clear that the CGCM incorporates the effects of such variables indirectly into the hedonic price or the commodity demand function. This is obvious by noting that the derivatives that form the basis for these functions follow uniquely from an assumed underlying consumer utility function U. Clearly the parameters of this function U for an individual consumer are derived from the individual's sociological, psychological, and demographic makeup. Income is an operational variable allowing the consumer to take action on that utility function. Prices are choice or rationing variables forcing the consumer to allocate that income. But ultimately the consumer's desire to purchase a commodity in any amount is governed by the inherent underlying parameters of the respective utility function.

## Consumer Choice and Demand Models

Another dimension to the theory of demand comes from the notion that consumers' observed choices among alternatives derive from the maximization of a stochastic utility function (McFadden 1974). The primary difference between this concept and more traditional demand concepts is that consumers discrete choices are of interest and not the actual quantity purchased. How choice attributes or characteristics of the chooser influence the particular choice is the primary focus. Following McFadden, consider the more general specification of the consumer's choice problem. Suppose that an individual faces $m$ choices. There exists a latent variable $Y^*$, which denotes the level of indirect utility associated with the $i$th choice. The observed variables $Y_i$ are defined as:

$$Y_i = 1 \qquad\qquad \text{if } Y_i^* = \text{Max}(Y_1^*, Y_2^*, \ldots, Y_m^*) \qquad\qquad (16.1)$$

$$Y_i = 0 \qquad\qquad \text{otherwise}$$

If we write $Y_i^* = V_i(X_i) + \epsilon_i$, where $X_i$ is the vector of attributes for the $i$th choice and $\epsilon_i$ is a residual that captures unobserved variations in tastes and in the attributes of alternatives and errors in the perception and optimization by the consumer.

If the residuals $\epsilon_i$ are independent and identically distributed with the type I extreme-value distribution whose cumulative distribution function (CDF) is

$$F(\epsilon_i < \epsilon) = \exp(-e^{-\epsilon_i}) \qquad\qquad (16.2)$$

and whose probability density function (PDF) is

$$f(\epsilon_i) = \exp(-e_i - e^{-\epsilon_i}) \qquad\qquad (16.3)$$

then we can show that

$$\text{Prob}\,(Y_i/X) = \frac{e^{v_i}}{\Sigma_{j=1}^{m} e^{v_j}} \qquad\qquad (16.4)$$

With this model of choice behavior we can estimate the probability that a given choice will be selected. If we have a set of $N$ individuals faced with $m$ choices, we can define

$Y_{ij}^* = $ the level of indirect utility for the $t$th individual making the $j$th choice

$Y_{ij} = 1$ for the $t$th individual making the $j$th choice
$Y_{ij} = 0$ otherwise                                                        (16.5)

In this model the decision variable $Y_i$ represents a simple binary choice for the consumer. The probability of the $i$th consumer choosing to use the product is then given as

$$P_{ij} = \text{Prob}(Y = 1) = \frac{1}{1 + e^{\beta' x_{ij}}} \qquad (16.6)$$

and the influence of the $j$th chooser-specific variable on the probability, or equivalently the frequency of product use, is given by

$$\frac{\partial}{\partial x_{ij}} L(x'_{ij} \beta) = \phi(x'_i \beta) \beta_j \qquad (16.7)$$

This model has been extended to choice situations which involve more than the simple binary situation (Maddala 1983). In these multinomial choice models the general specification is to allow each choice to be a function of both the attributes of the choices themselves and the chooser, where $X_{tj}$ is the vector of values of the attributes of the $j$th choice as perceived by the $t$th individual and $Z_t$ are individual-specific variables characterizing the chooser, then the probability of the $t$th individual selecting the $j$th choice is:

$$P_{tj} = \text{Prob}(Y_{tj} = 1) = \frac{e^{\beta' x_{tj} + \alpha'_j z_t}}{\sum_{k=1}^{m} e^{\beta' x_{tj} + \alpha'_k z_t}} \qquad (16.8)$$

The difficulty with this choice model when there is more than a simple binary decision is that it embodies what has become known as the "independence of irrelevant alternatives" (IIA). In short, the model posits that if the individual is offered an expanded choice set, that does not change the odds ratio (Madalla 1983). A number of modifications to this model have been proposed of interest in this study is referred to as the "nested multinomial logit model" (NMNL) developed by McFadden (1983). In summary, the NMNL model posits that the individual chooses in a hierarchical fashion. For example, the choice will be made whether to purchase or use a product or not. And then based on the outcome of this choice, the individual will decide on what level or how much of the good to purchase or use. In this fashion the choice problem does not involve the IIA problem. McFadden has shown that this model can be derived from the theory of stochastic utility maximization. While application of the NMNL model is very appealing, for the purpose of this study the binary (0/1) model is used as the basis for the first stage of analysis. The results of this binary model are presented below.

## Research Method

The AUTS data does not directly record quantity of use data. Instead, panel members are asked a series of questions whereby they record the frequency of use over a given time period. This frequency of consuming milk and dairy products is treated as a binary response (0/1) in this study. Never Use is classified as one group and Use as the other, both for regular whole milk, lowfat skim milk, any cheese except cottage cheese, and butter. In addition, AUTS panel members are asked to respond to an extensive set of questions on each product category and food use and attitudes in general. For example, in the panel survey, members are asked to respond to statements such as: Lowfat or skim milk tastes flat and watery. The respondent is then presented with an attitude scale variable ranging from 1: definitely disagree, to 6: definitely agree. From this type of question and response, the correlation between use/no use and definitely disagree/definitely agree can be calculated. Hypothetically, it would be expected that non-users of lowfat skim milk would also indicate a scale value close to 6 on this example question.

## Estimation

The logit model has two measurement techniques. These are the grouped data approach and the microdata approach. The former employs weighted least squares (WLS), while the latter is done by means of maximum likelihood estimation (MLE). The microdata approach with the maximum likelihood iterative procedure will be employed for this study.

The MLE estimates are found by maximizing the likelihood function with respect to the parameters of interest. The likelihood function is a joint probability distribution of the sample and is equal to the product of consumption probability of all individual observations. The primary appeal of applying MLE is that this technique possesses the asymptotic properties, i.e., consistent, asymptotically efficient, and asymptotically normal.

## Data

Data used in this study are from the Marketing and Economic Research Division of the United Dairy Industry Association, Consumer Attitude and Usage of Dairy Product Survey. This survey was conducted annually from 1972 through 1978, and has been conducted biennially beginning with 1980.

Data from surveys prior to 1976 were not available for this analysis. The sample observations include 3,659 panel members in 1976, 4,042 panel members in 1978, 4,170 panel members in 1980, 3,778 panel members in 1982, 4,044 panel members in 1984, 3,500 panel members in 1986, and 3,600 panel members in 1988. Panel members are selected and managed to be representative of the continental U.S. population, age 13 and older. This survey contains a rather large number of product, demographic, social, and attitudinal questions. Those are addressed to dairy product usage and other product usage. The large number of items addressed required that many questions not be addressed in this analysis. Those items selected were based on the judgment of the authors according to their importance, and reflect consumer attitudes toward fat or cholesterol or heart disease types of concerns. It is assumed that if the consumer is changing his or her food preferences in response to concerns about health issues, then these variables should be influential in an analysis of those use versus no use decisions.

For the purposes of this analysis, several determinations were made. Usage questions for each product category are numerous; therefore only frequency of consumption is employed, and is treated as a binary group— drink versus no drink, and use versus no use. Explanatory variables include annual household income, family composition, education of panel member, education of spouse, occupation of panel member, occupation of spouse, household size, race, and selected attitude scale variables (see Table 16.2).

## Statistical Models and Variable Specification

The statistical models for each product group are given as follows:

Fluid Whole Milk:

$$
\begin{aligned}
FWM = a_0 &+ a_1 MT + a_2 FT + a_3 F5 + a_4 F6\text{-}12 + a_5 FE \qquad (16.9) \\
&+ a_6 ED1 + a_7 ED2 + a_8 ES1 + a_9 ES2 \\
&+ a_{10} OC1 + a_{11} OC2 + a_{12} OS1 + a_{13} OS2 \\
&+ a_{14} IN1 + a_{15} IN2 + a_{16} IN3 \\
&+ a_{17} HOS + a_{18} RAC \\
&+ a_{19} AFTM + a_{20} CH2M + a_{21} HATM + a_{22} REFM
\end{aligned}
$$

Fluid Lowfat and Skim Milk:

$$
\begin{aligned}
FSM = b_0 &+ b_1 MT + b_2 FT + b_3 F5 + b_4 F6\text{-}12 + b_5 FE \qquad (16.10) \\
&+ b_6 ED1 + b_7 ED2 + b_8 ES1 + b_9 ES2 \\
&+ b_{10} OC1 + b_{11} OC2 + b_{12} OS1 + b_{13} OS2 \\
&+ b_{14} IN1 + b_{15} IN2 + b_{16} IN3 \\
&+ b_{17} AFTM + b_{18} RAC
\end{aligned}
$$

$$+ b_{19}\text{AFTM} + b_{20}\text{CH2M} + b_{21}\text{HATM} + b_{22}\text{REFM}$$
$$+ b_{23}\text{WATL}$$

Any Cheese (except cottage):

$$\text{FCH} = c_0 + c_1\text{MT} + c_2\text{FT} + c_3\text{F5} + c_4\text{F6-12} + c_5\text{FE} \qquad (16.11)$$
$$+ c_6\text{ED1} + c_7\text{ED2} + c_8\text{ES1} + c_9\text{ES2}$$
$$+ c_{10}\text{OC1} + c_{11}\text{OC2} + c_{12}\text{OS1} + c_{13}\text{OS2}$$
$$+ c_{14}\text{IN1} + c_{15}\text{IN2} + c_{16}\text{IN3}$$
$$+ c_{17}\text{HOS} + c_{18}\text{RAC} + c_{19}\text{HEAC}$$
$$+ c_{21}\text{FATC} + c_{22}\text{CHOC}$$

## Economic and Demographic Variables

The first five explanatory variables (MT, FT, F5, F6-12, and FE) represent family composition; male teenager, female teenager, female panel member with child 0–5 years old, female panel member with child 6–12 years old, and female panel member. The next variables are panel member education (ED1, ED2), spouse education (ES1, ES2), panel member occupation (OC1, OC2), spouses occupation (OS1, OS2). The variables (IN1–IN3) refer to three different annual household income groups. RAC indicates Caucasian race. The decomposition of family composition, education, occupation, and race represents this study's attempt to capture the differential impacts of the separate groups on the probability of drinking or using milk and dairy products. HOS is the indicator of household size of the respondent's family.

## Selected Attitude Variables

Variables regarding a respondent's attitude toward milk or dairy product characteristics represent scale variables for an attitude. The choices for these variables range from 1 to 6. One and 6 refer to definitely disagree and definitely agree, respectively. That is, a variable with higher mean value indicates respondent tends to agree with the related statement (Table 16.3).

In the milk model the attitude variables selected were: milk leaves a bad aftertaste (AFTM), milk is high in cholesterol (CH2M), milk can cause heart disease (HATM), milk is refreshing (REFM). The AFTM and REFM variables reflect a basic like/dislike for the product while CH2M and HATM reflect the consumer's health concerns. In addition to the above six variables, one additional variable was added for lowfat skim milk modeling: lowfat

**Table 16.2. Definition of model variables**

|  | Endogenous variables | |
| --- | --- | --- |
|  | Variable = 1 | Variable = 0 |
| FWM | If drink regular whole milk | If never drink |
| FSM | If drink skim/lowfat/2% milk | If never drink |
| FCH | If use of any cheese except cottage | If do not use |

|  | Exogenous variables | |
| --- | --- | --- |
| MT | Male teens (13–18) | Other category |
| FT | Female teens (13–19) | Other category |
| F5 | Female with child less than 6 | Other category |
| F6-12 | Female with child 6–12 | Other category |
| FE | Female, no children | Other category |
| OPM | (omitted group = males) | |
| ED1 | 1–4 years of high school | Other category |
| ED2 | At least 1 year of college | Other category |
| ED3 | (omitted group = 8 or less years of grade school) | |
| ES1 | Spouse 1–4 years high school | Other category |
| ES2 | Spouse at least 1 year college | Other category |
| ES3 | (omitted group = 8 or less years of grade school) | |
| OC1 | Blue collar/crafts occupation | Other category |
| OC2 | White collar/professional | Other category |
| OC3 | (omitted group =not employed) | |
| OS1 | Blue collar/crafts occupation | Other category |
| OS2 | White collar/professional | Other category |
| OS3 | (omitted group = not employed) | |
| IN1 | Annual household income $10,000 – $19,000 | Other category |
| IN2 | Annual household income $20,000 – $29,999 | Other category |
| IN3 | Annual household income over $30,000 | Other category |
| IN4 | (omitted group = less than $10,000) | |
| RAC | White | Other category |
| NWR | (omitted group = other) | |
| HOS | Household size | Continuous |

milk tastes flat and watery (WATL). In the cheese model, HEAC, FATC, HATC, and CHOC refer to cheese is a healthful food; cheese is fattening; cheese can cause heart disease; and cheese helps produce cholesterol, respectively.

**Table 16.3 Attitudes variables**

|  | Survey question summary |  |
| --- | --- | --- |
| FLUID MILK | ---------------------------- | ----------------- |
| AFTM | Milk leaves a bad aftertaste. | SD(1) . . . .SA(6) |
| CH2M | Milk is high in cholesterol. | SD(1) . . . .SA(6) |
| HATM | Milk can cause heart disease. | SD(1) . . . .SA(6) |
| REFM | Milk is refeshing. | SD(1) . . . .SA(6) |
| RELM | Milk is relaxing. | SD(1) . . . .SA(6) |
| BALM | Milk is required for diet. | SD(1) . . . .SA(6) |
| WATL | Lowfat milk tastes flat and watery. | SD(1) . . . .SA(6) |
| CHEESE | ---------------------------- | ----------------- |
| HEAC | Cheese is a healthful food. | SD(1) . . . .SA(6) |
| TASC | I like the taste of cheese. | SD(1) . . . .SA(6) |
| FATC | Cheese is fattening. | SD(1) . . . .SA(6) |
| HATC | Cheese can cause heart disease. | SD(1) . . . .SA(6) |
| CHOC | Cheese helps produce cholesterol. | SD(1) . . . .SA(6) |

## Net Effects of Health Variables

The maximum likelihood estimates for the logit models for FWM, FSM, FCH, and FBU along with the summary statistics of the estimation are given in Tables 16.4 through 16.6. In each year the logit model is estimated by product category. Use or nonuse is a function of the demographic and attitudinal variables. Each column lists the estimated logit model for a specific year. The number of observations, the proportion of (0/1), and the likelihood ratio Chi-square for the entire model are also listed for each year. This Chi-square statistic is equivalent to a joint test of all of the estimated parameters in the specified model. The results of the parameter estimation are interpreted by comparing parameter estimates across years. Those variables that are statistically significant in explaining the frequency or probability of use are identified and checked for consistency across all of the years. In this way, if a variable, such as concern about cholesterol CH2M, consistently influences the use decision by lowering the probability of use from the mean level, it will show up as a consistently significant variable in each year.

Looking first at the results for regular whole milk in Table 16.4, it is apparent that after accounting for the effects of the demographic and income variables on the decision to use regular fluid milk, concerns about cholesterol levels CH2M or heart disorders HATM related to the use of regular fluid milk of the product do not consistently help identify no use versus use. This is demonstrated by the fact the these variables are not at all significant over the period 1976–88.

Table 16.4  Comparison of logit models: Whole fluid milk 1976–1988

| | Logit model by year | | | | | | |
|---|---|---|---|---|---|---|---|
| | 1976 | 1978 | 1980 | 1982 | 1984 | 1986 | 1988 |
| CONST | -0.346 | -0.88 | -0.06 | 0.06 | 0.34 | -0.08 | 0.49 |
| MT | — | — | 0.97 | 0.48 | 0.42 | 0.24 | 0.45 |
| FT | — | — | — | — | — | — | — |
| F5 | — | -0.39 | -0.28 | — | -0.39 | -0.33 | — |
| F6-12 | — | -0.86 | -0.72 | -0.61 | -0.72 | -0.69 | -0.27 |
| FE | -0.71 | -0.5 | -0.78 | -0.78 | -0.64 | -0.67 | -0.69 |
| ED1 | — | — | — | — | — | — | — |
| ED2 | — | — | — | — | — | — | -0.49 |
| ES1 | — | — | — | — | — | — | -0.26 |
| ES2 | -0.54 | — | — | — | — | -0.29 | -0.42 |
| OC1 | — | — | — | — | — | 0.35 | — |
| OC2 | — | — | 0.20 | 0.16 | — | — | — |
| OS1 | 0.72 | — | 0.59 | — | 0.53 | 0.19 | 0.21 |
| OS2 | — | — | 0.24 | — | 0.53 | — | — |
| IN1 | — | — | -0.31 | -0.39 | -0.48 | — | -0.40 |
| IN2 | — | -0.49 | -0.48 | -0.39 | -0.56 | — | -0.56 |
| IN3 | — | -0.68 | -0.72 | -0.58 | -0.69 | — | -0.79 |
| HOS | — | — | — | 0.09 | 0.09 | 0.12 | 0.08 |
| RAC | — | — | — | — | -0.87 | -1.03 | -0.67 |
| AFTM | -0.19 | -0.14 | -0.04 | -0.04 | -0.06 | -0.06 | -0.04 |
| CH2M | — | — | — | -0.07 | — | — | — |
| HATM | — | — | -0.05 | -0.03 | -0.07 | — | — |
| REFM | 0.37 | 0.27 | 0.27 | 0.30 | 0.20 | 0.23 | 0.21 |
| RELM | — | — | — | 0.09 | 0.08 | — | 0.06 |
| BALM | 0.09 | 0.10 | — | — | 0.12 | 0.10 | 0.07 |
| NOBS | 2843 | 3423 | 3769 | 3192 | 3598 | 3498 | 3407 |
| "0" | 588 | 880 | 1022 | 901 | 1196 | 1230 | 1365 |
| "1" | 2255 | 2543 | 2747 | 2291 | 2402 | 2268 | 2042 |
| $X^2$ | 296 | 289 | 442 | 347 | 407 | 336 | 358 |

NOTE: — indicates not statistically significant at $\alpha = 0.10$. NOBS indicates number of sample observations. "0" indicates number of nonusers. "1" indicates number of users.

The case for lowfat skim milk is very similar to that of regular whole milk. Table 16.5 presents the logit models for the lowfat skim milk product category. After accounting for the demographic and income effects, the two most influential variables in the no use versus use decision are REFM and WATL. In fact the consumers' dislike for the taste of lowfat skim milk is quite strong and consistent across all surveys. The fat and cholesterol variables HATM and CH2M do not exhibit any significant influence on use decisions across the time period. This suggests that while health concerns are acknowledged by consumers, the product dimensions such as refreshing or flat and watery taste are the primary characteristics influencing consumer use

**Table 16.5   Comparison of logit models: Lowfat/skim milk products 1976–1988**

| | Logit model by year | | | | | | |
|---|---|---|---|---|---|---|---|
| | 1976 | 1978 | 1980 | 1982 | 1984 | 1986 | 1988 |
| CONST | -1.45 | -0.96 | -1.55 | -0.91 | — | -1.57 | -1.56 |
| MT | — | -0.25 | — | — | — | 0.27 | — |
| FT | — | — | — | — | — | 0.30 | — |
| F5 | 0.43 | 0.38 | 0.38 | 0.49 | 0.39 | 0.27 | — |
| F6-12 | — | — | 0.25 | — | — | — | — |
| FE | — | — | — | — | — | — | — |
| ED1 | — | — | — | — | — | — | 0.49 |
| ED2 | — | — | — | — | 0.55 | 0.64 | 0.84 |
| ES1 | — | — | — | — | — | — | — |
| ES2 | 0.34 | — | — | — | — | 0.39 | — |
| OC1 | — | — | — | — | 0.32 | — | — |
| OC2 | — | — | 0.02 | 0.22 | — | — | — |
| OS1 | — | — | -0.22 | -0.22 | — | — | — |
| OS2 | — | 0.26 | — | — | — | — | — |
| IN1 | — | 0.22 | — | 0.26 | 0.25 | — | — |
| IN2 | — | — | 0.32 | 0.24 | — | — | 0.26 |
| IN3 | — | — | — | 0.25 | 0.37 | — | 0.40 |
| HOS | — | — | 0.06 | 0.06 | -0.06 | — | — |
| RAC | 0.52 | 0.81 | 0.38 | 0.52 | 0.70 | 0.80 | 1.31 |
| AFTM | — | — | — | — | -0.12 | — | -0.09 |
| CH2M | — | — | — | — | — | — | — |
| HATM | — | 0.06 | 0.07 | 0.09 | 0.07 | 0.11 | 0.09 |
| RELM | 0.05 | — | 0.04 | — | 0.08 | 0.09 | — |
| REFM | 0.21 | 0.19 | 0.19 | 0.30 | 0.28 | 0.15 | 0.21 |
| BALM | 0.08 | 0.07 | 0.08 | — | 0.11 | 0.08 | 0.07 |
| WATL | -0.36 | -0.31 | -0.30 | -0.44 | -0.33 | -0.44 | -0.39 |
| NOBS | 2790 | 3358 | 3735 | 3217 | 3570 | 3474 | 3213 |
| "0" | 1107 | 1372 | 1433 | 1119 | 1343 | 1182 | 995 |
| "1" | 1683 | 1986 | 2302 | 2098 | 2227 | 2292 | 2218 |
| $X^2$ | 449 | 439 | 494 | 629 | 826 | 674 | 575 |

NOTE: — indicates not statistically significant at $\alpha = 0.10$. NOBS indicates number of sample observations. "0" indicates number of nonusers. "1" indicates number of users.

decisions. Advertising or promotion expenditures would most likely be better addressed to these issues. Given the magnitude of the response to the flat taste dimension, perhaps the greatest return would be from a higher solids fortification of the product rather that a promotional campaign designed to fool the consumer. In any event, health-related product dimensions as measured in these attitude scales do not appear to account for the increased consumption of lowfat or skim milk products.

The logit models for cheese are presented in Table 16.6. The three

Table 16.6  Comparison of logit models: Cheese products 1976–1988

|         | Logit model by year | | | | | | |
|---------|-------|-------|-------|-------|-------|-------|-------|
|         | 1976  | 1978  | 1980  | 1982  | 1984  | 1986  | 1988  |
| CONST   | 3.67  | 4.65  | 3.19  | 4.98  | 5.06  | 4.68  | 4.21  |
| MT      | —     | —     | —     | —     | —     | —     | —     |
| FT      | —     | 0.30  | —     | —     | —     | —     | —     |
| F5      | —     | -0.24 | —     | -0.44 | -0.35 | -0.39 | -0.34 |
| F6-12   | -0.30 | —     | —     | —     | —     | 0.24  | —     |
| FE      | —     | —     | —     | —     | —     | —     | 0.54  |
| ED1     | —     | —     | —     | —     | -0.76 | -0.71 | —     |
| ED2     | —     | —     | —     | -0.80 | 1.03  | -0.89 | —     |
| ES1     | —     | —     | —     | —     | —     | —     | —     |
| ES2     | —     | —     | —     | -0.40 | -0.32 | —     | —     |
| OC1     | —     | —     | —     | —     | —     | —     | —     |
| OC2     | —     | —     | —     | —     | —     | —     | —     |
| OS1     | —     | —     | —     | —     | -0.31 | -0.21 | —     |
| OS2     | —     | —     | —     | —     | —     | —     | —     |
| IN1     | -0.35 | -0.37 | —     | —     | —     | —     | -0.28 |
| IN2     | —     | -0.66 | —     | —     | —     | —     | —     |
| IN3     | -0.40 | -0.72 | —     | —     | 0.29  | —     | —     |
| HOS     | —     | —     | —     | —     | —     | —     | —     |
| RAC     | -0.98 | -0.87 | 0.80  | -0.80 | -0.69 | -0.54 | -1.25 |
| HEAC    | -0.34 | -0.37 | -0.38 | -0.32 | -0.45 | -0.42 | -0.37 |
| FATC    | 0.06  | —     | —     | —     | —     | —     | 0.08  |
| CHOC    | —     | —     | 0.09  | —     | 0.06  | —     | —     |
| HATC    | 0.07  | —     | —     | 0.12  | —     | —     | —     |
| NOBS    | 2894  | 3190  | 3484  | 3185  | 3528  | 3460  | 3288  |
| "0"     | 604   | 680   | 804   | 705   | 826   | 725   | 709   |
| "1"     | 2290  | 2510  | 2680  | 2480  | 2702  | 2735  | 2579  |
| $X^2$   | 88    | 106   | 101   | 135   | 167   | 155   | 151   |

NOTE: — indicates not statistically significant at $\alpha = 0.10$. NOBS indicates number of sample observations. "0" indicates number of nonusers. "1" indicates number of users.

attitudinal variables of interest are: FATC, HATC, and CHOC. Very little can be said about the cheese model. It appears that consumers use this commodity because they perceive it to be a healthy food to consume. Health issues do not appear to be very important in this regard.

## Conclusions

This paper reports on a research study that investigated the relative importance of various attitudinal variables to the frequency and per capita use of milk and dairy products. The consumer survey data (AUTS) was used to estimate a maximum likelihood logistics model for whole milk and for lowfat skim milk products. The frequency of product usage was estimated as a function of traditional socioeconomic variables and specific consumer attitude variables. The latter variables measured consumer perception of specific taste and health characteristics of the fluid milk products.

Relative price changes and shifts in consumers' real incomes play important roles in the changes observed in consumption patterns of dairy products. Oftentimes these variables do not offer a complete explanation of shifts that we observe to take place in consumers' purchasing habits. In the case of milk and dairy products, the 1970s and 1980s were a time when consumers shifted from consuming regular whole milk to lowfat skim milk. This was also a period in which interest in generic promotion and producer financed advertising was offered as one way to stimulate consumer demand.

From this research it was determined that certain perceptions of product quality and/or characteristics are more important to consumers than others. These characteristics need to be the focus of promotional strategies and advertising campaigns designed to increase demand. Consumer use of whole milk and lowfat milk are most sensitive to taste characteristics and less so to health related characteristics of the products. In the case of low fat milk products it appears that a significant consumption increase could be generated by either changing consumer perception that the product has a flat, watery taste, or possibly making direct modification to the product to eliminate this undesirable characteristic.

The results of this study suggest that an advertising campaign aimed at changing consumer attitudes toward milk taste would be most effective for increasing consumer frequency of consumption. The analysis of the health variables indicates that consumers are less sensitive to health attributes as compared to other product dimensions.

# 17 Discussion: Communicating Economic Research

BARRY D. PFOUTS

As director of marketing for the National Pork Producers Council of Des Moines, Iowa, and as a student and practitioner of consumer product marketing and advertising, I felt decidedly overwhelmed when asked to be a discussant at this prestigious academic gathering.

And in a fit of uncomfortable self-evaluation regarding my qualifications in this area I arrived at the conclusion that perhaps I could better serve this gathering by pleading a case for the customer.

For the past twenty-five years or so it has been my primary responsibility to develop and implement marketing plans in such diverse areas as sales promotion, food service, public relations, consumer and trade advertising and merchandising—principally for consumer products. These programs were all designed to change the public's perceptions in a positive direction, hopefully leading to increased consumer demand, consumption, and in turn increased profit for my clients.

From the beginning, the primary question I have faced has been: Is the program effective relative to our level of spending? The answer, at least in terms of any individual activity, has always been nebulous at best.

On the other hand, I am aware of no successful marketer who would consider eliminating his advertising program in order to generate long-term corporate health and profits. As the widely quoted cliche expresses so well: "I know that half my advertising dollars are wasted! What I don't know is which half!"

Nonetheless, the exhaustive chase continues for that holy grail of truth in advertising or at least truth in terms of the profitable effectiveness of dollars invested in advertising.

Branded product marketers have at their disposal numerous tools through which satisfactory data, relative to program effectiveness, can be obtained. Actual factory sales are supplemented by such syndicated services as Nielsen Audits and SAMI warehouse withdrawals. (For more information about the services provided by Nielsen and SAMI, see Forker et al.) Thus with reasonable accuracy, predicted results of marketing programs, particularly advertising campaigns, can be proven — at least after the fact.

But as we know all too well, such information gathering and analysis in the vast world of food commodity marketing are considerably more difficult. The size of these markets alone is boggling. Pork sales totaled $27 billion; dairy, $37 billion; and beef, $44 billion. Then, of course, the only regular sales or tonnage data available are provided by the U.S. Department of Agriculture and that data can be unwieldy, or often useless, particularly in terms of measuring advertising effectiveness against specific targets or geographic areas.

We need not at this time belabor the rationale for generic advertising of commodity food products. Suffice it to say that producers today have come to the realization that they must begin to market their products to the consumer. To depend on manufacturers, packers, or processors to provide economic health or to look after producer interests is a perilous course indeed. To the modern, sophisticated producer, the "farm gate" is only the beginning. Not until the sale is rung up at the supermarket checkout counter, or by the restaurant cashier, is the marketing process completed.

Consequently, through various means, producers have generated their own marketing funds and established their own organizations. These associations have been charged with the responsibility to provide the specific customized marketing programs that producers feel they need to sway consumer attitudes and perceptions, and thus increase consumer demand for their products. Like all enlightened marketers, the producer leaders of these organizations and their boards of directors and officers need to measure their return-on-investment and report these findings to the producer membership at large.

Thus we as professional marketers, along with our producer employers, frequently turn to the academic world to provide direction as we attempt to compete for consumer attention and dollars in the same arena as the Proctor & Gambles, Kelloggs, General Foods, and McDonalds of the world— as we attempt to make measurable changes in vastly larger markets with our much smaller budgets.

Here, as they say, is where the rubber meets the road. Can the highly diverse and varied role of a commodity support group such as National Pork Producers Council, United Dairy Industry Association, or the Beef Industry Council really deliver a significant return-on-investment in the extremely competitive world of modern consumer marketing? And if so, how can they provide reasonable "proof of performance" within a reasonable time frame and at a reasonable cost?

At NPPC we have established a set of conditions and ground rules to help us approach this admittedly difficult task and to provide a general, and we hope not confining, framework for research.

1.  We assume that all levels of our producer investors are interested and require regular evaluations of all producer funded activities.
2.  They want those evaluations to be thorough, accurate, objective, and above all, understandable to the membership and actionable for the professional staff.
3.  They are willing to invest reasonable sums for these evaluations just as they do for their other programs designed to obtain data.
4.  They are open to, and encourage, outside help from either private business or academia.
5.  Producers expect meaningful, actionable results. (They will not invest in research for its own sake.)
6.  In spite of this, producers are open to different, innovative approaches to obtain optimum results. They will not provide for variances simply to establish new conditions for analysis.
7.  Researchers must work with producer organizations to fully understand their objectives, strategies, and promotion approaches — not in isolation, and definitely not from an adversarial posture.
8.  Researchers must also honor any required nondisclosure agreements pertaining to databases or from other proprietary sources. (Obviously, shared organizational confidences between producers/staff and researchers carry the same prohibition.)
9.  Producers appreciate outside suppliers who make real efforts to learn their organization's "persona" and who provide constructive and positive recommendations for future actions.
10. Researchers who immerse themselves in the industry/organization, who learn the problems and opportunities unique to that structure, and who then market themselves accordingly, will be rewarded with future projects.

None of the foregoing is unique, yet the number of organizations who violate many of these common sense guidelines is astounding!

At this point, I would like to focus the balance of my remarks on a primary area near and dear to my heart — clearly the product of my professional background — communications!

As I mentioned earlier, our producers and staff want evaluations that are thorough, accurate, objective, and above all understandable. The action word here is understandable.

Let me position my next remarks with two unattributed quotations, and for the moment try to pretend you're a concerned and responsible hog producer or dairy farmer leader:

Equations (4), (5), and (6) form a recursive system in consumption, attitude, and recall. An estimation procedure was used to control for a selectivity problem in the data. This selectivity problem results from the condition structure of the hypothesized recursive system. A two-stage estimation procedure adjusting in equations (5) and (6) for this selectivity problem used the inverse Mills ratio as a correction factor and yielded consistent results for the parameters of the model (Maddala; Lee). A maximum likelihood probit estimation was carried out on each equation. The effect of the advertising message was carried through to the attitude and consumption equations by the inverse Mills ratio of the $M^*$ variable. Similarly, the effect of attitude was carried through to the consumption equation by the inverse Mills ratio of the $A^*$ variable.

And here's another:

The logit model has two measurement techniques, these are the grouped data approach, and the microdata approach. The former employs weighted least squares (WLS), while the latter is done by means of maximum likelihood estimation (MLE). The microdata approach with the maximum likelihood iterative procedure will be employed for this study.

The MLE estimates are found by maximizing the likelihood function with respect to the parameters of interest. The likelihood function is a joint probability distribution of the sample, and is equal to the product of consumption probability of all individual observations. The primary appeal of applying MLE is that this technique possesses the asymptotic properties, i.e., consistent, asymptotically efficient, and asymptotically normal.

As I see it, these are both extreme examples of researchers talking to themselves, when the objective was to evaluate a particular program and then communicate its effectiveness to producer leaders and their staffs.

You may ask what level of communication is necessary for producer groups and staffs? Well, starting at the top in my organization, for example, our president Ray Hankes has a farrow-to-finish operation. He markets 5,000 to 6,000 hogs per year and row crops between 300 and 400 acres of corn and soybeans in central Illinois. Ray operates a medium size family farm in that area. Ray, by the way, has a Ph.D. in ruminant nutrition and meat science from the University of Illinois. Others in our leadership have graduate and undergraduate degrees from Yale, Harvard, Princeton, and Eaton, plus all the universities in the Big Ten, the Big Eight, and on and on. Their degrees vary from agriculturally related areas to political science and English. And oh, yes, we have a staffer with a master's degree in agricultural economics from Ohio State.

But perhaps with the exception of the latter, very few of us have a daily working knowledge of univariate and multivariate analysis, ordinary least squares, or $t$-tests. For many of us, the closest we get to negative elasticity is a pair of failed suspenders, and a dummy variable is the boss who rejects your request for time off.

None of the foregoing should be construed as criticism of the intensely sophisticated disciplines of economics, statistics, or research. We recognize the years of research and analytical effort that went into the development of the highly refined tools and techniques and the body of data necessary to tackle the immensely complex problems of measuring marketing programs.

Our concern is with the modes and means of communicating such findings and recommendations to specific audiences.

I would paraphrase a modern cliche as follows: What you say is important only to the degree that how you say it is understood. Let me demonstrate with an apropos advertising example.

When our current ad agency, Bozell, Jacobs, Kenyon & Eckhardt, was first attempting to gain the NPPC account, they had developed several creative approaches to advertise pork to consumers. Through long and difficult background work and research they had developed the hypothesis that the nutritional improvements in modern pork products (i.e., 50 percent less fat than twenty years ago and a calorie and cholesterol story on par with the current nutritional holy grail — breast of chicken, skin removed) would have a very strong consumer appeal. As a result, they developed an extremely appealing test commercial saying exactly that. Test audiences loved the commercial. There was just one problem. Audiences did not believe the direct comparison claims that pork compared nutritionally with chicken.

This, of course, was the catalyst for the development of the now famous "Pork — The Other White Meat" campaign — a campaign, by the way, that consumers seem to have little trouble understanding, believing, or acting upon. This is the case despite some early negative concerns from several consumer advocacy groups around the country.

We recognize the difficulty in measuring both the individual and collective economic impact of programs as complex and varied as marketing, public relations, animal research, legislative affairs, and foreign trade. We recognize the need to make economic assumptions, and applaud the development and utilization of computer modeling techniques. We recognize the need to document, in excruciating detail, the exacting methods taken to develop conclusions, recommendations, and next steps.

But we believe that for our purposes — the purposes of industry organizations like NPPC — these tools and techniques need to be relegated to their proper position in the hierarchy of presentation. The first consideration should be the audience.

In terms of presentation, a producer and staff audience is most interested in more clearly understanding what happened, why it happened, and what should be done next. Although the arcane details of mathematical and statistical technique are of academic interest and appropriate for peer review, producer and staff audiences (for the most part) couldn't care less how you got there. To paraphrase another old expression, when we ask what time it is, don't tell us how to build a watch!

One other area that deserves additional comment is presentation tone. Even negative findings should be viewed as being valuable information. They should also be presented with recommendations for remedial actions and positive program adjustments or replacements.

While it shouldn't even have to be mentioned, how often are we faced with a presentation style or attitude that gives the appearance of talking down to the audience? This is only compounded by materials that are clearly outside or beyond the expertise of the audience. Suffice it to say that what an audience doesn't understand, it will not like. Of course this attitude may also project itself upon the messenger.

As a rather nondescript, but extremely wealthy, dairy farmer once told me after I made a rather self-congratulatory advertising presentation: "Boy, if you is so smart, how come you ain't rich?" Well, he's still rich and I'm still poor, but I learned something about communication that day.

In summation, I would like to say that we as staff, and our producer employers, admire you and more importantly respect what you do. Furthermore we have a desperate need for more and better proof and evaluations for what we are attempting to accomplish. We need your guidance as to how we can better execute our programs and how we can develop new and even more effective programs for the future. We ask that you help us to help ourselves, and our whole producer constituency, to reach a healthy economic future. Although I've outlined a number of things, the most important steps that you can take are to develop a better understanding of your audience and then to communicate with them.

# 5 Supply Response and Optimal Control Models of Advertising

# 18 Measuring Wool Promotion Response with Household Survey Data

## JOE DEWBRE and STEVE BEARE

Australian organizations spent US $140m in 1987–88 on overseas promotion of its three major agricultural exports: wool (US $121m), beef (US $11m), and wheat (US $8m). Government contributed to this expenditure, but the greatest share was paid from proceeds of grower levies.

Promotion expenditures were channelled through three statutory marketing organizations: the Australian Wool Corporation, the Australian Meat and Livestock Corporation, and the Australian Wheat Board (from whose annual reports the above figures are taken). Australian rural products have long been promoted overseas, but the level of such expenditures has increased dramatically in recent years. Major new programs of wool promotion have been undertaken in the past five years in the United States, Western Europe, and Japan. There has also been significant expansion of promotion of Australian beef in the United States and in Japan in the last couple of years. Further increases in both wool and beef promotion were planned for the coming year.

There are no published assessments of the effectiveness of past expenditures on overseas promotion of Australian beef or wheat. However, in the case of wool, a recent joint study by the Australian Wool Corporation and the (then) Bureau of Agricultural Economics analyzed the effects of wool apparel advertising in the United States (Australian Wool Corporation and Bureau of Agricultural Economics 1987). The results of that study provided some quantitative evidence of the benefits from promoting wool, and have had an influence on promotion spending decisions by the industry. The present paper contains an account of one major phase of that analysis.

Wool promotion is conducted by the International Wool Secretariat on behalf of the wool growers of its member countries. This organization, which uses the familiar Woolmark symbol in its promotion campaigns, is jointly funded by the wool exporting countries: Australia, New Zealand, Uruguay, and South Africa. It promotes wool in the major wool consuming markets around the world: principally in Western Europe, the United States, and Japan. The analysis reported here was undertaken in conjunction with a five-year program of increased advertising of wool apparel initiated in the United States in 1984. The overall aim of the study was to provide a measure of the influence of that program, to guide decisions about its continuance beyond its initial five-year horizon.

## Conceptual Issues

An important distinction between wool and other commodities subject to the influence of generic promotion is that, for the most part, wool is not directly the object of consumer choice. Promotion expenditures are typically directed at increasing the demand for final products in which wool is an attribute. The presence of wool in a garment may be regarded by consumers as an indicator of desirable characteristics, such as being of good quality, comfortable and fashionable, which together augment its utility. Houthakker (1952) extended the utility maximization framework of consumer theory to include choices of both quantity and quality characteristics, and demonstrated that consumer choice under utility maximization yielded ordinary demand curves for product characteristics.

The quantity of apparel wool consumed is determined by consumer choice among a wide and continuous range of wool and non-wool types of apparel. These choices are conditioned by the usual demand variables — prices, incomes, and factors which affect consumer taste and preference, which in the present case include promotion.

The term *promotion* as used in this study refers to a set of marketing activities undertaken by the International Wool Secretariat aimed at increasing consumer demand for wool products. The most important of these activities has been media advertising of wool apparel. In this paper the effect on consumer demand for wool apparel of the total expenditure on marketing activities directed at increasing such demand is analyzed.

In past studies there have been two general approaches to specifying response to advertising, within the utility maximization framework of consumer theory. In one, advertising is assumed to influence consumer tastes and preferences directly. That is, exposure to advertising increases the utility of consumption of a product. In the other, advertising is viewed as information, used by consumers to obtain utility more efficiently through their consumption decisions. These theories have identical implications for the general form of ordinary consumer demand equations that include advertising as an explanator along with the usual price and income arguments:

$$Q = f(P_1, \ldots, P_n, Y, A) \tag{18.1}$$

where

$Q$ is the quantity demanded of some good in the current period;
$f(\ldots)$ denotes a general functional relationship (for reasons discussed subsequently, a simple linear form was chosen);
$P_1, \ldots, P_n$ are the prices of the good and its close substitutes or complements;
$Y$ is the consumer's income; and
$A$ is the advertising exposure of the consumer.

It is widely accepted that advertising in any one period has carryover effects in subsequent periods. In the simplest case, these are the residual effects of past advertising. However, such advertising retention is not the only source of carryover effects on consumer demand. Wool apparel is a durable good. Though advertising (as well as changes in incomes and prices) may alter a consumer's desired wardrobe, consumers are not likely to discard their existing apparel in the short run. Consequently, they may only partly adjust their wardrobe toward a desired composition in any given period, and the adjustment process is then carried over into subsequent periods. Models of consumer purchase behavior based on partial adjustment, first introduced by Nerlove (1958), have been used in analyses of demand for a number of different commodities, particularly durables (see Phlips 1974).

The most common method of capturing advertising carryover effects, whether from advertising retention or partial consumer stock adjustment, is to include past levels of consumption as an additional explanator of current consumption in a demand equation. This was the procedure adopted in the present analysis. Limitations on the length of the time series of household wool consumption data (eleven years) prevented consideration of more general issues in the dynamics of advertising response.

The response of consumer demand to changes in advertising may depend on the existing level of advertising: there may be a decreasing or increasing marginal response at different base levels of advertising; furthermore, the response to advertising may change with price, income, and other variables. Thus, in general, the sales-to-advertising relationship is nonlinear.

Advertising researchers generally assume that demand exhibits a diminishing marginal response to advertising (Kinnucan 1985) — that is, that successive equal increases in advertising expenditure result in smaller and smaller increases in demand. In that case, it should be possible to identify an optimum level of advertising expenditures: that level below which additional advertising returns more than it costs and above which it costs more than it returns.

Theoretically, however, the marginal response of demand to advertising need not be diminishing over all ranges of the observed data. Figure 18.1 shows a full range of theoretically possible marginal responses of demand to advertising. The intercept on this graph — point $d_0$ on the vertical axis — represents the level of demand in the absence of any advertising. Over the range of advertising expenditures $a_0$ to $a_1$ the marginal response of demand is zero. Over some initial range of effective advertising expenditure, $a_1$ to $a_2$, the marginal response of demand to sales could plausibly be increasing. Over a higher range of advertising expenditures, $a_2$ to $a_3$, the demand to advertising relationship is represented with the diminishing marginal response usually assumed. Finally, it is possible that, once advertising expenditures reach some saturation level $a_3$, the response of demand to advertising would be negative.

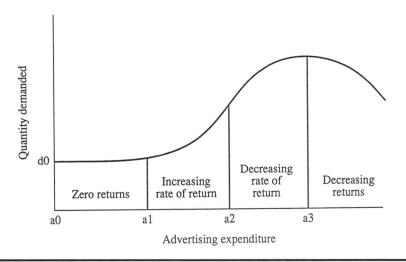

**Figure 18.1. Generalized response of demand to advertising.**

Diminishing marginal response is not the only source of nonlinear effects of advertising on demand. Advertising may also affect the price and income elasticities. It has been argued — by Quilkey (1986), for example — that advertising produces its effects *exclusively* through its influence on these other demand parameters.

Empirical estimates of the marginal response of demand to advertising will depend critically on the range of data over which the relationship is estimated. In this analysis, a linear demand equation was chosen after experimentation with more general functional forms. In preliminary regression analyses, a quadratic approximation to the general form of demand in equation (1) was applied to the data on consumption of wool in apparel, prices, incomes, and promotion expenditure. First, a general quadratic response-surface model was estimated to decompose the explained variation in wool consumption into linear, interactive, and squared effects (without distinguishing the independent variables). Virtually no explanatory power was attributable to interactive effects, indicating that the historical influences of promotion on price and income responses were negligible. Approximately 5 percent of the explained variation was attributed to squared effects — sufficient to warrant additional investigation into possible decreasing or increasing returns to promotion spending. A model with linear and quadratic promotion terms was estimated. The squared promotion term was not statistically significant, indicating that the question of increasing or decreasing returns to promotion spending could not be accurately determined from the existing data.

It was concluded that the available data did not cover a wide enough range of variation in advertising expenditure per person to permit estimation of nonlinear effects. Total expenditure by the International Wool Secretariat on advertising of wool apparel in the United States has varied significantly, mainly as a consequence of changes in the number of markets (both regional and end-use) in which promotion is undertaken. The variation in expenditure is not attributed to changes in the rates of advertising expenditure per person within particular markets.

## Data

The data used to measure the quantity and price of wool in apparel were derived from apparel purchase records of a sample of households in the United States. These records were obtained from two market research firms: the Market Research Corporation of America and the National Purchase Dairy Company. It was considered necessary to obtain data from both sources to ensure a sufficiently large sample: because wool apparel items are not purchased frequently by households, the number of purchase records available from either source alone was initially considered too small. Both firms have panels of households that are selected as a stratified quota sample of all households in the United States. Table 18.1 shows the numbers of sample households in these surveys for the years 1974–85. Participants are required to give detailed information each month on their purchases of

**Table 18.1 Numbers of households in the surveys**

|                                          | Years   | Annual number |
| ---------------------------------------- | ------- | ------------- |
| Market Research Company                  | 1974–81 | 7,500         |
| Market Research Corporation of America   | 1982–85 | 11,500        |
| National Purchase Dairy Company          | 1977–84 | 6,500         |
|                                          | 1985–88 | 500           |

a wide range of goods, including those items of apparel covered in this analysis.

Households were originally chosen for membership in the panels on the basis of statistical requirements for representativeness across a number of geographic and demographic dimensions. In the present analysis, household purchases were assigned to specific geographic regions corresponding to markets as defined by the International Wool Secretariat. For the most part these market definitions correspond very closely to U.S. Bureau of Census definitions of Statistical Metropolitan Areas.

The purchase records contain financial details on the transaction itself (for example, price, type of garment, sex of wearer, fiber composition) and socioeconomic information on the household making the purchase (for example, size of family and, in particular, geographic location and income). The apparel records used for this analysis were for all purchases of menswear, womenswear, boyswear, and girlswear (as listed in Table 18.2).

**Table 18.2. Apparel categories included in the analysis**

| Menswear      | Womenswear    | Boyswear | Girlswear |
| ------------- | ------------- | -------- | --------- |
| Coats         | Coats         | Knitwear | Knitwear  |
| Outer jackets | Outer jackets | Suits    |           |
| Jackets       | Jackets       |          |           |
| Knitwear      | Knitwear      |          |           |
| Socks         | Dresses       |          |           |
| Accessories   | Skirts        |          |           |
| Trousers      | Trousers      |          |           |
|   dress    | Suits  |          |           |
|   casual   |        |          |           |
|   other    |        |          |           |
| Suits         |               |          |           |
|   leisure  |        |          |           |
|   other    |        |          |           |

The wool content of individual garment purchases was calculated by multiplying the reported percentage wool content by the International Wool Secretariat estimates of average garment weights. The total of these calculations provided an estimate of the consumption of wool for each household for every year of the sample.

The International Wool Secretariat undertakes expenditure on a wide variety of promotional activities designed to shift the demand for wool apparel. Advertising has been directed primarily toward consumers and, to a lesser extent, to other decision makers in the marketing system — retailers, manufacturers, and distributors. Most wool apparel advertising sponsored by the Secretariat has been in the largest cities — principally in the urban Northeast—of the United States. There has been considerable variation, however, in levels of advertising expenditure between the various cities and over time, due to the geographic and end-use specific nature of many of the apparel advertising programs.

The single most important category of advertising expenditure undertaken by the Secretariat is retail cooperative advertising. It results from agreements between the Secretariat and various apparel retailers to share costs of newspaper advertisements, catalogues, and related promotion. The Secretariat has a range of requirements for such advertisements (for example, the advertised item cannot be price discounted) in addition to the primary requirement that the "Woolmark" or "Woolblendmark" label be prominently featured.

Some modeling considerations arise from the voluntary nature of these programs. Retailers in markets where wool apparel consumption is relatively high are more likely to participate in cooperative advertising than those where it is relatively low. Similarly, apparel retailers in general may be more willing to advertise in years when wool apparel demand is high than at other times. Retailers may also be aware of regional differences in consumer responsiveness to advertising of wool apparel, regardless of the existing level of wool demand. Regional dummy variables were included in the demand equation to capture any underlying static differences in wool apparel demand (though not in advertising responsiveness) between regions. Preliminary analysis also included year variables, which were subsequently dropped because of statistical insignificance of their estimated coefficients.

The data on promotion expenditures were calculated annually and were associated with households on a regional basis. Most promotion expenditure was specific to individual regional markets. Larger scale promotion expenditure was allocated among regions using additional data, such as subscription rates for relevant national publications. Total promotion expenditure in each geographic market was divided by the total number of households within that market to obtain promotion expenditure per household. The household population data used were obtained from Arbitron Ratings Company (1984).

Other data required included consumer price indexes specific to the selected regional markets. The U.S. Bureau of Labor Statistics (1986) published such indexes specific to 25 of the 195 regional markets included in this analysis. It also publishes consumer price indexes, cross-tabulated by population size, for four census regions and four population size groups in the United States. The remaining 170 markets were therefore classified by population size and census region, and consumer price indexes were assigned accordingly.

The distribution of sample households by region and income class did not match the corresponding distribution of households in the U.S. population in any year of the sample. In addition, the sample size grew more quickly than the population over the estimation period. It was therefore necessary to weight the sample to be more representative of the population. Weights were computed for each household in the sample based on a comparison of the proportions of sample households in each income and region class with the corresponding proportions in the general population.

Geographic and income cell proportions in the U.S. population were computed using U.S. Bureau of the Census data on the distribution of household incomes by census region (U.S. Department of Commerce, Bureau of the Census 1986). There were nine census regions. There were seven income categories for the years 1975 to 1978, but the categories were increased to nine in 1979 when additional data became available. This reduced the problem of bracket drift due to inflation, as the U.S. Bureau of the Census publishes data on the distribution of households by nominal income only.

## Analysis

### IMPLICIT PRICES

The raw price data available from apparel purchase records consisted of prices paid for individual wool garments. These data provide no measure of the value or price of wool in apparel. Annual implicit prices of wool in apparel were estimated using an hedonic price function (Griliches 1971). Implicit price equations of the following form were estimated for each category of apparel listed in Table 18.2, for each year of the study period:

$$GP_{ij} = a_j + b_j X_{ij} \qquad (18.2)$$

where

$GP_{ij}$ is the price paid for garment $i$ in apparel category $j$;

$a_j$ is the average implicit price of non-wool components in all purchases of garments in category $j$;

$b_j$ is the average implicit price of one percentage point of wool content in all purchases of garments in category $j$; and

$X_{ij}$ is the percentage wool content in garment $ij$.

The implicit price estimates obtained from regression analysis of equation (18.2) are biased. Beside the usual sources of bias, such as omitted variables and incorrect functional form, there is in this case a bias because of an identification problem peculiar to the use of a percentage as the measure of wool content. The identification problem and its implications for the analysis of consumer demand for wool can be examined, with little loss in generality, by considering the fiber component of garment prices in terms of only two fibers, wool and other. The linear hedonic price equation is written:

$$gp_{ij} = \alpha_j + ß_{jw}x_{ijw} + ß_{jk}(1 - x_{ijw}) \tag{18.3}$$

where $GP_{ij}$ is the price of the garment $i$ in apparel category $j$; $x_{ijw}$ is the percentage of wool fiber in garment $i$ of apparel category $j$; and $\alpha_j, ß_{jw}$ and $ß_{jk}$ are parameters ($w$ indicating wool and $k$ other fibers).

The coefficient $ß_{jk}$ may be interpreted as the price per percentage point of other fiber in garment category $j$. However, as the percentages of fiber content sum to 100, the model is not fully identified and the price of one fiber type must serve as a reference price.

The equation was estimated in the form:

$$
\begin{aligned}
GP_{ij} &= \alpha_j + b_j x_{ij} \\
a_j\ &= a_j + ß_{j0} \\
b_{jw} &= ß_{jw} - ß_{j0}
\end{aligned}
$$

The estimated price coefficient $b_{jw}$ must therefore be interpreted as the price premium for a percentage point increase in wool content. This premium will vary with both the price of wool in apparel and with the price of other fibers. In effect, the implicit prices estimated in these circumstances can be interpretated as implicit price premiums per 1 percent wool; that is, as expressing the price of wool relative to the price of other fibers. In the context of the demand model to be estimated, the use of a relative price is equivalent to an exact linear restriction. It imposes the condition that the derivative of the quantity of wool demanded with respect to the price of wool is equal (and opposite) to its derivative with respect to the price of other fibers. Consequently, own-price effects are likely to be understated while cross-price effects are likely to be overstated.

An important issue is whether the estimate of the elasticity of wool demand with respect to promotion expenditure is affected by the use of biased price data or by the imposition of restricted estimates of the demand parameters. The question hinges on whether the bias in the price data is systematically related to promotion expenditure. There is no obvious reason for suspecting such a correlation. The restrictions on the own- and cross-price parameters may lead to biased estimates of promotion effects if promotional spending is correlated with fiber prices. The most important correlation would be between promotional spending and wool prices. As own-price effects are likely to be understated, this correlation would tend to result in a downward bias in the estimated effect of promotion.

The $a_j$ and $b_j$ coefficients in equation (18.3) were estimated by ordinary least squares regression. Estimated implicit price premiums per percentage point part of wool content are not directly comparable across apparel categories, as such prices will vary with garment weights. That is, the price per 1 percent of wool content in suits may exceed the corresponding price of wool in skirts (in part, because there is more fabric in a suit). To calculate an average implicit price across apparel categories it was necessary to convert from a percentage wool content basis to a weight of wool content basis, as follows. The implicit expenditure premium on wool in each garment purchase was first calculated, by multiplying the percentage wool content in each garment by the corresponding estimate of the implicit price per 1 percent of wool content. The expenditure premium per garment was then totalled for each household in each year to produce an estimate of the total implicit expenditure on wool in apparel. This expenditure and the total weight of wool in the garments purchased by the sample households were calculated for each year from 1974 to 1985. The ratios of total implicit expenditure to total weight in each year were used as estimates of the annual average implicit price of wool per unit of weight.

## Demand

The wool demand equation finally chosen for the analysis was:

$$q_{it} = B_0 + B_1 P_{jt} + B_2 Y_{it} + B_3 A_{jt} + B_4 q_{i,t-1} + C'Z_{it} + u_{it} \qquad (18.4)$$

where

$q_{it}$ is quantity of wool apparel purchased by household $i$ in year $t$;
$B$ and $C$ are model coefficients to be estimated;
$P_{jt}$ is the real implicit price premium for wool in apparel purchased in region $j$ in year $t$;
$Y_{it}$ is real income of household $i$ in year $t$;
$A_{jt}$ is real promotion expenditure in region $j$ in year $t$; and
$Z_{it}$ is a vector of demographic variables for household $i$ in year $t$ (including household size, presence of children, and geographic region).

To simplify the exposition and to focus the discussion more specifically on the economic relationships, no further references to the demographic variables or their coefficient estimates will appear in this paper. A complete report of those results can be found in Australian Wool Corporation and Bureau of Agricultural Economics (1987).

In the construction of real variables — income, prices, and promotion — a regional consumer price index was used. This choice is readily defensible for the income and price variables, where the index was used to account for the effects of all other consumer prices. An advertising or marketing cost index would have been preferred for the promotion variables, but none could be found that corresponded to the promotion data definitions. It seems likely that the costs of promotion activities were very closely correlated with the general consumer price index, providing some justification for its use as a proxy for promotion cost inflation.

In estimating the parameters of the above demand equation from household data, a problem arises from the fact that many households may not make a relevant purchase in a given period. Some households do not purchase wool apparel at all, and even in purchasing households most wool garments (like other semi-durable products) are purchased infrequently. The effect of infrequent or zero purchase observations is that ordinary least squares estimates of the demand parameters will be biased (Tobin 1958). In this situation, consistent estimates of the demand parameters may be obtained using a censored regression model. The model incorporates a purchase threshold price, above which no purchase is made. The threshold price is the price-axis intercept of a demand curve drawn in the usual price-quantity diagram. For a more detailed discussion of the model, see Beare (1988).

The resulting conditional demand equation is written (with dummy variables and household, region, and time subscripts dropped):

$$q_w = \beta_0 + \beta_1 p_w + \beta_2 Y + \beta_3 A + \beta_4 q_w(-1) \text{ if } p_w \leq p_w^* \qquad (18.5)$$
$$0 \text{ if } p_w > p_w^*$$

The threshold price, $p_w^*$, is a latent variable, in the sense that it is not directly observed. It is assumed that threshold prices are distributed randomly about a conditional mean, given by the inverse of the demand function evaluated at $q_w$ equal to zero:

$$p_w^* = -[\beta_0 + \beta_2 Y + \beta_3 A + \beta_4 q_w(-1)]/\beta_1 + u \qquad (18.6)$$

where $u$ is a random variable. Equations (18.4) and (18.5) yield the Tobit censored regression model which, in simplified matrix notation, is:

$$q_w = \beta^T x \text{ if } \epsilon \geq -\beta^T x \qquad (18.7)$$
$$0 \text{ if } \epsilon < -\beta^T x$$

where

$\epsilon = \beta^T u;$
$\beta$ is the vector of coefficients $\beta_0$, $\beta_1$, $\beta_2$, $\beta_3$, and $\beta_4$; and
$x$ is the combined vector of the right-hand side variables—income, price, promotion, and the lagged dependent.

Several methods for estimating the Tobit model have been proposed. Maddala (1983) provides a detailed review. The procedure outlined here is a modification of the two-stage estimator developed by Heckman (1976). It is based on the assumption that the distribution of the disturbance term $\epsilon$ is logistic. A complete derivation of the results presented here may be found in Australian Wool Corporation and Bureau of Agricultural Economics (1987), and an extension of the results to systems estimation may be found in Beare (1988).

The unconditional expectation of $q_w$ is:

$$E(q_w) = E[q_w \mid \epsilon \geq -\beta^T x] Pr[\epsilon \geq -\beta^T x]$$

where $E$ denotes an expected value and $Pr(a)$ denotes the probability of event $a$. This expression is simply the expected quantity purchased, given that a purchase is made, multiplied by the probability that a purchase is made. The equation may be rewritten:

$$E(q_w) = \{\beta^T x + E[\epsilon \mid \epsilon \geq -\beta^T x]\} \, Pr[\epsilon \geq -\beta^T x] \qquad (18.8)$$

The term $E[\epsilon \mid \epsilon \geq -\beta^T x]$ is the expected value of the truncated disturbance term, which may be expressed:

$$\frac{g(-\beta^T x)}{1 - F(-\beta^T x)}$$

where

$$g(-\beta^T x) = - \int_{-\infty}^{\beta^T x} \epsilon f(\epsilon) d\epsilon$$

and

f is the density function of ε, and
F is the cumulative density function of ε.

The probability of purchase can be rewritten:

$$1 - F(-\beta^T x) \tag{18.9}$$

Assuming the distribution of ε is logistic, the probability of purchase may be expressed:

$$Pr(q_w \geq 0) = 1 - [1 + \exp(-\beta^T x/\sigma)]^{-1} \tag{18.10}$$

where σ is a scale parameter measuring the dispersion of the logistic error distribution. The unconditional expectation of $q_w$ given by equation (18.8) may be expressed:

$$E(q_w) = \sigma \ln [1 + \exp(\beta^T x/\sigma)] \tag{18.11}$$

Equations (18.10) and (18.11) constitute the model finally subjected to regression analysis. Equation (18.10) is the underlying probability equation for the logit model for discrete choice (McFadden 1974). Equation (18.11) may be regarded as the market or average household demand equation. The coefficient estimates were obtained in two steps.

In the first step a logit procedure was used to estimate the scaled coefficients in equation (18.10): $\beta_1/\sigma$, $\beta_2/\sigma$, . . . , $\beta_n/\sigma$. The data used for this purpose were, for right hand side variables (price, consumer income and promotion expenditure), the observed annual averages per sample household for the period 1978 through 1986. The dependent variable representing the purchase decision was assigned values of either 1 or 0: 1 if the sample household bought some wool apparel during the year, 0 if not. On average

30 percent of all sample households purchased some wool apparel in each year of the study period.

In the second step the scale parameter $\sigma$ was estimated from an ordinary least squares regression of equation (18.11). The data used for this purpose were: for the dependent variable, the observed quantities of wool apparel purchased by sample households during each year of the study period; and for the right-hand side variable (the expression in outer brackets in equation (18.11)), values calculated using results obtained in estimating equation (18.10), specifically the predicted probabilities of purchase.

Equation (18.11), when evaluated at the mean level for the explanatory variables, is an expression for average household level demand. The average effect on household demand of a change in one of the explanatory variables can be calculated from the derivative of equation (18.11) with respect to the $k$th element of $x$:

$$\frac{\partial q}{\partial x_k} = \frac{\beta_k}{1 + \exp\left(\dfrac{-\beta^T x}{\sigma}\right)}$$

This yields a short-run elasticity:

$$e_k^s = \frac{\beta_k x_k}{\left[1 + \exp\left(\dfrac{-\beta^T x}{\sigma}\right)\right] q} \tag{18.12}$$

To compute a long-run elasticity, the expected and lagged quantities purchased in equation (18.11) may be equated, as an equilibrium quantity $q^*$. This revised expression may then be differentiated implicitly with respect to $q$ and $x_k$ to yield:

$$\frac{\partial q^*}{\partial x_k} = \frac{\beta_k}{1 + \beta_4 + \exp\left(\dfrac{-\beta^T x}{\sigma}\right)}$$

and a corresponding long-run elasticity formula:

$$e_k^L = \frac{\beta_k x_k}{\left[1 + \beta_4 + \exp\left(\frac{\beta^T x}{\sigma}\right)\right]q} \tag{18.13}$$

## Results

Tables 18.3 and 18.4 contain first- and second-stage coefficient estimates, and their standard errors, for the principal explanatory variables in the wool apparel demand equation. Table 18.5 contains elasticity estimates for the combined first- and second-stage results.

The last column of Table 18.3 contains estimates of impact multipliers, which measure the expected short-run change in average probability of purchase caused by a 10 percent increase in a demand variable. For example, a 10 percent increase in real promotion expenditure could be expected to produce a 0.18 percentage point increase in the average probability of purchase or, equivalently, in the proportion of households who buy some wool apparel.

The significance levels of all estimated coefficients in the first-stage regressions are greater than 0.999, and the coefficients all have the hypothesized signs. The wool price effect yields the largest estimated multiplier on purchase probability — that is, a given percentage change in price produces a greater change in the proportion of households who purchase wool than does the same percentage change in any other variable.

The pseudo $R^2$ is a goodness-of-fit measure similar to the multiple correlation coefficient of a normal regression. It is a measure of the degree of accuracy with which the model predicts discrete purchase decisions for individual households. Its relatively low value is not surprising, since it

**Table 18.3 First-stage logit model estimates for the wool purchase decision**

| Variable | Scaled coefficient | Standard error | Impact multiplier |
|---|---|---|---|
| Real income | 0.0039 | 0.0001 | 0.011 |
| Real promotion | 2.632 | 0.202 | 0.0018 |
| Real wool price | -4.849 | 0.355 | -0.026 |
| Lagged wool demand | 0.823 | 0.016 | 0.0044 |

Pseudo $R^2 = 0.300$

**Table 18.4  Second-stage regression estimate of the scale parameter $\sigma$**

| Variable | Coefficient | Standard error |
|---|---|---|
| $-\ln[1 - Pr(q > 0)]$ | 0.627 | 0.003 |
| $R^2 = 0.277$ | | |

**Table 18.5  Estimates of short- and long-run elasticities of demand for wool in apparel**

| | Mean elasticity | |
|---|---|---|
| Variable | Short-run | Long-run |
| Income | 0.431 | 0.527 |
| Promotion | 0.070 | 0.086 |
| Wool-in-apparel price | -1.104 | -1.349 |

would be expected that individual household purchase decisions would be subject to a large number of random effects excluded from the model.

The elasticities of demand with respect to real promotion expenditure by the International Wool Secretariat are the central result of this study. For the whole sample period, a 1 percent increase in real promotion expenditure is estimated to have resulted in a 0.07 percent increase in average household wool consumption. When allowance is made for full adjustment to changes in price, income, or promotion, longer run elasticities are obtained which are somewhat higher than the corresponding short-run elasticities.

## Conclusions

Household survey data are a useful but little used source of information for evaluating the effectiveness of commodity promotion. To exploit these data fully, however, it is necessary to have adequate variation in proportional spending within the sample. Here, proportional spending data were obtained which varied on a regional and time-series basis.

In the early stages of the analysis there was some concern that the combined sample was too small to draw confident inferences about promotion response. This concern was dispelled; from some additional analysis (not reported here) using subsamples of the complete data set, it was evident that confident conclusions about wool promotion response could have been drawn with balanced samples of as few as 5,000 households per year. Naturally, this possibility depends upon the regional and temporal dispersion of promotion expenditures.

The major difficulty with the use of household purchase data, and more generally with time-series analysis of wool promotion response, is that of consistency of data definitions across the time series. The combination of changes in fashion, changes in client composition of the market research firms, and the general evolution of data services offered by those firms required considerable effort and compromise in the choice of purchase categories used in calculations of wool apparel consumption.

Wool promotion, prices, and household income were all found to be statistically significant variables in a household level wool-in-apparel demand equation. An average short-run elasticity of promotion response of 0.07 was estimated. The corresponding long-run elasticity (which is achieved within a relatively short four-to-five-year response period) was estimated to be 0.09.

The analysis reported here was part of a larger study of the payoff to added wool promotion expenditures in the United States (Australian Wool Corporation and Bureau of Agricultural Economics 1987). The conclusion of that study was that such expenditures were profitable. Based on those results and other considerations, decisions were taken to continue the wool advertising program.

A number of secondary issues regarding the impact of wool apparel promotion were also examined. Perhaps the most important issue is whether there is increasing or decreasing marginal response to further promotion expenditure. This question remains unanswered.

# 19    Impacts of Promotion on the Livestock Sector: Simulations of Supply Response and Effects on Producer Returns

## H. H. JENSEN, S. R. JOHNSON, K. SKOLD, and E. GRUNDMEIER

The growth in nationally mandated commodity promotion programs in the last five years has generated increased interest in evaluating industrywide effects of agricultural commodity programs. Do producer-funded generic promotion schemes enhance producer welfare? What indicators might be used to evaluate the impacts of promotion programs? If promotion programs succeed in increasing the price that consumers are willing to pay, will producers respond to these prices by increasing the quantity supplied, eliminating any return to advertising? What are the impacts on the industry?

From both the industry and public policy perspective, these questions are important. Industry leaders make decisions on the multiple uses of funds obtained through commodity check-off, as well as on the timing of industry initiatives. Reliance on certain indicators, such as those derived by looking only at demand effects within one industry, may mask other measures of impact such as market share. Furthermore, underlying cycles within the livestock industry suggest considering appropriate timing of promotion programs to enhance industry stability.

Because consumption changes are likely to be subtle, and evaluation of promotion programs may require several years of data from controlled market studies, simulations using model-based parameter estimates can provide a means to better understanding of responses to promotion in the livestock sector. This paper demonstrates the effect on producers of a successful commodity promotion program using a quarterly model of the U.S. livestock sector.

Among indicators of success are the impact on commodity price, net returns, and market share. By simulating effects over a number of years, it

The National Live Stock and Meat Board provided funding for this research. This paper reflects the views of the authors, however, and not those of the NLSMB.

is possible to distinguish immediate and long-term industrywide effects. This prospective type of analysis is important to industry leaders and public policymakers charged with weighing producer welfare and market effects. Impacts of other policies considered by the industry could be evaluated in a similar manner. The example used is drawn from promoting a single meat commodity: beef. Promoting beef affects beef demand directly. Although direct cross-commodity advertising effects may also exist, for purposes of this paper, they were assumed to be zero.

## Selected Studies of Promotion

The experience with promotion of agricultural commodities over the last several years provides a context for using the livestock models to analyze the potential impacts of a beef promotion campaign. Recent commodity promotion programs to be studied are: fluid milk, cheese, grapefruit, and frozen orange juice concentrate. Based on these evaluations, several factors are apparent (Table 19.1):

**Table 19.1 Summary of selected agricultural commodity promotion studies**

| Study | Commodity | Data | Ad effect | Carryover effects |
|-------|-----------|------|-----------|-------------------|
| Ward and Myers (1979) | frozen orange juice concentrate | quarterly (1967–75) | positive ad effect, increasing ad effect over time | approx. 3 quarters |
| Lee (1981) | grapefruit | quarterly (1971–78) | positive | 3 quarters |
| Kinnucan (1982) | fluid milk | monthly (1971–80) | positive (peak effect at 2–4 months) | 6 months |
| Ward and McDonald (1986) | fluid milk | monthly | positive (peak effect at 5–6 months) | 12 months |
| Blaylock, Smallwood, Myers (1987) | cheese | monthly (1982–86) | natural cheese—generic ad positive-branded, not significant | 1 month |
| | | | processed cheese—positive | over 2 years |

Table 19.1 (cont.)

| Study | Commodity | Data | Ad effect | Carryover effects |
|-------|-----------|------|-----------|-------------------|
| Ward and Dixon (1987) | fluid milk | monthly (1978–86) | ad effect not significant for first year of campaign; ad effect significant and positive for second year | 12 months |
| Liu and Forker (1988) | fluid milk | monthly (1971–84) | positive ad effect after 2 month lag | 6 months |

1. Advertising effects take time to appear, often due to a period of "buildup."
2. Advertising effects, in terms of increased purchase of the commodity, are relatively small.
3. There are both "carryover" effects and "decay" of advertising effects as consumers remember then forget the ad message. The decay period in several recent studies has been found to occur over two or three quarters.
4. Relatively little is known about the effect of supply adjustments on impacts of advertising. Few studies have considered supply response. (Lee 1981 and Liu and Forker 1988 are two exceptions.)

## Methods of Analysis

The impacts of a structured generic beef promotion program were evaluated using industry livestock models developed at the Center for Agricultural and Rural Development (CARD) at Iowa State University, and thus both changes in consumer and producer behavior are included. The types of demand changes introduced are typical of those found in other product studies. Two likely types of demand changes were used to illustrate the model's flexibility: a one-year advertising campaign and a sustained advertising shock.

The CARD livestock models incorporate the important structural parameters of the livestock sector and simultaneously determine the equilibrium levels of supply, demand, and price for the beef, pork, and poultry sectors. They are described in detail in Grundmeier et al. (1989). Quarterly time-series data are used to estimate the models. When operated together, the three sector models simultaneously interact through retail prices on the demand side as depicted in Figure 19.1.

On the demand side, prices are determined at the retail level because by assumption supply is fixed in the short term. The retail demand, derived in a demand systems context, explicitly accounts for both short-run and long-run changes in demand using an error-components model (Kesavan et al. 1988). The underlying assumption in formulating the demand component is that consumers do not instantaneously adjust to changes, but attributable in part to information or adjustment costs, they make adjustments over time.

Consumer behavior, consistent with economic behavior, is an embedded long-run structure that systematically accounts for the persistence or "stickiness" in short-term consumption decisions. However, consistent long-run consumer behavior implies certain restrictions on the short-run market outcomes. These effects are shown in the simulation of the structured advertising impacts. The demand price and expenditures elasticities are reported in Table 19.2.

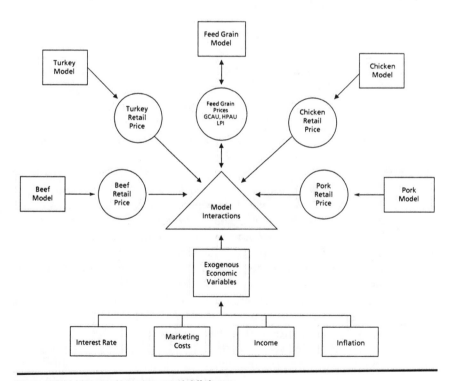

Figure 19.1. Livestock sector model linkages.

**Table 19.2** Estimated parameter for general dynamic demand model with homogeneity and symmetry imposed in long run and homogeneity imposed in short run (estimation period 1967–1986)

|            | Beef    | Pork    | Chicken  | Expenditure     | Lag adj. |
|------------|---------|---------|----------|-----------------|----------|
| **Beef**   |         |         |          |                 |          |
| Short run  | -0.52   | 0.23    | -0.14    | 0.43            | 0.33     |
|            | (0.08)  | (0.05)  | (0.05)   | (0.20)[a]       |          |
| Long run   | -0.80   | 0.30    | -0.028   | 1.06            |          |
|            | (0.07)  | (0.06)  | (0.02)   | (0.30)          |          |
| **Pork**   |         |         |          |                 |          |
| Short run  | 0.42    | -0.70   | -0.06    | 0.19            | 0.25     |
|            | (0.06)  | (0.05)  | (0.04)   | (0.17)          |          |
| Long run   | 0.62    | -0.60   | 0.13     | 0.68            |          |
|            |         | (0.07)  | (0.07)   | (0.23)          |          |
| **Chicken**|         |         |          |                 |          |
| Short run  | 0.06    | 0.19    | -0.63    | 0.0004          | 0.17     |
|            | (0.08)  | (0.06)  | (0.06)   | (0.23)          |          |
| Long run   | -0.17   | 0.34    | -1.05    | 1.24            |          |
|            |         |         | (0.06)   | (0.27)          |          |

SOURCE: Kesavan et al. 1988.
[a]The figures within parentheses indicate standard error.

## Simulations

The beef advertising simulations were conducted as intercept shifts in the price-dependent retail demand equation, and simulated from baseline convergent values from the three models: beef, pork, and poultry. Setting the livestock models at convergent values removes all extraneous factors that determine prices and supply levels. Thus, movements in feed prices, interest rates, inflation, and other exogenous variables are held constant and do not blur the impacts of the advertising campaign. Also, seasonal behavior in prices and supply variables does not enter into the solutions or the simulations.

When the livestock models are set at the 1984–86 mean levels of the exogenous variables and simulated sufficiently to allow initial conditions to work through the system, the endogenous variables of the models converge to constant levels. These "steady state" values of the endogenous variables are conditioned therefore on the levels of the exogenous variables. The constant levels of total beef supply, retail price, and the other endogenous variables form the baseline solution of the advertising simulations. Then, simulated advertising campaigns can be introduced and resulting impacts compared with the baseline solution.

In this study, the effects of two alternative simulated ad campaigns were delineated and evaluated in the short run and in the long run. The simulations were at the mean levels of the exogenous variables. In the first simulation, the campaign was assumed to begin in quarter 0, and last through the fourth quarter, or for one full year. In the second set of simulations, the campaign was assumed to begin in quarter 0, with sustained impact at the initial level. The models were simulated for 10 years after the beginning of the campaign to allow for complete long-run adjustments.

A qualification to be noted is that these effects are relative to the levels of the exogenous variables. Mean values for the 1984–86 period were used. The derived steady state values would change if the levels of the exogenous variables were different. Nonlinearities of the model imply different responses at different levels of the exogenous variables, and therefore the selection of steady state values is an important one.

The beef, pork, and poultry sectors interact through retail prices; this allows for the cross-commodity influence of the pork and chicken sectors on beef. In the analysis reported here, this response is only on the demand side, given the structure of the models. That is, the interactions among beef, pork, and chicken depend on cross-price demand elasticities in the meat demand system of the model, but not on interaction through feed costs. (The effect of including feed costs would be to slightly dampen supply responses in all sectors.)

In sum, the simulations were conducted using the following approach.

1. Simulations were made at the 1984–86 mean levels of the exogenous variables.
2. The models used were the livestock supply models and the demand system with beef, pork, and chicken.
3. Baseline simulations were made without beef advertising.
4. Simulations were then made with beef advertising effects.
5. Advertising demand shocks were made in the form of intercept shifts in the price-dependent beef demand equations.
6. Comparisons were made between baseline simulations and simulations with advertising. Variables of particular interest were the retail price of beef, the slaughter price of beef, beef supply, beef consumption, changes in competing meat products' prices and supply, market share, and net returns to cow/calf and feeder finisher producers.

## Demand Shocks

The two demand shocks were chosen somewhat arbitrarily in terms of the demand shift that would likely result from an advertising campaign. For the first it was assumed that in each of the four quarters of the first year of the simulation, the demand shift was worth about 7.0 cents per pound in the retail price. That is, in the first quarter, the advertising changed consumer behavior such that in the aggregate, consumers were willing to pay 7.0 cents per pound more for beef than before the advertising. The amount of the initial 7.0 cents per pound demand shift is 3 percent of the 1984–86 retail beef price level.

In the second period of advertising, the same impact was introduced, and in addition a 50 percent decay rate defined the carryover effect from the previous quarter of advertising. Similar demand impacts and carryovers were felt in the remaining two quarters of the advertising campaign. While the 7.0 cent impact was not based upon an empirical finding for beef advertising, the patterns of the assumed changes were similar to those observed for other commodities such as fluid milk and citrus fruit.

For the first illustration, the advertising campaign was assumed to conclude at the end of the first year. Demand shifts after this time were due only to the carryover effect of the ad campaign, as shown in Figure 19.2. Clearly, the decay rate is very important in determining the extent of carryover and the impact of the advertising. Lower decay rates would shift the demand curve further in subsequent periods during the advertising period and also help to maintain higher demand levels after the campaign has ended. The decay rate of 50 percent is similar to that found for fluid milk (Ward and McDonald 1986; Kinnucan 1985).

The second demand shock was based on the assumption that advertising effects a permanent change in demand. The shift was initially of the same magnitude as the first, converging to an aggregate 6 percent level in the demand shift, as shown in Figure 19.2. This was accomplished by the initial shift resulting in an increase of 3 percent in the first quarter, and continuing 3 percent shocks to the initial (base) levels. The decay rate assumed again was 50 percent. Other types of advertising impacts could be constructed with similar modifications.

## Illustration 1

The results of the simulations related to the first single-year advertising shock are presented in terms of percentage changes from the baseline in which no advertising was assumed. The supply effects and the demand

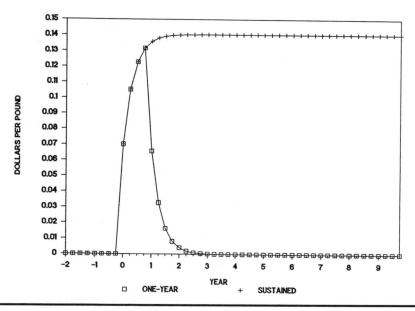

**Figure 19.2. Assumed advertising demand shocks.**

related cross-commodity influences were included in simulations. These model simulations provide insight into the dynamics of the beef demand and supply movements. The price increase from the advertising shock was transmitted to the farm-level in terms of an increase in slaughter steer price. The initial slaughter steer price increase caused producers to begin holding back heifers that would have been added to the breeding herd. Eventually, the breeding herd buildup resulted in increased slaughter, increased beef supplies, and lower prices. The cross-commodity effects were of two forms. On the demand side, initially the effects of advertising had little effect on consumption of pork and chicken. After the initial change in beef prices, consumers adjusted to higher relative beef prices brought about by the beef supply changes by substituting other meats, particularly pork, in their diets. The changes in demand for pork and chicken led to increases in pork and chicken retail prices, which in turn brought on changes in pork and chicken production and subsequent consumption.

Thus, the increased demand for beef changed the demand for pork and chicken because the initial beef retail price response was above the advertising effect. Pork and chicken producers reacted just as beef producers to a demand change and, as expected, increased their production capabilities. Since pork and chicken have shorter production cycles, their response to the demand shift was more rapid. The retail price increase for beef was affected by the relative shifts in pork and chicken demand and supply, and their subsequent feedback to the beef sector. The cross-commodity effects were constrained by the level of the responsiveness (cross-price elasticities) in the demand system.

Selected results are shown in Figures 19.3 to 19.6. The initial impacts of the advertising campaign on beef prices and production were to increase beef prices, and to slightly increase beef production during the first year (Figure 19.3 and 19.4). Beef producers can respond by increasing slaughter weights. The intermediate impacts of the demand shift demonstrate that cross-commodity effects are important determinants of price and production movements. The introduction of the pork and chicken sectors induced cyclical behavior in production and prices not found in other simulations, which isolated the beef industry by holding competing meat prices constant.

Similar movements in pork and chicken retail price exacerbated the initial price increase in beef (Figure 19.3). The shorter production cycles of pork and chicken, which in turn created shorter price cycles, had a dampening effect on the cyclical movements of beef prices and production. Strong cross-price effects with pork led to large cyclical swings in the pork industry as a result of the beef ad campaign. As supply responded in the livestock sector, beef retail prices moved downward. By the ninth quarter following the start of the one-year campaign, beef prices drop below the baseline and continue in that manner for nearly three years. Basically, increased supplies of beef and pork called forth by the higher beef prices contributed to the dampening of prices.

Another indicator of the effect of advertising is the market share of beef. Market shares of beef under the baseline and after the advertising campaign are plotted in Figure 19.5. Market shares generally followed beef supplies. That is, market shares were higher when supplies were higher and vice versa. As indicated, after the initial increase in supplies and market share in the advertising period, market shares declined, but then increased in later periods when supply had a chance to build. Market value for beef producers carried large percentage increases through the first two years following the introduction of the campaign. Market value was lower than starting levels for the next three years.

Effects of the advertising campaign for typical beef producers are illustrated in Figure 19.6, which depicts the movements of cow/calf producers' and feed lot operators' returns from the baseline in terms of dollars per head from an assumed zero baseline. Producer costs included the cost of the $1 per head check-off assessment. Since feed costs were held fixed at their 1984–86 means, the returns follow the movements in slaughter steer prices. Feeder finishers experienced large increases, then declines in their net returns. After almost six years, the campaign effects on net returns were dissipated.

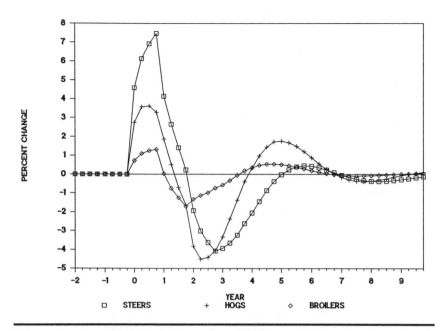

**Figure 19.3.** Farm-level price response for beef, pork, and chicken with the beef, pork, and chicken models (one year campaign).

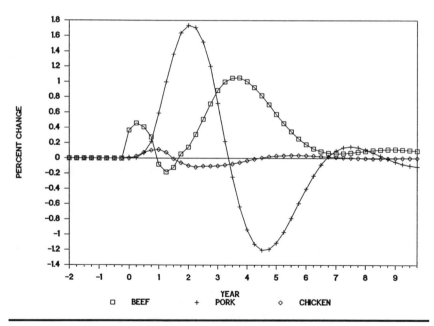

**Figure 19.4.** Livestock supply response for beef, pork, and chicken with the beef, pork, and chicken models (one year campaign).

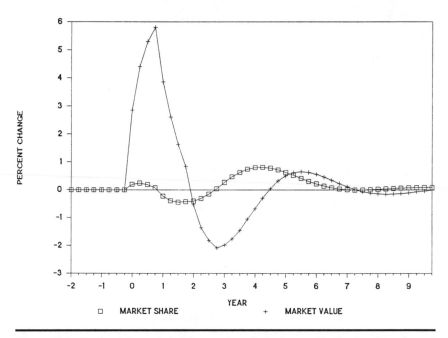

**Figure 19.5.** Beef retail market value and market share with the beef, pork, and chicken models (one year campaign).

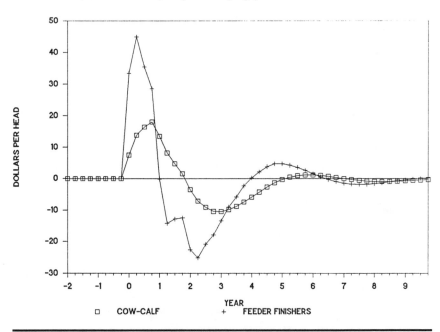

**Figure 19.6.** Cow/calf and feeder cattle returns with the beef, pork, and chicken models (one year campaign).

In summary, beef demand shocks were made in the total livestock model. Beef supplies were allowed to respond to higher beef prices. Likewise, the pork and chicken sectors were allowed to respond to higher beef prices. Results indicated the following:

1. The initial price response was enhanced as beef and competing meat producers expanded production.
2. Although initially beef prices reached a higher level, in effect, with decay, they fell due in part to cross-commodity effects. The downward pressure on beef, pork, and chicken prices was a result of expansions of the respective commodity production levels.
3. Increases in beef retail prices caused an expansion of pork and chicken production as consumers changed consumption of the other meats.
4. The initial beef price increase, while higher, did not result in a significantly greater level of beef production because prices fell sooner and faster with the cutoff of the advertising campaign. This reduced the length and rate of the expansion period.
5. The cross-price elasticities in the demand system were key factors in determining the response of pork and chicken to the demand shift in beef.
6. The one-year campaign caused the gross market value of beef to increase in the short run as price increases were higher than supply reductions. Gross value subsequently declined, then moved above the baseline, and equilibrated after seven years.
7. The market share of beef closely followed the supply of beef. After the first year, the beef campaign lowered market share slightly but, in the long run, market share was higher.
8. After the first year of the advertising campaign, net returns fell for cow/calf and feeder finishers. The initial level was not regained until after four years for the feeder finishers.

## Illustration 2

The sustained advertising shock represents the case of an advertising program that was able to bring about a "permanent" shift in demand. The results, again, are presented in terms of percentage change from the baseline in which no advertising was assumed. The results are shown in Figures 19.7 through 19.10. In the case of a sustained advertising shock, the overall retail price increase is higher, over 6 percent. The retail price increase continues after the first year, rising to a total impact of 6.75 percent, due to supply adjustments and declines thereafter. Slaughter steer prices rise almost 9 percent, before falling during the second year (Figure 19.7). At the end of ten years, beef prices are higher than the baseline, but not by the full 3 percent. Beef and pork supplies increase, and dampen the impact of the price increase (Figure 19.8).

The impacts of a successful beef promotion program differ for beef, pork, and broiler producers as shown in Figures 19.7 and 19.8. The price of all three rise initially, although hog and broiler prices fall after two years. Beef production increases initially with heavier weights and continues to increase throughout the period in response to higher beef prices (Figure 19.8). Likewise, pork production, stimulated through the demand response to higher beef prices, is positive throughout a ten-year period. That is, rising beef prices lead to higher pork production. After the second year, the market adjusts, beef prices fall, and pork producers respond with a lower rate of increased production. The story is different for chicken producers. Although there is some initial response to the higher beef prices, the overall impact in production in the poultry industry is very small. This is due primarily to the very small cross-price effects between beef and chicken.

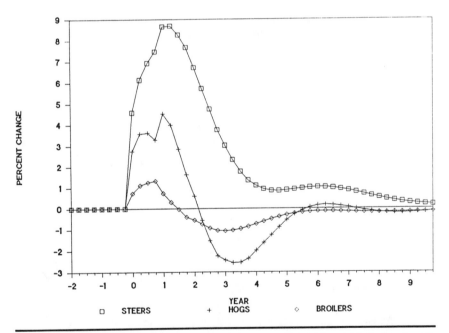

Figure 19.7. Farm-level price response for beef, pork, and chicken with the beef, pork, and chicken models (sustained demand shift).

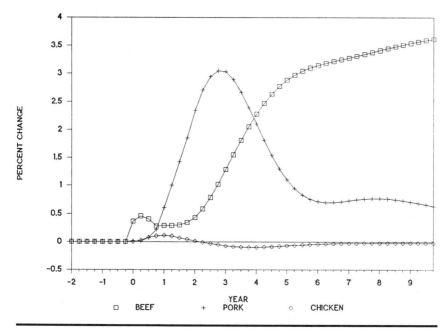

**Figure 19.8.  Livestock supply response for beef, pork, and chicken with the beef, pork, and chicken models (sustained demand shift).**

The market value of beef increases markedly during the first six quarters, then falls to a level of over 4 percent throughout the remaining period (Figure 19.9). The beef market share rises slightly then falls below the baseline before increasing to just less than 2 percent. The effect of consumers substituting pork and chicken for the now higher priced beef dampens the switch to beef. However, in the long run, the sustained promotion impact increases beef's market share and market value.

For producers, the sustained successful advertising program brings about continued increase in prices to cow/calf operators, as well as feeder finishers, through the first three years (Figure 19.10). The feeder finisher returns are higher initially during the first two periods but fall and, as with the cow/calf returns, approach the baseline values after five years. Alternative specifications that include feed cost adjustments dampen the increase in returns to the producers, but do not alter the overall pattern of responses. Thus, even with a permanent shift in demand for beef, supply and cross-price adjustments dampen changes in net returns to producers in the long run. Results indicated the following:

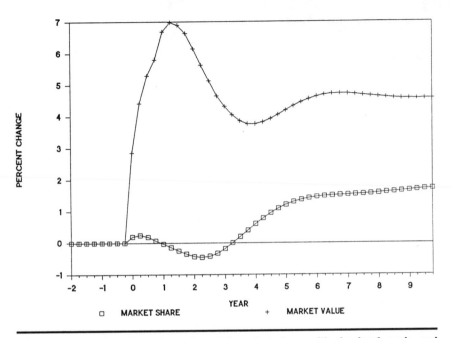

Figure 19.9  Beef retail market value and market share with the beef, pork, and chicken models (sustained demand shift).

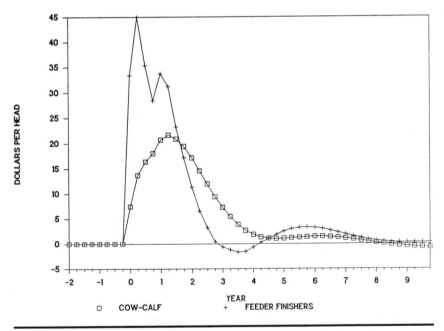

Figure 19.10.  Cow/calf and feeder cattle returns with the beef, pork, and chicken models (sustained demand shift).

1.  The short- and long-run effects of a generic beef campaign depend to a large extent on decay rates, and the sustainability of a campaign.
2.  An advertising campaign may cause a drop in beef supply as well as beef consumption as producers build herd size.
3.  The increase in beef prices attributable to advertising eventually results in larger beef supplies.
4.  Larger beef supplies in later periods cause lower beef prices in those later periods.
5.  Pork and broiler sectors respond to beef prices, although the broiler change in response is relatively small.
6.  The effectiveness of advertising campaigns cannot be judged on the basis of short-run indicators alone.
7.  The initial impact of the campaign is to decrease market share slightly. As supplies increase, however, so does market share. Market value increases and is maintained at a new higher level by the effective promotion.

## Summary and Implications

The estimated livestock models, simulated with advertising impacts suggested by results from other product promotion studies, illustrate the magnitude of induced industry changes.

1.  Increased demand due to advertising had different effects on beef prices depending on the decay rate of the advertising effect.
2.  Beef consumption fell in the short run due to reductions in cow slaughter and additions to the breeding herd, reducing near term supply.
3.  The increased price due to advertising resulted in longer term increases in beef supplies as producers responded to implied profit incentives.
4.  The beef promotion affected pork and poultry prices indirectly. Effects on the pork industry are stronger than for poultry.
5.  The responses of pork and chicken producers increased short-term price effects but resulted in a period of lower farm prices for all three producers.

There are several implications of these results for the design of promotion programs for the beef industry, or any other livestock industry. Very careful analysis is required to identify advertising impacts and these impacts should be assessed in the context of full models of the livestock industry.

1. Promotion campaigns should not be designed based on short-run goals alone. The short-run impacts can be deceiving relative to implications of advertising for broad indicators of industry performance.
2. Due to production cycles and impacts of external factors on the livestock industry, the timing of beef advertising campaigns may be an important consideration.
3. Implementing advertising campaigns during periods of large beef supply may be more advantageous than during periods of herd buildup.
4. Evaluation of promotion impacts should concentrate on market share, size of the industry, and stability rather than profit per head. Increased profitability on a per-head basis can be influenced by promotion only in the short run.
5. Results from controlled experimental studies are needed to add to the information available from industry or market models in evaluating advertising campaigns.

# 20 An Economic Analysis of the New York State Generic Fluid Milk Advertising Program Using an Optimal Control Model

DONALD J. LIU, JON M. CONRAD,
and OLAN D. FORKER

Generic dairy promotion is big business. The 1983 Dairy and Tobacco Adjustment Act requires that all dairy farmers pay a promotion assessment of 15 cents per hundredweight on all milk sold commercially. Of the total assessment, up to 10 cents may be retained locally to fund regional or state dairy product advertising. The funding for national and state programs combined totals over $200 million annually. Thus, the program involves high stakes and, if not well conducted, can result in substantial losses to dairy farmers. The size of the potential losses emphasizes the importance of understanding the economics of dairy promotion and the need to increase the efficiency of promotional effort.

The continuing effects of advertising on sales after the original period of expenditure is a well-recognized phenomenon, aptly summarized by Waugh's statement that "old advertisements never die — they just fade away." Advertising's lingering impact has led analysts to seek a dynamic setting in which to explore promotion issues. Thus far, most of the attention has been focused on quantifying the sales-advertising relationship within the context of distributed-lag econometric models (e.g., Liu and Forker 1988a). Using such models, an ex-post evaluation of the costs and benefits of a promotion program is made by comparing actual sales during a given period with a sales level simulated under the assumption of no advertising.

Another important application of the sales-advertising models is the simulation of sales under various levels of advertising expenditures with the goal of identifying the optimal spending policy for the promotion agency. A drawback of this approach, however, is that the truly optimal solution may be missed since it is impractical to exhaust all possible policy scenarios in the simulation; a situation that is especially true when there exists an

---

A version of this paper originally appeared as D. J. Liu and O. D. Forker, "Optimal Control of Generic Fluid Milk Advertising Expenditures," *American Journal of Agricultural Economics,* 72 (November 1990):1047–1055.

optimal seasonal allocation pattern. Additional complications are introduced if the interest is in long-term policy, in which case a time path for advertising must also be selected. In light of these drawbacks, the identification of a more comprehensive optimization framework for the study of optimal dairy promotion policy remains an important gap in the existing literature.

The purpose of this study is to identify the optimal advertising expenditures for the New York State fluid milk promotion program. New York State is the third largest milk producing state and the size of its consuming population is second only to California. Currently, New York dairy farmers invest $15 million annually in dairy promotion efforts. The optimization problem is cast in a deterministic optimal control framework with the goal of choosing the optimal advertising spending level for major cities in the state. Though the analysis focuses on markets at the state level, the model can be extended to determine the optimal level for national advertising expenditures across states or regions. In this paper, both analytical insights into the solution structure and empirical results pertaining to New York State are presented.

## A Conceptual Framework

Within the past thirty years several authors have examined advertising expenditure as a problem of optimal control. Nerlove and Arrow's capital theoretic approach treats advertising as investment in the firm's goodwill, which in turn affects current and future sales. In Vidale and Wolfe's sales response model, advertising is viewed as a means to acquire the uncaptured portion of a market's potential. Gould's diffusion approach to advertising explicitly admits the interaction between the uncaptured and the captured portions of the market either through inanimate media advertising or through word of mouth. (For a more detailed review on optimal advertising control models, see Liu and Forker 1988b). Each of the various theoretical models has yielded useful analytical insights into the structure of optimal advertising policy and has provided a framework for empirical studies by other researchers. For example, Rausser and Hochman used an adapted version of Vidale and Wolfe's sales response model to study the optimal orange juice advertising policy for the Florida Department of Citrus.

However, the above models were monopolistic in the sense that, in addition to being able to affect demand through advertising, the firm in question is assumed to have control over the price or quantity of the good supplied. Obviously, this is not the case for generic dairy promotion. In order to reflect more accurately the market structure of the dairy sector, the model developed in this paper includes an endogenously determined farm milk price, and the subsequent supply response arising from an advertising-induced change in farm price.

Our analysis is simplified by the assumption that the federal order minimum prices always apply. In the New York market, dairy farmers receive a blend price based on the federal order class prices and the utilization percentages. As a result, the farm milk price is a function of fluid sales and the farm milk supply, given the exogenous Class 1 differential and Class 2 price. The fluid advertising model to be constructed includes the evolution of retail fluid sales for major cities in the state, the evolution of farm milk supply for the entire state, and an equation for the average farm milk price. The objective of the promotion agency is to maximize the discounted net revenue stream from farm milk sales with the control variable being the level of fluid advertising expenditures in each city.

### RETAIL FLUID SALES EQUATION

The demand for fluid milk is specified as a function of advertising and other factors such as prices and income. Denote time $t$ fluid milk sales in market $i$ ($i = 1, 2, \ldots, I$) as $A_{i,t}$ and advertising expenditures as $U_{i,t}$. Since consumers need to hear, absorb, and act on the advertising message, it is assumed that there is a one-period time lag between the exposure of message and the action of purchasing. Further, since consumers will gradually forget the advertising messages, sales are assumed to decay over time if there is no continuing effort on advertising. The evolution of fluid milk sales can be specified as:

$$A_{i,t+1} - A_{i,t} = \Phi_i(U_{i,t}, A_{i,t}) + Z_{i,t+1} \tag{20.1}$$

where $\Phi_i(U_{i,t}, .)$ captures the positive impact of time $t$ expenditures on $t+1$ fluid sales, $\Phi_i(., A_{i,t})$ accounts for the negative impact of sales decay, and $Z_{i,t+1}$ incorporates the contemporaneous effect of all other variables on $A_{i,t+1}$.

Denote $\partial \Phi_i / \partial U_{i,t}$ as $\Phi_{U_i}$ and $\partial \Phi_i / \partial A_{i,t}$ as $\Phi_{A_i}$. Also, denote the sum of advertising expenditures across all markets as $U_t$ and the sum of fluid sales as $A_t$:

$$\Sigma_i U_{i,t} = U_t \tag{20.2}$$

$$\Sigma_i A_{i,t} = A_t \tag{20.3}$$

## FARM MILK SUPPLY EQUATION

The supply of raw milk is specified as a function of the expected farm milk price and other factors such as production capacity and variable production costs. For simplicity, it is assumed that farmers have naive price expectations, so the expected next period price equals the current price. Thus, the time $t+1$ supply of milk $(S_{t+1})$ is in part a function of the farm milk price from the previous period $(p_t^f)$. The evolution of farm milk supply can be specified as:

$$S_{t+1} - S_t = f(p_t^f, S_t) + W_t \tag{20.4}$$

where $f(p_t^f, \cdot)$ captures the part of $S_{t+1}$ contributed by $p_t^f$, and $f(\cdot, S_t)$ accounts for the negative impact of depreciation in the farm production capacity. Finally, $W_t$ incorporates the lag impact on $S_{t+1}$ of other variables such as variable production costs at period $t$.

The farm milk price $p_t^f$ is endogenous. Under the rules of the federal milk marketing order program, processors buy raw milk from dairy farmers paying a base price called Class 2 price $(P_t)$ for all the milk sold plus a premium called Class 1 differential $(\delta_t)$ for milk sold in the fluid market. As such, the average farm milk price is:

$$p_t^f = \delta_t (A_t/S_t) + P_t \tag{20.5}$$

where $\partial p_t^f/\partial A_t > 0$ and $\partial p_t^f/\partial S_t < 0$. Given (20.5), the supply transition in (20.4) can be written as:

$$S_{t+1} - S_t = \Psi(A_t, S_t \mid \delta_t, P_t) + W_t \tag{20.6}$$

where $\Psi(A_t, S_t)$ is conditional on the exogenous variables $\delta_t$ and $P_t$. Denote $\partial\Psi/\partial A_{i,t}$ as $\Psi_A$ (since $A_t$ is linear in $A_{i,t}$) and $\partial\Psi/\partial S_t$ as $\Psi_S$. Notice that $\Psi_A$ measures the positive impact of a change in current sales on the subsequent farm milk supply $[(\partial f/\partial p_t^f)*(\partial p_t^f/\partial A_t)]$. Similarly, $\Psi_S$ measures the negative impact of a change in current supply on the subsequent supply, including the price effect of $(\partial f/\partial p_t^f)*(\partial p_t^f/\partial S_t)$ and the depreciation effect of $\partial f/\partial S_t$.

## INEQUALITY CONSTRAINTS

In order for the solution to make sense, some restrictions are needed. The sum of the fluid sales across all markets cannot be greater than the supply of milk:

$$A_t \leq S_t \tag{20.7}$$

Also, the sum of advertising expenditures across all markets can be no greater than the available budget which, under the current dairy promotion program, equals a fixed assessment rate ($\tau$) times the quantity of milk sold (since carryover of funds has not been significant in practice, it is assumed that if the budget constraint is not binding at the optimal solution, the remaining money will go to manufactured dairy product advertising):

$$U_t \leq \tau S_t \tag{20.8}$$

Finally, the following non-negativity constraints are imposed:

$$A_{i,t} \geq 0 \tag{20.9}$$

$$U_{i,t} \geq 0 \tag{20.10}$$

$$S_t \geq 0 \tag{20.11}$$

## THE OBJECTIVE FUNCTION

For given initial state conditions $A_{i,0}$ and $S_0$, the agency's problem is to choose the time path for the control $\{U_{i,t}; t = 0, 1, \ldots, T - 1\}$ so as to drive the states $\{A_{i,t}; t = 1, 2, \ldots, T\}$ and $\{S_t; t = 1, 2, \ldots, T\}$ over time in an optimal path that maximizes the discounted revenue stream from farm milk sales, net of advertising cost:[1]

$$Z = \Sigma_{t=0}^{T-1} \, \rho t \{p_t^f S_t - U_t\} + \rho^T V(A_T, S_T)$$

where $\rho = (1 + r)^{-1}$ and $r$ is the interest rate; and $V(A_T, S_T)$ is a salvage term including terminal cash flow and terminal value of the states $A_{i,T}$ and $S_T$. Using (20.5), the above objective can be expressed as a function of the exogenous class prices ($\delta_t$) and ($P_t$):

$$Z = \Sigma_{t=0}^{T-1} \, \rho^t \{\delta_t A_t + P_t S_t - U_t\} + \rho^T V(A_T, S_T) \tag{20.12}$$

## Solution Insight

The framework presented in the previous section can be characterized as a dynamic nonlinear-nonautonomous optimization problem with multiple state variables. The nonlinearity is due to $\Phi_i$ and $\Psi$ while the nonautonomy arises from the time varying nature of $(\delta_t)$, $(P_t)$, $(Z_{i,t+1})$, and $(W_t)$. As such, a complete analytical solution for the problem is not readily available, leaving the alternative of numerical analysis. Before carrying out the empirical analyses, however, insight into the solution can be gained by examining the set of necessary conditions for optimality and deriving the steady state solution.

To simplify the exposition, we assume an interior solution and, hence, ignore the inequality constraints in (20.7) to (20.8). We also suppress the exogenous variables $Z_{i,t+1}$ and $W_t$ in state equations (20.1) and (20.6). Then, the problem is to maximize the objective in (20.12) by choosing $(U_{i,t})$, $(A_{i,t})$, and $(S_t)$, subject to the modified version of (20.1) and (20.6). The Lagrangian is:

$$
\begin{aligned}
L = \Sigma_{t=0}^{T-1}\, \rho^t \{ &\delta_t A_t + P_t S_t - U_t + \rho\, \Sigma_i\, \lambda_{i,t+1}\, [\Phi_i(U_{i,t}, A_{i,t}) \\
&+ A_{i,t} - A_{i,t+1}] + \rho\, \mu_{t+1}\, [\Psi(A_t, S_t) + S_t - S_{t+1}] \} \\
&+ \rho^T V(A_T, S_T)
\end{aligned}
$$

where $\lambda_i$ and $\mu$ are the current-value adjoint variables for the state variables $A_i$ and $S$, respectively, and they can be interpreted as the shadow prices of their corresponding states. The necessary conditions include (Kamien and Schwartz 1981):

$$
\rho\, \lambda_{i,t+1}\, \Phi_{U_i} = 1 \tag{20.13}
$$

$$
\rho\, \lambda_{i,t+1} - \lambda_{i,t} = -\delta_t - \rho\, \mu_{t+1}\, \Psi_A + \rho\, \lambda_{i,t+1}\, \Phi_{A_i} \tag{20.14}
$$

$$
\rho\, \mu_{t+1} - \mu_t = -P_t - \rho\, \mu_{t+1}\, \Psi_S \tag{20.15}
$$

$$
\lambda_{i,T} = \partial V / \partial A_{i,T} \tag{20.16}
$$

$$
\mu_T = \partial V / \partial S_T \tag{20.17}
$$

$$
A_{i,t+1} - A_{i,t} = \Phi_i(U_{i,t}, A_{i,t}) \tag{20.18}
$$

$$
S_{t+1} - S_t = \Psi(A_t, S_t) \tag{20.19}
$$

The optimality condition (20.13) reflects that the last dollar spent in advertising must equal the shadow value of the additional fluid sales. The adjoint equations (20.14) and (20.15) dictate the change in the shadow value of the state variables over time while the transversality conditions (20.16) and (20.17) specify their terminal values. Finally, conditions (20.18) and (20.19) reflect the need for the optimal solution to observe the physical motion of the state variables.

To gain insight into the steady state, let $(\delta_t)$ and $(P_t)$ take their respective long-term constants $\delta$ and $P$ and let the time horizon $T$ be infinity. By definition, in the steady state $U_{i,t+1} = U_{i,t}$, $A_{i,t+1} = A_{i,t}$, $S_{t+1} = S_t$, $\lambda_{i,t+1} = \lambda_{i,t}$, and $\mu_{t+1} = \mu_t$. Denote the above values in the steady state as $U_i$, $A_i$, $S$, $\lambda_i$, and $\mu$, respectively. Now, with the assumption that the terminal value function $V(\cdot)$ is finite, the terminal term in the Lagrangian vanishes as $T$ goes to infinity and, hence, the transversality conditions become $\lim_{t \to \infty} \lambda_{i,t} A_{i,t} = 0$ and $\lim_{t \to \infty} \mu_t S_t = 0$. Replacing variables with their steady-state values and making use of $\rho = (1 + r)^{-1}$, other necessary conditions require:

$$\rho \lambda_i = 1/\Phi_{U_i} \tag{20.20}$$

$$\rho \lambda_i \left( r + \Phi_{A_i} \right) = \delta + \rho \, \mu \, \Psi_A \tag{20.21}$$

$$\rho \mu \left( r - \Psi_S \right) = P \tag{20.22}$$

$$\Phi_i(U_i, A_i) = 0 \tag{20.23}$$

$$\Psi(A, S) = 0 \tag{20.24}$$

Substituting (20.20) and (20.22) into (20.21), one has:

$$r + \Phi_{A_i} = \Phi_{U_i} \left\{ \delta + \frac{P \, \psi_A}{r - \psi_S} \right\}$$

The interpretation for (20.25) is that the optimal steady state expenditure level is such that the marginal opportunity costs of advertising equal the marginal benefits of advertising. The marginal opportunity costs of advertising include time costs $(r)$ and the depreciation costs in the fluid sector $(\Phi_{A_i})$. The marginal benefits of advertising include the Class 1

premium from the additional fluid sales ($\delta \Phi_{U_i}$) and the base revenue from
the subsequent additional raw milk supply ($P\Psi_A \Phi_{U_i}$). However, the benefit
from additional farm supply is discounted by the opportunity costs of that
additional farm supply which includes time costs ($r$), and the cost of farm
capacity depreciation, as well as that of farm price change ($-\Psi_S$).

## The Econometric Model

The econometric model consists of retail fluid sales equations for three
major cities in New York State and a farm milk supply equation for the
entire state. The markets included in the analysis are New York City,
Syracuse, and Albany.

Other major cities in the state such as Binghamton, Buffalo, and
Rochester are not included. Fluid sales data for Binghamton are not
available, while Buffalo and Rochester had independent programs and are
not part of the New York–New Jersey federal marketing order region
covering most of New York State.

The estimation is based on monthly data from January 1983 to
September 1987. The sales data are derived from fluid plant surveys, while
advertising data are based on audits of the invoices of the New York State
promotion unit. Other data are from public sources. A detailed listing of the
data and their sources can be found in Liu and Forker (1989).

### RETAIL FLUID SALES EQUATIONS

In accordance with (20.1), the dependent variable for the retail fluid
sales equation is the change in sales ($A_{t+1,i} - A_{t,i}$). To account for the sales
impact of changes in population, $A$ is measured on a per capita basis. The
independent variables are lag fluid advertising expenditures deflated by the
consumer price index for all items ($U_t/\text{CPI}_t$), lag fluid sales ($A_t$), and other
factors which include the price ratio between retail fluid milk price and food
and beverage price index ($\text{PR}_{t+1}$), average per capita weekly earnings of
production workers deflated by the consumer price index ($\text{DINC}_{t+1}$), and a
set of harmonic variables (SIN and COS). In the case of New York City, a
time trend (TIME) is also included.

The advertising variable includes the prorated national fluid expenditures to account for the promotion effort of National Dairy Board which
started its program in September 1984. The lag dependent variable measures
the sales decay over time. The price for food and beverage is used as a proxy

for prices of fluid milk substitutes. Average weekly earnings serve as a proxy for income. Since the dependent variable exhibits a regular seasonal pattern from year to year, the harmonic variables are used to account for the seasonality. The variables COS1 to COS6 in Table 20.1 are the first to the sixth wave of the cosine term while SIN1 to SIN5 are the first to the fifth wave of the sine term. The selection of harmonics involves initially specifying all the eleven harmonics in the equation. Then, based on significance tests, "superfluous" harmonics are eliminated. Since each harmonic is orthogonal to other variables in the equations, statistical efficiency is unaffected by the elimination of the superfluous harmonics (Doran and Quilkey 1972). Finally, the trend variable for the New York City equation captures the sales impact of the gradual change in the ethnic composition of population over time; it is generally observed that nonwhites tend to consume less milk and the nonwhite population is growing faster than the white population in that city (see e.g., Kinnucan 1986).

**Table 20.1 Estimation results[a]**

New York City retail fluid sales:

$$\ln A_{+1} - \ln A = 0.0254 \ln (U/CPI)_{+1} - 0.8219 \ln A - 0.1806 \ln PR_{+1}$$
$$\quad (2.9) \qquad\qquad (-4.6) \qquad\quad (-1.5)$$
$$+ 0.3603 \ln DINC_{+1} + 0.0223 \; COS1_{+1} - 0.0088 \; COS6_{+1}$$
$$\quad (2.1) \qquad\qquad (2.7) \qquad\qquad (-1.9)$$
$$+ 0.0095 \; SIN3_{+1} + 0.0308 \; SIN5_{+1} - 0.0280 \ln TIME_{+1}$$
$$\quad (1.5) \qquad\qquad (3.9) \qquad\qquad (-2.8)$$
$$+ 0.2777 \; MA(1)$$
$$\quad (1.2)$$

Adjusted $R$-squared:  0.72   Durbin-$h$: 0.05

Syracuse retail fluid sales:

$$\ln A_{+1} - \ln A = 0.0362 \ln (U/CPI) - 0.7137 \ln A - 0.0055 \ln PR_{+1}$$
$$\quad (2.3) \qquad\qquad (-5.5) \qquad\quad (-0.1)$$
$$+ 0.3656 \ln DINC_{+1} + 0.0097 \; COS1_{+1} - 0.0156 \; COS6_{+1}$$
$$\quad (3.2) \qquad\qquad (1.1) \qquad\qquad (-2.2)$$
$$+ 0.0139 \; SIN3_{+1} + 0.0329 \; SIN5_{+1}$$
$$\quad (1.4) \qquad\qquad (3.3)$$

Adjusted $R$-squared:   0.51   Durbin-$h$: 1.15

Albany retail fluid sales:

$$\ln A_{+1} - \ln A = 0.0140 \ln (U/CPI) - 0.5214 \ln A - 0.1060 \ln PR_{+1}$$
$$\quad (0.9) \qquad\qquad (-4.5) \qquad\quad (-0.5)$$
$$+ 0.1942 \ln DINC_{+1} + 0.0243 \; COS1_{+1} - 0.0176 \; COS6_{+1}$$
$$\quad (1.1) \qquad\qquad (1.9) \qquad\qquad (-2.1)$$
$$- 0.0239 \; SIN3_{+1} + 0.0317 \; SIN5_{+1}$$
$$\quad (-1.9) \qquad\qquad (2.6)$$

Adjusted $R$-squared:   0.45   Durbin-$h$: 0.15

**Table 20.1 (cont.)**

New York State farm milk supply:

$$\ln S_{+1} - \ln S = 0.0994 \ln(p^f/\text{FCI}) - 0.0616 \ln S - 0.1491 \ln \text{DPCOW}$$
$$\phantom{\ln S_{+1} - \ln S =}(3.0) \phantom{0.0994 \ln(p^f/\text{FCI})} (-5.8) \phantom{0.0616} (-5.4)$$
$$- 0.0097 \text{ MDP} - 0.0205 \text{ DTP} - 0.0198 \text{ COS2}$$
$$(-1.6) \phantom{0.0097 \text{ MD}} (-3.0) \phantom{0.0205 \text{ DT}} (-5.7)$$
$$+ 0.0136 \text{ COS6} + 0.0351 \text{ SIN1} - 0.0063 \text{ SIN2}$$
$$(5.5) \phantom{0.0136 \text{ COS}} (8.9) \phantom{0.0351 \text{ SI}} (-1.8)$$
$$- 0.0211 \text{ SIN3} - 0.0280 \text{ SIN4} - 0.0538 \text{ SIN5}$$
$$(-6.1) \phantom{0.0211 \text{ SI}} (-8.2) \phantom{0.0280 \text{ SI}} (-15.5)$$

Adjusted $R$-squared:   0.91   Durbin-$h$: 1.28

[a]Figures in parentheses are the $t$-ratios of the coefficients.

The equations are specified in double logarithmic form and estimated individually. The estimation results are in Table 20.1. For the New York City equation, the advertising variable is lagged two months. The two-month lag specification yields the most significant advertising coefficient and the result is consistent with that found in Liu and Forker (1988a). Based on the estimated autocorrelation function and partial autocorrelation function of the residuals, a first order moving average $(MA[1])$ error structure is included to correct for serial correlation. (The imposition of the moving average error term is consistent with the transfer function specification in Liu and Forker 1988a.) All the coefficients remain stable after imposing the moving average term.

For the Syracuse equation, the price ratio variable is not significant and the adjusted $R^2$ is not as high as it was for the New York City equation. However, other variables are significant and the Durbin-$h$ statistic does not indicate the existence of the serial correlation. On the other hand, the Albany equation appears less satisfactory. The insignificant variables include advertising, price, and income.[2] Given the limited availability of individual city data on a monthly basis, however, an alternative specification does not seem feasible at this time.

Over all, the coefficients for advertising and lagged dependent variable are fairly robust among alternative choices of the included variables; the major differences occur in the estimated parameters for such exogenous variables as price and income. This is a desirable result given the advertising focus of the study. Monthly slope dummy variables are included in the preliminary analysis to ascertain whether there exist seasonal variations in the advertising coefficient (Kinnucan and Forker 1986). However, most of the slope dummies are found to be insignificant. The inclusion of the slope dummies also makes the price and income coefficients become less significant. Furthermore, a structural dummy variable is included to test whether there is an upward shift in the advertising coefficient since the inception of the national dairy promotion program (Ward and Dixon 1989). However, due to the fact that most of the sample periods coincide with the history of the national program, the resulting coefficient is insignificant. The exclusion of the structural dummy does not change other coefficients significantly.

Finally, the semi-logarithmic sales equations are also estimated. The statistical qualities such as the goodness of fit, the significance of variables, and the extent of serial correlation resemble those found in the double-logarithmic specification. Additionally, the magnitudes of the advertising elasticities are similar. For example, the short-run and long-run advertising elasticities for New York City are 0.024 and 0.029, respectively (versus 0.025 and 0.031 under the double-logarithmic specification). However, with semi-logarithmic specification, the magnitude of the coefficients for advertising and lagged dependent variable appear to be quite sensitive to alternative choices of the included variables. Preliminary analyses also indicate that the semi-logarithmic model tends to suffer numerical problems in the optimization run.

## FARM MILK SUPPLY EQUATION

In accordance with (20.4), the dependent variable in the farm milk supply equation is the change in supply $(S_{t+1} - S_t)$. The independent variables are lagged farm milk price $(p_t^f)$ over lagged feed cost index (FCI$_t$); lagged supply $(S_t)$; and other factors which include lagged slaughter cow price deflated by the index of price paid by dairy farmers (DPCOW$_t$); two dummy variable (MDP and DTP) which equal 1 for January 1984 through June 1985 and for April 1986 through September 1987, respectively; and a set of harmonic variables.

The feed cost index captures the effect of variable production cost while the lagged dependent variable measures the farm capacity depreciation over time. The slaughter cow price accounts for the opportunity cost of keeping the dairy cow on farm. The two dummy variables capture the supply effect of the 1984–85 Milk Diversion Program and 1986–87 Dairy Termination Program, respectively. The harmonic variables capture the seasonal pattern of farm milk supply. The estimation results are in Table 20.1.

## The Optimization

The estimated retail sales equations can be transformed readily into the form specified in (20.1) by allowing for the conversion of per capita quantity into market-wide quantity and collapsing all the terms as $Z_{i,t+1}$, except advertising expenditures $(U)$ and lag sales $(A)$. Similarly, the estimated supply equation can be transformed into that specified in (20.4) by collapsing all the terms as $W_t$, except farm milk price $(p_t^f)$ and lag supply $(S)$.

The remaining problem is to maximize the objective function in (20.12) subject to the state equations (20.1) and (20.4), the farm price formula (20.5), and the inequality constraints from (20.7) to (20.11). Since the state promotion unit retains two-thirds of the total dairy promotion funds, the assessment rate $\tau$ in (20.8) is specified as 10 cents per hundredweight of milk sold. The interest rate is specified as 7 percent per annum which is the average rate of the three-month Treasury Bills during the time period considered in this study. The terminal value function $V(\cdot)$ in (20.12) includes cash flow in the last period ($\delta_T A_T + P_T S_T$), and the values of the state variable $A_{i,T}$ and $S_T$ which are computed as the future income stream from those two states, discounted by the interest rate ($\rho$) and their respective decay (depreciation) rate. To make the computation of the future income stream possible, $\delta_T$ and $P_T$ are assumed to prevail indefinitely into the future. The optimization problem is solved for the period from January 1984 to September 1987, with the prorated national fluid advertising expenditures taken as given.[3]

Table 20.2 presents the average monthly observed values of the three endogenous variables (advertising, retail sales, and farm milk supply), as well as the average ratios of the optimal to the observed values. Upon taking into account the prorated national fluid expenditures, the levels expended by the New York State promotional unit are 8 percent and 11 percent too high in New York City and Albany, respectively. On the other hand, the optimal spending level for Syracuse is about three times that of the observed one. Due to the relatively large expenditure level in the New York City market, it is interesting to note that the 8 percent reduction in the observed spending of that market is about enough to cover the needed three-fold increase in the Syracuse market. Thus, the result suggests only a reallocation of the existing level of the total expenditures across the three markets.[4]

Given the average monthly values and the optimal/observed ratios for the fluid sales reported in the Table 20.1, it can be shown that the total sales could have been slightly increased if the advertising spending had been optimal. With the reallocation, the average monthly sales for Syracuse would have increased by 887.8 thousand pounds (i.e., 4.6 percent) which is more than enough to outweigh the corresponding combined sales decrease in New York City of 594.6 thousand pounds (0.3 percent) and Albany of 71.2 thousand pounds (0.4 percent). Finally, the result indicates that farm milk supply response due to a higher profit from the reallocation of advertising expenditures is at most minimal with the average monthly output increase at about 42.1 thousand pounds (0.007 percent).

Another observation that can be drawn from the optimal solution is the seasonal pattern of the advertising spending level. To demonstrate this, Figure 20.1 shows the percentage of the average monthly optimal expendi-

**Table 20.2  Average monthly observed values and the ratio of optimal to observed values of the endogenous variables**

|  | New York City | Syracuse | Albany | New York State |
|---|---|---|---|---|
| Advertising expenditures[a] | | | | |
| observed level | 270.4 | 12.5 | 17.6[b] | |
| optimal/observed | 0.92 | 3.27 | 0.89 | |
| Retail fluid sales | | | | |
| observed level | 198.2 | 19.3 | 17.8[c] | |
| optimal/observed | 0.997 | 1.046 | 0.996 | |
| Farm milk supply | | | | |
| observed level | | | | 601.0[c] |
| optimal/observed | | | | 1.00007 |

[a]Net of expenditures of the national program.
[b]Advertising expenditures are measured in thousand dollars.
[c]Quantities are measured in million pounds.

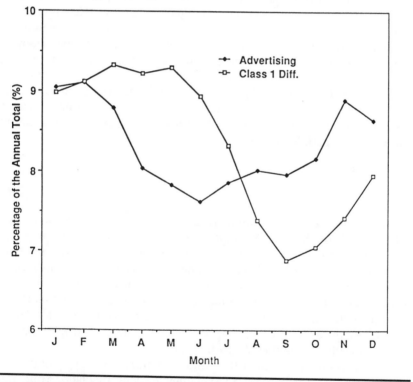

Figure 20.1.  Optimal seasonal advertising pattern and the class 1 differential, 1984–87 (New York City).

tures to the average annual optimal expenditures for the New York City market. The optimal expenditures in the figure include those expended by the national program which are regarded as given in the optimization exercise. The figure indicates that it is optimal to advertise more during the winter season and less during the late spring and early summer. This finding is consistent with the simulation result obtained by Kinnucan and Forker. Since the benefit of the fluid advertising is in part a function of the Class 1 differential, Figure 20.1 also plots the seasonal pattern of the differential. Bearing in mind that there is a two-month advertising delay in the New York City equation, it is evident that the seasonal distribution of the optimal spending pattern is in large part a consequence of the seasonal variation in the Class 1 differential.

The optimal seasonal pattern in Figure 20.1 cannot be used as the prescribed policy for the New York State promotion unit because it includes the prorated national spending. After accounting for the observed seasonal spending pattern of the national program, the optimal seasonal policy for the New York unit is quite different. In Figure 20.2, the pattern labeled exclude NDB is the optimal seasonal pattern for the New York State promotion unit, given the observed pattern of the national spending. A causal examination of the optimal and the observed seasonal patterns of the New York unit indicates that the observed pattern is far from optimal (see Figure 20.3). The result reveals an important fact. To maximize the effectiveness of dairy farmers' promotional monies, coordination between the state and national promotional units is essential; the optimal spending pattern of the New York unit depends critically on the seasonal expenditure pattern of the national program.

## Summary

The purpose of this study is to identify the optimal advertising expenditures for the New York State fluid milk promotion program. The problem is cast in a deterministic optimal control framework with fluid sales equations for major cities in the state and the farm milk supply equation for the entire state as the time-evolving equations. The objective of the model is to choose the optimal spending level for each city with the goal of maximizing the discounted future revenue stream from farm milk sales, net of advertising expenditures. Using the model, analytical insights into the nature of optimal solution are discussed.

Upon taking into account the prorated national fluid expenditures, the results indicate that advertising spending level by the New York State promotional unit in New York City and Albany could be reduced by about

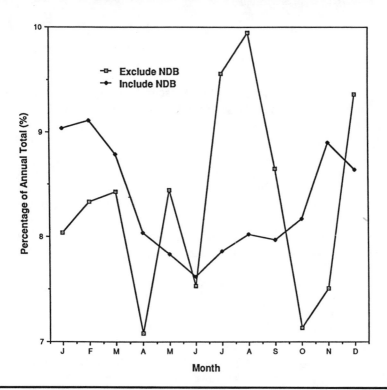

**Figure 20.2. Optimal seasonal advertising pattern, with and without national expenditures, 1984–87 (New York City).**

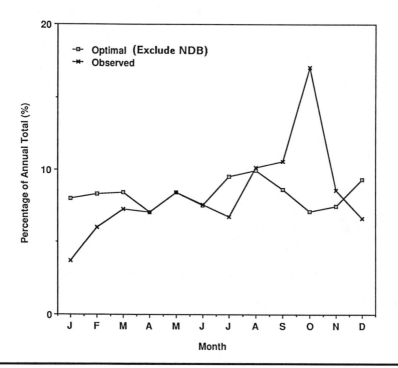

10 percent, while the spending level for Syracuse could be increased by three times. Due to the relatively large expenditure level in New York City, this solution suggests only a reallocation of the existing total expenditures across the three markets. The analysis also shows that it is optimal to follow a seasonal pattern in allocating advertising funds. Advertising should be intensified in the winter and at a lower rate during the late spring and early summer so as to take advantage of the seasonal variation in the Class 1 differential. Moreover, the prescribed seasonal spending pattern for the New York State promotional unit should take into account the pattern of the national program as it affects the sales in the state as well. Since both the optimal spending level and seasonal pattern of the state promotional unit depends critically on the expenditure level of the national program, coordination between the two units is essential to achieve optimality.

## Notes

1. The objective function is formulated from the perspective of the promotion agency. Certainly, a reasonable alternative would be net profit to producers which accounts for costs of farm production as well. With this alternative formulation, the analysis will be slightly complicated as one has to subtract the area under the farm milk supply curve from the objective function in (20.12). The two formulations, however, will not yield significantly different advertising policies as the farm supply response due to advertising has been shown to be minimal (Liu and Forker 1988a).

2. The estimated advertising elasticities are 0.025 for New York City, 0.036 for Syracuse, and 0.014 for Albany. The smaller advertising elasticity pertaining to Albany can be explained by a higher media cost in that market. Since the population is older, it is more expensive to reach the target group aging between 18 and 45 in the Albany market. The cost per thousand persons is $15.38 in Albany, compared to $13.20 and $13.28 in New York City and Syracuse, respectively.

3. The optimal solution is in part a function of the initial state values. Since there is considerable uncertainty in the estimated transition equations, it is important to update the state variables each period and resolve the optimization problem with a rolling horizon scheme when using the model in a planning context. In the ex post evaluation context of the current study, the observed shocks are added to the system so as to deal with the problem of estimation errors.

4. In Liu and Forker (1988a), it was found that the spending level for New York City from 1980 through 1984 should be reduced by 35% to achieve economic optimum. The near-optimal spending level for New York City during 1984 through 1987 found in the current study can be attributed to the following three reasons. First, as was found in Ward and Dixon, there has been an upward shift in the advertising effectiveness since the inception of the national dairy promotion program. Second, the Class 1 differential in New York State has increased from a monthly average of $2.20/cwt in 1984 to $2.66/cwt in 1987. Thus, the benefit of fluid advertising has

increased. Finally, since the current study allows the seasonal advertising pattern to deviate from the observed one, the opportunity set in the current optimization problem is enlarged and, hence, a higher solution found.

# 21 Discussion: Supply Response and Optimal Control Models of Advertising

BRUCE L. DIXON

The papers by Jensen, Johnson, Skold, and Grundmeier (JJSG) and Liu, Conrad, and Forker (LCF) are both commendable studies that raise some important issues. While these studies have some common themes, particularly with respect to supply response, they use different methods of selecting advertising expenditures.

The study by JJSG arbitrarily selects two different advertising scenarios, the first essentially a short-run scenario on the impacts of a one-year advertising campaign and the second a comparison of those results with results from the same type of program sustained over a ten-year horizon. Alternatively, LCF utilize a supply and demand model and optimize with respect to an objective function and determine an optimal trajectory of advertising levels. As a byproduct, LCF are able to also discuss supply response but in reference to an optimal trajectory. However, their analysis is narrower than that of JJSG because it is confined to one commodity. Since optimal advertising rates are the major empirical issue from the producers' point of view, my remarks concern themselves with optimal control as a method of analysis; within this framework, I will address specific comments to the JJSG and LCF papers.

Optimal control in its deterministic form is a means of obtaining a solution to an intertemporal optimization problem. In that respect it is no different from dynamic programming or, for that matter, nonlinear mathematical programming models. Canon, Cullum, and Polak (1970) show this equivalence. The big advantage of optimal control over these latter techniques of solution is that under appropriate smoothness conditions the maximum principle of Pontryagin et al. (1962) can be used to derive necessary conditions in each period that generally have an illuminating interpretation. LCF demonstrate this point by deriving rules for optimal advertising that have considerable economic logic as we would expect. However, a shortcoming of the maximum principle is that it does not

**336**

indicate a method of obtaining an actual numerical solution.

A further use of deterministic control, despite its numerical difficulties, is obtaining a steady state solution in both qualitative and quantitative terms. The latter could be obtained by the various numerical techniques mentioned above but the former is readily obtained from casting the problem as one of optimal control and application of the maximum principle by assuming that various exogenous variables are at some fixed level. LCF obtain a steady state solution in both qualitative and quantitative ways. Because of the parameter estimates used in their model, advertising is not very important. If advertising were important, I would question the usefulness of the steady state solution because of the fact that they use a monthly model with very significant seasonal effects.

My intuition is the more meaningful steady state solution would be a steady state trajectory of the controls throughout a year. With both demand seasonality (summer is a low demand period because of children being out of school) and supply seasonality, this type of trajectory is likely to be of more use, particularly since television viewing habits probably also vary seasonally if we consider television media. This raises the problem of differing effectiveness of an advertising dollar at different points in time, an issue that has been examined by Kinnucan and Forker with respect to fluid milk advertising.

Wisely, LCF do not use a stochastic optimal control approach. Solving a nonlinear deterministic optimal control problem is difficult enough without interjecting uncertainty. Stochastic control is appealing because of its so-called duality aspects. That is, when the model is acknowledged to be based on sample data, one is also faced with the problem of designing today's control actions with the thought in mind that the resulting observations on the endogenous (state) variables can also be used to update (reestimate) the parameters of the model before taking any control actions in the next period. Even with a relatively well-behaved linear-quadratic control problem, such problems are enormously difficult to solve (Rausser and Freebairn 1974).

Moreover, my personal work with dual control models indicates that even after going through the tortures-of-the-damned to get such solutions, the impact of the learning aspect is so small that it is not worth the effort. This type of control only tells us how to optimally lessen uncertainty about a parameter, it does not give the cost of uncertainty about model choice, i.e., what variables to include in our model and in what form. From an empirical point of view this is by far a more important question, amply demonstrated by the two papers, and one that is most important to researchers. To state the research issue more plainly, what data should be collected to estimate models to measure the impact of advertising and to direct the most efficient allocation of advertising dollars? Forker, Liu, and Hurst (1987) give this issue some consideration for dairy advertising.

The issue of model choice provides a convenient departure for specific remarks about the two studies. LCF conclude that advertising has been way too high in the three markets they model, particularly in New York City. This result is much different than the result obtained in Kinnucan and Forker (1986) and Liu and Forker (1988) which are studies applied to the same geographical area but use different databases in terms of periods included. However, the differences among the studies has such magnitude that an explanation is required. My personal guess is the form of the demand (sales) equation is so different that it is likely the root of the change in advertising effectiveness.

The differences are many. In the LCF study advertising expenditures only show up lagged one period. This is a distinct departure from Kinnucan and Forker and Ward and Dixon where advertising shows up with a distributed lag in both studies. In addition, the lagged dependent variable shows up as an explanatory variable. This is different from Kinnucan and Forker (1986) and Ward and Dixon (1989) but is in conformance with Liu and Forker. However, the structure of the lag in Liu and Forker is much more complex than in LCF. Additionally, the sales (dependent) variable is entered linearly whereas in the other three studies it is entered as its natural logarithm. Why the differences? My suspicion is that LCF were very interested in structuring their model as a first-order difference equation to fit the requirements of a standard statement of a discrete optimal control problem. In theory this is not necessary; Chow (1975) shows how to convert higher order models into a first-order form. Moreover, finite lags on the control variables, advertising in this case, can also be handled in Chow's form.

Because LCF come to such a different and important conclusion, I think it is necessary for them to estimate their sales equation in some of the past forms and put them into the optimal control model to see what the resulting control trajectory would be. If this were infeasible because of the problem dimensionality (and this is a real possibility), then at least the optimal trajectory derived from the present study could be substituted into the reestimated models to see what the resulting sales would be. In addition, the results of these simulations could be compared with simulating these reestimated models with the advertising expenditure strategies derived in Kinnucan and Forker and Liu and Forker. Such analysis would help put the current findings into a more reassuring perspective. As a final comment on LCF, with minimal effort it should be possible to obtain advertising expenditures by the National Dairy Promotion and Research Board. These expenditures would make the advertising data in the estimation phase of the

LCF study more nearly represent the total expenditures being made.

The need for more data is all too clear in the study by JJSG. The only way they can model advertising's effect is to shift the intercept of the demand equation. This is clearly a naive approach but it is probably not any worse than trying to borrow parameter estimates from, say, the fluid milk models and trying to estimate a reasonable parameter for advertising. In any event, the analysis could be expanded to tell us how much would be generated in terms of check-off funds to get some idea of the maximum funds available for advertising.

Additional uses of the work by JJSG would be to pursue further whether seasonality of advertising is important in initiating a program. That is, use different intercept shifts for their quarterly model of the demand for beef to see if advertising should be sensitive to seasonal movements or, in the case of beef, to longer term cyclical movements in supply. Their present results seem to indicate this. Such analysis would not indicate absolute allocations but it could help in determining relative allocations. Also, when utilizing fundamental regression concepts, it might be useful to advise the advertisers to inject considerable time-wise variability into the advertising levels initially. This will provide for the richest possible data set for estimating the impact of the advertising when relatively few observations are available in early periods. Such variability of advertising levels has been evident in the National Dairy Board expenditures.

Two other uses can be of the JJSG approach. The first would be to investigate the impact of advertising by other commodity groups. That is, JJSG have the model to investigate what would happen if the pork producers initiated a campaign in response to what they perceive as loss of market share to beef because of the promotion of beef. Indeed, it is clear that poultry is being advertised but, for the most part, I would speculate, by large firms in the poultry industry. Thus there are data somewhere on poultry advertising but it might take nothing short of a court order to obtain them. Nonetheless the model used in JJSG could be manipulated for pork and poultry in the same way as it has been for beef to try to trace out the impact of advertising competition. My experience with fluid milk indicates that fluid milk producers are interested in the impact of other beverage advertising on the sales of milk. A concrete answer, however, is yet to be forthcoming. JJSG might be in a position to shed at least some rough estimates on the impact of competitive advertising on beef producers.

The very real prospect and fact of advertising by numerous commodity groups brings up what some have termed the "whole stomach hypothesis." That is, if all commodity groups start advertising, who will be the losers and who will be the gainers? One sure gainer appears to be the advertising agencies but they are not normally listed in most public policy agendas along with consumers, commodity producers, and widows and orphans. It seems that modeling such as JJSG have done gives us a chance to measure the overall impact of multicommodity advertising campaigns, perhaps through the use of such measures and consumer and producer surplus less advertising costs.

The two studies have offered some tantalizing results, particularly in an empirical setting that enriches our understanding. My intuition is that while it is necessary to compute optimal solutions as LCF do, the biggest gains to understanding advertising's impact are in model selection. Thus in pursuing more elegant optimization methods, these methods should also be used to assess the adequacy of the model and data.

# 6 Future Directions for Advertising Research

# 22 Government Policy and Program Information Needs

CHARLES R. BRADER, KEVIN M. KESECKER,
and HAROLD S. RICKER

Generic promotion has become an increasingly important part of marketing agricultural products during the 1980s. In 1982 American producers spent about $44 million on domestic promotion under federal programs. By 1988, producers had increased their expenditures to over $300 million. These amounts represent only expenditures on promotion under federal programs. Total collections under federal programs with promotion provisions are in excess of $440 million. Expenditures on generic advertising and promotion have increased by over 580 percent in the last six years. Currently, there are over 250 state promotion programs in more than 40 states covering approximately 50 commodities. There are also nearly 40 federal programs. A list of the programs and their funding levels is provided in Tables 22.1–22.3. In addition, a national program for watermelons is currently in referendum.

The Agricultural Marketing Service (AMS) of the U.S. Department of Agriculture has the responsibility for administering federally sanctioned commodity promotion programs which fall into two broad categories. There are those authorized by marketing orders issued under the Agricultural Marketing Agreement Act of 1937. They include 22 fruit and vegetable marketing orders and three milk marketing orders (down from six), all of which contain advertising provisions. One reason for the decline in the dairy orders is the establishment of a national program with mandatory assessments. The second group contains 11 commodity-specific research and promotion programs authorized by free-standing statutes.

As the number of commodity programs and the expenditures on generic advertising grow, there is increasing concern among producers, government, consumers, and researchers over the efficiency and effectiveness of these programs. On the other hand, whether a generic advertising and promotion program is effective or not depends upon the perspective of various groups.

**Table 22.1  Commodity research and promotion programs authorized by federal statute[a]**

| | Most recent 12-month period – dollars in thousands | | | | | Expenditures for | | |
|---|---|---|---|---|---|---|---|---|
| | Total collections | Assess rate | Net collected after refund | Percent participation based on $ | Total funds available including interest, etc. | Promotion | Research | Other programs |
| National Wool Act of 1954 American Sheep Producers Council | 4,872 | d | Refunds not authorized | — | 6,176 | 4,386 | Not authorized | 873[q] |
| Mohair Council of America | 810 | e | Refunds not authorized | — | 1,110 | 232 | Not authorized | — |
| Cotton Research and Promotion Act of 1966 – Cotton Board | 39,181 | f | 25,540 | 65 | 38,375 | 16,412 | 3,874 | 1,855 |
| Potato Research and Promotion Act of 1971 – Potato Board | 5,800 | g | 4,740 | 82 | 4,753 | 4,300 | — | — |
| Egg Research and Consumer Information Act of 1974 – American Egg Board | 3,650 | h | 2,010 | 55 | 2,223 | 5 | 1,000[p] | 1,140[r] |
| Dairy and Tobacco Adjustment Act of 1983 – National Dairy Promotion and Research Board | 77,500 | i | Refunds not authorized | — | 95,800[m] | 69,300 | 10,268 | 7,812[s] |
| Honey Research, Promotion, and Consumer Information Act of 1984 – Honey Board | 2,527 | j | 2,286 | 90.5 | 2,200 | 1,678 | 55 | 100[t] |
| Beef Promotion and Research Act of 1985 – Cattlemen's Beef Promotion and Research Board | 46,396[b] | k | 41,704 | 90 | 46,908 | 28,092[n] | 715 | 5,761 |
| Pork Promotion, Research, and Consumer Information Act of 1985 – National Pork Board | 24,800[c] | l | 22,876 | 90 | 24,326 | 11,350[o] | 750 | 11,360 |

**Table 22.1 (cont.)**

Programs Disapproved in Producer Referendum
  Beef Research and Consumer Information Act of 1976 — Beef Board
  Floral Research and Consumer Information Act of 1981 — Floral Board
Programs Terminated
  Wheat and Wheat Foods Research and Nutrition Education Act of 1977 — Wheat Industry Council
Program in Other Departments
  U.S. Department of Commerce, National Fish and Seafood Promotion Council, $6.5 million advertising budget
Pending Order
  Watermelon Research, Promotion and Consumer Information Act of 1985 — Watermelon Board

[a] Authorized by individual legislation administered by industry boards February 1989.
[b] Collections of the Board only — states control 50 percent of domestic assessments.
[c] Annual collections.
[d] Deducted from incentive payment to wool growers.
[e] Deducted from incentive payment to mohair growers.
[f] $1 per bale plus .6 of 1 percent of value of bale.
[g] 1 cent per 100 pounds handled. Authority for increase to 2.3 cents April 12, 1984.
[h] 5 cents per 30 dozen cases of eggs handled.
[i] 15 cents per hundredweight on all milk marketed by producers. Credit of up to 10 cents is allowed for producer contribution to state and regional qualified promotion programs.
[j] 1 cent per pound of honey or honey used in honey products collected from producers and importers. Program began February 1987.
[k] $1 per head sold domestically and an equivalent amount on imported cattle and beef.
[l] .25 of 1 percent of the value of hogs sold and an equivalent amount on imported hogs and pork.
[m] The egg industry started an 18-month mandatory assessment program January 1, 1989 which will be followed by a referendum.
[n] Includes carryover from previous period.
[o] Board promotion — states control 50 percent of domestic assessments which are not shown.
[p] Board promotion — states and the National Pork Producers Council expend about 50 percent of funds, listed as "Other" but includes promotion.
[q] Funding for egg nutrition center and cholesterol action program.
[r] Industry services and market information.
[s] Consumer education, cooperative funding with states, foodservice promotion, and industry relations.
[t] $5,032 for nutrition education and $2,780 for program evaluation.

345

Table 22.2 Commodity research and promotion programs authorized by the Agricultural Marketing Agreement Act of 1937 — milk marketing orders, February 1989

| | | Most recent 12-month period — dollars in thousands | | | | Expenditures for | | |
|---|---|---|---|---|---|---|---|---|
| | Total collections | Access per 100 wt. (cents) | Net collection after refund[b] | Percent producer participation | Total funds available including interest, etc. | Total promotion | Nutrition research and education | Other programs |
| E. Ohio-W. Pennsylvania[a] | 3,667 | 10 | 3,137 | 87 | 3,671 | 2,424 | 670 | 28 |
| Indiana | 1,647 | 10 | 1,646 | 89 | 1,676 | 1,500 | 469 | 18 |
| Greater Kansas City | 725 | 10 | 725 | 100 | 744 | 291 | 457 | 4 |
| Middle Atlantic | 6,292 | 10 | 5,062 | 79 | 7,333 | 4,984 | 935 | 220 |
| Nebraska-W. Iowa | 1,204 | 10 | 1,094 | 94 | 1,246 | 706 | 356 | 8 |
| Total | 13,535 | ... | 11,664 | ... | 14,670 | 9,904 | 2,895 | 277 |

[a]Administered by federal market administrators.
[b]Producer refunds are not allowed, but up to 10 cents per hundredweight may be contributed to the National Dairy Board or another qualified program.

**Table 22.3.** Commodity research and promotion programs authorized by the Agricultural Marketing Agreement Act of 1937 — fruit and vegetable marketing orders[a]

Most recent fiscal year — dollars in thousands

| Expenditures for | Promotion | Research | Expenditures for | Promotion | Research |
|---|---|---|---|---|---|
| TX Citrus | 461 | . . . | HI Papayas | 119 | 8 |
| FL Limes | 7 | 108 | CA Olives | 1,573 | 59 |
| FL Avocados | 6 | 53 | ID-OR Onions | 595 | 42 |
| CA Nectarines | 1,580 | 59 | TX Onions | 141 | 79 |
| CA Peaches | 1,179 | 38 | FL Celery | . . . | . . . |
| CA Pears | 713 | 26 | FL Tomatoes | 391 | 108 |
| CA Plums | 1,650 | 59 | TX Lettuce | . . . | . . . |
| WA Cherries | 4 | . . . | TX Melons | 121 | 51 |
| WA-OR Prunes | . . . | 3 | CA Almonds | 744 | 170 |
| CA Tokay Grapes | 26 | . . . | CA Walnuts | 639 | 254 |
| OR-WA-CA Winter | | | CA Dates | 135 | . . . |
| Pears | 2,246 | 110 | | | |
| Totals: | Promotion | 12,330 | Research | 1,227 | |

NOTE: Assessments on handlers for promotion and research activities are established each year through a budget process. Assessments are based on the projected quantity of the commodity handled. The level can vary from year to year. (Assessments are mandatory.)
[a]Administered by industry committees.

Producers, who request the establishment of a generic program and pay for its operation, are usually interested in its impacts on sales and returns. Upon seeing their advertisements (assuming they like them), producers may tend to believe they are effective. But what producers like may not result in increased sales. They tend to be less concerned about the impacts on, for example, producers of substitute products.

Advertising agencies and program managers tend to be more interested in the immediate issues such as consumer recall of specific advertising slogans and campaigns. They also have obvious self interests in the continuation and development of these programs.

Consumers are likely to be concerned about the impact on their expenditures and welfare such as product information and use, nutritional value, and truth in advertising.

Public policymakers responsible for enactment of new promotion legislation or supplementation of existing laws that create various generic promotion programs are interested in the real and perceived impacts on their constituents.

Academic goals should be to objectively evaluate the effectiveness of generic advertising and promotion programs. However, objectivity is jeopardized when funding and much of the data for evaluation are provided directly by the commodity boards, who have a vested interest in the outcome.

While often discussed as promotion, there is a distinction between generic advertising and promotion. The former is paid media advertising, while the latter may include in-store promotions, couponing, special allowances, demonstrations, and the like. The effectiveness of promotion efforts can be readily evaluated in terms of changes in sales because, while other factors may have some impact, the promotion is often very specifically targeted in a known and somewhat controlled market environment. Generic advertising is much more difficult to evaluate because of its broader reach and the fact that many other uncontrollable factors may influence sales. The smaller federal programs tend to place more emphasis on promotion programs than generic advertising.

An objective of the AMS is to encourage comprehensive and reliable evaluations of federally sanctioned generic promotion programs. The role of AMS and some of its concerns in this area will be presented, and then some thoughts on data and the evaluation of generic programs will be offered for discussion.

## Evolving Role of AMS in Commodity Research and Promotion Programs

Federal involvement in research and promotion programs began in the mid-1950s with the passage of the National Wool Act of 1954. This act contains a section authorizing advertising and promotion for wool, mohair, sheep, and goats. In the same year, similar authority was added to the Agricultural Marketing Agreement Act.

In the mid-1960s, these programs developed into the form that exists today. The first free-standing commodity-specific legislation, the Cotton Research and Promotion Act, was passed in 1966.

AMS's administration of commodity research and promotion programs has been largely free of major controversy. A fundamentally "hands off" oversight policy by AMS coupled with responsible administration by a relatively small number of commodity boards contributed greatly to this atmosphere. Before the mid-1980s, there were several common constraints on program activities. Together these factors helped to minimize controversy within each affected industry and between that industry and its competitors. Beginning in the mid-1980s, however, many constraints were modified or eliminated in new research and promotion legislations.

Prior to the mid-1980s, most programs were based on referenda that required approval by a two-thirds majority of those affected. Producers paying assessments were able to obtain refunds on demand if they did not support the program objectives. Information regarding refunds was kept confidential so that those who requested refunds could not be ostracized for their actions. Unwarranted claims against competing products were prohibited. Also, all the activities of the program boards were subject to oversight by the U. S. Department of Agriculture.

Today, producer groups have opted for a reduced government role and have been successful in removing or altering some statutory constraints. The Dairy and Tobacco Adjustment Act of 1983, which authorized the Dairy Promotion and Research Board, moved the timing of the referendum to after the establishment of a national staff and an active advertising program. One could argue that it was not far enough after the start of the program to adequately determine the effects, but it was after the program was under way, rather than at the start. The statute was also the first federal research and promotion legislation that did not contain a refund provision. This program legislation also mandates an independent evaluation of the effectiveness of the total program by the USDA with an annual report to Congress.

The 1986 Beef Research and Consumer Information Act contained most of the typical constraints at that time, but the program could not be established through referendum, failing to pass twice. The Agricultural Adjustment Act of 1985, which contained authorities for both a beef and a pork program promotion authority, emulated the delayed referendum procedure established in the dairy program. A referendum was passed in favor of the beef program 22 months after its initiation. Pork producers passed their referendum 24 months after it had been put into effect. Both programs do not provide for refunds. Neither of these programs requires the type of evaluation that the dairy program requires.

The Egg Research and Consumer Information Act of 1974 allows for refunds and has been experiencing a refund rate of approximately 40 percent. There were continuing efforts in the egg industry to eliminate the refund option with success coming on January 1, 1989, when a mandatory program for 18 months was put in place. It will be voted on in referendum in mid-1990. The American Egg Board must hold 10 percent of all revenues in case the referendum should fail.

Some producers in the cotton industry, which also has a promotion program with a high refund rate under an "old" statute, have discussed legislative amendments to preclude refunds. They almost accomplished their goal last year, but lost out in Congress. They will likely continue to explore ways of achieving this goal.

The changing climate surrounding the research and promotion programs has thus affected AMS's oversight role and policies, even with respect to comparative advertising. The agency has discouraged comparative advertising from the inception of these programs to avoid the possibility of antagonism or negative advertising between commodity groups. More recently, some positive comparisons have been approved.

Another major change has been the coupling of national and local programs. Under the dairy legislation, two-thirds of the assessment income may go directly to local/regional promotion groups with minimal federal oversight. Likewise, under the new beef statute, state councils keep part of the assessment income, also with limited federal oversight. The oversight responsibilities of AMS in this area are not clearly defined. Yet the secretary of agriculture is responsible for enforcement at both the national and local levels. Should controversy develop over activities of the relatively autonomous local entities, the AMS expects to be tested.

Another area of concern for AMS is the promotion-lobbying relationship. Commodity groups are prohibited from using funds collected under the promotion programs for lobbying activities. However, an organization involved in lobbying may also be permitted to carry out promotion activities on behalf of the federally-sanctioned program. This is the case, for example, with the Pork Producers Council and the pork program. Specific groups aside, this kind of activity may also challenge AMS's oversight responsibilities.

The commodity research and promotion legislation of the 1980s has provided for a higher level of funding for generic promotion activity. At the same time it has provided substantially fewer statutory constraints. The appropriate role of the USDA in this environment will continue to evolve and will not be free of controversy. With the exception of the dairy program, there has been no mandate for AMS or any government involvement in evaluating the effectiveness of these programs. However, uncertainty about the value of these programs will persist until more convincing evidence about the effectiveness of generic promotion is produced.

With the increasing number of generic promotion programs, other competing commodity groups may feel pressured to develop their own. This might be construed as an indication that they are convinced that generic promotion works, or confirms the notion that it has become a necessary cost of marketing to help maintain market share. The consumer may get more and better product information, but it comes at a higher price. Under these circumstances, the government continues to provide oversight to try to ensure fairness, and no group is likely to cut its programs without some unlikely unilateral action by all.

## Data Needs and Evaluation of the Effectiveness of Generic Programs

A vast array of literature and studies exist on the subject of evaluating the effectiveness of generic programs. Most of the research efforts have focused on the effects of individual programs on sales. However, each study invariably resulted in one of two conclusions: either the promotion program is claimed to be effective or there is inadequate data.

Data needs for evaluating the effectiveness of generic advertising have been debated and discussed for a number of years. It is recognized that available data were not designed and are incomplete for program evaluation. But, little real progress to resolve the problem is evident. A systematic approach for evaluating the growing number of promotion programs should be developed and implemented soon. As part of this effort three fundamental principles should be considered.

First, data should be collected under the guidance of promotion objectives, economic theories, and analytical methods. The long-term goals, target audiences, and intentions of the promotion campaigns should be well understood before data collection or analytical methods are even considered. They are the focal factors for evaluation. At the same time, it is necessary for researchers to not only identify the necessary data but also justify the underlying reasons for the needs.

Second, the capacity of an individual to consume food is limited. Increased consumption of one product will be at the expense of competing products. At present, beef, pork, eggs, cheese, and seafood all have some type of generic promotion. Obviously, they are direct substitutes. It follows that the direct and the cross effects of advertising must be considered in evaluating these programs. This implies that a unified data collection approach should be taken for all commodities, or at least for competing commodities in a food group.

Third, the issue of data quality must be addressed. It should be recognized that data represents only incomplete and imperfect records of outcomes that are quantifiable. Statistics or estimates of parameters derived from data are subject to both sampling and nonsampling errors, which may be minimized through design but not eliminated. When the magnitude of these errors is ignored, sophisticated analyses and precise results may become meaningless.

To evaluate the effectiveness of a generic promotion program, a basic requirement is that good records must be kept on all relevant local, regional, and national promotion activities. Program evaluations cannot be considered complete without these records. In this regard, there are at least two types of data to be collected: accounting data, including the actual expenses on advertising and promotion by type of media; and activity data, including the date, timing, frequency, exposure, and target audiences of actual promotion activities.

It is desirable to develop a standard bookkeeping procedure for recording this type of information consistently across all commodity programs. The procedure could be developed jointly between a group of researchers and representatives of commodity groups involved in generic promotion activities. The researchers should lead by specifying and justifying the data needs for evaluation; accountants could be called upon to develop a simple, easy-to-use procedure; and the promotion boards must be willing to participate and cooperate on a regular, committed basis. These tasks are undoubtedly complex and difficult, but accountability is essential when public funding is involved. The responsibility for collecting this basic set of data has been placed upon the researchers to identify reasonable requirements and the promotion boards to provide.

Given the diverse interests of producers, public policymakers, consumers, program boards, advertising agencies, researchers, and others, when can a commodity promotion program be considered effective? In the past, this question has hampered research efforts, primarily because a unified and systematic approach has not been formulated to determine program effectiveness. Consider the following list of questions:

1. Has generic advertising and promotion improved the consumer's opinion and attitudes toward the image of the product? The consumer's understanding of the nutritional value of the food product? The consumer's intentions to purchase the product?
2. Has generic advertising and promotion increased, or slowed the decrease in, sales or consumption of the product?
3. Has generic advertising and promotion positively impacted the net return to producers?

If the generic promotion program has resulted in affirmative answers to the above questions in a cost effective manner, there should be general agreement that the program can be judged effective. However, the government must also assure that the gain of one commodity group is not at the unfair expense of another group.

As one proceeds through the above set of questions, the data requirements and the degree of difficulty in collecting the data increase in a progressive manner. As more answers are demanded, the intensity of the data collection effort will increase and the total cost of evaluation will multiply. A realistic compromise is needed to achieve balance between these conflicting factors.

There are real difficulties in isolating the impact of generic advertising from other factors that may have influenced commodity sales. For example, the Economic Research Service (ERS) of the USDA identified changes in prices, incomes, and donations of dairy products as having the largest impacts on consumption levels during the past several years. This did not mean that other factors, such as advertising, were not important. It is also difficult to separate the impacts of brand advertising from generic. A complicating factor for all researchers is the reluctance of brand manufacturers and commodity boards to share all of the relevant advertising data needed for evaluations.

Awareness and attitude data collected from opinion surveys are often used as a guide to advertising effectiveness. Alternatively, sales or consumption impacts due to generic promotion may be estimated by econometric and other statistical methods based on data from household panels, supermarkets, food service establishments, and government agencies. Both of these approaches are useful and complementary.

Much of the needed data are available from public sources. For example, the Census Bureau provides data on demographic factors. However, the demographic data have not been sufficiently utilized in most evaluation efforts. Other needed data can be obtained from the private sector. What is needed, but not readily available from either public or private sources, has not been clearly specified.

From our perspective, a designed, systematic approach for a comprehensive national database is desirable for evaluating generic advertising programs. Opinion and consumption data for the major food groups, such as grain, meat, dairy products, fruits and vegetables, and beverages, along with demographic, economic, and life-style data, should be collected over time. Meaningful comparisons based on accurate and reliable data between different time periods can then be made to determine whether consumption patterns have changed for the targeted population.

## Summary

In conclusion, the commodity research and promotion legislation of the 1980s has provided for a higher level of financial funding for generic promotion activity, and there are substantially fewer statutory requirements. Vigorous promotion boards have been created, and they have the financial resources and organization to conduct sophisticated national advertising campaigns. This is generating new opportunities for commodity groups. However, with greater opportunity comes greater risk. There is likely to be increased controversy over the appropriate role of government in this continually changing environment.

The role of generic advertising in the marketing of agricultural products is still being debated. The effects of generic advertising on producers and consumers are important issues. Even though the promotion programs began in the mid-1960s, evaluation of these programs and their data needs are still questioned and remain unresolved.

Much of the difficulty in these areas is attributed to the lack of reliable data. However, researchers have also failed to develop an approach and identify the corresponding analytical methods, which in turn determine the kind of data to be collected. Otherwise, promotion boards collect available data on an ad hoc basis, hoping they will one day be useful for long-term evaluation. Studies collected in this manner are not proactive; they have obvious limitations.

To complete a thorough and effective evaluation of advertising and promotion programs will require a cooperative effort and trust between the commodity boards and researchers that does not exist in most cases today. For obvious reasons, each board wishes to keep program details proprietary.

Measuring the effect of generic advertising is not an exact science, but precise public accountability for funds collected under federal programs is necessary. Opinion surveys, econometric modeling, analysis of household consumption data, and various other approaches have both merits and limitations. All of them are useful and complementary, but the development and implementation of a systematic approach is needed. A choice must ultimately be made on the appropriate level of investment for evaluation efforts.

# 23 Generic Advertising: A Commodity Perspective

**ARCHIE MACDONALD and PETER GOULD**

In this chapter we discuss the things that users or commodity groups need and want from economic research measuring the effectiveness of advertising. Collectively, generic advertisers currently spend a lot of money, with the likelihood that, as new check-off programs become mandated, the total value will increase significantly. In fact most, if not all, advertising activities include a significant research component, but it is generally not the econometric research that is discussed in this book. Millions of dollars are spent on market research, while very little expenditure has been made to satisfactorily address questions about the "bigger picture." This should not be interpreted as commodity groups not having specific objectives or taking their advertising/promotional activities very seriously. Ultimately, decisions about advertising are made by producer representatives, using what information and processes they have available. Of necessity, contemporary producers are shrewd and discerning business people. They need better information to make better decisions on matters that, potentially, have a widespread impact. What we really are going to talk about in this chapter is the information that will allow producers or producer groups to make better decisions about the level and allocation of advertising dollars.

## Why Advertise?

At an aggregate level, there can only be one ultimate reason to advertise and that is to affect product demand in a positive way. This can be accomplished by either shifting the demand curve or increasing its slope, e.g., closer to vertical than horizontal. Having said this, it must be borne in mind that the effect on the demand curve is relative, e.g., compared to what it would have been in the absence of advertising.

The process of advertising and its various components is complicated by the fact that there are numerous vehicles for delivering an advertising message and similarly there are many potential messages. This whole area is not getting any less complex as consumers become more sophisticated and sensitized, and marketers seek any advantage available. Advertising effectiveness is a function of our strategy. At one level, we attempt to inculcate attitudes that milk is a beverage suitable for all occasions for teenagers and young adults. Traditionally, milk consumption has gone into the abyss once younger adults switch to coffee, beer, wine, and soft drinks.

At another level, we try to influence a consumer's short-term decision with an in-store cheese sample or a chocolate milk flyer in a restaurant. With respect to nutrition education, we help teachers learn about good nutrition in the expectation that students will learn good eating habits and that good eating habits include basic and real foods such as milk and dairy products, meat, fish, fruit, vegetables, and so forth. Good habits, like bad habits, can be hard to break. Dairy nutritionists work with health professionals in both the dental and medical fields. An emerging area with significant and growing potential is geriatric care.

Advertising is used to disseminate information either proactively or reactively. We can promote the positive attributes in our foods like calcium and hope to persuade some consumers to switch or continue to consume milk and dairy products. Unfortunately, or fortunately depending on the perspective, a lot of energy and money is spent in what we call the "health arena" where "truths" based on "scientific research" are debated in the interest of information and education. The issues are fat, cholesterol, hormones, toxins, chemicals (added or otherwise), and carcinogens. The intentions may be laudable, the stakes are high, and the results are often confusing.

## Problems and General Observations

Having identified this range of objectives and avenues, the questions still remain: Have we accomplished what we had hoped to? Have we gotten a fair return on our investment?

We are dealing with items that have different time horizons from a payoff perspective, and we need to find a basis of standardizing the comparisons somewhat akin to a discounted cash flow analysis before we can make sense of proper allocations.

I am prepared to suggest that we really don't have good methods for evaluating the effectiveness of generic advertising programs. In micro terms, advertising tends to be evaluated in relation to how audiences/consumers/

target groups respond or react to advertising messages such as awareness of the ad, degree of recall, understanding the message, persuasion, liking or not liking it, and similar hypothetical parameters. Consumers are also routinely tested to monitor attitudes towards a product, e.g., do they consider it natural? healthy? a good source of vitamin Q? and so forth. This information is valuable feedback to the creative and marketing people in terms of monitoring changes in attitudes and perceptions and identifying the impact of newly introduced factors, such as the release of research results or the reporting on a conference related to health issues. However, these methods do not provide sufficient insight into what effect advertising is having on the demand function. A more direct, obvious, and necessary approach is to correlate advertising and sales. Much of the work done to date in this area has to be categorized as preliminary or groundbreaking. "Simplistic" approaches that only incorporate advertising expenditure as an additional variable to a demand model that includes basic economic and demographic variables are just not good enough.

Rigorous attention to quality of data and market specification must be made in the analysis of advertising effectiveness. Model testing without regard to the relevance of the data is dangerous.

The advertising function and its role in consumer behavior is complex. A host of factors including price, quality, competition, substitution, demographic changes, and other advertising are all interacting. This is further compounded by the advertisers' objectives, level of expenditure, quality of creative, and ability to make good media purchases.

The first thing that users/commodity groups need from researchers is caveats with appropriate emphasis. Researchers, in that sense, are no different than any other marketer: they perceive a strong advantage in getting their product to the market first. This, to some extent, has resulted in a "widely held belief" that generic advertising is not a prudent way to spend money. If it is not, why are we doing so much of it? Surely, it can't all be misspent. That gets closer to the heart of the matter. Commodity groups are, through their advertising initiatives, sincerely attempting to either expand the total market, maintain the market, decrease the rate of decline and/or increase profitability. A case could be made that some of these programs perform a public service, particularly in the nutrition education area, provided that the program was relatively unbiased.

In the final analysis, someone is spending real dollars, either as a board of directors on behalf of all producers or in some other fashion. These expenditures have opportunity costs at the farm level. Alternatives include debt repayment, a new piece of equipment, or buying a government savings bond; at the industry level, choices may include things like supporting production research or investing in new product development. The latter is not generally a component of Canadian farm marketing/promotional organization marketing programs.

Advertising/promotional activities should not be taken as given — they must serve a discernable purpose, although one espoused rationale is maintaining a presence because that is what the competition is doing.

Our producer directors have a difficult time deciding how much money to allocate to advertising activities. To characterize the decision-making process as arbitrary may be unfair, but it certainly contains a degree of truth. As opportunities increase in terms of target audiences/groups including segmentation based on age, sex, ethnicity, and special health needs; market segmentation including in-home and out-of-home; delivery vehicles including alternative media, packaging, and special events, the demand for resources and dollars increases. That dollar demand is compounded by media inflation outstripping overall inflation, reduced on-farm margins, and farm-gate and/or retail prices being squeezed by the competition or oversupply. Commodity decision makers have to make choices both about the overall level of expenditure and the allocation amongst programs. Our producer directors are not well positioned to objectively make those decisions — as I suspect is the case for most, if not all, similar organizations. The decision-making process is based on judgement relative to market needs and affordability and is in large part influenced by the persuasiveness and clarity of the person making the budget request. It is generally accepted that it would be a rare event if a marketing (read promotion) group proposed a decrease in the level of advertising/promotional expenditures. (This is not intended to be a criticism.)

The initiatives and developments of recent years as reflected in this symposium are welcomed by commodity groups such as ours as timely and necessary. The following section addresses some specific items decision-makers and/or the advertising people need from the economic researcher.

## Research Needs

Before getting to specifics, I want to make two points. The first relates the expectations that might be created from research on the effectiveness of advertising. It is difficult to get objective results from what is essentially a subjective activity, advertising. I am making this point to emphasize the fact that we don't expect any research results to be categoric. One study may find that generic advertising may not be effective — e.g., a low or negative payback — while another may show the opposite. If reality could be measured, we recognize that both results might be correct. Users can and should only expect a measure of the probability that the findings are accurate within a specified confidence interval.

The second point is that commodity groups sincerely believe that their advertising/promotional activities result in, all things being equal, market expansion — that the various facets of advertising help achieve their objectives within the marketing function. It is in this latter context that commodity organizations need tools to assess the effectiveness of their programs.

The needs are based on common sense and sound management practices.

1. It would be helpful to know if advertising generates a positive return on the investment. These expenditures have opportunity costs and there may well be better ways to allocate the funds—one of which is to not collect them.
2. If it can be shown that there is a positive return, it can be assumed that this level is by definition not optimal. Therefore, in which direction should expenditures go to move in the direction of optimum?
3. Conversely, if advertising is not efficacious, what are the reasons? Is it possible that there is a minimum threshold level, which if not attained, results in insufficient exposure to affect behavior? What period of time and what level of penetration are required to shift the demand for a product generically?

If the aggregate-level questions can be addressed, it then becomes necessary to provide guidance in a comparative context. If it is determined that more total dollars should be spent, then where should they be spent? Alternatively, if budgets are constrained, in what programs should the reductions occur?

Advertising is a mix of nonhomogeneous activities. To address the above questions, I have identified five areas that need differentiation to assess the relative effectiveness.

1. Can the impact of alternative media (e.g., print, TV, radio) and programs (e.g., nutrition education, contests) be differentiated? That is, if one is going to cut back or expand, what is the best way to do it?
2. Can the econometric analysis take into account the differing objectives and time horizons of advertising, which range from the desired short-term effect of a discount coupon to the life-style reinforcement/alternatives of a TV campaign to the long-term habit formation theory that underlies nutrition education?
3. The problem is further compounded by the likelihood that most commodities will have a number of concurrent campaigns or programs.

To illustrate this simply, on the fluid side we promote milk and chocolate milk while the industrial side includes cheese, butter, ice cream, and so on.

4.   One of the overriding issues is that of "quality," which by its nature is qualitative but again could benefit from its quantification. Using the Ontario Milk Marketing Board as an example, decision making to a degree is influenced by the perceived quality of the advertising, when in fact quality is equated to likability. While liking or not liking should not be totally discounted, much more emphasis should be placed on "effectiveness" and would, if a reliable means could be found to measure effectiveness and that analysis, be made available to the board. Should it be taken as given that if a pool of money exists or is created that it will be well spent? To that end some differentiation between the quality of campaigns or creatives has to be incorporated into the equations.

5.   The fifth area that needs differentiation is the output of advertising. Traditionally, dollars have been used as a proxy for the "product" of advertising expenditures. However, what we are really trying to measure is something like "messages sent and received" and these should be measured (and possibly weighted) in such a way that they can be added across media and/or programs. This is particularly critical in a time-series context. One can probably be categorical in asserting that analysis using expenditure data for the variable is likely to be unsatisfactory. We need a standard of measure that will truly reflect the impact of advertising rather than a crude proxy for it!

In the overall scheme of things, it would seem that the effectiveness of our own advertising must also relate to the level of our competitors' advertising as well as the level of total advertising. In a similar vein, there are factors at play, particularly in the food sector, that can have a significant impact on product perceptions. These factors are often beyond the control of commodity groups and, in fact, themselves become a reason for advertising. Examples include issues related to cholesterol, fat, irradiation, "growth hormones," sugar, and chemical residues. Producers feel a need to counteract either misinformation or accurate information that gets distorted or overplayed in media reporting. This type of "advertising" is geared to reducing the potential negative impact of "information" and may result in a lower rate of decline versus a measurable increase in consumption. This notion is very important and somehow must be incorporated in the analysis. These effects have been very significant in consumer reaction to butter and the red meats, for example, and conversely have impacted in a positive way on substitutes or replacements.

## Conclusions

1. Commodity groups make multimillion-dollar decisions based on the belief that advertising works and that the risks (costs) of not advertising may be even higher.
2. Accordingly, tools are needed to make the management decisions more meaningful and relevant. Questions that need answering include:
   - Is there a minimum threshold level below which expenditures are essentially wasted?
   - Is there a positive net return to investing in advertising?
   - Should the level of expenditure be higher or lower?
   - Can returns be differentiated between programs and/or media?
3. Perceptions about generic advertising are relatively deeply rooted. Those perceptions can and will change in proportion to the related research initiatives. Therefore, it is very important that the results or comments be erudite.
4. Similarly, producer decision makers may react to research results. Accordingly, it is important to convey results in a way that will more likely be understood than misunderstood. Producer directors and/or government administrators, and many others as well, often don't think like econometricians — which is probably just as well. The research community should keep in mind the very real potential consequences in contrast to the theoretical implications of their work.
5. To be effective, the analytical tools must mirror reality to the greatest extent possible, including accounting for the objectives of advertising, exogenous factors, the structure of the industry, the nature of the market, and the quantification of the messages sent (or received).
6. There is a need for researchers to understand the advertising process from the producer check-off through "traditional" means of measuring effectiveness. I believe very strongly that if progress is going to be made in this area, let alone the achievement of success, the effort will have to be based on a team approach including econometricians, market researchers, agency people, and commodity people.
7. While all above factors are important, perhaps the most important is trying to maintain a realistic set of expectations. Academics are in pursuit of knowledge, research dollars, and publications. Advertisers are in pursuit of simple answers and vindication for both past and future activities. In reality, it is not likely that the effect of advertising or behavioral response can be accurately modeled. The process is complicated as already indicated. There is branded advertising, generic advertising, and a hybrid branded generic type, e.g., "Wisconsin/New York/California Cheese." There are also situations where promotional

expenditures in one area such as out-of-home are intended to cause sales increases in another area, like retail. It is to be hoped that all parties can maintain a sense of perspective and always attach probabilities to outcomes. What commodity groups ultimately should be looking for is a consistent methodology that can be repeated and used as an independent and objective measure of their advertising activities.

8. This leads to the last point. I have always had lingering doubts about whether or not we are trying to do something that cannot be done. Why are we now trying to develop methodologies for the purpose of measuring advertising effectiveness?

Part of the answer lies in the accountability that commodity organizations have to their members/producers. Success cannot readily be measured by profit and loss as in the case of private companies. Whether funds are collected by legislated check-off as is the case with many U.S. commodities or mandatory check-offs that we have in Canada, there is an element of public trust. We have an obligation to ensure that producer funds are spent as well as they can be.

To help ensure that, there is a further obligation to support the development of new evaluation techniques. This is sometimes difficult when funds are already perceived to be scarce and economic research considered to be esoteric, to be kind.

Nonetheless, the Canadian dairy industry is keenly interested in the recent and ongoing developments in this area. There appears to be a critical mass attained that should result in progress. Events such as the symposium that produced this book not only provide an opportunity for learning and exchanging views, they help maintain momentum, providing impetus for the future.

Commodity groups must be prepared to look down the road for at least five years and perhaps longer. And if developing useful methodologies is really a goal, then we will also have to make a commitment in terms of funding, data, and expertise. The Ontario Milk Marketing Board and Dairy Bureau of Canada are excited about the contribution that effectiveness of advertising research can make to more efficient advertising.

# 24 Future Directions for Advertising Research: A Researcher's Perspective

STANLEY R. JOHNSON

The increase in producer financed advertising and promotion of agricultural commodities has raised a number of far reaching research issues. In general, these issues involve methods of assessing impacts of advertising and promotion for market demand and public policy questions on producer and societal benefits of generic advertising and promotion. New data sources, extensions of consumer theory incorporating attitudes and perceptions, additional attention to correspondences ences between individual and market demand, and other advances have been stimulated by the associated research. The result has been improved integration of research methods from marketing and economics.

While there has been a significant increase in advertising and promotion research, the full implications of these programs for producers and society are still in question. Impacts of advertising and promotion on consumer attitudes and perceptions have been demonstrated. And, statistically significant coefficients of proxies for advertising effects in demand contexts have been estimated. Still, there is neither clear nor convincing evidence on the magnitudes of shifts in demand brought about by advertising, how demand is shifted by advertising and promotion, or the incidence of the benefits from such shifts. Supply response, cross-commodity effects, and the decay rates for information are among the factors complicating evaluation research.

## Analytical Approaches

The commonly used analytical approaches are for estimating direct impacts of advertising and promotion on consumption or commodity sales, and for identifying the benefits of advertising and promotion more generally viewed. For the former, the analytical approaches that have evolved represent an interesting merging of concepts from marketing and economics. For the latter, there has been less research activity, perhaps because of the priority given to the estimation of direct effects of advertising and promotion. But, it is in this latter research area that the results critical to the future of these programs will come, establishing the benefits of advertising and their incidence.

## DIRECT EFFECTS

The research approaches that have been used in identifying direct impacts or indicators of impacts for advertising and promotion programs are shown in Figure 24.1. Generally, the approaches integrate methods, models, and data used in economics and marketing in varying degrees. More traditional economic approaches utilize demand specifications and incorporate advertising impacts through scaling and translation. Indicators of impacts of advertising are then obtained as estimated demand shifts and/or shifts in consumption and sales projections under alternative assumptions on prices, income, other scaling and translating variables, and the advertising or promotion program.

Marketing approaches place important emphasis on the message conveyed in the advertising or promotion campaign. Indicators of outcomes are more for measures of changes in attitudes or perceptions than for final consumption or sales projections. Direct research approaches focus on cognizance of the advertising message and relationships between awareness of the message and attitudes or perceptions about the associated commodity.

In the generic promotion and advertising evaluations, the researchers in economics and marketing have drawn on concepts that can be viewed as extending or elaborating traditional analytical frameworks. As shown in Figure 24.1, these include household decisions, information processing, supply response, group decisions, and the food supply. Generally, the integration of approaches has joined the analytical frameworks at the stages of the analysis indicated in the figure: demand functions and systems for economics, and promotion program design for marketing. These expanding research approaches are producing estimates of indicators of impacts of advertising and promotion programs that are more easily understood, more useful in program design, and more successful in identifying and attributing benefits of advertising and promotion.

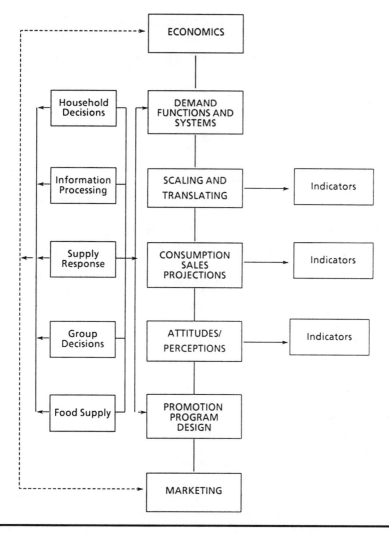

**Figure 24.1.  Integrating approaches to the study of consumer behavior.**

## BENEFITS/COSTS

Many of the producer funded advertising and promotion programs have been justified on the basis of increased profitability. From the viewpoint of the individual producer, this choice of a benefits indicator is highly questionable. Agriculture is a competitive industry. Accordingly, there is free entry into the markets for agricultural commodities. With free entry it is easy to show that impacts of advertising and promotion work themselves out in the dynamics of the commodity markets, and that the long-run equilibrium rate of return is unaffected.

Using an industry viewpoint, alternative conclusions are possible and rate of return or other measures of producer benefits can be demonstrated. In simple terms, if market share can be increased and a normal rate of return obtained, there is an industry-wide benefit of advertising. In economic jargon, if the demand function for the commodity is shifted, benefits of advertising or promotion can be estimated as additions to producer surplus. The latter measure, an appropriate focus for industry and producer groups, is illustrated in Figure 24.2.

In this figure, a hypothetical shift in demand due to advertising and promotion has been indicated as $D^1D^1$. Alternative supply functions are SS and $S^1S^1$. P and $P^1$ are the equilibrium prices. The shaded areas identify increases in producer surplus from the demand shift, depending on whether there is a corresponding shift in supply. For illustration, the supply functions selected are at extremes, representing no shift and a supply shift $S^1S^1$ yielding the equilibrium price P.

The results in Figure 24.2 show that for the industry there are potential

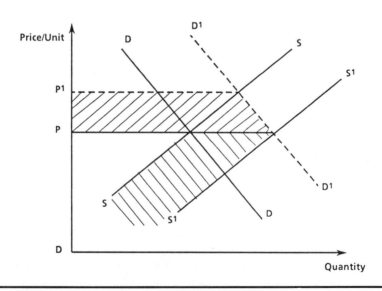

**Figure 24.2. Industry impacts of advertising and promotion.**

benefits from advertising and promotion. With the surplus measures appropriately calculated it is, in principle, possible to justify taxing the producers to establish the demand shift $D^1D^1$. In simple terms, $t$, total "normal" profits for the industry, increases with market share. This seems to be the argument best defining the position of those supporting check-off programs.

The result is not, however, so clear from a societal viewpoint. Even from a producer viewpoint the result is not as simple as indicated by the stylized illustration in Figure 24.2. Cross-commodity effects are important. It is possible, for example, that the entire impact of the initial advertising and promotion shift could "leak" to other markets. Leakage can be estimated using cross-price elasticities between the target commodity and substitutes. For agricultural commodities, substitution effects are typically high. Thus, even for producers, the estimation of industry benefits from advertising and promotion represents a complex of analytical issues.

If the scope of the benefit analysis is broadened, the analytical issues become even more complex and the impacts of advertising less clearly understood. The general question involves the benefits to society of investing resources in advertising and promotion. In principle, these benefits can be established using economic surplus measures. But the surplus measures required are multimarket. And, if uncertainty is used as a justification for introducing information through advertising, the appropriate surplus concepts require additional theoretical structure. In stylized economywide models, advertising and promotion can be shown as increasing or decreasing welfare.

## Data Sources

A number of specialized research questions that require new information sources have been raised by evaluations of advertising and promotion. The generation and use of data in evaluations have been influenced by the marketing and economic questions as well as new measurement technologies. Applying economic theory to advertising makes use of available data and highly structured assumptions about the consumer decision process. In contrast, marketing approaches use less structured models for evaluation. The emphasis in marketing research is more on elicitation of specialized data and controlled experiments. In a sense, marketing approaches substitute experimental design for the *a priori* structure used in the economic approaches for assessing impacts of advertising and promotion.

Merging economics and marketing in the study of advertising has provided additional added structure for analyses and new data sources for economists. These new data have spawned extensions in theory that may yield important results in the future. Examples of data available for adding to models motivated by economic theory include attitude measures, scanner panels, surveys on recall of promotion messages, and so on. From economics, hierarchical methods and cross-commodity effects can be added to marketing analyses.

New technologies for data gathering perhaps offer the most potential for integrating economics and marketing for evaluating direct impacts of advertising and promotion. Unfortunately, these new data sources have not yet been well adapted to the requirements of economic theory. Tracking study data that do not identify consumption, scanner data that tend to concentrate only on single commodities, and failure to integrate scanner and other experimental data with national surveys (BLS and NFCS) are examples of unnecessary limitations of new data sources available for evaluating advertising and promotion. Minor changes in current collection procedures, more cooperation by producer groups and marketing firms and economists, and direct involvement of government agencies responsible for national surveys could yield valuable results on impacts of advertising and promotion.

The least available and most difficult to acquire data are those required for estimating societal benefits. Obtaining results in this area will take time and careful analysis. However, simulation models using partial demand systems, supply response, cross-commodity effects, and different response rates for advertising and promotion have been developed. These simulation models can at least indicate experimentally the industry-wide and societal impacts of advertising and promotion. In a sense, the experimental models represent a new data source. Experimental results can be applied to the design of advertising and promotion programs, and they will afford clearer perspectives on the impacts of advertising and promotion.

## Future Research Issues

Several future research issues are suggested by the results to date of the policy questions raised by producer funded advertising and promotion programs. Selected issues are delineated here to stimulate discussion on possible research initiatives and to suggest the scope of the research task for clearly establishing impacts of advertising and promotion.

1.  Advertising and promotion campaigns, and interest in evaluation, have generated new data that can be used in understanding consumer behavior. Unfortunately, these new data sources have not been widely shared or integrated with some traditional data systems generated by

government agencies. Associated issues involve: the propriety or nature of market research data, integration of market research and government sponsored surveys, use of structure from theory in designing specialized surveys, coordination of specialized surveys among commodity promotion boards, sharing of survey results, and establishment of protocols to ensure comparability.

2. The integration of concepts from economics and marketing is continuing. Research in this area should be supported along with more direct assessments of advertising impacts. Associated research issues in the modeling area include: identifying more fully the role of information in consumer decisions, aggregation of individual-to-market level impacts, cross-commodity effects, household decisions and commodity characteristics, linking of promotion programs to measurable performance outcomes, and theoretical advances needed to support more robust impact analyses.

3. Producer financed promotion programs have major public policy implications. Are the producers being well served by the promotion programs that they are financing? Issues in this area include: short-and long-term impacts of advertising and promotion, types of messages that are incorporated in advertising campaigns, partial vs. full analysis of societal or market impacts, responsibilities for government and the private sector in producer check-off financed advertising, appropriate performance measures for assessing societal and producer impacts, regulation of advertising, efficiency of advertising, and promotion programs in achieving desired impacts.

The results to date on advertising and promotion are encouraging. Extensive theoretical and applied research results useful to producers and regulators in better understanding impacts of commodity advertising and promotion are becoming available. Unfortunately, many of the research results raise more questions than they answer. This is simply a manifestation of the complexity of the assessment problem, however. Clearer and more definite estimates of direct advertising impacts will be required. Also, estimates of producer and societal benefits more soundly grounded in welfare theory must be established. These results will contribute to the efficiency of advertising programs, more strategic positioning of advertising and promotion programs, development of improved theories of consumer behavior and markets, and more extensive and diverse databases for research on individual and market demand.

# REFERENCES

Albion, M., and P. Farris. 1981. *The Advertising Controversy: Evidence on the Economic Effects of Advertising.* Boston: Auburn House.

Alt, F. F. 1942. "Distributed Lags." *Econometrica* 10:113–28.

Amemiya, T. 1981. "Qualitative Response Models: A Survey." *Journal of Economic Literature* 59:1483–1536.

Amuah, A. K. 1985. "Advertising Butter and Margarine in Canada." Master's thesis, University of Guelph.

Anderson, G., and R. Blundell. 1982. "Estimation and Hypothesis Testing in Dynamic Singular Equation Systems." *Econometrica* 50:1559–71.

_____. 1983. "Testing Restrictions in a Flexible Dynamic Demand System: An Application to Consumers' Expenditures in Canada." *Review of Economic Studies* 50:397–410.

Appel, V. 1966. "On Advertising Wear Out." *Journal of Advanced Research* 11:11–13.

Arbitron Ratings Company. 1989. *Universe Estimates Summary: 1984–85.* New York.

Aronson, J. E., D. A. Eiler, and O. D. Forker. 1973. *Attitudes Toward and Consumption of Milk and Other Beverages in Selected New York State Markets, Fall 1972: Baseline Data for Evaluating Milk Promotion.* Ithaca, NY: Cornell University. Department of Agricultural Economics, Agricultural Experiment Research.

Associated Milk Producers, Inc., personal correspondence.

Australian Wool Corporation and Bureau of Agricultural Economics. 1987. *Returns from Wool Promotion in the United States: An AWC/BAE Analysis.* BAE Occasional Paper No. 100. Canberra: Australian Government Publishing Service.

Aviphant, P., J. Y. Lee, and M. G. Brown. 1988. "Advertising and the Demand for Fruit Juices: A Demand Subsystem Approach." Paper presented at the American Agricultural Economic Association Annual Meeting, Knoxville, TN, August.

Bagozzi, R. P. 1983. "A Holistic Methodology for Modeling Consumer Response to Innovation." *Operations Research* 31:128–76.

Barnett, W. A. 1979. "Theoretical Foundations for the Rotterdam Model." *Review of Economic Studies* 46:109–30.

_____. 1981. *Consumer Demand and Labor Supply.* Amsterdam: North Holland.

Barten, A. P. 1964a. "Consumer Demand Functions under Conditions of Almost Additive Preferences." *Econometrica* 32:1–38.

_____. 1964b. "Family Composition, Prices, and Expenditure Patterns." In *Econometric Analysis for National Planning,* edited by P. E. Hart, G. Mills, and J. K. Whittaker. London: Butterworth.

_____. 1977. "The Systems of Consumer Demand Functions Approach: A Review." *Econometrica* 45:23–52.

Basmann, R. 1956. "A Theory of Demand with Variable Consumer Preferences." *Econometrica* 24:17–58.

Bass, F. M., and D. G. Clarke. 1972. "Testing Distributed Lag Models of Advertising Effect." *Journal of Marketing Research* 10:298–300.

Beare, S. 198. "Logistic Estimation of Censored Demand Systems." Paper presented at the 1988 Australian Economics Congress, Australian National University, Canberra, August 28–September 2.

Becker, G. S. 1965. "A Theory of the Allocation of Time." *Economic Journal* 75:493–517.

Belsley, D. A., E. Kuh, and R. E. Welsch. 1980. *Regression Diagnostics: Identifying Influential Data and Sources of Collinearity.* New York: John Wiley and Sons.

Bewely, R. 1980. *Allocation Models: Specification, Estimation, and Applications.* Cambridge, MA: Ballinger.

Bhattacharya, N. 1967. "An Application of the Linear Expenditure System." *Economic and Political Weekly* 2:2093–8.

Blaciforti, L., and R. Green. 1983. "An Almost Ideal Demand System Incorporating Habits: An Analysis of Expenditures on Food and Aggregate Commodity Groups." *Review of Economics and Statistics* 65:511–15.

Blaylock, J. R., and W. N. Blisard. 1988. "Effects of Advertising on the Demand for Cheese." USDA's Report to Congress on the Dairy Promotion Program (Exhibit G). Washington, D.C.: Government Printing Office.

Blaylock, J. R., and D. M. Smallwood. 1983. *Effects of Household Socioeconomic Features on Dairy Purchases.* Technical Bulletin No. 1686. Washington, DC: Economic Research Service, U.S. Department of Agriculture.

Blaylock, J. R., D. M. Smallwood, and L. H. Myers. 1987. "Econometric Analysis of the Effects of Advertising on the Demand for Cheese." Report to the National Dairy Promotion and Research Board by the Economic Research Service, U.S. Department of Agriculture, May.

Board of Governors, Federal Reserve System. *Federal Reserve Bulletin,* selected issues. Washington, DC.

Boehm, W. T. 1975. "The Household Demand for Major Dairy Products in the Southern Region." *Southern Journal of Agricultural Economics* 7:187–96.

Boehm, W. T., and E. M. Babb. 1975. *Household Consumption of Beverage Milk Products.* Bulletin No. 75. West Lafayette, IN: Purdue University, Department of Agricultural Economics, Agricultural Experiment Station.

Brown, M. G., and J. L. Lee. 1985. "Subgroup Demand: An Application of Dynamic Linear Expenditure System to a Fruit Juice/Drink Commodity Subgroup." Paper presented at the Southern Agricultural Economics Association Winter Meetings, Biloxi, AL, February.

―――――. 1989a. "Advertising Effects in Systems of Demand Equations: Some Alternative Approaches." Paper presented at the NEC-63 Research Conference on Commodity Advertising and Promotion, Orlando, FL, February.

―――――. 1989b. "Theoretical Overview of Demand Systems Incorporating Advertising Effects." Paper presented at the NEC-63 Research Conference on Commodity Advertising and Promotion, Orlando, FL, February.

Canon, M.D., C. D. Cullum, Jr., and E. Polak. 1970. *Theory of Optimal Control and Mathematical Programming.* New York: McGraw Hill.

Capps, O., Jr. 1988. "Utilizing Scanner Data to Estimate Retail Demand Functions for Meat Products." Technical Article No. 22976. Texas Agricultural Experiment Station, Texas A&M, August.

CARD (Center for Agricultural and Rural Development). 1988. "Measuring the Effectiveness of Beef Promotion and Advertising Programs." Report to the National Live Stock and Meat Board, June.

Chang, H., and H. Kinnucan. 1989. "Evaluating Canadian Butter Advertising and Using the AIDS Model." Paper presented at the NEC-63 Research Conference on Commodity Advertising and Promotion, Orlando, FL, February.

_____. 1990. "Advertising and Structural Change in the Demand for Butter in Canada." *Canadian Journal of Agricultural Economics* 38:295–308.

_____. 1991. "Advertising, Information, and Product Quality: The Case of Butter." *American Journal of Agriculture Economics* 73:1195–1203.

Chang, H. S. 1988. "Measuring the Effects of Advertising in Food Demand Subsystems." Ph.D. diss., Department of Agricultural Economics, University of California, Davis.

Chang, H. S., and R. Green. 1989. "Measuring the Effects of Advertising on Income and Price Elasticities Using Time-Series/Cross-Section Data." Paper presented at the NEC-63 Research Conference on Commodity Advertising and Promotion, Orlando, FL, February.

Chang, J. A. 1988. "A Theoretical Model of Generic and Brand Advertising." Ph.D. diss., University of Florida, Gainesville.

Chavas, J. P. 1983. "Structural Change and the Demand for Meat." *American Journal of Agricultural Economics* 65:148–53.

Choi, Y. 1988. "Generic and Brand Advertising Using Characteristic Demand Analysis." Working paper, The Ohio State University.

Chow, G. C. 1975. *Analysis and Control of Dynamic Economic Systems.* New York: John Wiley and Sons.

Christensen, L. R., D. W. Jorgenson, and L. J. Lau. 1975. "Transcendental Logarithmic Utility Functions." *American Economic Review* 65:367–83.

Christensen, L. R., and M. E. Manser. 1977. "Estimating U.S. Consumer Preferences for Meat with a Flexibly Utility Function." *Journal of Econometrics* 5:37–53.

Clarke, D. G. 1976. "Econometric Measurement of the Duration of Advertising Effect on Sales." *Journal of Marketing Research* 13:345–57.

Clement, W. E. 1963. "Some Unique Problems in Agricultural Commodity Advertising." *Journal of Farm Economics* 45:183–94.

Clements, K. W., and A. Selvanathan. 1988. "The Rotterdam Model and Its Application in Marketing." *Marketing Science* 7:60–75.

Connor, J., and R. W. Ward, eds. 1989. *Advertising and the Food System.* North Central Regional Research Publication 287, N.C. Project 117, Monograph 14. Madison, WI: University of Wisconsin.

Connor, J. M., R. T. Rogers, B. W. Marion, and W. F. Mueller. 1985. *The Food Manufacturing Industries: Structure, Strategies, Performance, and Policies.* Lexington, MA: D. C. Heath and Co.

Cox, T. L. 1989a. "A Rotterdam Model Incorporating Advertising Effects: The Case of Canadian Fats and Oils." Paper presented at the NEC-63 Research Conference on Commodity Advertising and Promotion, Orlando, FL, February.

————. "A General Conceptual Framework for the Analysis of Advertising Impacts on Commodity Demand." In *Market Demand for Dairy Products,* edited by Z. A. Hassan, D. P. Stonehouse, and S. R. Johnson. Ames: Iowa State University Press (forthcoming).

*Dairy Market Statistics.* Washington, DC: United States Department of Agriculture, Agricultural Marketing Service, various issues, 1980–85.

Deaton, A., and J. Muellbauer. 1980a. "An Almost Ideal Demand System." *American Economic Review* 70:312–26.

————. 1980b. *Economics and Consumer Behavior.* Cambridge, MA: Cambridge University Press.

Diamond, P., D. McFadden, and M. Rodriguez. 1978. "Measurement of the Elasticity of Factor Substitution and Bias of Technical Change." In *Production Economics: A Dual Approach to Theory and Application,* Vol. 2, edited by D. Fuss and D. McFadden. Amsterdam: North Holland.

Dixit, A. K., and V. Norman. 1978. "Advertising and Welfare." *The Bell Journal of Economics* 10:1–17.

Doran, H. E., and J. J. Quilkey. 1972. "Harmonic Analysis of Seasonal Data: Some Important Properties." *American Journal of Agricultural Economics* 54:646–51.

Duffy, M. H. 1987. "Advertising and Inter-Product Distribution of Demand." *European Economic Review* 31:1051–70.

Eiler, D. A., and C. B. Cook. 1977. "Teenage Consumers' Beverage Habits." *New York's Food and Life Sciences* 10:10–11.

Eiler, D. A., and S. R. Thompson. 1974. "Adult Attitudes Toward Major Beverages in Seven New York Metropolitan Markets." *SEARCH* 4:1–47.

Erlich, I., and L. Fisher. 1982. "The Derived Demand for Advertising: A Theoretical and Empirical Investigation." *American Economic Review* 72:366–88.

Fishbein, M. 1967. *Readings in Attitude Theory and Measurement.* New York: John Wiley and Sons.

Fisher, F. M., and K. Shell. 1968. "Taste and Quality Change in the Pure Theory of the True Cost-of-Living Index." In *Value, Capital and Growth: Papers in the Honour of Sir John Hicks,* edited by J. N. Wolfe. Chicago: Aldine.

Fomby, T. B., R. Carter Hill, and S. R. Johnson. 1984. *Advanced Econometric Methods.* Amsterdam, Holland, and New York: Springer-Verlag.

Forker, O. D., D. J. Liu, and S. J. Hurst. 1987. "Dairy Sales Data and Other Data Needed to Measure Effectiveness of Dairy Advertising." Research Paper 87-25. Department of Agricultural Economics, Cornell University, Ithaca.

Frank, G. L. 1985. "Generic Agricultural Promotion and Advertising: An Overview." In *Proceedings of Research on Effectiveness of Agricultural Commodity Promotion Seminars,* edited by W. J. Armbruster and L. H. Myers. Arlington, VA: Farm Foundation, and U.S. Department of Agriculture.

Galbraith, J. K. 1958. *The Affluent Society.* Boston, MA: Houghton Mifflin.

Gallant, A. R., and D. W. Jorgenson. 1979. "Statistical Inference for a System of Simultaneous, Non-Linear, Implicit Equations in the Context of Instrumental Variable Estimation." *Journal of Econometrics* 11:275–302.

Goddard, E. 1988a. " Modelling Advertising Effects in a Demand Systems Framework." Working Paper WP88/1, Department of Agricultural Economics and Business, University of Guelph, January.

_____. 1988b. "The Demand for Canadian Fats and Oils: A Case Study of Advertising Effectiveness." Unpublished manuscript, Department of Agricultural Economics and Business, University of Guelph.

_____. "The Impact of Advertising Butter and Margarine in Canada." In *Market Demand for Dairy Products,* edited by Z. A. Hassan, D. P. Stonehouse, and S. R. Johnson, Ames: Iowa State University Press (forthcoming).

Goddard, E., and A. K. Amuah. 1988. "Advertising in the Canadian Fats and Oils Market." Working Paper WP88/8, Department of Agricultural Economics and Business, University of Guelph, April.

_____. 1989. "The Demand for Canadian Fats and Oils: A Case Study of Advertising Effectiveness." *American Journal of Agricultural Economics* 71:741–49.

Goddard, E., and B. Cozzarin. 1989. "Effectiveness of Generic Advertising of Milk, Butter, Cheese, Eggs, and Meat in Canada." Paper presented at the NEC-63 Research Conference on Commodity Advertising and Promotion, Orlando, FL, February.

Goddard, E., and A. Tielu. 1988. "Assessing the Effectiveness of Fluid Milk Advertising in Ontario." Unpublished manuscript, Department of Agricultural Economics and Business, University of Guelph.

Goddard, E. W., H. Kinnucan, A. Tielu, and E. Beleza. "Advertising Fluid Milk in Ontario." In *Market Demand for Dairy Products,* edited by Z. A. Hassan, D. P. Stonehouse, and S. R. Johnson. Ames: Iowa State University Press (forthcoming).

Gorman, W. M. 1976. "Tricks with Utility Functions." In *Essays in Economic Analysis,* edited by M. J. Artis and A. R. Nobay. Cambridge: Cambridge University Press.

Gould, J. P. 1970. "Diffusion Processes and Optimal Advertising Policy." In *Microeconomic Foundation of Employment and Inflation Theory,* edited by E. S. Phelps. New York: Norton.

Green, R. 1985. "Dynamic Utility Functions for Measuring Advertising Responses." In *Proceedings of Research on Effectiveness of Agricultural Commodity Promotion, Seminar.* Arlington, VA: Farm Foundation, and U.S. Department of Agriculture.

Green, R., and J. Alston. 1989. "Elasticities in the AIDS Models." Working Paper, Department of Agricultural Economics, University of California, Davis.

Greenberg, A., and C. Suttoni. 1973. "Television Commercial Wearout." *Journal of Advanced Research* 13(5):47–54.

Griliches, Z. 1971. *Price Indexes and Quality Change.* Cambridge, MA: Harvard University Press.

Grundmeier, Eric, K. Skold, H. H. Jensen, and S. R. Johnson. 1989. "CARD Livestock Model Documentation Beef." CARD Technical Report 88-TR2, Ames, IA: Center for Agricultural and Rural Development, Iowa State University.

Haidacher, R. C., J. R. Blaylock. 1989. "Why Has Dairy Product Consumption Increased?" *National Food Review* 11:28–32.

Haidacher, R. C., J. R. Blaylock, and L. H. Myers. 1988. *Consumer Demand for Dairy Products*. Agricultural Economics Report Number 586, Washington, DC: Economic Research Service, U.S. Department of Agriculture.

Hanemann, W. M. 1984. "Discrete/Continuous Models of Consumer Demand." *Econometrica* 28:244–57.

Heckman, J. 1976. "The Common Structure of Statistical Models of Truncation, Sample Selection and Limited Dependent Variables and a Simple Estimator for Such Models." *Annals of Economic and Social Measurement* 5:475–92.

Heien, D. M., and C. R. Wessells. 1988. "The Demand for Dairy Products: Structure, Prediction, and Decomposition." *American Journal of Agricultural Economics* 70:219–28.

Henning, John. 1986. "An Econometric Model of the World Wheat Market by Class: Evaluating Alternate Canadian Export Regimes." Master's thesis, University of Guelph.

Hoerl, Arthur E., and R. W. Kennard. 1970. "Ridge Regression: Applications to Nonorthogonal Problems." *Technometrics* 12:69–72.

Hoover, S., M. Hayenga, and S. R. Johnson. 1989. "A Comprehensive Program Evaluation." Report to the National Pork Board, January.

Houthakker, H. S. 1952. "Compensated Changes in Quantities and Qualities Consumed." *Review of Economic Studies* 19:55–64.

_____. 1960. "Additive Preferences." *Econometrica* 28:244–57.

Houthakker, H. S., and L. D. Taylor. 1970. *Consumer Demand in the United States 1929–1970*, 2nd ed. Cambridge, MA: Harvard University Press.

Huang, C. L., and R. Raunikar. 1983. "Household Fluid Milk Expenditure Patterns in the South and United States." *Southern Journal of Agricultural Economics* 15:27–33.

Huang, K. S. 1985. *U.S. Demand for Food: A Complete System of Price and Income Effects*. Technical Bulletin Number 1714, Washington, DC: Economic Research Service, U.S. Department of Agriculture.

Ichimura, S. 1951. "A Critical Note on the Definition of Related Goods." *Review of Economic Studies* 18:179–83.

*International Financial Statistics*. 1970–87. Washington, DC: International Monetary Fund.

Jastram, R. W. 1976. "A Treatment of Distributed Lags in the Theory of Advertising Effect on Sales." *Journal of Marketing Research* 13:345–57.

Jensen, H., and T. Kesavan. 1987. "Generic Advertising of Food Product Characteristics." In *Proceedings of the 33rd Annual Conference of the American Council on Consumer Interests*. Denver, CO, April 1–4.

Jensen, H. H., S. R. Johnson, K. Skold, and E. Grundmeier. 1989. "Impacts of Promotion on the Livestock Sector: Simulation of Supply Response and Effects on Producer Returns." Paper presented at the NEC-63 Research Conference on Commodity Advertising and Promotion, Orlando, FL, February.

Johnson, S. R., Z. A. Hassan, and R. D. Green. 1984. *Demand Systems Estimation: Methods and Applications*. Ames: Iowa State University Press.

Jones, E. 1987. "Impacts of Economic and Socioeconomic Changes on Potato Use." *Vegetable Situation and Outlook Report* TVS-2422, ERS.

Jones, E., and R. Ward. 1984. "A Simultaneous Model of the U.S. Potato Subsector." Paper presented at the annual meeting of the AAEA, Ithaca, NY.

Jones, J., and J. Weimer. 1980. "A Survey of Health and Nutrition Related Food Choices." *National Food Review* 12:16–18. Washington, DC: U.S. Department of Agriculture.

Jorgenson, D. W., and L. J. Lau. 1975. "The Structure of Consumer Preferences." *Annals of Economic and Social Measurement* 4:49–101.

Joseph, P. 1968. "Application of the Linear Expenditure System to N.S.S. Data: Some Further Results." *Economic and Political Weekly* 609-15.

Judge, G. G., W. E. Griffiths, R. C. Hill, and T. C. Lee. 1980. *The Theory and Practice of Econometrics.* New York: John Wiley and Sons.

Judge, G. G., R. C. Hill, W. E. Griffiths, H. Lutkepohl, and T. C. Lee. 1982. *Introduction to the Theory and Practice of Econometrics.* New York: John Wiley and Sons.

Kamien, M. I., and N. L. Schwartz. 1981. *Dynamic Optimization: The Calculus of Variations and Optimal Control in Economics and Management.* New York: North Holland.

Kesavan, T., S. R. Johnson, and H. H. Jensen. 1988. "Dynamic Systems for U.S. Meat Demand Using an Error Correction Mechanism." CARD Working Paper 88-WP38, Ames, IA: Center for Agricultural and Rural Development, Iowa State University.

Kinnucan, H. W. 1982. "Demographic Versus Media Advertising Effects on Milk Demand: The Case of the New York City Market." Department of Agricultural Economics Staff Paper No. 82–5. Ithaca, NY: Cornell University.

———. 1983. "Media Advertising Effects on Milk Demand: The Case of the Buffalo, New York Market." Department of Agricultural Economics Research Paper No. 83–13. Cornell University, Ithaca, NY, February.

———. 1985. "Evaluating Advertising Effectiveness Using Time Series Data." In *Proceedings of Research on Effectiveness of Agricultural Commodity Promotion Seminar,* edited by W. Armbruster and L. H. Myers. Arlington, VA: Farm Foundation, and U.S. Department of Agriculture.

———. 1986. "Demographic versus Media Advertising Effects on Milk Demand: The Case of the New York City Market." *Northeastern Journal of Agricultural and Resource Economics* 15:66–74.

———. 1987. "Effect of Canadian Advertising on Milk Demand: The Case of the Buffalo, New York Market." *Canadian Journal of Agricultural Economics* 24:181–96.

Kinnucan, H. W., and D. Fearon. 1986. "Effects of Generic and Brand Advertising of Cheese in New York City with Implications for Allocation of Funds." *North Central Journal of Agricultural Economics* 8:93–107.

Kinnucan, H. W., and O. D. Forker. 1986. "Seasonality in the Consumer Response to Milk Advertising and Implications for Milk Promotion Policy." *American Journal of Agricultural Economics* 68:562–71.

———. 1988. "Allocation of Generic Advertising Funds Among Products: A Sales Maximization Approach." *Northeastern Journal of Agricultural and Resource Economics* 17:64–71.

Kinnucan, H. W., and M. Venkateswaran. 1990. "Effects of Generic Advertising on Perceptions and Behavior: The Case of Catfish." *Southern Journal of Agricultural Economics* 22:137–51.

Kirkland, J. T., and J. Sipple. 1987. "Fluid-Milk Demand in Pennsylvania: What Factors Influence Consumption?" Cooperative Extension Service, The Pennsylvania State University.

Kmenta, J. 1971. *Elements of Econometrics*. New York: Macmillan.

_____. 1986. *Elements of Econometrics,* 2nd ed. New York: Macmillan.

Knutson, R. D., C. A. Hunter, Jr., and R. B. Schwart, Jr. 1981. *The Texas Dairy Industry: Trends and Issues*. Publication No. B-1362, Texas A&M University, Texas Agricultural Extension Service.

Knutson, R. D., R. Schwart, and E. G. Smith. 1988. "Milk Self-Sufficiency: A Desirable Goal?" *Food and Fiber Economics*. Texas A&M University, Texas Agricultural Extension Service, 17, 8.

Kokoski, M. 1986. "Demographic Variations and Consumer Preferences." *American Journal of Agricultural Economics* 68:894–907.

Kotowitz, Y., and F. Mathewson. 1979. "Advertising, Consumer Information, and Product Quality." *The Bell Journal of Economics* 10:566–88.

Ladd, G. W. 1979. "Survey of Promising Developments in Demand Analysis: Economics of Product Characteristics." In *New Directions in Econometrics of Agriculture: Modeling and Forecasting*. Amsterdam: North Holland.

Ladd, G. W., and V. Suvannunt. 1976. "A Model of Consumer Goods Characteristics." *American Journal of Agricultural Economics* 58:504–10.

Lancaster, K. J. 1966. "A New Approach to Consumer Theory." *Journal of Political Economy* 74:132–57.

Lavidge, R. C., and G. A. Steiner. 1961. "A Model for Predictive Measurements of Advertising Effectiveness." *Journal of Marketing* 25:59–62.

Leading National Advertisers. *Ad$ Summary,* various issues.

Leamer, Edward E. 1983. "Let's Take the Con Out of Econometrics." *American Economic Review* 73:31–43.

Lee, J. Y. 1977. "An Economic Analysis of Florida Citrus Advertising Programs." Paper presented at Southern Agricultural Economics Association Winter Meetings, Atlanta, GA, February.

_____. 1981. "Florida Department of Citrus Advertising Research Program." *Advertising and the Food System,* edited by J. M. Conner and R. W. Ward. North Central Regional Research Project NC117. Monograph 14, 179-196.

_____. 1981. "Generic Advertising, FOB Price Promotions, and FOB Revenue: A Case Study of the Florida Grapefruit Juice Industry." *Southern Journal of Agricultural Economics* 13:69–78.

_____. 1984. "Demand Interrelationships Among Fruit Beverages." *Southern Journal of Agricultural Economics* 16:135–43.

Lee, J. Y., and R. M. Behr. 1988. "Advertising and the Demand for Fruit Juices: A Household Production Theory Approach." Paper presented to the Southern Agricultural Economics Association Winter Meeting, New Orleans, LA, February.

Lee, L. F. 1981. "Fully Recursive Probability Models and Multivariate Log-Linear Probability Models for the Analysis of Qualitative Data." *Journal of Econometrics* 16:51–69.

Lewbel, A. 1985. "A Unified Approach to Incorporating Demographic or Other Effects in Demand Systems." *Review of Economic Studies* 52:1–18.

Little, Arthur D., Inc. 1986. "Econometric Analysis of the Effect of Generic Advertising on Fluid Milk, Cheese, and Butter Demand." Appendix in *Report to Congress on the Dairy Promotion Program*, by the Secretary of Agriculture. Washington, DC: U.S. Department of Agriculture.

Little, J. D. C. 1979. "Aggregate Advertising Response: The State of the Art." *Operations Research* 27:629–67.

Liu, D. J., and O. D. Forker. 1988a. "Generic Fluid Milk Advertising, Demand Expansion, and Supply Response: The Case of New York City." *American Journal of Agricultural Economics* 70:229–36.

_____. 1988b. *In Search of Optimal Control Models for Generic Commodity Promotion.* Working papers in Agricultural Economics, No. 88-5, Department of Agricultural Economics, Cornell University.

_____. 1989. *Optimal Fluid Milk Advertising in New York State: A Control Model.* Working Papers in Agricultural Economics, No. 89-2, Department of Agricultural Economics, Cornell University, June.

Liu, D. J., J. Conrad, and O. D. Forker. "Optimal Control of Generic Dairy Promotion: Some Preliminary Results on the New York State Fluid Program." Paper presented at the NEC-63 Research Conference on Commodity Advertising and Promotion, Orlando, FL.

Liu, D. J., H. M. Kaiser, O. D. Forker, and T. D. Mount. 1988. "Estimating Endogenous Switching Systems for Government Interventions: The Case of the Dairy Sector." Working Paper No. 88-11, Department of Agricultural Economics, Cornell University, September.

_____. 1989. *The Economic Implications of U.S. Generic Dairy Advertising Program: An Industry Model Approach.* Working Paper, No. 89-22. Department of Agricultural Economics, Cornell University, November.

McEwen, W. J. 1985. "Awareness, Recall, and Advertising Effectiveness." In *Proceedings of Research on Effectiveness of Agricultural Commodity Promotion Seminar,* edited by W. J. Armbruster and L. H. Myers. Arlington, VA: Farm Foundation, and U.S. Department of Agriculture.

McFadden, D. 1974. "Conditional Logit Analysis of Qualitative Behavior." In *Frontiers in Econometrics,* edited by P. Zarembka. New York: Academic Press, 105–42.

_____. 1983. "Modelling the Choice of Residential Location." In *Spatial Interaction Theory and Planning Models.* Amsterdam: North Holland.

Maddala, G. S. 1977. *Econometrics,* New York: McGraw-Hill.

_____. 1983. *Limited-Dependent and Qualitative Variables in Econometrics.* New York: Cambridge University Press.

Manser, M. E. 1976. "Elasticities of Demand for Food: An Analysis Using Non-Additive Utility Functions Allowing for Habit Formation." *Southern Economic Journal* 43:879–91.

Mercer, R. L. 1986. *Potato Spotlight*. Denver, CO: National Potato Promotion Board.

Morrison, R. M. 1984. *Generic Advertising of Farm Products*. Agricultural Information Bulletin No. 481. Washington, DC: Economic Research Service, U.S. Department of Agriculture.

Mountain, D. C. 1988. "The Rotterdam Model: An Approximation in Variable Space." *Econometrica* 56:477–84.

Muellbauer, J. 1974. "Household Composition, Engel Curves, and Welfare Comparisons between Households." *European Economic Review* 5:103–22.

———. 1975. "The Cost of Living and Taste and Quality Change." *Journal of Economic Theory* 10:269–83.

Myers, L. H. 1987. "Research Needs and Future Directions in Advertising and Promotion Evaluation." Dairy Product Demand Symposium, Atlanta, GA, October.

National Potato Promotion Board. *Potato Board Spotlight,* various issues.

Nelson, P. 1970. "Information and Consumer Behavior." *Journal of Political Economy* 78:313–29.

———. 1974a. "Advertising as Information." *Journal of Political Economy* 81:729–54.

———. 1974b. "The Economic Value of Advertising." In *Advertising and Society,* edited by Y. Brozen. New York: New York University Press.

Nerlove, M. 1958. "Distributed Lags and Demand Analysis." *Agriculture Handbook,* No. 141. Washington, DC: U.S. Department of Agriculture.

Nerlove, M., and F. V. Waugh. 1961. "Advertising Without Supply Control: Some Implications of a Study of the Advertising of Oranges." *Journal of Farm Economics* 43:813–37.

Nerlove, M., and K. J. Arrow. 1962. "Optimal Advertising Policy under Dynamic Conditions." *Economica* 29:129–42.

Nichols, L. M. 1985. "Advertising and Economic Welfare." *American Economic Review* 75:213–18.

Nielsen, A. C., Company. "Selected Citrus and Other Fruit Products — Consumer Sales," selected issues.

NPD Research, Inc. "Market Summary of the Beverage Category Prepared for the Florida Department of Citrus," Annual Reports 1980–85.

Ostheimer, R. H. 1970. "Frequency Effects over Time." *Journal of Advanced Research* 10:19–22.

"P & G Opens Spout for O.J." 1983. *Advertising Age.* October 17:1, 82.

Phlips, L. 1974. *Applied Consumption Analysis*. Amsterdam: North Holland.

———. 1983. *Applied Consumption Analysis,* 2nd ed. Amsterdam: North Holland.

Pindyck, R. S., and D. L. Rubinfeld. 1981. *Econometric Models and Economic Forecasts*. New York: McGraw-Hill Book Company.

Pollak, R. A., and M. L. Wachter. 1975. "Thee Relevance of the Household Production Function and Its Implications for the Allocations of Time." *Journal of Political Economy.* 83:255–77.

Pollak, R. A., and T. J. Wales. 1969. "Estimation of the Linear Expenditure System." *Econometrica* 37:611–28.

_____. 1978. "Estimation of Complete Demand Systems from Household Budget Data: The Linear and Quadratic Expenditure Systems." *American Economic Review* 68:348–59.

_____. 1979. "Welfare Comparisons and Equivalence Scales." *American Economic Review* 69:216–21.

_____. 1980. "Comparison of the Quadratic Expenditure System and Translog Demand Systems with Alternative Specifications of Demographic Effects." *Econometrica* 48:595–612.

_____. 1981. "Demographic Variables in Demand Analysis." *Econometrica* 49:1533–51.

Pontryagin, L. S., V. G. Boltyanskii, R. V. Gamrelidze, and E. F. Mishchenko. 1962. *The Mathematical Theory of Optimal Processes.* New York: John Wiley and Sons.

Pope, R. D. 1985. "The Impact of Information on Consumer Preferences." In *Proceedings of Research on Effectiveness of Agricultural Commodity Promotion Seminar,* edited by W. J. Armbruster and L. H. Myers. Arlington, VA: Farm Foundation, and U.S. Department of Agriculture.

Powell, A. A. 1974. *Empirical Analytics of Demand Systems.* Lexington, MA: Heath.

Prato, A. A. 1973. "Milk Demand, Supply, and Price Relationships, 1950–1968." *American Journal of Agricultural Economics* 55:217–22.

Quilkey, J. J. 1986. "Promotion of Agricultural Products — A View from the Cloister." *Australian Journal of Agricultural Economics* 30:38–52.

Rausser, G. C., and E. Hochman. 1979. *Dynamic Agricultural Systems: Economic Prediction and Control.* New York: North Holland.

Rausser, G. C., and J. W. Freebairn. 1974. "Approximate Adaptable Solutions to U.S. Beef Trade Policy." *Annals of Economic and Social Measurement* 3:177–203.

Ray, R. 1980. "Analysis of a Time Series of Household Expenditure Surveys for India." *Review of Economics and Statistics.* 62:595–602.

_____. 1982. "The Testing and Estimation of Complete Demand Systems on Household Budget Surveys." *European Economic Review* 17:349–69.

Richardson, C. L. 1973. "The Advertising Response for Processed Oranges: A Distributed Lag Approach." Master's thesis, University of Florida.

Rozmarin & Associates, Inc. "Pork Attitude and Perception Study." Advertising tracking study conducted for National Pork Producers Council, February 1987–May 1988.

Salathe, L. E. 1979. *Household Expenditure Patterns in the United States.* Technical Bulletin Number 1603. Washington, DC: U.S. Department of Agriculture.

Schmalensee, Richard. 1972. *The Economics of Advertising.* Amsterdam: North Holland Publishing Company.

Schmura, G. 1952. "Complementarity and Shifts in Demand." *Metroeconomica* 4:1–4.

Schroeter, John R. 1988. "Analysis of Behavior Scan Data and Beef Consumption Responses to Promotion and Advertising." In *Report to the National Live Stock and Meat Board.* Ames, IA: Center for Agricultural and Rural Development, Iowa State University, June.

Schwart, R. B., Jr. 1988. "Federal Milk Marketing Orders." *Dairy Fact Sheet.* Publication No. L-2053, Texas Agricultural Extension Service, Texas A&M University.

Seton, N. J. 1985. "Future Growth in the Texas Dairy Industry." Unpublished Master's thesis, Texas A&M University.

Simon, J. L., and J. Arndt. 1980. "The Shape of the Advertising Response Function." *Journal of Advertising Research* 4:11-28.

Stigler, G. J. 1961. "The Economics of Information." *Journal of Political Economy* 69:213-25.

Stigler, G. J., and G. S. Becker. 1977. "De Gustibus Non Est Disputandum." *American Economic Review* 67:76-90.

Stone, R. 1954. "Linear Expenditure Systems and Demand Analysis: An Application to the Pattern of British Demand." *Economic Journal* 64:511-27.

Texas Milk Market Report. *Statistical Summary,* various issues, 1980-85. Carrollton, Texas, C. E. Durham, Market Administrator.

Theil, H. 1965. "The Information Approach to Demand Analysis." *Econometrica* 33:67-87.

_____. 1976. *Theory and Measurement of Consumer Demand,* Vol. 2. Amsterdam: North Holland.

_____. 1980a. *Systems-Wide Explorations in International Economics, Input-Output Analysis, and Marketing Research.* Amsterdam: North Holland.

_____. 1980b. *The Systems Wide Approach to Microeconomics.* Chicago: University of Chicago Press.

Thompson, S. R., and D. A. Eiler. 1975a. "Multivariate Probit Analysis of Advertising Awareness on Milk Use." *Canadian Journal of Agricultural Economics* 23:65-73.

_____. 1975b. "Producer Returns from Increased Milk Advertising." *American Journal of Agricultural Economics* 57:505-8.

_____. 1977. "Determinants of Fluid Milk Advertising Effectiveness." *American Journal of Agricultural Economics* 59:330-35.

Tintner, G. 1952. "Complementarity and Shifts in Demand." *Metroeconomica* 4:1-4.

Tobin, J. 1958. "Estimation of Relationships for Limited Dependent Variables." *Econometrica* 26:24-36.

Tsujimura, K., and T. Sato. 1964. "Irreversibility of Consumer Behavior in Terms of Numerical Preference Fields." *Review Of Economics and Statistics* 46:305-19.

United Dairy Industry Association (UDIA). *Tape Formats—Dairy Usage and Trend Study,* 1976, 1978, 1980, 1982, 1984, 1986, and 1988.

U.S. Bureau of Labor Statistics. 1986. *Monthly Labor Review.* Washington, DC: U.S. Government Printing Office.

U.S. Department of Agriculture. *Agricultural Statistics,* selected issues. Washington, DC.

_____. *Livestock and Poultry Situation and Outlook Report,* various issues. Washington, DC: Economic Research Service, U.S. Department of Agriculture.

_____. 1983. *Food Consumption: Household in the South, Seasons of the Year 1977–78.* Nationwide Food Consumption Survey 1977–78, Report H–6. Washington, DC: Human Nutrition Information Service, U.S. Department of Agriculture, August.

_____. 1985. *Nationwide Food Consumption Survey, Continuing Survey of Food Intakes by Individuals: Women 19–50 Years and Their Children 1–5 Years, 1 Day.* NFCS, CSFII Report No. 85–1. Washington, DC: Human Nutrition information Service, U.S. Department of Agriculture.

_____. 1987a. *Food Marketing Review, 1986.* Washington, DC: Economic Research Service, U.S. Department of Agriculture, February.

_____. 1987b. *Nationwide Food Consumption Survey, Continuing Survey of Food Intakes by Individuals: Women 19–50 years and Their Children 1–5 Years, 4 Days.* NFCS, CSFII Report No. 85–4. Washington, DC: Human Nutrition information Service, U.S. Department of Agriculture.

_____. 1988. *Crop Production.* Washington, DC, October.

U.S. Department of Commerce. 1987. *Statistical Abstract of the United States 1987.* Washington, DC.

_____, Bureau of the Census. 1986. *Money Income of Households, Families and Persons in the United States.* Washington, DC: Government Printing Office (and previous issues).

Varian, H. R. 1978. *Microeconomic Analysis.* New York: W. W. Norton, Inc.

Vidale, M. L., and H. B. Wolfe. 1957. "An Operations Research Study of Sales Response to Advertising." *Operations Research* 5:370–81.

Wallis, K. F. 1974. "Seasonal Adjustment and Relations Between Variables." *Journal of the American Statistical Association,* (Applications Section) 69:18–31.

Walters, C. G. 1978. *Consumer Behavior: Theory and Practice,* 3rd ed. Homewood, IL: Richard D. Irwin, Inc.

Ward, R. W. 1973. "Evaluation of Generic Advertising Effectiveness with Econometrics." Paper presented at the Southern Regional Workshop on Market Dynamics, May 30–June 1.

_____. 1974. "An Economic Analysis of the Florida Department of Citrus Advertising Rebate Program." *ERD Report* 74-1, Gainesville, FL: Economic Research Department, Florida Department of Citrus.

_____. 1975. "Measuring the Effectiveness and Interaction of Generic and Branded Citrus Advertising: An Application of Maximum Likelihood Estimator." Unpublished paper, Gainesville, FL: Economic Research Department, Florida Department of Citrus.

_____. 1976. "Measuring Advertising Decay." *Journal of Advertising Research* 16:37–41.

_____. 1988a. "Evaluation of the Economic Gains from Generic and Brand Advertising of Orange Juice." Comments to the Advertising Committee, Florida Citrus Commission, Lakeland, FL, April.

_____. 1988b. "Advertising Expenditure Implications from the Generic and Brand Advertising Model for Orange Juice. Comments to the Advertising Committee, Florida Citrus Commission, Lakeland, FL, May.

_____. 1988c. "The Case for Fluid Milk." Paper presented to the AAEA Symposium on Advertising Data. Knoxville, TN, August.

Ward, R. W., and B. L. Dixon. 1987. *An Econometric Analysis of the National Dairy Promotion Board's Fluid Milk Advertising Programs.* Report to the National Dairy Promotion and Research Board, Arlington, VA, March.

_____. 1988. "The Economic Impact of Fluid Milk Advertising on Milk Consumption." In USDA's *Report to Congress on the Dairy Promotion Program* (Appendix F). Washington, DC: Government Printing Office.

_____. 1989. "Effectiveness of Fluid Milk Advertising Since the Dairy and Tobacco Adjustment Act of 1983." *American Journal of Agricultural Economics* 71:229-36.

Ward, R. W., and J. A. Chang. 1985. "Theoretical Issues Relating to Generic and Brand Advertising on Agricultural Commodities." In *Proceedings of Research on Effectiveness of Agricultural Commodity Promotion, Seminar,* edited by W. J. Armbruster and L. H. Myers. Arlington, VA: Farm Foundation, and U.S. Department of Agriculture.

Ward, R. W., and J. G. Davis. 1978. "A Pooled Cross-Section Time Series Model of Coupon Promotions." *American Journal of Agricultural Economics* 60:393–410.

Ward, R. W., and L. H. Myers. 1979. "Advertising Effectiveness and Coefficient Variation Over Time." *Agricultural Economics Research* 31:1–11.

Ward, R. W., and W. F. McDonald. 1986. "Effectiveness of Generic Milk Advertising: A Ten Region Study." *Agribusiness* 2:77–90.

Ward, R. W., J. A. Chang, and S. R. Thompson. 1985. "Commodity Advertising: Theoretical Issues Relating to Generic and Brand Promotions." *Agribusiness* 1:269–76.

Waugh, F. V. 1959. "Needed Research on the Effectiveness of Farm Products Promotions." *Journal of Farm Economics* 41:364–77.

White, K. J. 1988. "A General Computer Program for Econometric Methods—SHAZAM." *Econometrica.* 46:239–40.

Wilson, R. R., and R. G. Thompson. 1967. "Demand, Supply, and Price Relationships for the Dairy Sector, Post–World War II Period." *Journal of Farm Economics* 49:360–71.

Wohlgenant, M. K. 1982. "Structural Shifts in Demand for Meats: Taste on Quality Change?" Paper presented at the AAEA Annual Meetings, Logan, UT.

Wu, J. S., K. M. Kesecker, and R. J. Meinhold. 1985. "Discussion on Analytical, Empirical, and Measurement Issues in Evaluating Advertising Program Effectiveness." In *Proceedings of Research on Effectiveness of Agricultural Commodity Promotion, Seminar,* edited by W. J. Armbruster, and L. H. Myers, Arlington, VA: Farm Foundation, and U.S. Department of Agriculture.

Zielske, H. A. 1959. "The Remembering and Forgetting of Advertising." *Journal of Marketing* 23:239–43.

# INDEX

Advertisement
  apple, 4
  effectiveness of, 70
  location of commodity item in, 15–16
  size of, 13–14, 16–22
  translating advertising message into, 70
Advertisers, 7–8, 21
Advertising
  brand. *See* Brand advertising
  changes in, 3, 10–11, 14–15, 22–23
  commodities in Canada, 120–38
  commodity, xiv–xv, 3, 206–21
  cooperative effort needed for evaluating, 354
  data, 49
  decay effect, 207–8
  demand elasticities and, 90–91, 101–19
  demand systems incorporating, 79–100, 181–92, 205
  dollar effectiveness of, 276–77
  economics of, 166–68
  effectiveness, 166, 223
    for orange juice, 209–10, 212–13
    research, 358–60
    in view of competition advertising, 360
  effects
    on consumer behavior, 167–68
    on demand, 148
    on demand elasticities, 112–13
  evaluation, 120
    with split-cable scanner data, 58–69
    using AIDS model, 165–80, 187–88
  expenditures
    made at feature prices, 67–68
    as measure of, 3
  experiment for beef, 61–69
  farm market impact, 53–55
  frequency for apples, 6–8
  household level analysis of, 59
  household production theory and, 95–98

  impact
    on consumption, 141–45
    on endogenous variables of dairy industry model, 51–53
  inserts and pictures, 14–15, 21
  lag structure, 73
  manufactured dairy product, 41–42
  marginal impacts of, 55–56
  measurement of, 3, 70, 182, 207–8, 356–58
  message, 70
  national, campaigns. *See* National advertising campaigns
  newspaper, 3–23
  print, 237, 257–58
  and proportion of meat purchased at feature prices, 68
  radio, 34, 36–38, 72, 195
  reasons for, 355–56
  rebate program, 225
  relationship to sales, 319
  research, 182–88, 363–69
  retail market impact, 53–55
  retail sources of, for apples, 6–8
  in Rotterdam model, 139–64
  scaling and translating for, 183
  seasonality in initiating a program, 339
  split-cable scanner data use in evaluating, 58–69
  strategies, 22
  television. *See* Television advertising
  theoretical model of, 196–98
  timing of, 12–13
  unusual production conditions affecting, 5–6
  variables in beef experiment, 66–67
Age, 109
Agricultural Adjustment Act, 349
Agricultural Marketing Agreement Act, 343, 348
Agricultural Marketing Service (AMS), 343, 348–50

**385**